ISBN 978-1-331-28845-9
PIBN 10169382

1 MONTH OF
FREE
READING

at

www.ForgottenBooks.com

By purchasing this book you are eligible for one month membership to ForgottenBooks.com, giving you unlimited access to our entire collection of over 1,000,000 titles via our web site and mobile apps.

To claim your free month visit:

www.forgottenbooks.com/free169382

English
Français
Deutsche
Italiano
Español
Português

www.forgottenbooks.com

Mythology Photography **Fiction**
Fishing Christianity **Art** Cooking
Essays Buddhism Freemasonry
Medicine **Biology** Music **Ancient
Egypt** Evolution Carpentry Physics
Dance Geology **Mathematics** Fitness
Shakespeare **Folklore** Yoga Marketing
Confidence Immortality Biographies
Poetry **Psychology** Witchcraft
Electronics Chemistry History **Law**
Accounting **Philosophy** Anthropology
Alchemy Drama Quantum Mechanics
Atheism Sexual Health **Ancient History**
Entrepreneurship Languages Sport
Paleontology Needlework Islam
Metaphysics Investment Archaeology
Parenting Statistics Criminology
Motivational

THE COLLECTED PAPERS

OF

FREDERIC WILLIAM MAITLAND

IN THREE VOLUMES

VOLUME III

CAMBRIDGE UNIVERSITY PRESS
London: FETTER LANE, E.C.
C. F. CLAY, Manager

Edinburgh: 100, PRINCES STREET
Berlin: A. ASIIER AND CO.
Leipzig: F. A. BROCKIIAUS
New York: G. P. PUTNAM'S SONS
Bombay and Calcutta: MACMILLAN AND CO., Ltd.

THE COLLECTED PAPERS

OF

FREDERIC WILLIAM MAITLAND

DOWNING PROFESSOR OF THE LAWS OF ENGLAND

EDITED BY

H. A. L. FISHER

VOLUME III

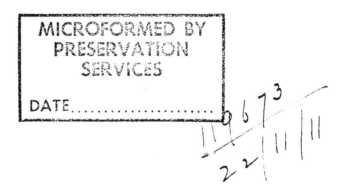
Cambridge:

at the University Press

1911

Cambridge:

PRINTED BY JOHN CLAY, M.A.
AT THE UNIVERSITY PRESS

TABLE OF CONTENTS

VOLUME III

Papers of a less technical character are marked by an asterisk.

vi　　　　　　　　　　*Contents*

THE TRIBAL SYSTEM IN WALES[1]

IT is probable that by this time all who take a serious interest in those problems of remote economic history, which are the theme of Mr Seebohm's study, will have read this book[2]. It is certain that if they have read they have admired it, and have fallen once more under that charm which has made *The English Village Community* one of the classical books of our time. Therefore there is here and now no need to expend many words of general praise. The earlier part of this new volume and the precious appendixes that it contains seem to me to be beyond praise. By the earlier part I mean the part which fills the first pages. This explanation may be necessary, for Mr Seebohm still works "from the known to the unknown," so that in his hands the last becomes first and the first last. Perhaps, however, we should say that he works rather from the knowable than from the known. Of the Wales of the thirteenth and fourteenth centuries very little has been known hitherto by the

[1] *Economic Journal*, Dec. 1895.

[2] *The Tribal System in Wales* by Frederick Seebohm. Longmans, 1895.

M. III.

generality of Englishmen and Welshmen.   A great deal now is knowable in these delightful pages, a great deal that is well attested by accurate and authentic documents that are here printed in full and are elucidated by an ingenious commentary.   One part of that charm of which I have spoken consists in the author's strong desire to see things in the concrete, and to make his readers see them in the same fashion, and we can now see in the concrete certain bits of Welsh life as that life was lived in the thirteenth century.

Beyond this lies the unknown.   Must we say the unknowable?   Mr Seebohm will not expect from us a ready answer to that question.   He would very properly despise us if, in an off-hand way, we declared that he had solved the many problems of ancient Welsh history.   What he has given us on the present occasion is but, as the first words of his preface tell us, "the first part of an essay."   "It is confined to an attempt to understand the *structure* of tribal society in Wales.   The *methods* of tribal society in Wales and the extension of the inquiry to other tribal systems are left to form the subject of another volume."   Now in the exposition of any social system we may well give one chapter, or one book, to structure and another to functions; this is a convenient arrangement.   But when we are actually engaged in the task of reconstruction or are examining the results of another man's reconstructive labours, we cannot thus separate the two topics.   The proof of the model is in the working. We cannot tell whether or no the organs of the hypothetically restored beast have been correctly shaped until we know what purposes they are going to serve. Therefore, Mr Seebohm would have little but contempt for a critic who at this moment broke forth into indiscriminate laudation. His procedure indeed may have been intended to obtain from some of his readers a statement of those difficulties that they would like to see dissolved so that he may have an opportunity of dissolving them in his next volume. In this spirit of suggestion I offer a few remarks.

Until the day comes (whether it ever will or ever can come I do not know) when those who are skilled in Celtic philology will have sorted that miscellaneous mass which we know as the Ancient Laws of Wales, the materials which will be at the service of investigators will be of an extremely dangerous and unsatisfactory kind. I am not hinting at forgery; the forgery of codes of law would be an uncommon event. I am referring to what is a very common and, at a certain stage of society, an unavoidably common process, namely, the accretion and fusion in the hands of lawyers of rules and institutions which had their origin in widely remote periods. At any given moment the law of a nation contains things new and old. In 1819 the law of England comprised a mass of rules touching trial by battle; it also comprised a mass of rules about negotiable instruments. There is no fear of our saying that the judicial combat and the bill of exchange are institutions which belong to one and the same age. We know the *caput mortuum* when we come upon it in modern times. We have continuous records and a continuous tradition. But do we know the *caput mortuum* when we come upon it in ancient times?

Some Welsh lawyer has collected things new and old. Possibly he was bound to copy down some rules that were well-nigh but not quite obsolete when he copied them.   In 1819 an English lawyer who wished to make a complete statement of English law would have been bound to speak of trial by battle as of one of the methods by which lawsuits could be decided.   We know well from our own history how apt were the lawyers of past ages to fuse the old with the new, to borrow rules from the most various sources, without telling us whether those rules were practicable or impracticable, living or dead, imported novelties or obsolescent survivals of a forgotten age.   We seem almost entitled to say that it is improbable *a priori* that the Welsh Laws, even in their purest form, represent to us the life of the people as it was being lived, really and truly lived, at any one moment of time. We seem almost bound to frame some theory of development which will mark some rules as new and others as old.   But how to obtain such a theory, that is the difficulty.   Out of the laws themselves we shall hardly obtain it, while at present no other body of rules has been brought sufficiently near the Welsh to afford us the means of critical comparison.   Philology may have something in store for us.   The heir apparent, or successor designate, of the Welsh chieftain is called the *edling* ; on this side of Offa's dyke he would be called the *ætheling.*   Are these two words two, or who has done the borrowing ?   It has long ago been pointed out that in Wales the bondman is a *taeog* and in England a *theow.*   Has there not from a very remote age been going and coming between Taffy's house and my house, and did not the Lords Marchers even at a pretty recent time claim the right of selling English criminals as slaves to the Welsh? But even when philology has done its utmost, we shall, I fear, be compelled to admit that some of the main principles of that "tribal society" which is described in the Welsh laws are susceptible of more than one explanation, and until we have Mr Seebohm's theory of "methods," we can pronounce no sure judgment on his account of "structure."

Let us take, by way of example, what seems to me a matter of cardinal importance. We see set before us a system of mutually exclusive clans. Each has its chieftain; each is an organized unit; the nation, tribe, race is built up out of these units. They can be, and they are, mutually exclusive, because each of them is constructed in accordance with the agnatic principle. Except in an exceptional case, one cannot inherit through a woman: *Mulier est finis familiae.* For all economic, proprietary, possessory purposes the members of each clan cling closely together. All this seems fairly simple. But so soon as there arises a question of blood-feud, of wergild (or *galanas*, as the Welsh call it), this clan system seems to fall to pieces. The "galanas-group," by which we mean the group which is entitled to receive and liable to pay the blood-money, is defined by a principle radically different from that which gives the clans their shape. It traces consanguinity both through men and through women. The consequence is that the "galanas-groups" are not, and cannot be, mutually exclusive unless there is strict endogamy within each group.

Let us put a concrete case. I belong to a "kindred." The members of that kindred trace their blood from a common ancestor through an unbroken series of males. Also I belong to a proprietary or possessory group which is smaller than the kindred; but this also is agnatically constituted. In the particular case we will suppose that I am living in intimate communion with a number of men who are my paternal first cousins, being sons of the sons of my father's father. All my economic interests are bound up with theirs. This is put before us as a common case. And now one of these men slays my mother's brother. *Quid iuris?* This, we may say, is a question of arithmetic. I am both debtor and creditor, for I belong to two different "galanas-groups." So we have but to set off the debit and credit and perform a subtraction sum. Now this may be a tolerable solution in days when revenge has given place to blood-money; but can we translate it into the language of a time when the blood-feud is not merely permitted by law, but demanded by all that is sacred? My mother's kinsmen are swooping down on the cluster of huts in one of which I live; they are coming to burn and to slay. What is my duty? What is my natural impulse? Shall I defend the cousin who slew my uncle, or shall I make common cause with the raiders? " Divided duties" there will always be; were it otherwise, this would be a poor world for lawyers. But here we seem to have an easily possible case in which the problem goes to the very root of morality and religion. Can we suppose that a state of society which permits, which necessitates, the emergence of such problems, is a normal and stable state? Can it be other than a transitional state in which two different conceptions are contending for the mastery?

Mr Seebohm says (p. 104): "The payment of galanas was therefore a matter between two kindreds." Now this is just what we should like to say; but unless there has been some fundamental change in the constitution of the "galanas-group," or in the constitution of the "kindred," these two have never been coterminous, but have been fashioned by two thoroughly different principles. It would be difficult or impossible to improve the excellent exposition that Mr Seebohm has given of the nature of the "galanas-group," but it brings out in sharp outlines this fact that the blood-feud unit is not a kindred, and may or must be composed of men who belong to different kindreds. This has long seemed to me to be the central difficulty of the Welsh laws. I had hoped that Mr Seebohm would have solved or at all events attacked it, and I still hope that he will attack it in his next volume. This problem occurs not only in Wales, but in some other parts of the world, and I venture to think that until we have loosened it we have hardly begun the explanation of tribal society.

Again, let us hope that Mr Seebohm has not said his last word about patriarchism. "It can hardly be doubted," he says (p. 95), "that the Welsh *weles* resemble in their structure much more closely the 'patriarchal family' under its *patria potestas* than what is known as the 'joint family' with its joint ownership under a chief who is only *primus inter pares*." This may be very true, and yet we may be obliged to add that the gulf between the Welsh *wele*, as it is described in the codes and the Roman system of *patria potestas* is almost immeasurably wide.   In the Wales of the codes there is nothing that ought to be called *patria potestas* without a qualifying note.   The young tribesman when he attains the age of fourteen years is commended to a lord and becomes a fully free man, "and he is himself to answer for every claim that may be made on him."   If there was a time when the full-grown son remained in his father's power that time has gone by; but I cannot think that Mr Seebohm has as yet proved that it ever existed.

If the Welsh laws are treacherous, still more treacherous are those Welsh diplomata, would-be deeds of conveyance and the like, which claim an ancient date.   Mr Seebohm puts more faith in the Liber Landavensis than I dare put until Mr Haddan's unfavourable judgment has been impugned and re-versed.   Mr Seebohm, though he treads cautiously on this dangerous ground, seems at times to be scarcely aware of the full extent of the danger.   At one point (p. 177) he seems inclined to accept as a basis for inferences about the Wales of the sixteenth century, a charter which concedes to a church a full-blown and elaborate "immunity."   The church is to hold its lands "with complete legal cognisance of thief, of theft, of violence, of slaying, of waylaying, of in-cendiarism and contention with blood and without it."   Now surely with this document before us we must say one of two things, either that it is a gross forgery, or that Wales, far from being a country in which archaic or primitive phenomena can be studied, is the land which led the van of the nations in their progress from tribalism to feudalism. If we translated this document into Latin and supposed it to come from England, the reign of Canute or of Edward the Confessor would be the earliest age to which we could refer it, and if we supposed it to come from France or Germany we should, to say the least, find few to believe that it was Merovingian. Welsh philologists may say of it what they will, but the dilemma is not to be escaped. If this flamboyant immunity belongs to the sixth, seventh, or eighth century, Welsh ecclesiastics and Welsh conveyancers were far in advance of their foreign brethren. However, though I do not think that Mr Seebohm has been quite sceptical enough in his dealings with these highly suspicious documents, I must not suggest that his use of them vitiates the main argument of his book.

So sparse are the genuine documents which come from the Wales of ancient days that the temptation to eke them out by other evidence is strong. In a few instances it seems to me that Mr Seebohm has yielded too easily to this temptation. To illustrate the Celtic custom of tonsuring serfs he calls to his aid (p. 129) a passage in the Scottish law-book *Quoniam attachiamenta*, in which I can see no tonsure, and nothing Celtic, but merely the Normano-Anglian law of the Scottish lowlands which copies from English law-books, and which tells how the man who submits to become a serf delivers himself to his master " by the front hairs of his head," a practice of which we have a good deal of evidence coming from Frankland. But this is a small point, and the other instances in which

Mr Seebohm might be accused of similar mistakes are of no great moment.

His second volume we shall eagerly await, and he will easily understand that only because there is a second volume to come has this review of the first been devoted rather to a statement of difficulties than to an expression of the gratitude that is due to him for an excellent piece of work.

THE MURDER OF HENRY CLEMENT[1]

ANY English document of the thirteenth century which shows us witnesses being examined separately as to the perpetration of a crime is of so rare a kind that the following extract from a Coram Rege roll seems worthy to be printed. It relates to the murder of Henry Clement in the year 1235 of which Matthew Paris has told us[2]. Clement was a clerk whom Maurice Fitzgerald, the justiciar of Ireland, had sent as envoy to the king. It will be seen from the following record —and this we might learn from Paris also—that the guilt of the murder was attributed to two very different persons. On the one hand suspicion fell on Gilbert Marshall, Earl of Pembroke, for Clement, it was said, had bragged of having a hand in the death of Richard Marshall, Gilbert's brother, who perished in Ireland in the year 1234. On the other hand there were some who laid the murder of Clement at the door of William de Marisco, whose father, Geoffrey de Marisco, was supposed to have taken part in the plot which lured

[1] *English Historical Review*, April, 1895.
[2] Matth. Par. *Chron. Maj.* III. 327, IV. 193–6; *Royal Letters*, ed. Shirley, I. 469–70; Sweetman's *Calendar of Irish Documents*, Nos. 2262, 2291, 2321.

Richard Marshall to his fate. This of course is strange; it is much as if we were certain that some modern Irish crime had been committed either by Fenians or by Orangemen, and yet knew not which party to accuse. It suggests that there was a triangular quarrel between the Marshalls, the Fitzgeralds, and the family of Marsh or Dumaresque. The truth may be that Clement had been babbling and had thus incurred the enmity of all parties. The end of the matter was that Gilbert Marshall proved his innocence, while William de Marisco was outlawed, took to piracy, and in 1242 was hanged as a traitor. We know also that Gilbert Marshall was suspected of shielding William de Marisco from justice[1].

The following record stands on Curia Regis Roll No. 115 (18–19 Hen. III), m. 33 d. It has been copied by Miss Salisbury. The roll is in bad condition; some words are illegible and the words here printed within brackets are barely to be read. I have endeavoured to write out in full the words which are contracted in the original document. I have read no other record of this age which shows us a similar attempt to obtain evidence of a crime from witnesses who are examined one by one.

MIDD. { *Henricus Clement nuncius Iusticiarii Hybernie occisus fuit apud Westmonasterium in domo Magistri Davidis le Cirurgien.*

Et Willelmus Perdriz nuncius domini Regis tunc fuit in domo illa et dicit quod post mediam noctem[2] ante diem Lune proximum

---

[1] Sweetman's *Calendar*, No. 2321.
[2] This seems to be the night between 13 and 14 May 1235.

ante Ascenscionem Domini venerunt v. homines armati vel sex vel ibi circiter et plures alii[1] nec nescivit numerum ad domum praedicti Davidis et fregerunt hostium aule et postea intraverunt aulam et ascenderunt versus unum solium et hostium solii fregerunt et ibi occiderunt predictum Henricum et vulneraverunt predictum Magistrum Davidem. Et quesitus si sciret qui ipsi fuerunt dicit quod non. Quesitus eciam[2] ipse fecit dicit quod non fuit ausus aliquid facere propter metum predictorum armatorum et dixit predicti homines dicebant sibi quod teneret se in pace et quod non oporteret eum timere. Et dicit quod credit quod plures extra domum fuerunt in vico quia cum idem Henricus vellet in fugam convertere et abire et cum vellet exire per quandam fenestram retraxit se propter multitudinem gentium quam vidit extra in vico.

Et Brianus nuncius Iusticiarii Hybernie tunc fuit in curia in quadam domo forinseca in quodam stabulo et dicit quod neminem vidit nec aliquid scivit antequam factum illud perpetratum fuit et tunc levavit clamorem sed dicit quod nescivit qui fuerunt sed dicit quod homines Willelmi de Marisco minati fuerunt eidem Henrico de corpore suo quia dicebat quod idem Henricus fuit in curia et secutus fuit curiam domini Regis et ipsum et alios de Hibernia impedivit quod negocia sua facere non potuerunt in curia. Et dicit quod habet in suspicione ipsum Willelmum et suos et homines Marescalli sed dicit quod nescit aliquem nominare. Et dicit quod suspicionem habet de quodam valeto Ricardi Syward[3] sed nescit illum nominare.

Willelmus garcio predicti Henrici dicit quod iacuit in quodam stabulo in curia et quod nichil inde scivit antequam factum illud factum fuit[4] quod nescit qui illi fuerunt sed dicit quod predictus Henricus sepius dixit in hoc dimidio anno quod homines Marescalli ei minati fuerunt sepius. Et quesitus si aliquem nominavit unquam dicit non quod.

Et Willelmus homo ipsius Perdriz venit et dicit quod iacuit in aula et dicit quod plures venerunt in domum circiter duodecim vel

---

[1] *Et plures alii* interlined.   [2] Supply *quid*.

[3] Richard Siward was a friend of the Marshalls. This witness, who is a servant of Fitzgerald, seems to suspect both Marshall and Marisco.

[4] Supply *et*.

ampliores[1] videbatur ei quod domus plena erat sed non fuit ausus
clamare sed cooperuit capud suum quadam barhudo.   Et dicit
quando recesserunt ipse secutus fuit eos cum clamore usque ad
cimiterium Westmonasterii et unus eorum reverti voluit super eum
et ipse in domum intravit et non fuit ausus ulterius sequi.   Et dicit
quod tres vidit euntes versus cimiterium cum gladiis extractis.

Sander Scot garcio Thome le Messager dicit quod iacuit in domo
et dicit quod vidit sex armatos quolibet genere armorum et caligis
ferreis et quidam tulerunt quandam grossam torchiam tortam in[2]
manu sua usque ad hostium solarii et quando perceperunt quod
Henricus fuit in solio tunc illam extinxerunt et intraverunt ad facien-
dum illud factum.

Alicia hospita ipsius Magistri Davidis dicit quod iacuit in quadam
camera in domo sua et famula sua similiter et pueri sui cum ea et
quando audivit frangere hostium aule versus vicum ipsa voluit exire
sed non fuit ausa exeundi pro famula sua et ipsa levavit clamorem
et aperuit quandam fenestram versus curiam et nullum de garcionibus
qui iacuerunt in stabulo potuit evigilare.   Quesita si aliquem cog-
noscebat vel videret dicit quod non, set dicit quod audivit eundem
Henricum dicentem Dominica qua occisus fuit eadem nocte quod
timebat sibi ne interficeretur et voluit potius esse in Hibernia quam
in Anglia.

Et Hawisia famula ipsius Alicie dicit similiter quod fuit in camera
illa sed neminem vidit nec aliquem cognovit.   Et filia ipsius Alicie
nichil aliud dicit.

Rogerus de Norwico qui iacuit in tentoriis ante portam domini
Regis dicit quod audivit homines euntes super calcetam et vidit
plures circiter sexdecim et quorum quidam fuerunt armati et ha-
buerunt gladios extractos set neminem cognovit et dicit quod equi
eorum fuerunt in cimiterio et plures illic tendebant et unus ivit
versus villam.

Godefridus Sutor qui similiter iacuit in tentoriis dicit quod audivit
equos et fremitum equorum et tunc post parvum intervallum fregerunt hostium aule et intraverunt sed nescit quid tunc ibi fecerunt sed
audivit ictus gladiorum.

---

[1] Supply *et*.

[2] Three preceding words interlined; *quandam grossam* on erasure.

Johannes filius Rogeri de Norwico similiter dicit quod neminem vidit sed audivit tumultum sed nullam scit certitudinem.

Ricardus Tremle iuratus[1] dicit quod nichil inde scit nisi quod audivit clamorem nec ab aliquo audivit nec inquirere potuit si aliqui ei minati essent vel quod aliquis ei aliquid vellet nisi bonum.

[Dictus] Magister David[2] iuratus dicit quod neminem cognovit sed armati fuerunt circiter quinque vel sex de illis qui...ascenderunt in solium et ipsum vulneraverunt[3] et cum ipse Henricus aperuisset fenestram et vellet [exire retraxit se] propter multitudinem gentium qui fuerunt in vico. Et dicit quod ipsum Henricum interfecerunt... dominus Rex [esset] nuper apud Roffam venerunt quidam Henricus de Ponte Arche et Henricus de...[et] minati fuerunt ei ita quod in- secuti fuerunt eum supra pontem Roffe cum quodam garcione et ille [garcio] habuit cultellum [semitractum] ut idem Henricus dicebat et quando cepit se ad cultellum suum ille garcio...et recessit et idem Henricus de Ponte Arche dicebat quod habuit spinam in pede et... recederet a predicto Henrico. Et dicit quod quidam parvus nuntius Willelmi Marescalli cum minutis butonibus[4] venit cotidie et inqui- rendum...dictus Henricus ubi esset et hospitari vellet. Dicit eciam quod venerunt cum quadam magna torchia.

Willelmus de Cantilupo et Ricardus de Stafford milites de Hi- bernia iurati dicunt quod idem Henricus cum esset apud Roffam ita fuit insultatus ut ipse Henricus eis dicebat et secundum quod pre- dictus Magister David dixit et eciam apud Suttone insidiatum fuit ei ita quod premunitus fuit a quodam milite familiare domini Regis. Dicunt eciam quod cum dominus Rex nuper esset apud Windesores venit Willelmus de Marisco et dicebat eidem Henrico quod ipse Henricus impedivit eum quod non potuit negocia sua expedire et promovere in curia quia majorem habuit graciam quam ipse habuit

---

[1] It is not said of the previous witnesses that they were sworn.

[2] The surgeon in whose house the murder was done.

[3] The witness himself was wounded.

[4] The five preceding words are interlined. Instead of *Willelmi Marescall'* should we read *Willelmi de Marisco*? Can this be an early appearance of the boy in buttons?

erga dominum Regem et dixit quod lueret de corpore suo et quod si
ipsum interfecisset pacem faceret cum domino suo[1].

...xxiiij[or] [de vico] Westmonasterii et ultra la Cherringe et versus
Tathulle dicunt super sacramentum suum quod nullam...veritatem
nec aliquid audiverunt nec quis hoc potuit fecisse[2].

...[3] qui interfuerunt morti ipsius Henrici et qui utlagati sunt
Willelmus de [Marisco]...Burgundie Philippus de Dinant Thomas
de Erdinton...de Ponte Archi. Eustachius Cumin Rogerus de
Marisco[4].

---

[1] William de Marisco told Henry Clement that if William slew
Henry, William would be able to make his peace with Henry's master,
Maurice Fitzgerald.

[2] This jury of twenty-four is called in, not to draw inferences
from the evidence already given, but to give, if possible, additional
evidence.

[3] Supply *Nomina eorum* or the like.

[4] From other sources we learn that the names of the persons
outlawed were William de Marisco, William of Pont de l'Arche,
John Cabus, Walter Sancmelle, Philip of Dinant, Thomas of Erdinton,
Henry of Colombieres, Eustace Cumin and Roger de Marisco.

TWO CHARTULARIES OF THE
PRIORY OF ST PETER AT BATH[1]

THE Somersetshire Record Society will soon obtain a foremost place among our antiquarian societies if it can often command the services of Mr Hunt. His learning, patience, and industry make him an almost ideally good editor for a cartulary, and the first of the two cartularies with which he here deals—and this he publishes nearly in full—is one which is of very great and general importance. It is the beautiful twelfth-century cartulary of Bath Priory, which lies at Cambridge in the library of Corpus Christi College. Many of its contents have long been well known, for from it Kemble and others have derived some precious Anglo-Saxon land-books, profitable documents even if they are not all that they pretend to be. These Mr Hunt has treated judiciously. For one thing, his copy of such portions of the text as are written in the Old English tongue is guaranteed by Professor Skeat, who has been able to point out a few mistakes in the previous editions. For another thing, we have from Mr Hunt himself not only a long introduction, which, in truth, is an elaborate history of the monastery, but

---

[1] *English Historical Review*, July, 1895.

also excellent notes on the names of the persons who are supposed to witness the land-books. A dogmatic judgment as to the genuineness of these ancient documents Mr Hunt does not give, and his reticence is wise, for it is doubtful whether the man is yet born who combines all the many kinds of knowledge and skill which will be possessed by him who finally assigns to would-be Anglo-Saxon diplomata their proper places in the gently graduated scale of carelessness, improvement, and falsification which lies between unadulterated genuineness and wicked forgery. In the meanwhile the work must be done bit by bit, and the laborious *discussio testium* (if I may adopt an old phrase) which Mr Hunt has energetically pursued is work of just the right kind.

Again, it is highly expedient that the most ancient cartularies should be printed just as they stand. Of course there is also ample room for chronologically arranged collections of all the land-books, such as Kemble made and Mr Birch is making. Still each separate cartulary should be printed as it stands. A good instance of the necessity of this procedure appears in Mr Hunt's volume. To many readers the most attractive of the documents that he prints will be that which describes the services of the men of Tidenham; for has not Mr Seebohm made it classical? Now this document is undated; but the cartulary also contains a grant of Tidenham by King Edwy to the monastery, which tries to date itself in 956, and a lease of Tidenham to Stigand. A good deal in our conception of some early stages in manorial history may depend on the question whether this statement of the Tidenham services represents matters as they stood in the middle of the tenth century, or on the very eve of the Norman Conquest. In the cartulary it is placed far away from Edwy's grant and immediately precedes the lease to Stigand. This is not conclusive, but I do not think that for the future we can confidently speak of it as describing "a manor of Edwy's day."

Some of the charters of the Norman age that are here printed are even more interesting, because more unique, than their predecessors. We have here (p. 49), for example, Modbert's famous lawsuit, which has been made known to us by Madox and Mr Bigelow. It is perhaps the best of all the "Placita Anglo-Normannica" that have come down to us. Then there is (p. 52) a deed from 1123 in which a man agrees to do suit to the courts of the hundred and the county for a whole vill. There is (p. 62) a feoffment from 1153 under which the sixth part of the service of one knight is to be done. These are early specimens. But we must not descend to particulars, else we shall be noticing a grant *in pheodo* (p. 51), of which, despite a threat of modernised spelling, Mr Hunt has not had the heart to deprive us. On purpose I will say nothing of the matters which fill the largest space in his introduction, in particular the relations between the churches of Bath, Wells, and Glastonbury. A first-rate cartulary has many sides, and Mr Hunt's work successfully stands the test of being examined from a point of view that is not his own.

The second part of his volume consists of a calendar, elaborately annotated, of a later cartulary preserved at Lincoln's Inn. This, no doubt, will be of great service to the antiquarians of Somersetshire, and there are in it a few documents printed at length which deserve to be set before a larger circle of readers. No doubt Mr Hunt has here given as much as the finances of the society would permit him to give. Still it may be permissible to remind similar societies that there is a small but growing class of men who take an interest in the form of mediaeval documents, and who will buy books in which such documents are either given in full or translated word by word. Deeds of manumission, for instance, are not so common that they should be passed by with three or four words. One would like at least to know whether any reason was given for the enfranchisement of the villain, and whether any money passed. Early letters of credit also are curiosities which illustrate the growth of the law of agency. However, Mr Hunt has behaved so nobly by the earlier that we shall raise no complaint if his calendar of the later cartulary rather whets than satisfies our appetite.

To catch Mr Hunt in what one hopes to be a mistake is a rare pleasure. Whatever the cartulary may say, the fine on p. 27 can hardly come from 15 Henry III. The judges' names point to a date some ten years earlier. Gerard de Athée (p. 194) was not "one of John's Flemish mercenaries," but came from Touraine. At least there is much evidence that points in this direction.

THE HISTORY OF MARRIAGE, JEWISH AND CHRISTIAN[1]

ONE of the penalties that a learned man must now and then pay for the fame that his learning has brought him is that his lightest words will seem serious to others, and that if, passing for a moment outside the province that he has made his own, he falls into mistakes, those mistakes will be pointed out by critics who are incompetent to judge the strong points of his work. Dr Luckock's book on the *History of Marriage*[2] is so likely to become authoritative among a large class of readers and disputants, so likely to be regarded as an armoury of proved controversial weapons, that the ungracious task of pointing to passages in it that should either be amended or omitted is a task which some one, though he may be profoundly ignorant of biblical, patristic, and talmudic lore, ought to undertake ; and it falls to me to say that, whatever may be his title to write a history of more ancient or more modern affairs, of the text of Leviticus or the text of Lyndhurst's Act, what he has written of the middle ages requires careful revision.

Though I think that he has made several mistakes,

[1] *English Historical Review*, Oct. 1895.

[2] *The History of marriage, Jewish and Christian, in relation to divorce and certain forbidden degrees.* By H. M. Luckock, 1894.

it will be sufficient if I single out two paragraphs.   A
reconsideration of them might lead him to a correction
of other passages and a distrust of those writers who
have been his guides.   The error to which I shall refer
lies, not in an overstatement, but in an understatement
of what I take to be a part of his case, and therefore
bears witness to his candour, for he has in the following words (so it seems to me) made unnecessary concessions to those whom he regards as his adversaries,
besides needlessly tainting the fair names of a gallant
earl, a faithful countess, and two august popes.

From the Norman Conquest to the beginning of the seventeenth
century no new Ecclesiastical Laws were made on this subject [the
indissolubility of marriage].   Dispensations, however, for remarriage
after separation were from time to time sought and obtained from
the Pope.   There were two famous instances in the highest rank
of life.   King John had married Hadwisa, daughter of William, earl
of Gloucester, and lived with her for eleven years without any
scruple on the score of consanguinity, but being captivated by the
personal beauty of Isabella of Angoulême, he resolved to shelter
himself under the plea of nearness of kin to obtain a divorce.   The
evil was aggravated by the fact that his second wife was already
betrothed ; but those were days when kings claimed to be a law
to themselves, and a dispensation was readily granted for his adulterous union.

His example was followed not long after, in the reign of
Henry III, by Simon de Montfort, who appealed to Rome to obtain a ratification for a second marriage, while his lawful wife was
still living.   It was in direct opposition to the Canons and Constitutions of the Church, but again the dispensation was granted.
(Morgan, *On the Law of Marriage,* II. 218 ; Jebbs' [*corr.* Tebbs']
Essay, 204.)

Now as to Montfort's case, I cannot but think that, if
the dean of Lichfield will look for a few minutes at the
evidence, he will see the necessity of making honour-

able amends to Earl Simon and Pope Gregory, perhaps also to the countess Eleanor, or of revealing the name of that other wife. Surely he is not hinting at some hitherto undisclosed scandal about the dowager of Flanders, who, says M. Bémont, was old enough to be Simon's grandmother, and who swore that she had not married him. I fear that Dr Luckock's informants were ignorant of her existence. The names of his informants he gives us in the fairest way. They are not quite the names that we should have expected in such a context, not Bémont nor Pauli, not Prothero nor Creighton nor Norgate, but Morgan and Tebbs ; still any warrantors are better than none.

In the year 1822, the Society for Promoting Christian Knowledge in the diocese of St David's having offered a prize of fifty pounds, Mr H. V. Tebbs, proctor in Doctors' Commons, set to work, and within a short space of time—two months, if I read him rightly—produced an essay on the "Scripture Doctrine of Adultery and Divorce," which wandered through many ages and lands, and promoted Christian knowledge within the aforesaid diocese in manner following, that is to say :—

In 1199, King John being divorced from the duke of Gloucester's daughter was in the same year remarried to Isabell, the heiress of a noble family. And, indeed, king John's first wife had been, previously to her marriage with him, divorced from Henry de Leon, duke of Saxony.

Matthew Paris makes mention of the case of Simon de Montford, in Henry III's time, in which the pope, in opposition to the laws and canons of the church, granted a dispensation, and then ratified his second marriage. (Matth. Paris, *Hist.*, p. 455.)

Now it is always dangerous to speculate about the origin of error, for error is manifold; still if we suppose that by p. 455 Mr Tebbs meant p. 465 in Wats's edition, we shall come to a passage in which Matthew Paris speaks of a marriage contracted by Montfort and also of a papal dispensation. Had Mr Tebbs been in less haste to earn a prize and promote Christian knowledge, he might have turned over a few pages and come upon another passage in which Paris says more of that marriage and that dispensation. He would have come upon the well-worn story of the widowed girl's rash vow, and would have discovered that (to put the matter technically) the impediment to the marriage was not the *ligamen* of the husband, but the *votum* of the wife. I am inclined to think that, if he had carried his researches yet a little further, he would have found that no papal dispensation was necessary for the validation of this marriage; in other words, that Pope Gregory (who knew his canon law) decided, and was right in deciding, that a *votum casti-tatis*, however solemn, provided that it did not amount to a *professio* in some recognised religious order, was no *impedimentum dirimens*. Simon and Eleanor had sinned, but their marriage was a good marriage. As to that other wife, I fancy that the rapid Mr Tebbs invented her. He saw the words *Et dispensavit dominus Papa cum ipsa, prout sermo sequens declara-bit.* He had no mind or no time to look for the *sermo sequens*; he saw that the pope "dispensed with" some woman, and took this to mean that Simon was suffered to put away wife No. 1 (whether she was Eleanor or no he does not tell us) and marry wife No. 2. The pope of Rome used to do such things—in England and the year 1822 : Christian knowledge affirmed it.

In Dr Luckock's index we may read, "Cosin, bishop, his carelessness in quoting authorities—mischievous consequences of this—" I know not how careless Bishop Cosin was, or how much mischief his carelessness may have done, but I do not think that Mr Tebbs was careful, and he seems to me to have done more mischief than I should have thought him capable of doing, so artless were his ways. However, he succeeded in deceiving the Rev. Hector Davies Morgan, who (so the *Dictionary of National Biography* says) had gained another of these 50*l.* prizes by promoting Christian knowledge, and who in 1826 published a book on the doctrine and law of marriage. Morgan repeated what Tebbs had said, adding a generalising ornament of that kind which historical essayists used to think permissible and elegant. These sad cases of Simon and John he sets before us as mere examples of the sort of thing that your mediaeval pope would do. "The facility with which such dispensations were granted is strikingly illustrated by the case of King John." There are some marriages with which we who are not popes can dispense. One of Earl Simon's seems to have belonged to this class. I think that the dean of Lichfield will not be infringing any papal prerogatives if he dispenses with that marriage for the future.

Turning to King John, we feel almost angry with Dr Luckock for suppressing that thrilling episode in these Morgano-Tebbsian *Gesta Pontificum* which introduces us to Henry de Leon, duke of Saxony. And

I am not certain that something true might not be made of it, if we held that a count of Maurienne must be also count of Mortain (Mortain, Maurienne, Macedon, and Monmouth were much alike in the diocese of St David's), or that Clementia of Zäringen was identical with her own daughter, though in the latter case we might also have to hold that a boy but five or six years old could be irrevocably bound by a marriage contract. That little John should marry the divorced wife (or, in strictness of law, discarded mistress) of his sister's husband, adds a spice of horror to the tale and sets us thinking about that inscrutable mystery the *affinitas secundi generis*. Dr Luckock saw that there was something wrong with Henry "de Leon." The pity is that when his scepticism had been once aroused it fell asleep again and left the accusation against Innocent III unretracted. The pope is still supposed to do something wrong and to enable our bad king to be "a law to himself."

John's matrimonial affairs are not so plain as might be wished. Contemporary Englishmen seem to have been somewhat uncertain as to what really happened. We start of course with this, that he went through the form of marriage with Isabella, otherwise Avice, of Gloucester ; and that, if there was no dispensation in the case, this would-be marriage between two persons who stood to each other in the third degree of consanguinity was a nullity. John and Isabella are living together in incestuous concubinage ; it is John's duty to put Isabella away, and if Pope Innocent commands him to do so, we need not be surprised. Thus we may understand the rumour which found credence in an

English monastery to the effect that the pope issued such a command and that John obeyed it[1]. That is a consistent story. Nevertheless we may be fairly certain that it is not true. We learn from another and a trustier source that there had been some papal dispensation for the union between these second cousins, and we are told that the pope was vexed when certain French bishops pronounced a divorce, or, to use stricter language, declared that the marriage was null[2]. This they may well have done without questioning the pope's power of removing the impediment that lay between John and his kinswoman. For any one of twenty reasons they may have held that the document which John had obtained from the papal chancery did not meet the case. I am not defending them; I know not whether they need defence, but it seems quite possible that if an appeal to Rome had been made against their sentence it would have been reversed. Isabella, it may be, was not so anxious to retain the king of England as Ingeborg was to retain the king of France; we know that she tried two other husbands before she died. But, whichever story be true, the marriage with the Gloucester heiress was pronounced null by an ecclesiastical court. Indeed John seems to have been at pains to obtain a sentence from the Norman bishops[3] and another sentence from the bishops of his more southerly dominions[4]. John, then, if a wicked, was none the less an unmarried man. He required no dispensation if he wanted to marry.

---

[1] Coggeshall, 103.

[2] Diceto, II. 167; cf. *ibid.* 72.

[3] Diceto, II. 167.

[4] Hoveden, IV. 119.

One point, at all events, I should have said, was beyond all reasonable doubt, had not Dr Luckock written the paragraph that I have transcribed, namely, that the pope gave John no help in getting rid of Isabella of Gloucester. Innocent himself told Philip of France that John's case had never come before the Roman see. Mistaken he can hardly have been. Why should we not believe him[1]?

Dr Luckock, when he rejected the pretty tale about Henry de Leon's divorced wife, may have felt that he was depriving his readers of a harmless joy, and owed them some compensation. So John's crime and Innocent's complacency must be magnified. " The evil was aggravated by the fact that his second wife was already betrothed." Now no doubt John behaved scurvily to the Lusignans, and sorely was he punished for so doing; but we seem to have very good reason for believing that the contract between Hugh and Isabella was one which, according to the law of the church, she could avoid. We are told that when she said her *verba de praesenti* she was below the age at which a complete marriage was possible[2]. Hugh might be irrevocably bound, but she was free to avoid her contract, and if, when old enough to marry, she married John, her marriage with John would be valid without any dispensation. I have not come upon the authority which

---

[1] Innocentii III *Opera* (ed. Migne), i. 1015: *Licet autem praedictus Ludovicus quondam pater tuus et praesens etiam rex Anglorum ab his quas sibi iunxerant, praelatorum terrae suae iudicio fuerint separati, super divortio tamen non fuit ad sedem apostolicam querela delata. Unde quod a praelatis ipsis factum fuerat, cum nullus penitus reclamaret, noluit revocare.*

[2] Hoveden, iv. 119.

asserts that there was any dispensation at all relating to this bond (such as it was) between Hugh and Isabella, but I think that Dr Luckock would have considerable difficulty in proving that about the year 1200 it was unlawful or scandalous for a pope to dispense with a marriage that had not been consummated. Not so very long before that time such a marriage would hardly have been treated by the church as more 'than an agreement to marry. It may be formally true that after 1066 (the date that Dr Luckock chooses) "no new ecclesiastical laws were made" touching the indissolubility of marriage, but he does not, I take it, doubt that about a century after that date there was a very large change in the canonical conception of the manner in which a perfect and indissoluble marriage comes into existence.

"These were days," he says, "when kings claimed to be a law to themselves, and a dispensation was readily granted for his adulterous union." Yes, and these also were days when Innocent was laying France under an interdict in order that King Philip might be constrained to dismiss the German adulteress and take back the Danish wife. These popes were shamelessly inconsistent, were they not?

Unless Dr Luckock is in possession of information which leads him to believe that John's union with his cousin of Gloucester and Earl Simon's union with that anonymous lady were not consummated unions, or were contracted between persons who had never been baptised, he is, if I understand him rightly, charging two popes with having done what canonists of the classical age said that the popes never did, and even that no

pope could do; he is charging them with having dispensed with the impediment to marriage which consists
in a lawful and consummate *ligamen* uniting two Christians. This charge he has brought not merely against
two popes, but, to all appearance, against the two most
illustrious of all ecclesiastical legislators. He will, I
think, admit that his "two famous instances in the
highest rank of life" are mere illusions. He speaks
of them, however, as if they were examples of what
was done "from time to time" by popes who lived
after the middle of the eleventh century. If he has
some other and some better attested instances to offer,
he should give them to the world. I am too ignorant
to say that there are none to be found, but any which
can be found should certainly have a place in every
history of marriage law, for they are conspicuously
absent in some books which nowadays enjoy a higher
repute than the works of Messrs Morgan and Tebbs.

THE ORIGIN OF THE BOROUGH[1]

THE controversy as to the origin of the German towns goes on cheerfully. The matter in debate is many-sided, and the main questions are perplexed with collateral issues. The readers of this Review have before now had occasion to wish that Dr Keutgen would speak his mind at greater length than was possible in those notices of other men's books which he has contributed to these pages. This he has now done in a short but tightly packed book[2], wherein he passes judgment on most of the theories that have come to the front within recent years. His work is critical and eclectic, and it assumes in its readers a familiarity with the outlines of the dispute. It is not, therefore, an easy book for beginners and outsiders; but one member of that class can say gratefully that he has found in it many passages that are interesting and helpful. Certainly it is a book which any one who is going to speculate about the origins of our English towns ought to have read. Of its bearing on English history I will venture to say a few words.

[1] *English Historical Review*, April, 1896.
[2] *Untersuchungen über den Ursprung der deutschen Stadtverfassung.* Von Dr F. Keutgen. Leipzig: Duncker und Humblot. 1895.

Any theory as to the origin of the *Stadt* (in English the borough) must answer at least one question of legal history. There may, indeed, be many questions of economic history to be solved—for example, whether we ought to treat as aboriginal those mercantile and industrial elements which are prominent in the boroughs of the later middle ages. But one question of legal history there undoubtedly is : When, why, how does the town become a jurisdictional unit, a district which has a court in and for itself ? No mere accumulation of economic facts will enable us to answer that question. We are in search of a legal principle. It may be highly convenient that a thickly peopled spot should become a jurisdictional unit with its own court. But in the world of law things do not happen merely because they are convenient, and, after all, the world of law is a world of fact.

This, then, is one focus of the controversy. Now, of course it is allowed on all hands that when we speak of "the" origin of "the" *Stadt* or "the" borough we are not thinking of every *Stadt* or every borough. In particular we leave out of account the newer boroughs. When once some boroughs have come into existence, and a legal line has been drawn between *Stadt* and *Dorf*, between borough and rural township, then there can and there will be imitation. This point we need not labour; in England new boroughs have been made in this nineteenth century. Our interest lies in the oldest boroughs and in the days in which there could be no imitation, since there was nothing—at all events no borough—to imitate. In England we may exclude from our consideration more than half of those places which were boroughs when the boroughs first began to send burgesses to the king's parliaments.

This done, we cannot make "the" borough court grow out of "the" village court. In later times the village or township very often has a court of its own, a manorial court. In that case the village court may well become a borough court. Its lord grants a charter; he lightens the pressure of seignorial power; he consents to efface himself more or less completely, and to allow the quondam villagers to behave as burgesses are by this time behaving, to take the profits of the court, and so forth. But this almost certainly is not the history of the borough court in those ancient boroughs, the "county towns," which are throughout the middle ages our typical English boroughs. Unless our earliest evidence is very deceptive, we may speak of a time when the *burh* had a court, and the village, or *tún*, normally had none. If there are still among us any who would start from village courts as from primitive data, they can, indeed, afford to disregard a great deal of German and French controversy, but I cannot think that in other respects their lot is enviable.

The land becomes honeycombed with "immunities" and sokens. But another lesson that we are learning from Germany (and Dr Keutgen makes this prominent) is that the borough court is not the outcome of "immunity." As regards Germany this is a principle which must, so it seems, be fought for, because, as I understand, we first catch sight of the *Stadt* as a jurisdictional unit at a time when the jurisdiction over it has passed, or is in the act of passing, from the king

M. III.

or emperor to the bishop of the town, who is already a mighty "immunist"; hence complications and equivocal documents. I believe that in England this principle could be made good in much simpler fashion. The typical ancient *Stadt* of Germany is a bishop's see, and at a very early time in its history its bishop becomes its lord. In England, on the other hand, very many of the boroughs which have every right to be regarded as ancient and typical never were bishops' sees, and never had over them any lord but the king. The town itself becomes honeycombed with sokens, but from age to age the borough court has only the king above it. It is not the outcome of immunity; there is no immunist. It belongs to that order of courts to which the shire moot and the hundred moot belong.

Why should the borough have a court? That there is an intimate connection between the borough court and the special peace that reigns within the borough is not now to be denied. In England we begin to lose sight of that special peace (which, be it remembered, means specially severe criminal law) at a yet early time. In the twelfth century the whole of our criminal law was rapidly reconstructed on new lines. England was a small country, and its king was strong. Still in Domesday and elsewhere there are a good many relics of the old borough peace waiting for their collector; indeed it may be doubted whether the last of these relics will have disappeared until the enterprising burglar has "done a burgling." The English borough, like the German *Stadt*, has been the scene of specially severe laws against violence.

Whence this special peace? Here we come upon the dazzling *Marktrechttheorie.* Any one who has read Sohm's brilliant essay will echo the words in which M. Pirenne (*Revue Historique,* LIII. 78) has recently described its impetuous force. *On est sub-jugué, bon gré mal gré.* We abandon with regret this beautiful dogma ; still in the end we abandon it. Objections to it have been collecting in many quarters ; they are well stated by M. Pirenne and by Dr Keutgen ; several of them seem to me unanswerable, and in particular I cannot believe that in England the market ever was the legal essence of the borough. Of course it was not this in the later middle ages. The mere " market town " is one of the things that we contrast with the borough. For all legal purposes it is a village ; it has only the constitution of a village, but once or twice a week a market is held in it. Then, again, the borough as such has no market ; the right to have a market is a separate " franchise," which ought to have a charter behind it. Lastly, the market jurisdiction is distinct in kind from the jurisdiction of the borough court. To all this we may add the difficulty, on which many have commented, of making the essentially temporary market peace grow into the eternal peace of the borough.

It is here, so I think, that Dr Keutgen has performed his greatest service. He has insisted that, whatever else the German *Stadt* may be, it is a burg. He very truly remarks that in English this truth becomes a truism. Our English equivalent for *Stadt* is " borough," or, to put it another way, those thickly peopled spots which have a special peace, a special

law, an urban constitution, those thickly peopled spots
which are not mere villages or townships, are boroughs.
That is their legal name; in the middle ages it is also
their common, their only name, for every village is
a "town." Is it not, then, rather with a *Burgfriede*
than with a *Marktfriede* that we have to start?

I think it must be allowed that here in England in
the days of the Germanic invasions, and for some time
afterwards, the word *burh* meant simply stronghold,
and carried with it no hint of thick population, or, it
may be, of any population at all. The map of England
seems to tell us this. The hilltop that has been fortified
is a *bury*. Very often it will give its name to the
neighbouring village. But we have a large number of
places whose names end in *bury, borough, burgh* which
are not to all appearance connected with ancient camps,
and have never been, so far as we can tell, peculiarly
populous villages. There are, I believe, some two
hundred and fifty villages (to say nothing of hamlets)
which thus by their names aspire to be boroughs. In
Essex, again, it is common to find some house or
group of houses bearing the name of the village in
whose territory it is situated with the word "bury" by
way of distinctive addition. Thus in Harlow there
will be Harlowbury, in Netteswell there will be Nettes-
wellbury, and so forth. On the other hand, it is not
a little remarkable that in the first flight of those
places which became legal "boroughs" hardly more
than three—namely, Canterbury, Salisbury, and Shrewsbury—assert their right to be boroughs in their very
names. This, by the way, is but a poor tale to set of
against Augsburg, Regensburg, Strassburg, Magde

burg, Hamburg, &c. So our map seems to tell us that the legal differentiation of borough from village, though indubitably ancient, is by no means primeval.

There seems, however, to have come a time here in England when *burh* acquired a new sense, or rather underwent a specification. We may reasonably ask whether this process was not closely connected with that striking phenomenon, the extremely artificial character of a great deal of our old English political geography. Let us look at the boroughs and counties of Middle England as they appear at the date of the Norman Conquest. One might think that godless French republicans had been here already, so mechanical, so rationalistic, so utilitarian is the allotment. Each shire has its borough, in general its one and only borough, just in its centre, or, in other words, each borough has its shire arranged neatly around it ; the borough gives its name to the shire ; the borough is the *chef-lieu* of an *arrondissement*. Have we not here the outcome of a deliberate military policy ? Is not each district to have its stronghold, its place of refuge ? What is all this *burh-bót* of which we hear, this duty from which no landholder is to be exempt ? Is it not the duty of the men of the shire to maintain the fortifications (primitive enough) of the borough, the one borough, of the shire ?

Another striking sight meets our eye in the boroughs of Domesday Book. The *barones comitatus* have, and their predecessors, the great folk, hallowed and lay, of the old English shire, have had, houses and burgesses in the county town. These town houses, these burgesses, are often reckoned as belonging "for rating purposes" to rural manors of their lords which lie many miles away from the borough. What did the Anglo-Saxon thegn want with a town house? He was not going to spend "the season" there in order that he might take his wife and daughters to the county balls. Then, again, your ceorl who was "thriving to thegn right" was expected to have a *burh-geat-setl*, and what is this but a house in the gate of the *burh*? Is it not a duty of *burgward* which obliges the thegns of the shire to have houses and dependents in the *burh* of the shire?

If such a train of thought as this has occurred to us, much of what Dr Keutgen has written about the deliberate and systematic foundation of burgs in Saxony will seem to us suggestive and luminous. To me it seems that we enter on a new and a very hopeful line of speculation when we shift our attention from markets and handicraft and commerce to the military character of the ancient *burh*. For one thing, we are thus enabled to obtain our special peace, and our specially royal peace, on cheaper terms than those that are offered by the *Marktrechttheorie*. The fictitious royal presence we can obtain, and the royal court which is a public court, co-ordinate with the hundred moot. We have all read how the sphere of the king's peace is measured outwards from his *burh-geat*. We know how in later days any spot at which the peripatetic king may be is the centre from which the jurisdiction of a special tribunal, the court of the king's own household, radiates outwards. Whatever be the oldest application of the word *burh*, the *burh* which becomes the legal borough (in general a "county town") is a very royal place. It has been created, or at all events is being maintained, as a matter of national importance; it is maintained "at the expense of the nation" by the duty of *burh-bót*. This, so it seems to me, is what in later days prevents the borough from being engulfed in the system of land-ownership and manorial jurisdiction.

Let me endeavour to explain myself. The king is the lord of the borough. But the borough of which the king is lord is not a tract of soil. I am speaking of the great ancient typical boroughs. In later days there may often, in the earlier days there may sometimes, be boroughs of which the king is lord in every sense; he is the landlord of each burgess; each burgess holds his tenement immediately of the king. So also in later days we may find boroughs of which some other person is the lord. But in the ancient boroughs, the county towns, this was not the normal state of affairs at the date of the Domesday survey or at any later time. Of course when the feudal theory had been pressed home the king appeared as the lord, the ultimate lord, of every inch of soil in the borough. But he was this only in the sense in which he was the lord of every inch of soil in his realm. The important point is that many of the burgesses in a royal borough were not the king's immediate tenants; they did not pay their rents to him. The burgesses were a tenurially heterogeneous group. Some of them were reckoned to belong to divers distant rural manors of the *barones comitatus*. In later days the thread of tenure which connects a given burgess with the king will often run through the lord of a great honour. So the borough court is not founded on a tenurial or feudal principle; the burgesses are not peers of one tenure; but the borough court is a link between them, and above that court stands the king, who takes its profits. Thus in the king's hand "the borough" becomes a "thing incorporeal," like a hundred or a county, and the king can let it to farm. Ultimately the burgesses will become its farmers. Jurisdictional unity coupled with tenurial or proprietary heterogeneity is what we have to account for in our ancient boroughs. The structure of the borough is not very like the structure of a manor; it is far more like the structure of a hundred. The court that gives it its unity, and in course of time becomes the centre and organ of burghal liberty, seems from the first to be a national court. I believe that, for England at all events, Dr Keutgen is pointing in the right direction when he suggests that the *Burgfriede*, or special royal peace conferred upon fortified places which are military units, units in a system of national defence, is the original principle which serves to mark off the borough from the village.

The prominence given to the burg and its peace is, if I am not mistaken, the newest and most distinctive feature of Dr Keutgen's work. About other matters he is, as already said, critical and eclectic. As regards the economic history of the towns, so many different theories are before the world that probably the time for a wise eclecticism has come. One writer will attribute a larger, another a smaller place to the mercantile element, or again to the element of voluntary association which produces gilds; but then it is by no

means unlikely that this difference of opinion represents a real difference between the history of different
towns.   I think, however, that Dr Keutgen must be
right when he insists that, if once we can account for
the borough court, we may for the rest think of the
borough community as being essentially similar to the
other communities of the land.   There is a great deal
of English evidence which tends to show that the
borough community was regarded as being at bottom
one and the same thing as a village community.   The
borough is a privileged township.; but none the less, or
rather all the more, it is a township.   In the thirteenth
century we are quite right in speaking of the community
of London as a *villata*, and this is sometimes done in
official documents ; but the community of Little Peddl-
ington also is a *villata*.   At a time when most villages
have courts, manorial courts, there is the utmost difficulty
in drawing a well-principled line between the humbler
boroughs and the mere townships ; the sheriffs can
draw an unprincipled line pretty much where they
please.   And then gradually the word "town," which
has belonged to every village in the kingdom, is exclusively appropriated by those larger "towns," many
or most of which are boroughs.   All this would surely
have been otherwise if men had felt that there was
some radical difference between the *Dorfgemeinde* and
the *Stadtgemeinde*.   As the borough grows in size and
power, the borough community becomes much more
complex than the village community.   For many purposes the borough likens itself to a hundred, and for
those purposes the various "wards" or parishes within
the borough begin to look like the townships which

make up the hundred. Many problems remain to be solved. To me it seems that, whatever may be the case of the *Rat* in Germany, the borough council of our English towns grows out of the borough court. When first we meet with a select group of twelve burgesses which is beginning to be a council for the borough, its primary duty still is that of declaring the judgments or "deeming the dooms" of the borough. To account for the formation of this group of dooms-men is by no means easy; still we may doubt whether even here we have a phenomenon that is only to be found within borough walls. It is not unknown that a rural hundred will have just twelve doomsmen, and that the duty of providing them will be allotted among the great landowners of the hundred in a manner that looks extremely artificial. On the whole, the structural peculiarities which distinguish the borough community seem to disappear somewhat rapidly if we endeavour to pursue them behind the age of borough charters; *die Stadtgemeinde ist der Landgemeinde gleichartig.* The notion of a township which is also a hundred *vel quasi* is a good, though perhaps not an all-sufficient, clue.

A SONG ON THE DEATH OF SIMON DE MONTFORT[1]

THE following poem is written on a fly leaf in a manuscript belonging to Caius College (No. 85, formerly 167). That volume contains several treatises on the canon law—to wit, (1) the "Ordo Iudiciarius" of Tancred, archdeacon of Bologna (*ob. circ.* 1234); (2) the "Summa de Matrimonio" (written between 1234 and 1245) of Raymund de Pennaforte (*ob.* 1275); (3) an imperfect copy of the "Summa Aurea" of the Oxford canonist William of Drogheda (*ob.* 1245). In the last of these treatises, as here presented, the years 1262 and 1267 are mentioned as the dates of certain imaginary documents. If we may judge from marginal notes, this volume belonged about the year 1270 to a certain Walterus de Hyda. His name is introduced into various legal formulas, written in the margin, which may represent real or may represent imaginary transactions. If they are founded on fact, then we may gather from them that Walter had taken degrees in arts and canon law at Paris (*tam in artibus quam in decretis laudabiliter rexit Parisius*); also that though of gentle he was of illegitimate birth; also that some

---

[1] *English Historical Review*, April, 1896.

unnamed person had written to the pope asking that Walter might have a dispensation enabling him, though a bastard, to accept a bishopric in case one was offered; also that, on the presentation of a certain M. de B., knight, the bishop of Chichester instituted him in the church of N.; also that in 1272 he gave a bond to the lady A. Salvage, widow of R. Salvage; also, though this is less clear, that on the Monday before Easter in 1274 Adelinya[1] La Savage, lady of Brawatere (Broadwater), presented him to S[tephen Berkstead], bishop of Chichester, for institution as rector of Brawatere. Some of these would-be facts may well be true. Between 1262 and 1287 the bishop of Chichester's initial was S. A family named Salvage held Broadwater[2]. In 1278 a Master William (so the Vatican register has it) de Hyda, being then an acolyte and a proctor of certain English prelates, was sojourning at Rome and received a dispensation from the impediment caused by his illegitimate birth[3].

On a fly leaf at the beginning of the volume occurs our song. After this song was written there a legal formula was added, which supposes that W. de Hyda is bringing an action for defamation. A good many other notes stand on the same page. There is a short poem about St Nicholas, and there are some tags of jurisprudence and of moral and natural philosophy (e.g. *Nota quod fetor candele extincte iumentis et mulieribus dat aborcionis causam*). The poem is written in minute letters, and hardly fills half the page.

---

[1] The end of this name is not very plain.
[2] Dallaway, *Sussex*, vol. ii. part ii. p. 22.
[3] *Register of Papal Letters*, i. 454.

I must not pretend to have read through the whole of the Caius MS., but all that I have seen of it seems to favour the belief that this copy of the song was written within ten or twenty years after the battle of Evesham, while the last verses suggest that the song itself was composed very soon after the fatal day.

In substance and in form it is not unlike some of those other songs that have been printed by Mr Wright, Mr Halliwell, and Mr Prothero, though it is somewhat ruder than they are. Its Montfort is the Montfort of popular hagiology, who wears a hair shirt, treads in the footsteps of Becket, and fights for the ideas of Grosseteste. Its most distinctive traits seem to be the following: (1) Not content with Biblical heroes, such as Abel, Samson, and Nebuzaradan (the allusion to whom I do not understand), it introduces Hector, Achilles, and Ulysses. *Cadit Hector, Rachel flevit* is a charming specimen of mixed mythology. (2) It avoids naming or even describing the men against whom Montfort was fighting, except where it speaks for a moment of the fierce Welsh marchers. No word is said of any king. (3) It devotes no less than six stanzas to Simon's standard-bearer, Guy de Balliol, of whom we may, indeed, read a little, but not very much, elsewhere, and, on the other hand, it passes by in silence some more famous men who fell by the earl's side. For a moment I thought that these stanzas might send us to the newly founded Aula de Balliol at Oxford to find our poet; but its founder, John de Balliol, the lord of Barnard Castle, was a royalist, and Guy seems to have sprung from some more purely Scottish branch of the great family[1]. (4) The appear-

[1] See for Guy, Blauuw, *Barons' War*, p. 278.

ance of the Northumbrian king in company with the
braves of Greek and Hebrew legend is explained by
the calendar: Earl Simon was slain on the vigil of
St Oswald[1].

1. [2]Vbi fuit mons est vallis
   Et de colle fit iam callis
   Heus et strata publica.

2. Propter casum dire sortis
   Debilis est factus fortis
   Non per sua merita.

3. Bellicosus infirmatur,
   Alter Sampson[3] trucidatur,
   Lamentatur Anglia.

4. Symon pro simplicitate
   Marchionum[4] feritate
   Cadit cesus framea.

5. Die Martis[5] bellum creuit,
   Cadit Hector[6], Rachel fleuit
   Pro cesis in area.

6. Comparatur hic Uluxi,
   Nam pro fide crucifixi
   Non timebat uilia.

7. Rexit vigor in Achille,
   Sed et Symon talis ille
   Qui pugnat pro patria.

8. Primus natus[7] rexit frenum,
   Non permisit alienum
   Dare patri uulnera.

9. Dum durauit non expauit
   Pater[8] enses, sed certauit
   Propter pacis[9] federa.

10. Pater prole confortatur,
    Proles patrem consolatur
    Dum durarent prelia.

11. Non fuerunt duo tales
    In amore speciales
    Infra mundi climata.

12. Abel Ade sociatur;
    Abel prius immolatur,
    Cadit Adam postea.

13. In Henrico rosa vernat,
    Et in rosa si quis cernat
    Sat aperit[10] lilia[11].

14. Martir fertur per ruborem,
    Et per album fertur florem
    Virgo sine macula.

---

[1] *French Chronicle of London*, p. 7: " Mardi ... la veille de seint Oswold."

[2] The numeration of the stanzas and the punctuation are due to the editor.

[3] Part of this word has perished, but it is fairly clear.

[4] The Welsh marchers.   [5] Tuesday, 4 Aug.

[6] The *H* of *Hector* supplied above the line.

[7] Henry de Montfort.   [8] Apparently *pac*.

[9] Corrected from *patris*.   [10] Apparently *apererit*.

[11] A hole in the parchment; but I have little doubt of *lilia*.

15. Dixit quidam, ut Pilatus,
Qui in bello principatus
Tenuit dominia,

16. "Redde, redde, Comes fortis
Eris aut pro certo mortis
Datus ad suplicia."

17. "Hunc," fert alter, 'occidatis!
Ulli viuo non parcatis
De sua familia!"

18. Omnes clamant, "Moriatur!"
Comes instans meditatur
De superna patria.

19. "Reddo me omnipotenti,
Vitam meam do viventi
Deo pro victoria."

20. Tunc venerunt loricati
Nimis graues et irati
Cum magna superbia,

21. Cupientes preualere,
Non potentes amouere
Pedibus scansilia[1].

22. Firmiter incedit equo :
Cadit equus non ab equo[2]
Perforatus lancea.

23. Hunc occidunt conspirantes,
Introducunt ignorantes
In celi palacia.

24. Quando martir exspirauit,
"Montem fortem," excla-
mauit,
"Summe pater adiuua!"

25. Caput eius mutulatur
Et os eius perforatur
Certans pro iusticia.

26. Manus, pedes detruncantur,
Et de morte cuncti fantur
Vili sibi tradita.

27. Omnes illi confundantur
Per quos eius violantur
Nature virilia.

28. Thomas martir nuncupatur,
Sicut[3] Christus[4], sicut datur
Symon pro iusticia.

29. Passi sunt in ista terra
Pari pena pari guerra
Ambo cruciamina.

30. Symon gratis passus fuit
Et pro terra cesus ruit,
Thomas pro ecclesia.

---

[1] The ladder to heaven.

[2] A pun, as in "Amisi equum quia dixi equum quod non fuit equum."

[3] *Sit* or *Sic.* Should it be *Sicut*?

[4] The word seems to be *xs.* The only alternative is *s* preceded by the compendium for *pro*.

31. Comes regi sociatur
    Qui Oswaldus[1] nuncupatur
    Equa per certamina.

32. Nabuzardan subnervavit[2]
    Et hunc vita superauit
    Continens ieiunia.

33. Hic Robertum[3] sequebatur
    Cuius vita comendatur
    Certa per miracula.

34. Dictis eius vir obedit ;
    Fert Robertus, Symon credit
    De statutis talia :

35. "Si verum confitearis
    Et pro dictis moriaris
    Magna feres premia.

36. "Quod vir iustus paciatur
    Satis liquet et probatur
    Per magna tonitrua[4].

37. "Est lorica duplex ei
    Et examen huius rei
    Fit per eius spolia[5]."

38. Extra bene vir armatur,
    Quisquis videns hoc testatur
    Per signa bellifica.

39. Loricatur subtus stricte ;
    Hanc non tulit miles ficte
    Tendens ad celestia.

40. Nec contentus est hac veste;
    Invocato deo teste,
    Induit cilicia.

41. Symon,Symon modo dormis!
    Quam mors tua sit enormis
    Clamat vox ad sydera.

42. Ante tuum Christe uultum
    Non relinquas hunc inultum
    Pro tua clemencia.

43. Hii[6] coniuncti sunt victores,
    Et sunt vivis alciores
    Nam vivunt in gloria.

44. Firmiter sunt hii[7] ligati
    Qui nec morte separati
    Nec sunt in milicia.

---

[1] Oswald of Northumbria, slain by the heathen in battle.   His body, like Simon's, was mutilated.

[2] Apparently either *subuerauit* or *subnerauit*, with the "*er*" *in compendio.* I fail to find anything which connects Nebuzaradan with any hamstringing.   But *subnervare* occurs several times in the Vulgate.

[3] Robert Grosseteste.

[4] An allusion to the storm in which the battle was fought?

[5] Perhaps what I take to be a speech put into Grosseteste's mouth may extend beyond this point.

[6] Simon and his son Henry.   [7] *hii* interlined.

45. Et Radulfus, Basset dictus,
    Miles eius est conflictus
    Paciens pericula.

46. Et de Baylol dictus Guydo
    Signa feris corde fido
    Cunctis[1] aparencia.

47. Vires eius probitatis,
    Vir in fide constans satis
    Ostendebat dextera.

48. Quando Symon fuit cesus
    Guydo sicut nondum lesus
    Signum fert in lancea.

49. Signum iusti nunquam ruit,
    Semper exaltatum fuit
    Inter tua brachia.

50. Euasisse potuisti,
    Tamen magis elegisti
    Symonis consorcia.

51. Interfectis in agone
    Spe mercedis et corone
    Christe dona grandia.

52. Symon, Symon si vixisses
    Currere non permisisses
    Raptores in patria.

53. Quis nos potest defensare ?
    Venietne ultra mare
    Exspectata venia ?

54. Custos pacis heu necatur
    Et ad litus applicatur
    Nauis cum discordia.

55. Incessanter Angli flere,
    Modo possunt redolere,
    Non habent remedia,

56. Nisi Deus mittat eis
    Vindictam de dictis reis
    Qui fecerunt scelera.

57. Ne subuertant alieni
    Istam terram dolo pleni,
    Super hanc considera.

Amen.

[1] *Cuntis* in MS.

WYCLIF ON ENGLISH AND ROMAN LAW[1]

ANY passage in a mediaeval book which compares or contrasts the system of the civilians with our own English law should be treasured. Such a passage there is in Wyclif's *De officio regis*, a tract that was published by the Wyclif Society in 1887. The heresiarch is not a writer whose arguments are easily followed, for they are always taking unexpected turns, or at all events turns which will be unexpected by those who are not familiar (and I, for one, am not) with the theology and politics of the time. In this tract, for example, he is concerned to belittle the civilians. Apparently the quarrel that is really near his heart is the quarrel with the canonists. He wants to see a world and a church that have little law other than the law of God laid down in the Holy Scriptures, of which law neither civilians nor canonists but theologians are the custodians and interpreters. One of his reasons for praising, somewhat faintly, the law of England is that there is not very much of it.

"Et hinc leges regni Anglie excellunt leges imperiales, cum sint pauce respectu earum, quia supra pauca principia relinquunt residuum epikerie sapientum[2]."

[1] *Law Quarterly Review*, Jan. 1896.
[2] *De officio regis*, p. 56.

English law has but few principles, and much is left to the ἐπιείκεια of the wise.

Wyclif, however, has a feud with the bishops who have been fostering the study of "the civil law" in the universities. Thus they have been withdrawing men and means from theology. Of the two, the clergy of England had better read English than Roman law. But, says Wyclif, some will argue that there is more subtle reasoning and more justice in Roman civilian-ship (*civilitate Romana*); also that it must needs be studied if the canon law is to be understood ; also that it is necessary for the decision of causes according to "the law of arms." Now it must be confessed that there is much of reason in this *civilitas Romana*. Also that it has produced great statesmen.

"Sed non credo quod plus viget in Romana civilitate subtilitas racionis sive iusticia quam in civilitate Anglicana, et cum sit per se notum quod quecumque lingua, Latina, Greca vel alia, sit imper-tinens clerimonie vel racioni, cum racio sit ante linguam, patet quod non pocius est homo clericus sive philosophus in quantum est doctor civilitatis Romane quam in quantum est iusticiarius iuris Angli-cani[1]."

This is an early assertion of the right of the common lawyer, the justice of the law of England, to take his place beside the doctors of the civil law as a clerk and philosopher, or, as we should say, a learned and a libe-rally educated man. Wyclif goes on to argue that the canon law in its purity (that is, the canon law as he would like to see it) can be studied without the aid of the civil law; also that the true "law of arms" lies in the Bible.

---

[1] *De officio regis*, p. 193.

4—2

Elsewhere he is arguing for the disendowment of the civilians and canonists at the universities :—

"Unde videtur quod si rex Anglie non permitteret canonistas vel civilistas ad hoc sustentari de suis elemosinis vel patrimonio crucifixi ut studeant tales leges (hoc enim non sustinet de lege propria cui racionabiliter plus faveret) non dubium quin clerus foret utilior sibi et ad ecclesiasticam promocionem humilior ex noticia civilitatis proprie quam ex noticia civilitatis duplicis aliene[1]."

It would be better for the clergy to learn the civil system of their own country than the "doubly alien" system of imperial and papal Rome. Still, he adds, something should be known of this foreign matter, in order that men may understand that in old times the pope was subject to the emperor. A historical study of the civil and canon law will teach them how baseless are the pretensions of modern popes.

In attacking the papalists Wyclif had been making common cause with the imperialists of the continent. But he seems to think it necessary that he should dissociate himself from them lest he should be taken to allow the emperor some superiority over the king of England. The imperial theory, the theory of a world-wide monarchy, is attractive and once was useful. But the emperors have forfeited their claims by their folly in endowing "their bishop" (that is, the pope) contrary to Christ's religion and in allowing the clergy to usurp imperial rights. The empire no longer "lives imperially as it ought to live." So England will have none of it, nor of its laws. Therefore, once more, it is a scandal that our bishops should be licensing and encouraging the clergy to study the *ius civile*[2],

---

[1] *De officio regis*, p. 237.   [2] *Ibid.* p. 250.

which in tracts that are addressed to the vulgar in the vulgar tongue becomes "paynymes lawe" and "hethene mennys lawe."

There are not wanting some other signs that in the second half of the fourteenth century "the civil law" (thanks to such legally-minded prelates as Bateman) was looking up in the world. Wyclif's *De officio regis* is ascribed by its editors to the year 1379 or thereabouts. A few years afterwards, in the case of the lords appellant, we hear the famous declaration of the peers that this realm never has been and shall not be governed by the civil law. They were at the moment engaged in setting up a "law of parliament" (which, it is to be feared, meant law or lawlessness improvised for the purpose of vengeance) not only above the civil but above the common law[1]. However the mere fact that some one had proposed that "appeals" in Parliament should be conducted according to the civil law, that is, according to the system of procedure which the civilians and canonists had jointly elaborated, shows that this procedure was gaining ground, and we know that it was becoming the procedure of the nascent court of equity. Wyclif's protest in favour of English law is therefore of some interest. He was quarrelling with the clergy and was concerned to keep the laity, including the king, nobles, and common lawyers on his side.

---

[1] *Rolls of Parliament,* III. 236, 244.

"EXECRABILIS" IN THE COMMON PLEAS[1]

TOWARDS the middle of Edward III's reign, just when the national movement against papal "provisors" was coming to a climax, the king's legal advisers and the justices of the Court of Common Pleas took upon themselves to enforce a certain papal constitution, though to enforce it in an odd, lopsided fashion, favourable to their royal lord. The pope's weapons were to be wrested from his hand and used against him. The king was going to take possession of a great deal of ecclesiastical patronage which the pope had destined for himself. This clever move is partially revealed to us by certain discussions in the Year Books, which have never, I believe, been fully explained because they have never been compared with the plea rolls.

The constitution in question was none other than the famous *Execrabilis*, which fills a prominent place in the constitutional history of the Catholic Church. It is one of the stock examples of those covetously fiscal "extravagants" which are characteristic of the Avignonese papacy. For some time past popes and councils had been legislating against pluralism, that is,

[1] *Law Quarterly Review*, April, 1896.

against the simultaneous tenure by one clerk of more than one benefice involving a cure of souls[1]. Among the laws striking at this evil was a canon of the Fourth Lateran Council (1215), which began with the words *De multa*[2]. This canon is here mentioned merely because a tradition among English lawyers taught, and perhaps still teaches, that a reference was made to it in the cases which are to come before us; but we shall hereafter see that this tradition has its origin in a mistake. Legislation, however, was futile. The popes themselves made it futile by their dispensations, and those who do not like popes tell us that the laws were made in order that they might be dispensed with. At last, in November, 1317, John XXII issued a long and stringent constitution whose first word was *Execrabilis*[3]. It was stringent; it was retrospective; it attacked those clerks who were already holding several "incompatible" benefices, even though they had obtained dispensations. Such a clerk was, within one month after notice of this constitution, to resign all but one of his benefices, or else they were all to be vacant *ipso iure*. There were prospective besides retrospective clauses, and finally there was a clause in which we may, if we like, discover the legislator's main motive. All the benefices vacated by the "cession" of the pluralists were "reserved" to the pope, or, in other words, it was for him to fill the vacancies. This constitution was no idle word in England. In

---

[1] For a full historical account of the law see Hinschius, *Kirchenrecht*, III. 243 ff.

[2] Conc. Lat. IV. c. 29; c. 28, X. 3, 5.

[3] c. un. in Extrav. Joan. XXII, 3; c. 4 in Extrav. comm. 3, 2.

the next year we can see Pope John busily at work collating clerks to English benefices which have been vacated by the force of *Execrabilis*[1]. The English king was weak and worthless, and apparently the Holy Father was allowed to have his way.

A little later Edward III was on the throne, and the outcry against " provisors " was swelling. At this moment some of the king's lawyers seem to have caught at the idea that two could play at *Execrabilis*, and that, while the " reservation " was studiously disregarded, the main provisions of the bull might be enforced with advantage. It will be remembered that the amount of patronage that fell to the king's share was very large. To say nothing of the churches that were all his own, he exercised the patronage of infants who were in ward to him, and also the patronage annexed to bishoprics that were vacant. So any measure which emptied churches might do him a good turn and enable him to pay his servants.

In 1335 the king brought a *Quare impedit* against the bishop of Norwich for the deanery of Lynn[2]. The king stated in his count that John, late bishop of Norwich [that is John Salmon who died in 1325], had conferred the deanery on one Master Roger of Snet- tisham, who was already parson of the church of Cressingham, and who continued to hold both bene- fices for more than a month after his installation in the

---

[1] *Calendar of Papal Letters*, II. 172–182.

[2] De Banco Roll, No. 305, Hilary 10 Edw. III, m. 214 dors. An earlier stage on De Banco Roll, No. 303, Trinity 9 Edw. III, m. 236. I have to thank Miss Salisbury for searching and making extracts from these rolls.

deanery, "per quod per constitucionem de pluralite predictus decanatus vacavit ipso iure," and remained vacant until the temporalities of the bishopric of Norwich came into the hand of Edward II upon the death of bishop John. To this declaration the bishop demurred in that polite form in which we demur to the pleadings of kings. He said that he did not understand that the king desired an answer to the said declaration, "for therein he does not allege that the said deanery was vacant *de facto* in such wise that this Court might take cognizance of the vacancy, but merely alleges that it was vacant by the constitution against plurality, which does not fall within the cognizance of this Court." So the bishop craved judgment. The king replied that by the constitution against plurality the deanery must be adjudged to have been vacant *de iure* just as though the dean had been deprived thereof by sentence. So the king craved judgment. Here the record ends, and no more of the case has been found.

So much from the roll. In the Year Book we have discussion[1]. After some little fencing over the question whether the king ought to say that a "bishopric," or merely that the "temporalities of a bishopric" are in his hand when there is no bishop, the serjeants come to the main matter. For the bishop it is said, "Sir, you see how the king takes as the cause of the voidance the constitution touching plurality, and shows nothing that lies in any fact which would give cognizance to this Court, such as resignation, privation, death

[1] Y. B. 9 Edw. III, f. 22 (Trin. pl. 14); Y. B. 10 Edw. III, f. 42 (Hil. pl. 3).

or succession." Parning, who is arguing for the king, replies, "The constitution touching plurality was made by a general judgment that all should be deprived who held their *beneficia curata* for more than a month after the constitution, and this binds them more firmly as regards privation than a judgment that some certain person should be deprived, for the one might be afterwards annulled upon appeal; not so the other."

The Year Book, like the roll, tells of no judgment. Probably the king and the bishop came to terms. We can, I think, see that the king's advocates had rather a difficult course to steer. They were proposing to enforce a papal constitution directly and without any certificate from the English ordinary. What might they not have on their hands if they once began to administer the "extravagants" of Avignon? Parning's argument seems to be explicable by the retrospective character of *Execrabilis*. This, he urges, is "a general judgment." If a particular judgment of deprivation were given against a clerk and were certified to this Court, you would hold that the benefice was vacant. Well, here is a general judgment and one that is subject to no appeal. That the constitution in question was *Execrabilis* and not one of the earlier decrees (for example *De multa*) would, I believe, be clear even from this case, because of the mention made of the one month which is given to the pluralist for the resignation of his superabundant benefices. Happily, however, this is put beyond all doubt by the enrolled record of the next case, though it is left dubious in the Year Book.

In 1351, John of Gaunt, on behalf of the king,

brought a *Quod permittat* against Simon Islip, archbishop of Canterbury, for a presentation to the church
of Wimbledon in the county of Surrey[1]. The king's
declaration stated that Robert of Winchelsea, archbishop
of Canterbury, being seised of the advowson, collated
John of Sandale in the eleventh year of the reign of
Edward II, and that because Pope John, in the second
year of his pontificate (Sept. 5, 1317–1318) and the
ninth year of the said reign (July 8, 1315–1316)[2],
made a certain constitution called *Execrabilis*, to the
effect that no clerk should occupy two *beneficia curata*
beyond one month after the publication of the said
constitution without being deprived *ipso iure* of both
benefices, which constitution was published in the said
year of Edward II, and because the said John of Sandale occupied the church of Wimbledon and various
other churches [which are named] for days and years
after the said publication, the said church of Wimbledon by virtue of the said constitution became vacant,
and remained vacant until the temporalities of the
archbishopric came into Edward II's hands by the
death of archbishop Robert, and so the right to present a clerk pertained to Edward II, from whom it
descended to the now king.

Pausing here for a moment, we may remark that
to us who are blessed with books of reference, the
king's story is obviously false, for Robert Winchelsea
was dead, and Walter Reynolds had succeeded him
at Canterbury some time before the publication of
Execrabilis. But we must not allow this brutal matter

---

[1] De Banco Roll, Mich. 25 Edw. III, m. 41 dors.
[2] The slight discrepancy in the dates will be noticed.

of fact to spoil a discussion of matter of law. We learn from the Year Book[1] that the counsel for the archbishop were at first inclined to demur. The king, they said, founds his action on a matter that does not lie in the cognizance of this Court, and we do not think that this Court will take cognizance of a matter which ought to be pleaded in Court Christian. This was a very intelligible line of defence: it is not for the Court of Common Pleas to enforce directly a law against plurality. However, we are told that the archbishop's counsel dared not demur at this point, since if the Court was against them they would be allowed no other defence. So they, as both the report and the record show, traversed the king's statement that the church of Wimbledon fell vacant while the temporalities of the archbishopric were in the hands of Edward II. This is the plea that is upon the roll, where no notice is taken of the abortive demurrer. A jury was summoned and gave the king a verdict. The jurors said upon their oath that after the publication in England of the constitution called *Execrabilis*, for some six weeks and more, John of Sandale held the church of Wimbledon and certain other churches that they named, that thereby the said church became vacant, and that it remained vacant until by the death of archbishop Robert the temporalities of the archbishopric came into the hands of Edward II. Judgment was given that the king should recover his presentation and that the archbishop was in mercy[2].

[1] Y. B. 26 Edw. III, f. 1 (Pasch. pl. 3).
[2] See also the case against the bishop of Worcester, Y. B. 24 Edw. III, f. 29 (Trin. pl. 21).

On the roll this judgment is followed by a remarkable writ dated April 22, 1352. Much to our surprise the king confesses that he is now informed that the title to the presentation which he had successfully urged was feigned and untrue (*fictus et non verus*), and that the church did not become vacant while the temporalities of the archbishopric were in his father's hand. Therefore he revokes his presentation of a certain William of Cheston, declares that the judgment is not to be enforced, and forbids that the archbishop should be further molested. This writ comes to us as a surprise, for though, as already said, we happen to know that the jurors' verdict must have been false when it supposed that Winchelsea's death occurred after the publication of Pope John's constitution, still we are hardly prepared to see Edward III quietly resigning the fruits of a judgment. The interesting feature of the case, however, is the proof that the Court of Common Pleas was prepared to put in force one half of the notorious extravagant, and this without requiring any sentence of deprivation pronounced by an English ecclesiastical court. The pope had said that in a certain event a benefice was to be void ; void therefore it was, for the pope had power to make laws and even retrospective laws against pluralism. On the other hand, no word is said in record or report of the other half of the bull, for a "reservation" is plainly an attempt to touch that right of patronage which is a temporal right given by the law of the land, and such an attempt is *ultra vires statuentis*. The pope's law may turn an incumbent out, but, the church being vacant, the patron can exercise his right of presentation. A very pretty plan! But what would the English prelates say?

We can now understand a petition that the clergy presented to the king in the Parliament of 1351[1]. Probably it was occasioned by the action directed against the archbishop. " May it please you to grant that henceforth no justice shall hold plea of the vacation of any benefice of Holy Church by reason of insufficient age, consecration as bishop, resignation, plurality, inability, or other voidance *de iure*, for no such avoidance lies or can be in the cognizance of lay folk; but if our lord the king desires to take advantage of any such avoidance *de iure*, let a mandate be sent to the archbishop or bishop of the place where the benefice is, bidding him inquire touching this matter in the due manner according to the law of Holy Church as is done in the case of bastardy." In answer to this prayer the king willed that if title by avoidance came in plea before his justices, whereof the cognizance appertained to Court Christian, the party[2] should have his challenge, and the justices should do right. This somewhat enigmatical response was converted into a statute[3]. "Whereas the said prelates have prayed remedy because the secular justices accroach to themselves cognizance of the vacation of benefices, whereof the cognizance and discussion belongs to the judge of Holy Church and not to the lay judge, the king wills that the justices shall henceforth receive the challenges made or to be made by any

---

[1] *Rolls of Parliament*, II. 245.

[2] The statute suggests that the word should be *prelate* not *party.*

[3] 25 Edw. III, stat. 3, cap. 8.

prelates of Holy Church in this behalf, and shall do right and reason in respect of the same." This statute, like many others which touch the relation of the temporal to the spiritual tribunals, looks very much like an "As you were." Bishops and justices must fight the matter out : both parties should be reasonable ; but the king does not like to decide their quarrels.

I believe that the justices held their ground. The traditional law of Coke's day was that "by the constitution of the pope" if a clergyman accepts a second benefice "the first is void *ipso iure* and the patron may present if he will," although no sentence of deprivation has been passed[1]. In other words, the secular court would take direct notice of the ecclesiastical rule that avoids the one *beneficium curatum* when the other is accepted. Coke thought that the rule in question was the outcome of *De multa*, the canon of the Lateran Council of 1215. That canon would in fact have justified what was done by our Courts of common law, but when Coke proceeds to say that this is the constitution that is referred to in the cases of Edward III's day, he is mistaken. He had seen the Year Books, but did not know that the roll spoke expressly of Pope John and his *Execrabilis*.

Having mentioned John of Sandale and pluralism, it may be worth our while to observe that this distinguished clerk, while working his way upwards through the royal chancery towards the chancellorship of the realm and the bishopric of Winchester, had become a pluralist of the deepest dye. He, when yet a subdeacon,

---

[1] Holland's case, 4 Rep. 75 a ; Digby's case, 4 Rep. 78 b.

obtained the chancellorship of St Patrick's at Dublin, the treasurership of Lichfield, seven churches in seven dioceses, and three prebends at Wells, Howden and Beverley, and had leave from the pope to accept additional benefices to the value of £200[1].   The requisite dispensation he had obtained from Clement V at the instance of the king of England.   This is a good illustration of that viciously circular process from which an escape was impossible until the pope's claims were utterly denied.   The king's "civil service" must be maintained, but, such is the nation's impatience of taxation, that it can only be maintained out of the revenues of the churches.   The only method, however, by which these revenues can be secured for such an object consists in papal dispensations.   Therefore the pope's power to dispense with the laws that he has ordained must be acknowledged.   And then when the pope tries to make profit for himself out of the powers that we allow to him, we begin to complain and to pass statutes of "provisors" that we dare not enforce, lest the king's "civil service" should break down.   We cannot get on with the pope, and yet we cannot do without him, for rightly or wrongly we believe that he can legislate for the church.   It is an intricate and is not a pleasant tale; but it deserves telling, and yet will never be told in full until the Year Books have been properly edited.

[1] *Register of Papal Letters*, II. 9, 27, 88, 119.

CANON LAW[1]

By the Canon Law we here mean the mass of legal rules administered by the ecclesiastical Courts during the Middle Ages. We must not endeavour to describe, even in the briefest manner, the prolonged process of development which issued in the existence of ecclesiastical Courts wielding compulsory powers, and claiming to be independent of the State. Nor may we dwell upon what may be called the embryonic stage in the growth of the rules which these Courts enforced, a stage which was already beginning in the first days of Christianity. It must suffice that no sooner had Christianity become a tolerated religion than the bishops were suffered, or even required, by the Roman State to hear and decide disputes touching the internal affairs of the Churches, and that the great ecumenical councils which were held at the Emperor's command were settling the foundations not only of dogma but also of discipline. Books containing the rules or "canons" that were ordained by these councils became current among the Churches of the West. To these ecumenical canons, which might claim the authority of all the Churches or of an universal Church, transcribers added the canons of other famous but not

[1] Renton's *Encyclopedia of the Laws of England*, 1897.

ecumenical councils; and some of these were deemed to be hardly less authoritative. Also the pre-eminence of that *ecclesia* which had its home in the capital city of the world was already making itself felt. The Bishop of Rome was being consulted by other bishops, and his replies to their questions were preserved and reverenced. The germs of an elaborate system of appeal were already visible. In the Western world— the Orient we must leave out of sight—the Pope was slowly acquiring a power of declaring law which would in course of time become a power of making law.

A distinct stage is marked by the *Collectio Diony-siana*. It was compiled about the year 500 at Rome by Dionysius Exiguus (so he called himself), a monk of Scythian birth. He collected and translated the canons of famous Eastern councils, and to these he appended some letters issued by the popes from Siricius onwards (384–498). Already conciliar canons and "decretal" letters of popes were being set side by side. His work became current in the West. A version of it (*Dionysio-Hadriana*) was sent by Pope Hadrian to Charles the Great in 774. But other collections were current. Canons of very various origins, Oriental, African, Spanish, Gallican, were often transcribed into one book. The bishops of one province would borrow the collection which had been made in another province, and still enjoyed a considerable liberty of choosing the rules that should be accepted in their dioceses. Another celebrated collection of canons and decretals seems to have taken shape in the Spain of the seventh century. It has been known as the *Hispana* or *Isidoriana*, for without sufficient warrant it has been ascribed to St Isidore of Seville.

Then about the year 850 this Spanish collection, which had found acceptance in Frankland, became the foundation for a superstructure of forgery. Someone who called himself Isidorus Mercator, and who seems to have tried to personate St Isidore, foisted into the old book a large number of decretals which purported to come from the earliest popes, the immediate successors of St Peter. That he lived in Frankland seems plain, though attempts to fix his home more accurately have not as yet been perfectly successful. His objects we are beginning to understand; they can only be explained out of the difficult history of the Frankish Church in its darkest age. There seems to be no reason for supposing that he had specially at heart the interests of the papacy; but those interests he indubitably furthered, not only by his endeavours to weaken the power of the metropolitans over their comprovincial bishops, but also (and this is of the utmost importance) by his propagation of the belief that ever since the apostolic age the Bishops of Rome had been declaring law for the universal Church in decretal letters. By this belief the Middle Ages were ruled. Some of the forger's contemporaries seem to have had their doubts; but very soon the pseudo-Isidorian decretals were generally accepted in Rome and elsewhere.

The canonical materials had thus received a large accession. New and ampler collections were made, as bishop borrowed from bishop and transcriber from transcriber. Moreover, these books were beginning to take a more juristic form. A merely chronological arrangement of materials was abandoned in favour of a logical arrangement. The collector set himself to make what we might call a digest or manual of ecclesiastical law. The sphere of ecclesiastical law was now being rapidly widened. The Frankish empire was going to pieces. The State, if indeed we may talk of a State, was at its weakest, and the ecclesiastical tribunals were ever making new claims to jurisdiction over all causes in which the interests of the Churches or of the clergy were even remotely concerned. Then in the eleventh century the papacy emerged from an eclipse. It appeared as a reforming power making for righteousness. At the same time, in the schools of Italy, first at Pavia and then at Bologna, men were beginning ardently to study Justinian's law-books. Here were models of jurisprudence which the collectors of ecclesiastical rules would strive to imitate. Here also was a formidable rival, which threatened their theory of Church and State, for the emperor of Justinian's books is very truly supreme over all causes, ecclesiastical as well as civil, and will legislate even about dogma if he pleases. The jurisprudence of these renovated *leges* was to be met by an equally professional jurisprudence of *canones*. The study of ecclesiastical law could no longer be regarded as a department of theology; it was a jurisprudence to be taught in schools, to be debated in Courts, to be argued over and developed in a lawyer-like way by professional experts, by *canonistae* or *decretistae*. Many treatises, which in our own day are slowly coming to light, endeavoured to meet the new demand for scientific manuals. One treatise was so successful as to obliterate all others, and to usher in what we may call the classical age of the canon law.

About the year 1139, Gratian, a monk at Bologna, compiled a book which he called *Concordia discordantium canonum*, but which was soon universally known as the *Decretum Gratiani.* He wove together a large number of the authoritative texts (*auctoritates*), including many of pseudo-Isidorian origin, interspersing them with observations of his own (*dicta Gratiani*), which endeavoured to explain and harmonise them. This book, which was produced at the headquarters of the new secular jurisprudence, quickly supplanted all the older collections. The Church had now a text-book which could be compared with the civilian's Digest; it became the base of a large mass of gloss and comment. Among those who made abridgments of it was Roland Bandinelli, who became pope as Alexander III, and whose long pontificate (1159–81) is marked by a large number of important decretals. These newer decretals were collected by divers canonists; five of their compilations (*Quinque compilationes antiquae*) were especially famous; the third bore the sanction of Innocent III, and the fifth was issued by Honorius III. Then in 1230 Gregory IX charged his penitentiary, Raymond of Peñaforte, with the task of codifying all such decretals as had been issued since the date of the *Decretum* and were to be in force for the future. The outcome was the *Decretales Gregorii IX.* This code was published in 1234. The topics dealt with by its five books are indicated by the mnemonic line *Iudex, iudicium, clerus, sponsalia, crimen.* It was intended by its author to be a statute-book for the universal Church.

It is not a "code" in our modern sense of that term—
that is to say, it does not aim at being an exhaustive
statement of the whole law—but it was to be, like
the code of Justinian, a complete collection of all the
modern statutes. As such it was received by the
canonists, and it was soon surrounded by a large com-
mentatory apparatus. Innocent IV (1243–54) was
among the commentators. In 1298 Boniface VIII
published a new volume, compiled from the decretals
issued since 1234. This, when added to Gregory's
five *libri*, became the *Liber sextus decretalium*, or,
more briefly, the Sext. It was meant to be, and was
received as a statute-book, and as an exclusive statute-
book for the period between 1234 and 1298 ; in other
words, decretals that were not taken into it were
abrogated. In 1317, John XXII published a seventh
volume, consisting chiefly of decretals issued by his
predecessor, Clement V; this also had statutory authority; it is known as the Clementines. The great
legislative period was now at an end. John XXII
and his successors issued some decretals of considerable importance, but no official collection was made of
them. The most generally valuable of them were
read and glossed in the schools; as they were not
contained in the old statute-books, they were known
as "extravagants." In 1500 two collections of them
were added by Jean Chapuis to a Parisian edition of
the older books. The one contained Extravagants of
John XXII (1316–34), the other contained the best
known Extravagants of other popes (*Extravagantes
communes*), ranging from Martin IV to Sixtus IV
(1281–1484).

For some time past the title _Corpus Iuris Canonici_ had been given to the sum of the received books. A complete *Corpus* consists of six members—(1) the Decretum of Gratian, (2) the Decretals of Gregory IX, (3) the Sext, (4) the Clementines, (5) the Extravagants of John XXII, (6) the Common Extravagants. These six are not of equal force. The Decretum never received any formal sanction, and, according to the doctrine that prevails among the Roman Catholic canonists of modern times, no text (*auctoritas*) is any the better for being contained in that volume. Such a canonist would be quite free to say that a particular text was forged and of little, if any, value. As to the *dicta Gratiani*, they were never regarded as more than the opinions of a venerated master. However, an official edition of the Decretum was published by Pius V in 1582, and Catholics were prohibited from making changes in the text. On the other hand, the Decretals of Gregory IX, the Sext, and the Clementines are authoritative statute-books. Each of them is to be considered as a single whole published by a legislator at one moment of time, so that there can be no talk of one passage being prior to, and therefore abrogated by another and a later passage. Further, the book as a whole comes from a legislator; therefore no sentence in it can be invalidated by any discussion of its history previous to its insertion in that book, for the pope was free to alter the decretals that he was collecting and codifying. On the other hand, a passage in the Sext can overrule or abrogate a passage in the Decretals of Gregory IX, and a passage in the Sext may be overruled by a passage in the Clementines;

the one will be *lex prior*, the other *lex posterior*.
Lastly, the two books of Extravagants are unofficial;
no decretal is the better for being in them; no decretal
is the worse for not being in them. However, they
have been considered to contain the most generally
useful papal edicts of the period that they cover, a
period of degeneration in the history of the papacy.
Various portions of the *Corpus* were printed so soon
as the day for print had come. The whole appeared
in the Parisian edition of 1500. An official edition,
the work of a congregation of cardinals, the so-called
Correctores Romani, was issued in 1582. The *Corpus*
was edited in modern times by Richter (1839) and
Friedberg (1879–81); both editors were German
Protestants; the existence of the official edition has
hampered the Catholics. Friedberg's edition should
be in the hands of every student of the canon law;
but for historical purposes it is often necessary to use
an old edition which gives the gloss as well as the
text, for in the later Middle Ages the gloss was venerated. The classical gloss (*Glossa ordinaria*) on the
Decretum comes from Joannes Teutonicus (before
1215) and Bartholomew of Brescia (*circa*, 1236), that
on the Decretales Gregorii from Bernard of Parma
(*circa*, 1266).

An immense mass of legal literature, academic and
practical, grew up around the Corpus Juris. The
greater part of it comes from men who, if not Italians
by birth, had studied in the Italian Universities; but
France also produced many canonists of eminence.
There were faculties of canon law in both the English
universities. The doctors in canon law (*doctores in*

decretis, in iure canonico) took precedence of the civilians (*doctores in legibus, in iure civili*). The course of lectures and exercises required of a candidate for a degree was long, and a degree was necessary to anyone who wished for practice in the ecclesiastical Courts. But the books read in England were for the most part foreign, and England produced no canonist of first-rate rank. In the twelfth century we may claim Ricardus Anglicus, who, however, has been too hastily identified with a bishop of Salisbury (*Dict. Nat. Biog.* XLVI. 108); in the thirteenth, William of Drogheda, a portion of whose work still exists in manuscript; in the fourteenth, John de Athona; and in the fifteenth, William Lindwood. Of the two last we shall speak below.

By members of the Roman Catholic Church of the present day the mediaeval canon law is still regarded as law in so far as it has not been changed by any competent ecclesiastical authority; but very considerable changes were introduced by the Council of Trent, and during the last three centuries the popes have legislated from time to time about many matters. The three statute-books issued by Gregory IX, Boniface VIII, and John XXII, are still statute-books, but they are old statute-books, and the law that is contained in them has been definitely and expressly altered at numerous points. The decisions and practice of the various tribunals and " congregations " at Rome would also have to be considered by anyone desirous of knowing the existing law about any particular matter. How far this system of law can be actively enforced in any given country is a different question, which in some cases is answered, at least in part, by a "concordat." between the See of Rome and the civil power. By English Courts the canon law of the Roman Catholics can only be regarded as a system of rules voluntarily accepted by the members, or at all events by the clergy, of a "non-conforming" religious body. The existence of a particular rule would therefore be, not a matter of law, but a matter of fact to be proved by the evidence of experts. Much information touching this point will be found in *O'Keeffe* v. *Cullen*, specially reported by H. C. Kirkpatrick (Longmans, 1874).

According to the theory propagated by the canonists of the classical age there was a great mass of law which was common to the universal Church (*ius commune*). Some room was left for local variations. In the first place, a metropolitan might make statutes for his province, and a bishop might make statutes for his diocese, and these would be valid if they did not contradict law which proceeded from a higher source, in particular from the pope, and were in harmony with the first principles of ecclesiastical jurisprudence. In the second place, some respect was due to the customs of dioceses and provinces, provided that such customs were "prescript and laudable." Further, it was admitted that in certain cases a rule of statutory origin, even though it came from the apostolic see, might become obsolete, owing to non-observance. However, the space thus allowed for divergence from the *ius commune* was by no means very wide.

The two best known works of English mediaeval canonists deal directly with local English law. One John of Acton, Ayton, or Athon, a canon of Lincoln, published (1333-48) a glossed version of the constitutions given to the English Church by the papal legates, Otto and Ottobon. In 1430 William Lindwood, being then the principal official of the Archbishop of Canterbury, published a glossed version of the constitutions given to the southern province by its metropolitans from the time of Stephen Langton downwards. The object of both books (a good edition of both in one volume was issued at Oxford in 1679) was to harmonise these local statutes with the general system in the *ius commune*. Uniformity in the law was secured by the appellate jurisdiction of Rome. Appeals were permissible at almost every stage of every suit, though the inferior judge was not always bound to "defer to" (i.e. to stay proceedings during) an appeal which he considered frivolous. But further, the doctrine gained ground that the pope was the judge ordinary of every man, and therefore that a plaintiff, neglecting all lower Courts, might, if he pleased, go straight to the supreme tribunal. This procedure was very commonly adopted by English litigants in the twelfth and thirteenth centuries. The first step which the plaintiff took was to "impetrate" a writ from Rome, which usually committed the cause to two or three English prelates, who would hear it in England, and in so doing would be acting as the pope's delegates (*iudices delegati*). The writ sometimes gave them instructions as to the rules of law that they were to apply, and sometimes instructed to them no larger duty than that of deciding questions of fact.

The claims of the Church to jurisdiction when they

had reached their full latitude were exceedingly wide.
Any cause which, even remotely, concerned the doctrines, sacraments, or discipline of the Church was
claimed as the exclusive property of the ecclesiastical
tribunals *ratione materiae*. Thus, for example, the
whole province of matrimonial law was annexed.
Moreover, it was asserted that no criminal or "personal" action could be brought against a clerk before
a secular forum ; such an action would belong to the
Court Christian *ratione personae*. It is improbable
that these claims were ever admitted in all their ful-
ness by any secular power, unless this happened in
the States of the Church, where the pope was both
spiritual and temporal lord. Certainly both in France
and England the State's Courts actively and successfully resisted what were regarded as encroachments.
In particular, from Henry II's days onwards, the
temporal power in England, by means of "writs
of prohibition," kept to itself all litigation about
advowsons ; also the "benefit of clergy" that was
conceded in cases of felony was but a small part of
that immunity of the ordained from secular justice
(*privilegium fori*), which was comprised in the Church's
demand. It is unquestionably true therefore that
some parts of the canon law were not enforced in this
country. We must not, however, infer from this that
the ecclesiastical Courts did not consider themselves
bound to administer the law that they found in the
papal statute-books. It seems to be supposed by
some eminent writers that in the later Middle Ages
the rulers of the Church of England exercised a right
of rejecting or declining to follow the decretals of

Rome, even in matters which the State left to cognisance of the spiritual tribunals ; but this has ,hardly been proved.

In the nineteenth century the history of the canon law became the subject of a large literature, German, French, and Italian. The student should be warned that any book on this topic becomes antiquated very soon, owing to the rapid output of previously unpublished documents. Here, however, it may be sufficient to refer him to A. Tardif, *Histoire des sources du droit canonique*, Paris, 1887.

RECORDS OF THE HONOURABLE SOCIETY OF LINCOLN'S INN[1].

I.

THERE is, perhaps, no more serious gap in the history of mediaeval England than that which should be filled by the tale of the Inns of Court. They have a fair claim to be the most purely English of all English institutions, and the influence that they exercised over the current of our national life could not easily be overrated. For let us ask, What was it that saved English law when the day of strain and trial came in the sixteenth century? Why was there in England no "reception" of Roman law? We ought to pause before we answer these questions. We ought to look not only at Germany, but also at France and Scotland. The danger was very great. In "the new monarchy," as Mr Green called it, the monarch must often have felt that his legal tools were clumsy, and there were plenty of people to tell him where to look for apter instruments. As it was, our common law had a bad time under Henry VIII. In all directions its province was being narrowed by the new courts, the Star Chamber, the Court of Requests, the Council of the North, and so forth. There comes a moment when the stream of law reports, which has been flowing

[1] *English Historical Review*, Oct. 1898 and April, 1900.

ever since the time of Edward I, seems to be on the very point of running dry. Reginald Pole, the highly educated young man who is not far from the throne, is saying that the time has come for Roman law; every well-ruled nation is adopting it. The Protector Somerset is keenly interested in getting a great "civil law college" founded at Cambridge. To praise "the civil law" is a mark of enlightenment, and sometimes of advanced protestantism, for your common lawyer is apt to be mediaevally and even popishly inclined.

But there was a difference between England and other countries. For a long time past English law had been taught; it had been systematically and academically taught in and by certain societies or "fellowships" of lawyers. Did not that mark it off from every other mass of legal rules with which it ought to be compared? Roman law had been taught and canon law had been taught; they had been taught in England, as elsewhere; but had German or French or Scotch law been taught, taught systematically and academically? If the answer to this is No, then surely we have here a difference of the first importance. The taught system will be very much tougher than the untaught. In England the struggle is not between doctrine and traditional practice, but between doctrine and doctrine, and when the tyranny is overpast English mediaeval doctrine has its wonderful renaissance in the Elizabethan courts and the pages of Sir Edward Coke.

If this or anything like this be true, then every scrap of information that we can obtain about these Inns of Court should bear a high value in the eyes of all who care for English history. Happily at this

moment the rulers of more than one society seem
disposed to do all that in them lies towards stimulating
and satisfying our reasonable curiosity. A sumptuous
volume comes to us from Lincoln's Inn[1]. It is edited
by Mr J. Douglas Walker and Mr W. P. Baildon, and
their work has been well done. We must not omit to
say that this book contains an enormous mass of
miscellaneous information bearing on the life and
manners of the fifteenth and sixteenth centuries.
Merely as a record of prices and wages it would be
valuable, and there are instructive and amusing anecdotes. But the main matter is that we can now know
pretty thoroughly the constitution of this honourable
fellowship of Lincoln's Inn as it was between the years
1422 and 1586. In a careful preface Mr Walker has
said almost everything that can as yet be said with any
certainty. During this period the framework of the
society remains marvellously stable. What it was in
the days of Elizabeth it had been in the first year of
Henry VI, when it suddenly appears before us in the
first of its Black Books. "The system of government,"
says Mr Walker, "remains unaltered; admissions are
made more regular, education more effective, but the
changes are slight, so that it is possible from the casual
notices to say that the constitution which existed in
1422 was in force in 1586." This being so, we shall
agree with Mr Walker in thinking it "safe to infer
that so early as the former year the constitution had
become well suited to the wants of the society, and
that this completeness had been the growth of many

---

[1] *The Records of the Honourable Society of Lincoln's Inn. The
Black Books*, vol. I. 1422–1586. 1897.

years of use and wont." On the other hand, there is a limit beyond which we must not carry even the embryonic history of this or any kindred society. As a prerequisite we must have granted to us a considerable number of professional lawyers. Nor only that, for these societies consist not of fully graduated lawyers (if that phrase may pass), but of *apprenticii*. The "benchers" of these inns who give degrees (*vel quasi*) by calls to their bars and their benches are themselves mere apprentices. The full-blown *servientes* have an inn of their own ; and would that its history were known! All this seems to imply a demand for and supply of professional pleaders and advisers such as we should scruple to postulate for any reign earlier than Edward II's, or at earliest Edward I's.

Mr Walker holds out a little hope that about the time before 1422 he may have something to tell us in a future volume. He is postponing an account of the site, the local habitation, of the society, and it may be that there are leases or conveyances of land and buildings which will lighten the darkness. At present we end with a difficult problem. In 1422 we see a highly organised society. What has been its model, or to what other institutions may we liken it?

We are impelled to ask some such question, for the absolutely new grows rarer the more we read. It would be folly to rush in where Mr Walker has declined to tread, but it seems to me that we are more likely to find the germinal idea in the gild than in the college or in the university. Lincoln's Inn is acephalous ; it has no head, no master, or warden, or provost;

it has four annually elected "governors" or "rulers."
In this it is unlike a college, but not unlike some gilds.
The gild, though often it has a single "alderman" as
its head, has often four, just four, elected skevins
(*scabini*). If the primary object of the association is
that of providing lawyers with a common hall and
common meals, and with chambers in which they can
live cheaply, and for the time being celibately—they
do not bring their wives to town—then a certain
resemblance to the college seems to follow of necessity,
and it is increased by the common store of books
and the chapel. And then in the gild of the craft
or "mastery" there seems to be an element which
is potentially educational, and which may become
academic if the craft in question is a craft rather of the
head than of the hand. The gild seeks to regulate
apprenticeship. It assumes the duty of protecting the
public against bad work and its own members against
undue competition. Moreover there was a good deal
of gild-like festivity in the inn. Its "revels" were
prolonged and its records are tinged with the roseate
hue of good wine. Apparently it knew of no
"founder," of no foundation charter or founder's
statutes. It seems to have made its rules as it went
along. Also it was unendowed; it held the site upon
lease; it was self-supporting; it lived from hand to
mouth; there was no corporate revenue to be divided
among fellows. But it is easy to make wrong guesses,
and after all it is only for points of connexion that we
can ask, for the honourable fellowship is not a craft
gild, and the corporation (*vel quasi*) which begins to
teach English law by means of "readings" and

"moots" does something that is very new and very important. Perhaps nothing so important was done by any mediaeval parliament.

That *vel quasi* is one of the oddest points in the whole story; the "fellowship" or "society" never becomes corporate. It is as if English lawyers had said, "We will show you how all this can be done without any of your Italian trickery : we have no need of 'incorporation'; we can get all that we want by means of our own home-grown trust." One would think that at times the unincorporatedness of the inn must have occasioned difficulties and expense, but I suppose that lawyers knew how to avoid litigation, and, in the days when *quo warranto* was a terror, an inn may have been the safer because of its impersonality.

Be this as it may, the honourable society of Lincoln's Inn never acted more worthily of its illustrious past than when it decided to publish its records. We may hope that it will not be weary of well-doing and that we may soon know all that can be known of one at least of the Inns of Court.

II.

This volume is to the full as interesting as its predecessor, and does credit to those who have been concerned in its preparation, namely, Mr Douglas Walker and Mr Baildon[1]. The student of life and manners will find in it many stories which will be to his liking, and every now and again there is an entry

[1] *The Records of the Honourable Society of Lincoln's Inn. The Black Books*, vol. II. 1568–1660. 1898.

that bears on the grand struggles that were taking place in church and state. But the main value of the book consists in the light that it pours upon the continuous life of one of the most English of English institutions, the technically unincorporate society or fellowship of lawyers, which is practically performing public functions, since it controls the admission of advocates to the courts, but which none the less secures for itself almost as much autonomy as would be allowed to any private club.

"The lawyers of Lincolne's Inne were not incorporate, neither by Act of Parliament nor by any Letters Pattents from the King's Majestie." That was said to Charles I by Richard Montague, bishop of Chichester, whom we know in other contexts. He had determined to make a vigorous onslaught against the title by which the lawyers held their inn. Then there was a scene well worthy of the full account of it that the lawyers put into their Black Book (p. 332). Charles himself sat to hear the bishop's complaint. He sat at Whitehall on 23 Nov. 1635, "in the withdrawing room next the bed chamber." Laud was there, and so were the secretaries of state and some other ministers. Three masters of the bench appeared on behalf of the society, and took no exception to the king's hearing and deciding in his proper person what really was a suit for the recovery of land; perhaps they knew that even Charles could not decide that suit against them. Montague spoke a little evil of lawyers. He recalled that good old writ in which Edward I declared that sevenscore apprentices and attorneys would be enough for all England. He said that he would argue his own cause, hinting that since lawyers had become divines a divine might become a lawyer. Then he told how land had been given to his predecessor Ralph Neville by Henry III, how thereon a house had been built for the bishops of Chichester, how various leases of the house were granted to the benchers of the society, the last (it had lately expired) being a lease granted in 1535 by Bishop Sherborne for ninety-nine years at a rent of 16*l.* 13*s.* 4*d.* It then appeared, however, that in the next year Sherborne's successor, Bishop Sampson, sold the reversion for 200*l.*, and conveyed the freehold to two Syliards who were trustees for the society. The technical objections that Montague could bring against this transaction were not very formidable, and one after another they were overruled by Charles, who is represented as showing some skill in legal argument. Montague, however, told a discreditable tale of Sampson, suggesting that he got his bishopric by means of the influence of Eustace Syliard, one of the ushers of King Henry's bed chamber, and that the grant in favour of the society was part of a simoniacal bargain. In the end the lawyers were triumphant, and when Montague, abandoning legal claims, begged that the king's influence might secure for the bishops of Chichester a right to lodge in the inn that had once belonged to their see, he was told that since the conveyance the lawyers had spent 40,000*l.* in improvements. So with a *Liberavi animam meam* Montague desisted. But when he mentioned the unincorporate character of the society he was touching a curiously important point. What we know as our English " liberty of association "

was rendered legally possible by the law or the equity
about uses and trusts, which enabled a body of men to
perpetuate itself and in effect to own property, while
a screen of feoffees or trustees protected it from the
inquisitive scrutiny of the state. If we look abroad
we may fairly doubt whether our own lawyers of the
fifteenth and sixteenth centuries would have permitted
this arrangement, which, besides impairing the practical
operation of the statutes of mortmain, allows something
that can hardly be distinguished from corporateness to
be acquired without any authoritative act, had it not
been that they themselves were bred in societies that
just were not corporations. It is surely an easily
excusable slip of which Mr Walker, himself a master
of the bench, is guilty when he says (p. xxiv) that
"legal education largely occupied the attention of the
benchers in their individual and corporate capacity."

As to legal education, we may witness the decline
of the old system. It had proceeded on the mediaeval
theory, which was breaking down in the universities
also—namely, the theory that the man who has taken
a full degree is licensed to teach, can teach, and ought
to teach, and may rightly be coerced into teaching.
The publication of numerous law books, especially
Coke's, must have decreased the demand for the
somewhat rough and haphazard instruction that would
be given by a reader who was merely taking his turn
at the work. Unfortunately these ancient societies
were slow to put anything more modern in the place
of this outworn plan.

MAGISTRI VACARII SUMMA DE MATRIMONIO[1]

INTRODUCTION.

Of late years a good deal has been written about Vacarius. Very recently Dr Liebermann[2], to whom the students of English legal history already owed a heavy debt of gratitude, has summed up what is known of the life of this Italian legist and has added to the sum by calling attention to two works of his which are lying in manuscript at Cambridge. The one of these is theological, the other is devoted to the law of marriage. This latter will be printed in a later number of this Review. I have not that knowledge of the canon law which would enable me to edit this treatise scientifically; but I believe that I can give a fairly correct copy of it, and that it will be of some interest to a few Englishmen and to a few foreigners.

Of Vacarius himself I will say but very little, since I have nothing to add to what has been written by Dr Liebermann and others in accessible places[3]. Only

---

[1] *Law Quarterly Review*, April, 1897.

[2] *English Historical Review*, XI. 305.

[3] Rashdall, *Universities of Europe*, II. 335; Pollock and Maitland, *Hist. Engl. Law*, I. 97; Holland, *Oxford in the Twelfth Century* (Oxford Hist. Soc.).

let us remember, first, that in all probability he came to England as early as 1148, and was living here as late as 1198; secondly, that in the meanwhile he had dwelt under the patronage of Archbishop Theobald of Canterbury and afterwards of Archbishop Roger of York; thirdly, that we have some reason for supposing that his great book, the Summa of Justinian's Code, was finished in 1149; and fourthly, that we have fairly good evidence of his having taught Roman law in Oxford at some time in his long career.

The manuscript in question is preserved in the University Library at Cambridge (Ii. 3. 9), and its contents are described at some length in the printed catalogue (vol. III. pp. 412–415). For the more part they consist of various works of St Augustin. Better judges of handwriting than I am have said that this volume was compiled near, but rather before than after, the year 1200. At the beginning there is a table of contents which seems to be coeval with the body of the book. The portion of this which is most interesting to us runs as follows:—*Augustinus de agone christiano. Item eiusdem sermo Mulierem fortem*[1]. *Item de trinitate. Summa Magistri Vacarii de* [apparently *matrimonio* has been erased and then a later hand has added *assumpto homine*. *Item eodem* [*sic*] *de matrimonio*]. *Expositio S. Augustini contra paganos.* The pages are divided into two columns. A little way down in the second column on a certain page we find the rubric *Magistri Vagarii tractatus de assumpto homine incipit.* The treatise that is thus

---

[1] This, it is said, really comes not from Augustin, but from Bede.

introduced fills rather more than twenty columns. Then without interval comes the rubric *Hic incipit quedam summa de matrimonio Magistri Vacarii*, and on this at once follows our treatise, in the first words of which the writer speaks of himself as the author of an *opusculum de assumpto homine*. Our treatise fills rather less than twenty-six columns, and in the column in which it ceases another brief tract begins with the words *Omnium expetendarum prima est sapientia*. The writing is good, and I do not think that the scribe can be charged with many mistakes.

The disquisition *de assumpto homine* is heralded by a prefatory letter; this will be printed below by way of appendix. The author is concerned with "the assumption of man" by Christ. He is making an attack upon what he regards as a fashionable but erroneous philosophy. As I understand him, he seeks to prove that Christ assumed not only the reasonable soul and human flesh, but also the "substance" of man. The course of his argument I dare not attempt to describe. He is angry with certain adversaries who (so he says) fill the high places in the schools; but he does not name them. The only writers whom he expressly mentions are ancients, such as Augustin, Jerome, Claudian and Boethius. I should suppose that he is attacking that doctrine of the Incarnation which is known as Nihilianism, and that his vigorous words are aimed either at the great Peter Lombard himself or at some disciples of his who outran their master along a dangerous road[1]. They found another

---

[1] *Sentent.* lib. III. dist. 290. See Dorner, *The Person of Christ,* Eng. trans., Div. 2, vol. II., pp. 310 ff.; Baur, *Lehre von der Drei-*

enemy in a countryman of ours, one John of Cornwall[1], and their doctrine was condemned by Alexander III. In this case Vacarius seems to have been fighting on what by its success was to prove itself to be the orthodox side. It was otherwise when he wrote on marriage. Here he championed a losing cause, for this same Alexander dealt its death-blow[2].

The tract on marriage may speak for itself. I must not presume to comment upon it at any length, nor endeavour precisely to fix its place in the important controversy to which it belongs. In the main it will be intelligible to any one who will read a few modern books and keep a copy of the Decretum Gratiani open before him[3]. But two or three explanatory remarks I will venture to make.

In the middle of the twelfth century the Church throughout the Western world was successfully claiming for her courts an exclusive right to pronounce on the validity of marriages. But in truth she was not as

einigkeit, II. 548 ff. ; Rashdall, *Universities*, I. 54. The watchword of the school was : *quod Christus, secundum quod est homo, non est aliquid.*

[1] Martène et Durand, *Thesaurus Novus*, v. 1657 ; *Dict. Nat. Biog.* s.v. John of Cornwall.

[2] In the preface to the *De assumpto homine* the hand of the civilian seems to be betrayed when its author says, "Cum lege cautum sit nullam esse interpretationem que tantum valeat ut preiudicare possit manifesto sensui." I have not, however, been able to trace the origin of this maxim.

[3] See von Scheurl, *Entwicklung des kirchlichen Eheschliessungsrechts*, Erlangen, 1877 ; Freisen, *Geschichte des canonischen Eherechts*, Tübingen, 1888 ; Esmein, *Le mariage en droit canonique*, Paris, 1891 ; Friedberg, *Lehrbuch des Kirchenrechts* (ed. 4, Leipzig, 1895), pp. 408–413.

yet equipped with any doctrine of wedlock sufficiently definite to serve as a legal theory. A few brief texts in the Bible; a few passages in the works of the Fathers, some of which were but too mystical, while others were but too hortative; a few canons and decretals that were not very consistent with each other —these were the unsatisfactory materials out of which law was to be made. And the law was to be cosmopolitan. The very nature of the claim to treat marriage as a spiritual matter, a divinely ordained institution, prevented the Church's lawgivers and lawyers from laying a decisive stress upon any rites or usages that were merely national. A cosmopolitan law of marriage cannot make any ceremony or formality essential. It must compose its marriage out of those elements which we can conceive as common to the marriages of all people.in all ages, such as the agreement to marry, the beginning of cohabitation, and the sexual union. Difficulties which in any case would have been great were complicated by the supposed necessity of proving that marriage is in some sort—but who shall say what sort?—a *sacramentum*, and of giving the name of marriage to such union as the Christian legend would allow St Joseph to contract with the Blessed Virgin.

Gratian (circ. 1139–42) made a determined endeavour to obtain a consistent theory out of the materials that he collected[1]. He holds that the *sponsalia*, the agreement to marry hereafter, constitute an "initiate marriage," which however only becomes a

---

[1] See especially C. 27. q. 2.

"consummate marriage" at the moment of physical
intercourse. Were we to translate his doctrine into
modern terms, we should say that really there is no
marriage until such intercourse has taken place, though
from this principle he would not draw all the inferences
that would be drawn from it by modern law. About
the same time Peter Lombard[1] was developing a new
distinction, the famous distinction between *sponsalia
de futuro* and *sponsalia de praesenti*. Espousals by
words of present time, which are contracted if man and
woman express their agreement to be from henceforth
husband and wife, constitute a perfect marriage, though
the *copula carnalis* is necessary to introduce into the
union the sacrament of Christ and His Church. On
the other hand, espousals by words of future time are
no marriage; they are but an agreement that there
shall be a marriage hereafter.

Thenceforth there were two main theories before
the world. Gratian's was spoken of as the Italian or
Bolognese theory; Peter's became the theory of the
Gallican Church. Warm debates ensued. In particular, about the year 1156, the Italian canonist
Rufinus came forward as a vehement champion of
Gratian's cause[2]. But time was on Peter's side. His
doctrine had the advantage of being compatible with
the existence of a perfect marriage between St Mary
and her reputed husband. Pope Alexander III, while
he was but Magister Rolandus, had written on this
subject, and, though he accepted Gratian's principles,
expressed some doubt about the deductions that were

[1] Lib. IV. dist. 27.
[2] *Summa Rufini* (ed. Schulte, Giessen, 1892), p. 389.

drawn from them[1]. As pope he went over to Peter's side, and in the course of his long pontificate settled the law of the Church by a series of decisions that were promulgated in decretal letters. Peter's doctrine that consent *per verba de praesenti* constitutes a marriage became the law of the Church; but at the same time some traces of the opposite theory were retained, for by "consummation" a marriage gained an additional degree of indissolubility and perhaps of sacramentality.

Now Vacarius has a theory which differs from all of these. The true act of marriage, the act which marks the moment at which the marriage takes place, is the mutual delivery (*traditio*) of man and woman each to each. Of course as a condition there must exist a pact of the appropriate kind. The man delivers himself as husband, the woman delivers herself as wife. But it is not a mere expressed consent that makes the marriage; there must be a delivery, a "tradition." Again, as a condition there must be the natural power of effecting a carnal union; but the *carnalis copula* is unessential; it does not make the marriage; the marriage is made by the "tradition." In a startling passage and by way of *reductio ad absurdum* Vacarius brings the Bishop of Hippo to the side of the nuptial couch to upbraid the bridegroom for embracing a woman to whom he is not yet "perfectly" married. "Inciuiliter loqueris Augustine," is the man's reply, "for she is my wife, having become so by tradition, and the first embrace is as legitimate as the last." That harmful text about man and woman

---

[1] *Summa Rolandi* (ed. Thaner, Innsbruck, 1874), pp. 126–133.

becoming "one flesh" is cleverly encountered by another text. From the moment of the marriage, that is, from the moment of the tradition, the man has no power over his own body, or, in other words, his body is already his wife's and her body is his. Therefore this is the moment at which they become "one flesh." At this moment the law makes them "one flesh" by giving to each power over the other's body; the sexual union is mere matter of fact. We must distinguish between the perfection of a legal act and the fulfilment of obligations which that act creates. We must not blur this distinction by talk about "consummation." A marriage is a marriage, and it cannot become more of a marriage than it already is.

Vacarius is prepared to carry this thought into the mystical sphere of sacramentality. The marriage effected by "tradition" already contains the sacrament of Christ and the Church. At the moment of delivery the man and woman are made "one flesh" by a *vinculum iuris*. Further, he protests against a popular use of the word *ratum*, which would make it imply indissolubility[1]. This use is, for one thing, unclassical; no single sentence in the *Corpus Iuris Civilis* sanctions it. A marriage effected by tradition is a *matrimonium ratum*, and this it would be even if the law permitted a divorce *a vinculo*. We are bidden remember that even after the time of Christ, even after the time of

---

[1] dictum post c. 17, C. 28. q. 1: "Coniugium enim aliud est legitimum et non ratum, aliud ratum et non legitimum, aliud legitimum et ratum. Legitimum coniugium est quod legali institutione uel prouinciae moribus contrahitur. Hoc inter infideles ratum non est, quia non est firmum et inuiolabile coniugium eorum."

Justinian, divorce was possible; St Joseph and St Mary married under a law that allowed divorce. Logical to the last, Vacarius will even declare that the marriages of infidels are *rata*, and contain the sacrament of Christ and the Church.

This attempt to make all turn upon the mutual *traditio* does not indeed stand quite alone. A similar attempt seems to be made for a moment by the author of the book that is known as the *Summa Coloniensis*[1]. He is thought to have been a German, to have done his work about the year 1170 in the province of Köln, and to have been an adherent of the anti-pope Calixtus. At this point we shall do well to remember that our Henry II carried on a flirtation with the Calixtines, that Reinald von Dassel, Archbishop of Köln, who was the soul of the schism, visited our shores, and that Roger of Pont l'Evêque, Archbishop of York, was both the patron of Vacarius and the rival and enemy of Becket[2]. Some intercourse between Vacarius and the German canonist is not out of the question.

[1] The work was described by Schulte, *Sitzungsberichte der Wiener Akademie*, vol. 64, p. 93. The relevant passage is given by Scheurl, *op. cit.* p. 168, and Freisen, *op. cit.* p. 189: "Item cum in hoc pacto uterque dicat alteri *Trado me tibi*, si verba cum effectu accipiuntur, ex tunc caro utriusque alterius efficitur. Illud enim generale est in huiusmodi contractibus, ut traditione rei dominium transferatur. Proinde, ex quo sponsa viro tradita et cum eo velata atque traducta est, ex tunc caro eius viri est, etsi nuptiale mysterium nondum in ea completum sit, et hoc Gratianus post multas ambages sentire videtur."

[2] See, for example, the letter addressed by Henry to the Archbishop of Köln, telling how the Archbishop of York and others have gone as the king's envoys to threaten Pope Alexander; *Materials for the Life of Becket*, v. 428.

We may well think that the doctrine of Vacarius had much to commend it. On the one hand, it cannot have stood very remote from Germanic custom, while on the other, it was not out of harmony with the usage described in the Digest, for though some would teach us nowadays that the Roman marriage became in theory a merely consensual and formless transaction, still undoubtedly great stress was laid on the *deductio in domum* as being the usual and almost necessary evidence of a marriage. Also it was much in the vein of our own ancient lawyers that some change of "seisin," some *traditio vel quasi* (as Vacarius calls it), should be regarded as the act of marriage. However, unfortunately for the Church and unfortunately for the world, the Church's law of marriage took a different turn. The voice of Vacarius is *Vox clamantis in deserto*. To this may be due the fact, if fact it be, that his voice is transmitted to us by an unique manuscript.

At another point he opposes the triumphant doctrine of the canonists. A young girl who is in the power of parents or guardians cannot be married without their consent. If that be not given there will be no marriage, but at best a *contubernium*. He accuses his adversaries—and here he has both Gratian and Peter Lombard against him—of frittering away the clear words of Pope Evaristus[1] (100?–109?). Those words we now know to be the words of the Pseudo-Isidore[2]. Neither Vacarius nor his foes knew that, and in his eyes they are guilty of eluding a plain

---

[1] c. 1, C. 30. q. 5.

[2] Hinschius, *Decretales Pseudo-Isidorianae*, p. 87.

decree of a pope who was learned *in utroque iure.*
Here again he had morality, decency, ancient law, and
the remote future for allies ; but the current of sacra-
mentalism was too strong to be stemmed.

That he had Gratian's work before him seems
quite plain, though he never names Gratian nor the
Decretum. Also we may infer that the Decretum
was still new and had not yet established itself as the
one classical text-book of the canon law, for though he
quotes many of the "authorities" that are contained
in it, and also quotes some of the *dicta Gratiani,*
he never mentions any "distinction," "cause," or
"question," as assuredly he would have done had he
been writing near the end of the twelfth century.
Whether he had before him the "Paleae," that is, the
passages inserted in the Decretum by Gratian's pupil
Paucapalea[1], seems more doubtful. He quotes two
passages that are thus introduced; but from this it
does not follow that they stood in his copy of the
Decretum. To one of these two he repeatedly[2]
alludes, but whereas in the manuscripts which are the
base of the modern editions of Gratian's book this text
is ascribed to Augustin[3], Vacarius attributes it to Pope
Hormisda (A.D. 514–523). It is a passage which
appears also, and under Augustin's name, in the
Compilatio Prima[4] and in the Decretals of Gregory
IX.[5]

[1] Schulte, *Geschichte*, I. 62. 109.
[2] Vacarius, §§ 12, 19, 25, 26.   [3] c. 51, C. 27. q. 2.
[4] c. 1, *Comp. Prima*, 4. 4.
[5] c. 1, X. 4. 4. The other passage is quoted by Vacarius, § 22,
and is the Palea which stands as c. 18, C. 27. q. 2.

With the theory of marriage stated by Peter Lombard our author was familiar; but I cannot say that he takes any words from the Parisian schoolman, nor do I see any proof that he had read the Summa of Paucapalea, the Summa of Roland, or the Summa of Stephen of Tournay. On the other hand, it is pretty plain that he borrowed phrases from and directed much of his argument against Rufinus. This, if Dr von Schulte is right, would allow us to assign his treatise to any year after 1156[1].

If we place out of account the two " Paleae" which have been already mentioned, I believe that he cites but two other "authorities" which he could not have obtained from the Decretum. (1) The first of these[2] is a forged letter of Alexander, pope and martyr, that is, of Alexander I (109?–119?). This appears in the Summa of Rufinus[3], also in the Summa of Johannes Faventinus[4], also in the Collectio Lipsiensis[5]. It is a forged decretal, but it is not one of the Pseudo-Isidorian brood. No more seems to be certainly known of it than that it became current in the twelfth century. Not impossibly it was concocted in the course of the controversy about marriage in order to support the Bolognese against the Parisian theory. (2) The second of these two authorities[6] is a canon of the Council of Verberie, held in the year 753. This in

---

[1] *Summa Rufini;* ed. Schulte, p. xi.

[2] Vacarius, § 20.   [3] *Summa Rufini*, pp. xxxi, 396.

[4] Schulte, *Sitzungsberichte der Wiener Akademie*, vol. LVII., pp. 589, 590.

[5] Friedberg, *Quinque Compilationes*, p. 205; Freisen, *Eherecht*, p. 183.

[6] Vacarius, § 39.

its-original form[1], and in the form in which Vacarius knew it, distinctly contemplates the possibility of a true divorce in our sense of the term: that is to say, in a certain case a man whose wife will not follow him into a foreign country is allowed to marry another. Part of this canon appears in the Decretum, but the part which permits a divorce has been carefully excised[2]. Vacarius quotes, or rather paraphrases, the original form of the text, but only in order that he may show that strange things have occasionally been permitted. Possibly he found the whole canon in the pages of one of Gratian's predecessors, Regino of Prüm[3], for example, or Burchard of Worms[4].

In favour of an early date for the book we have not only the informal manner in which the authorities that lie in the Decretum are cited, and the assumption that the grand marriage question is still open, but also the fact that no notice is taken of the epoch-making decretals of Alexander III.[5] This is the more significant because one of the most decisive of those decretals was sent to England[6]. The popes, it is true, had hardly as yet made good their right to legislate on a large scale, and the canonists were still ready to say

---

[1] *Mon. Germ.*, *Capitularia*, ed. Boretius, I. 41; Freisen, *op. cit.* p. 783.

[2] c. 4, C. 34. q. 1.

[3] Regino, II. 123 (ed. Wasserschleben, p. 262).

[4] Burchard, IX. 54 (Migne, vol. CXL., col. 824); Freisen, *op. cit.* 801.

[5] Freisen, p. 191; Esmein, I. 127.

[6] c. 6, *Comp.* I, 4. 4 (Friedberg, p. 47); translated, Pollock and Maitland, *Hist. Engl. Law*, II. 369. See also Mansi, *Concilia*, XXII. 293.

upon occasion that a pope had gone wrong. We may
fairly suppose, however, that had Vacarius known
these Alexandrine decretals, he would have felt bound
either to hold his peace or to controvert them.
Magister Rolandus, when he had taken possession of
the chair of St Peter, was not a man who could be
quietly ignored. Unfortunately his pontificate (1159–
1181) was long, and few of his decretals have been
dated. Nevertheless if 1156 or thereabouts is the
earliest date to which we can attribute this Summa,
the latest date is, I should suppose, not much later.

That its author was the Vacarius of whom all of us
have heard, and not another person of the same name,
seems clear. We know Vacarius as a legist, and this
is just such a tract as would be written by a legist who
for the nonce was making an incursion into the
canonist's territory. Having before his eyes the
precision of his own beautiful Digest, he seems to feel
a sort of pity and even contempt for the boneless
scraps of exhortation and mysticism that are collected
in the Decretum. He complains that the law of the
Church is always shifting and wabbling[1]. He complains of the canonist's method. What is the use of
an attempt to make a concordance of discordant canons
when the canons are discordant[2]? His theory of

---

[1] Vacarius, § 16: "Ecclesiastica namque iura dissonas recipiunt
sentencias et varias formas, plerumque inutiles, quia non obser-
uantur."

[2] *Ibid.*, § 16: "Illi enim qui ad hoc frustra laborant ut quamlibet
passim contrarietatis *discordiam* reuocent ad *concordiam*, plerumque,
ut vicium huiusmodi contra veritatem evitare contendunt, in veritate
labuntur in peius." If we remember that Gratian called his book

marriage, too, is a legist's theory. It may not be just that which modern scholars will discover in Justinian's books, but it brings marriage into line with the conveyance of property. Other legal transactions, such as donation and partnership, are constantly before his mind, and in his eyes a word from Pomponius is enough to sweep away a lot of foolish talk about *matrimonia* which are and *matrimonia* which are not *rata*[1]. We should hardly be going too far were we to say that this is a civilian's protest against the mess that is being made of the law of marriage by canonists and divines. We might like, perhaps, to go further and to contrast an Oxonian with the Bolognese and with the Parisian theory of marriage, and thus to unite in one story the three great universities of the twelfth century. But we have no warrant for this. Vacarius's pamphlet (for it is no more) is no school-book comparable with the Decretum and the Sentences, and, for anything that we know, may represent the opinion of one solitary and protesting legist. That its author was both daring and acute is plain.

Another guess is inviting. If we attribute this tract to the years which closely follow 1156, we give it to a time when England and Rome, Normandy and Gascony were witnesses to the dogged litigiousness of that immortal plaintiff, Richard of Anesty[2]. Beginning his long suit in 1158, he triumphed in 1163. He had

Concordia discordantium canonum, this remark will seem pointed enough.

[1] Vacarius, § 36.

[2] *Joan. Saresberiensis Epistolae*, ed. Giles, vol. I. pp. 123–132; Palgrave, *English Commonwealth*, vol. II. pp. v–xxvii, lxxv–lxxxvii.

the professional aid of another Italian lawyer, whose name has elsewhere[1] been coupled with that of Vacarius, namely, of Master Ambrose[2]. Is it impossible that if Magister Ambrosius was of counsel for the plaintiff, Magister Vacarius was retained for the defence? Or again, if in 1159 Vacarius still remained an inmate of Archbishop Theobald's household, we can hardly doubt that he was consulted about a case which raised nice questions of matrimonial law and tasked the wisdom of the archiepiscopal court to its uttermost. One of these questions was whether a divorce pronounced in Stephen's reign by the legate Henry of Blois was valid. In Henry I's day one William had, so some asserted, married Albreda, while others maintained that this was no marriage and that at a later date he had married Adelicia. In Anesty's suit Archbishop Theobald's secretary, John of Salisbury (to whom Vacarius was "Vacarius noster" and from whom we learn of Stephen's attempt to silence the voice of Roman law), reported to Alexander III the story of these would-be marriages and the subsequent divorce. He said that the former marriage was upheld and the nullity of the second declared by Henry of Blois, who was acting in pursuance of a mandate from Innocent II (1130–1143). This mandate apparently supposed that some sort of formal "tradition" of Albreda by her father had taken place, but that William had never removed her from her father's house, and it was admitted that there had been no ecclesiastical ceremony and no sexual intercourse.

---

[1] Liebermann, *Engl. Hist. Rev.* XI. 313, 314.
[2] Palgrave, *op. cit.* p. vii.

Nevertheless, Innocent decreed that if there had been a consent to be thenceforth husband and wife, there had been a marriage, and that the subsequent union with Adelicia, though solemnly celebrated in church and blessed with offspring, was adulterous. In short, Innocent seems to have acted upon the theory of marriage which is now generally coupled with the name of Peter Lombard[1]. Now this was just such a case as would have set Vacarius a-writing his pamphlet. There might be a pact by "words of present time," but was there a marriage if Albreda was left under her father's roof[2]? Often what looks like a speculation of abstract jurisprudence has been the outcome of a concrete lawsuit, and is none the worse for having its origin in real facts. This is only a guess; but the temptation to connect together two men so famous in our legal history as the first teacher of Roman law and the heroic English litigant was not to be withstood[3].

[1] Innocent's mandate is set out in John of Salisbury's letter (I. 125). It appears also as c. 10, *Comp. Prima*, 4. 1 (Friedberg, *Quinque Compilationes*, p. 44). It must belong to the last years of Innocent's pontificate (1130–1143). Henry of Blois was appointed legate on March 1, 1139 (*Dict. Nat. Biog.*, s.v. Henry of Blois). Palgrave (*op. cit.* p. viii) thought that the divorce was pronounced in 1141 or 1143. The exact date of Peter Lombard's work has been a matter of controversy.

[2] According to Innocent there had been a *traditio* by Albreda's father, but the *traductio in domum mariti* was to take place upon a future day, and meanwhile she was *commendata* to her father.

[3] In the printed copy of the treatise the punctuation and the numeration of paragraphs will be due to the editor.

APPENDIX

Magistri Vagarii Tractatus de assumpto iiomine incipit.

Suo B. suus V. salutem. Post collationem de homine assumpto inter nos habitam, sepe cum plerisque aliis uestigia opinionis uestre sectantibus de re eadem tractatum habui, qui etiam rationem ipsius opinionis mihi exposuerunt precipuam. Summa uero eiusdem opinionis ea est ut non sit aliquis homo qui pro nobis interpelletur, quem susceperit deus uerbum, set animam et corpus tantum assump-sit. Eius autem urgentissimam rationem talem reddunt: quam[1] personam a uerbo assumptam esse, necesse est ut dicamus, si concesserimus eum assumptum esse qui ex anima et carne subsistat ut pro nobis interpellare possit. Nam cum dicimus dei sapientiam seu uerbum suscepisse humanam naturam uel hominem, nichil nisi rationalem animam et humanam carnem absque earum in unam substantiam conpage significamus assumptas. Hec est doctrina celebris a quibusdam modernis inuenta magistris. Hec est uia in scolis maxime frequentata et trita hodie. porro huiusmodi disciplina cum nullis auctoritatibus' roborari possit, licet aliquibus paucis uix aliquo modo colorari querat, regulas tamen suas habet et traditiones, quibus maiorum auctoritates eludere possit, ut suum defendat errorem. Nam si qua obiciatur auctoritas, promptam habent responsionem secundum suas regulas, ut si auctoritas est expositione indigeat et interpretatione, cum econtrario lege cautum sit nullam esse interpretationem que tantum ualeat ut preiudicare possit mani-festo sensui. Item ut tantum effugere possint ex leui occasione, nugari dicunt quemlibet urgentem eos. Naturamque humanam in Christo ita disponunt, ut dum totam eam Christo tribuere uideantur, animam rationalem et humanam ei carnem concedendo, totam ei auferant negando substantiam ipsius[2] hominis ex eis consistere. Vnde querenti mihi, Cum substantia fuerit infans ille quem magi adorauerunt, que substantia fuerit? responderunt quidam quod diuina fuerit substantia et non humana. Hec et alia his similia

---

[1] Possibly *quem*.

[2] *ipsius* repeated.

induxerunt me et inpulerunt ad scribendum, et quamuis ipsa rei
sublimitas et operis difficultas animum et uires mihi adimerent
scribendi, eius tamen inuocato nomine qui desperata etiam consueuit
petentibus donare, et ea paruulis pulsantibus aperire que sapientibus
et prudentibus celantur, eius inquam inuocato nomine, et oculis ad
celum erectis, opus meas extendens uires eius donatione inpleui,
quod discretioni uestre dilectionis eo studio inspiciendum, discutien-
dumque commisi quo scriptum est, ut ueritatis amore singula
diligenter examinetis, et si quid inprudenter ibi insertum fuerit,
industria uestre prudentie, antequam ad alium perueniat, corrigatur.
Euidentibus autem tam rationibus quam auctoritatibus pro ingenii
mei exiguitate studui demonstrare que pocius sententia ueritate
nitatur de homine assumpto, utrum ut anime et corporis assumptio
non composuerit unam hominis substantiam in Christo, an talis
omnino utriusque fuerit coniunctio ut ex eis unus subsistens fuerit
homo substantie humane perfecte sicut quilibet alius[1] homo.
[Rubrica] *De assumpto homine. quod substantia sit ex anima et carne
subsistens tam animalis quam hominis, nature*[2] *proprietatibus subiecta,
non autem diuina. et quod homo cum sit persona, ipse tamen assumptus
dicitur et non ipsa persona. et quod Christus et dominus glorie et gigas
gemine substantie duarum sint substantiarum nomina. et non deus.
et ideo ex dupplici substantia Christus esse una persona dicitur. et non
deus, non homo ita dicitur. et quod deus uere et proprie inde est aliquid,
quia est homo.* [3]Crebris itaque mutationibus et motibus....[4] sed est
secundum catholicos unius substantie humane specifica differentia
seu specificata proprietas seu forma quedam, que proprio nomine
humanitas uocatur, ut supra ostensum est. [Rubrica] *Hic incipit
quedam summa de matrimonio Magistri Vacarii.*

---

[1] *aliis*, MS.

[2] *n* with *e* above, preceded and followed by a stop, MS.

[3] Beginning of treatise.   [4] End of treatise.

LAND-HOLDING IN MEDIAEVAL TOWNS[1]

L'étude de la propriété urbaine au moyen âge a relativement peu attiré l'attention des érudits. With this sentence M. des Marez begins a very interesting book, and there is truth in these words. A good many years have gone by since Arnold published his *History of Ownership in the German Towns.* From that time onwards almost every one who has taken part in the controversies which have raged around urban institutions has had something to say about land ownership and land tenure, and we have all learnt that the existence of a form of tenure peculiar to the towns (*die städtische Erbleihe, Leihe zu Stadtrecht*) is one of the main facts that must be studied and explained. To Englishmen this should have come as an easy lesson, for a " burgage tenure " lies on the surface of our old and orthodox law books, and it cannot be said of us, as perhaps it might be said of some of our neighbours, that a juristic prejudice, demanding a sharp severance of matters of private from matters of public law, has had to be slowly surmounted. But, though not a little has been written on the continent touching the proprietary side of

---

[1] *English Historical Review*, April, 1899.

urban affairs, it seems very certain that much more must be written before the problem is solved, and that for a long time to come there will be ample room for books such as that which is now before us.

M. des Marez speaks of towns in general, but more particularly of the Flemish towns and most particularly of Gand. In so far as his book is a study of medieval Gand there can, I should suppose, be but one opinion about its interest or its value. His work culminates in a " Plan de la Condition Juridique du Sol de la Ville de Gand au Moyen Age," a plan drawn on a large scale and so coloured that we can tell whether a particular house is held as a *franc bien* (*Vrij Huus Vrij Erve*) or by the *tenure libre du droit urbain* or by a *tenure du droit domanial*. We should have something comparable to this if some one drew a map of an English medieval borough, distinguishing the houses that pay a haw-gafol, the houses, if any, which owe military service, the copyhold tenements, and so forth. The archives of Gand must be astonishingly rich in records of conveyances and leases, for they have enabled M. des Marez to perform such a feat of industry as has never yet been performed for any other town. It is very possible, however, that an equal wealth of materials may be found elsewhere, and that students will set to work upon it now that they can learn from this book that the task of making a map of the *condition juridique* of the soil of a borough need not end in pointless antiquarianism, but will certainly raise, even if it does not answer, questions that are of far-reaching importance in the history of institutions.

There is a great deal here that makes us wish for the day when comparative jurisprudence will be something better than a name. The coming of that day we have not hastened, but have retarded, by theories which flit from one end of the earth to another and mix up all the ages. The *condition juridique* of the soil of English and Flemish towns in the later middle ages would be a really good subject for comparative study. Gand was never very far from London. In the thirteenth century some of the most important people in Gand, some of the *markans et bourgeois hyrritavles*, knew England well. International aid should be possible, but difficulties stand in the way.

We see on the one hand so much economic similarity, and on the other so many legal differences, which, however, are differences between modes of thought rather than between practical rules. Though at the present moment we islanders might probably win most in the exchange, the gain would not lie all on one side. For example, M. des Marez, when speaking of those *rentes* which play a large part in the economy of the towns, finds it necessary to insist that there are *points de contact entre le cens foncier et la rente*. This truth might have been driven home by the remark that in England to this day the *cens foncier* is a *rent*, and that when an Englishman hears the word *rent* he thinks first and foremost not of what Frenchmen call a *rente*, but either of a *cens foncier* or of a *loyer*. So again in an interesting chapter we are told how *le louage* is developed in the towns. In the sixteenth century *les termes de loyer, location, preneur, bailleur sont parfaitement définis*. But at an earlier time there has, says our author, been a confused use of words which did not distinguish the *louage* from the *accensement*; for example, *à Ypres le loyer s'appelle rente, et prendre à rente est synonyme de louer.* Upon this we might remark that Englishmen stand to-day where the people of Ypres stood five centuries ago. Either a *loyer* is a *rent*, and to *take at a rent* is a good equivalent for *louer*, or else we ought to say that of *louage* we know nothing. But surely, the foreign inquirer might ask, you perceive a wide gulf between the *preneur* and the *censitaire*? *A la différence du censitaire, qui jouit d'un droit réel, le preneur ne peut opposer au bailleur qu'un droit de créance.* Our reply would be that long ago, and apparently at the persuasion of the Romanists, we tried that idea for a little while and then abandoned it. Since the middle of the thirteenth century we have denied that "sale breaks hire." Our *preneur* (if indeed we know such a person) has a *droit réel* and not a mere *droit de créance* ; the *loyer* that he pays is a *rent* and stands in one class of rents with the *cens foncier*. M. des Marez seems to hold that the prevalence of the principle *so brekt koep hure*, or *Kauf bricht Miete*, is not due to Roman influence. This is one of those questions about which the last word will hardly be said until the English is collated with the French and German evidence.

However, it is chiefly in the already prolonged discussion concerning the origin of the towns that this book means to leave its mark; and certainly it deserves consideration. M. des Marez, who seems to be following in the footsteps of M. Pirenne, to whom he dedicates his book, is against the derivation of the urban community from a rural or village community. In the typical case he sees neither an "old-free" (*altfreie*) community which slowly becomes urban, nor yet a servile or semi-servile group which gradually struggles into liberty and civic life, but a new community which from the first has been a community of *mercatores* and from the first has enjoyed a kind of land tenure such as was not to be found in the rustic world. He admits, indeed (or rather this is a main point in his theory), that the seat of this new community is very commonly to be found in close contiguity with the seat of some older and unfree community. The *mercatores* make their settlement close to the walls of some castle or some abbey, so that hard by the tract that they occupy there will be the homesteads and cottages of the count's or the abbot's villeins and serfs, who are living under a *droit domanial* or *Hofrecht*. At a later time, if this new "mercatorial" community is successful, it will extend its local limits; it will engulf and absorb the *vieux bourg*, and may take up into itself several different villages which have had different lords. Even then, however, old boundaries will often be visible if we make a map that shows the *condition juridique* of the soil. But if we look at what thus becomes the core of the great town, the centre from which this power of absorption radiates, then we have before us an area of which we may say that its first inhabitants were *mercatores*. At Gand, for example, this core is the *Portus Gandensis*, which is surrounded by the Lys and the Scheldt, and is thus divided from the *vieux bourg* where the counts of Flanders had a castle, and from the lands which were tilled by the villeins of the great abbey of St Peter. Now the first inhabitants of this *Portus Gandensis* were *mercatores*, and from the first the tenure by which they held their houses of the count of Flanders was markedly distinct from rural tenure.

That M. des Marez has fully proved his case even for Gand I cannot think. Beyond the mere word *portus* and an excellent commercial situation he seems to have very little evidence that the inhabitants of the port were mainly merchants until the year 1200 has been reached, and yet the supposed settlement seems to take place in the first half of the tenth century. An additional reason for hesitation I find in the instructive chapter which deals with the urban *allmende*. When the town of Gand has attained personality (*lorsque la ville devient une personne juridique*) it appears as the owner of a large piece of land, *un immense terrain*, situate within the limits of the *portus*, and M. des Marez (rightly, so I should suppose) sees in this the *allmende*, or the *upstal*, as they said in Flanders, of the community which inhabited the *portus*. But, we may ask, is a great tract of common land part of the natural equipment of a community which has always been mercatorial? And then one piece of this tract has been called the *cultura*.

Suppose, however, that a story of this sort, a story of immigrant merchants, can be proved for this, that, and the other town; dare we make it typical? In the later middle ages the towns were very imitative; it is clear at times that English townfolk have been

thinking of foreign models; also new towns are
deliberately manufactured by farsighted lords. We
can believe that something of the same kind went
on in remoter times, when once an example had been
set. But the theory that is now before us impels us
to ask whence these immigrant merchants come, for
we cannot go on indefinitely tracing them back from
town to town. Without denying the existence of
homeless traders who travelled in caravans, we may
gravely doubt whether such persons were strong
enough in numbers and wealth to obtain land from
bishops and counts on peculiarly favourable terms and
to found sedentary local communities of a new kind
and an abnormally free kind.

And M. des Marez will have from the first a
strong contrast between urban tenure and rural tenure.
He argues, indeed, that the *alleu urbain*, which is
found in the later middle ages (the *Vrij Huus Vrij
Erve* of Gand, for example), has no connexion with
the *alleu* of "the Frankish period." He is not
going to have in his town any of Arnold's aboriginal
Germanic freedom. The old *alleu* of the barbarian
time disappears, or rather survives only in circles with
which we have no concern. The new *alleu urbain* or
franc bien of the towns is a *censive* whose *cens* has been
remitted or redeemed. The characteristic phenomenon
is not allodiality, but a heritable tenure which, while
it yields rent (*cens*), is free (as we should say) from
every other "incident" or "casualty," free from
reliefs, heriots, and everything of the kind; it is a
pure "cash-nexus," to borrow a phrase from Carlyle,
between grantor and grantee. This *tenure urbaine*

libre differs radically from the *tenure du droit domanial*, which is what you find in the open country.

Is it not possible that M. des Marez has been painting his rural background a little too dark? Outside the towns all is given over to the sway of *le droit domanial*, by which phrase he renders the German *Hofrecht*. What minimum of service or unfreedom this *droit domanial* implies he does not exactly tell us; he is not writing of the open country; but apparently we might render his doctrine into English by saying that outside the sphere of burgage there is nothing but villeinage. In England that statement would not be true, nor even approximately true, for the socage of the thirteenth century and the sokemen of the eleventh are not negligible quantities. Ultimately in England our *tenure urbaine libre*, our *Leihe zu Stadtrecht*, our burgage tenure, appears as a mere subordinate variety of that *liberum socagium* which is found in the open country, and to define the specific mark of this variety is by no means easy. Now it is probably true that in Flanders and some other parts of the mainland the towns exercised such a dominating influence over the general stream of legal and institutional history as could not be claimed for our English boroughs; but when he descends to detail M. des Marez seems to confess that between the *tenure urbaine libre* and the rural tenures there are mediating shades. For example, he admits that urban law does not absolutely exclude *droits de mutation*—that is to say, dues to be paid to the landlord when there is a change in the tenancy. Such dues are to be found, though only sporadically, even in the *portus Gandensis*.

Then, again, it is allowed that the immigrant merchants could not in all cases obtain such good terms as were to be had in the island between the Scheldt and the Lys. A strong contrast is drawn between Gand and Arras: between the behaviour of a great lay lord, such as the count of Flanders, and that of a conservative abbot. The *mercatores* who come to Arras, and establish the *novum burgum* there, are settling on the land of St Vaast, and, though they do not become part of the servile *familia Sancti Vedasti*, still they have to submit to the abbot's *droit domanial*, so that the establishment of the free urban tenure comes by degrees and after many struggles. Here, then, we see a gradual development. *C'est dans cette terre de saint Vaast, enchaînée dans les liens du droit domanial, que nous verrons évolver la personne et le sol vers la liberté.* But if a slow transitory process of this kind is possible, must we needs call in those colonising merchants to set it agoing? And, on the other hand, if at a very early time the count of Flanders was getting nothing from the people in the *portus Gandensis* (of which he was *seigneur justicier*) except a light rent (*cens*), which *n'était en quelque sorte qu'une prestation récognitive de cette seigneurie*, can we be sure that the soil has ever been his to do what he pleased with, and that he has not acquired a justiciary seigniory over an old group of landowners? Still it is an interesting theory, this theory of mercantile colonies, and I must stop far short of saying that it does not hold good in some of the towns of Flanders and other lands.

AN UNPUBLISHED "REVOCATIO" OF HENRY II[1]

UNDER the above heading, in a recent number of this Review[2], Mr Herbert brought to light a document that he had unearthed from "a late fifteenth-century copy[3]." Grateful to him for his discovery, I none the less think that some one should enter a modest *caveat* against this document, more especially because all that concerns the murder of Becket still interests many people who have little time or taste for critical study. Now, if genuine, this instrument is of first-rate importance, for in clear words it tells us how Henry II in the hour of his penance formally and solemnly abandoned that profitable guardianship of vacant churches which was exercised by him, his predecessors, and successors, and whereout they sucked no small advantage. Here upon the threshold is a reason for circumspection. When compared with all the concessions that Henry unquestionably made at Avranches, a renunciation of *la régale*, as Frenchmen conveniently call it, would have been so supremely important that surely we should long ago have heard

---

[1] *English Historical Review*, Oct., 1899.
[2] *Ib.*, XIII. 507.   [3] Brit. Mus. Add. 34807.

of this splendid triumph won for the churches by the martyred archbishop.   And then, when this grand surrender was disregarded, and the king went back to the bad old way, surely a shameless breach, not merely of plighted faith, but of a written and producible charter, would have raised a storm of execration audible through all the ages.

Circumspecte agamus.   Let us look at the form of this instrument, for its form is very curious.   In reproducing its initial lines I will, within brackets, suggest two small changes (an ablative for a dative) which, so I think, will greatly improve the style, but fatally damage the substance.

In Dei nomine Amen etc.   Anno domini millesimo c. lxxiiij. Coram venerabilibus in Christo patribus et dominis Alberto divina dignacione tituli Sancti Laurencii in Lucina et Theodino tituli Sancti Vitalis presbiteris Cardinalibus et apostolice sedis legatis. Priori [*but read* legatis, Priore] et conuentui [*but read* conuentu] Ecclesie Cantuarie ac aliis quamplurimis regni Anglie personis in ecclesia conuentuali Sancte Trinitatis Cantuarie predicte congregatis. Nos Henricus Dei gracia Rex Anglie, Dux Normannie etc....in hiis scriptis publice et palam reuocamus...concedimus...volumus...pro-mittimus...Acta sunt hec anno supradicto.

Now Mr Herbert and his immediate warrantor, who lived in the fifteenth century, see here a letter addressed by Henry II to the prior of Canterbury and some other people.   Mr Herbert adds that " obviously the date should be 1172," not 1174, and suggests that the letter was written at Avranches, where Henry met the cardinals.   But, I would ask, have we often seen a mediaeval letter which took the following form ?

In the Name of God Amen. On such a day. In the presence of so and so. To so and so. We Henry...revoke...grant...promise. These things were done on such a day.

There is no *Salutem*, no *Noverit*, no *Sciatis*, no *Valete*, no *Data*, no reference to seal or signature. The names of the witnesses, if any, stand at the beginning. And who are the addressees? "The prior and convent of the church of Canterbury and very many other persons of the realm of England congregated in the aforesaid church of the Holy Trinity at Canterbury." Have we often seen the like of that address? And, on the other hand, do not the initial and final words of this instrument, the initial *In Dei nomine Amen* and the final *Acta sunt hec etc.*, seem to be those of no letter but of an "act," the record of an ecclesiastical court?

In truth a few strokes of the pen—nearly as few as will turn 1174 into 1172—will convert this highly irregular letter into a respectably regular "act." Thus :—

In the Name of God Amen. On such a day, etc., in the presence of the Legates, the Prior and Convent of Canterbury, and divers other persons of the realm of England congregated in the church of Canterbury, We, Henry...revoke...grant...promise... These things were done on such a day.

All now runs smoothly enough. We no longer find the addressees of a letter wedged in between the *coram cardinalibus* and the *nos Henricus*. The *quamplurimis personis*, being now in the ablative and safely governed by *coram*, will give no trouble. In such a context it is, I believe, usual and correct to mention the crowd of unnamed bystanders.

Yes, it may be objected, the document may run smoothly enough, but it will tell a plain untruth, for it will tell how the cardinals held a court in Canterbury Cathedral, before which court Henry accepted penance, revoked his innovations, and solemnly surrendered *la régale.*

To this my reply must be that this document seems to me to be trying its hardest to tell just that plain untruth. Not, perhaps, with guilty intent, for it may be the outcome of some innocent exercise in the art of composing *acta,* and a forger who thought that he could, with impunity, put a pair of papal legates just wherever he pleased would have had much to learn in his nefarious business.

As to the date, it confirms my suspicion. In 1174, as anybody might easily learn, Henry was at Canterbury, and a penitential scene was enacted in the cathedral. It was a memorable scene, even though the cardinals were not presiding and the guardianship of widowed churches was not renounced.

CANON MacCOLL'S NEW CONVOCATION[1]

WITH "the crisis in the Church" and "the Lambeth decision" this paper will have nothing to do. In the one I take no interest; the other I have not read. But I have been constrained of late to make some acquaintance with the first years of Elizabeth's reign, and whatever is written about that time by Mr Malcolm MacColl seems to me a serious matter; at all events, when it consists of the suggestion of hitherto unknown or disregarded facts. Mr MacColl has the public ear, and what he says, even by way of hypothesis, will soon be believed by the many, and will pass into the manuals. Therefore, I will venture to make public an appeal to him for the reconsideration of a doctrine that he has promulgated[2], touching the events of the year 1559, and more particularly touching a newly discovered convocation of the clergy.

He will agree with me that the Roman Church has not permanently profited by the consecration that was perpetrated at the sign of the Nag's Head. He will agree with me that the Anglican Church will not permanently profit by a convocation that is holden at

---

[1] *Fortnightly Review*, Dec., 1899.　　[2] *Ib.*, Oct., 1899.

the sign of the Cock and Bull.   He will agree with me
that the year 1559 is so fruitful of documents of all
sorts and kinds, that it is scarcely a time at which
guess-work should assemble bishops and clergy in
synods, of which no direct evidence has descended to
us.   We think of Parker's collections and Cecil's
memoranda, of the Zurich letters, of Feria, Quadra, and
Noailles, of the Roman attacks and Anglican apologies.
We think how easy it would be to prove, for example,
that in 1559 a colloquy between champions of two
creeds took place in Westminster Abbey during the
Easter recess of Parliament.   We think of these things,
and we say that at such a time important events are
hardly to be multiplied except at the call of contemporary testimony.   Let us leave room for the stroke of
genius.   Every now and again some master of the
historic art may be able to demonstrate that a parliament or a synod must have been assembled, although
he can show us no text that describes its doings, or
none that is not too late, anonymous and of unknown
origin.   Such exploits are for those who by years of
toil have taught themselves to fly.   Most of us have to
walk on foot.

Now Sir William Harcourt, so I understand, said
that "the Crown and Parliament enacted the Prayer
Book in the teeth of the bishops and clergy."   I am
not concerned to defend the phrase, and it is not that
which I should have chosen ; but if we are speaking of
what happened in the first year of Elizabeth's reign,
then we must either admit that Sir William's saying
does not fly very wide of the mark, or else we must
produce some facts that have been neglected.   We

supposed that no bishop voted in favour of the Act of Uniformity. We supposed that every bishop who was present in the House of Lords voted against it. We supposed that the lower house of convocation, at least in the southern province, uttered its mind in articles which breathe out Roman Catholicism of an uncompromising and militant sort. This being so, we had perhaps no warrant for talking of the clergy's teeth, but we seemed to have ample warrant for denying that the changes in worship that were effected in 1559 were authorised by any constitutional organ of the English Church. So far as I am aware, those historians and controversialists whose names Mr MacColl would more especially revere have been content to leave the matter thus, and to say (as well they might) that the Church accepted or received a book that it did not enact or propound.

In passing, let us notice Mr MacColl's treatment of the old evidence, for I must confess that I do not like it :—

"Of the twenty-six sees then existing, ten were vacant through death, leaving sixteen bishops as peers of Parliament. Nine of those voted against the third reading of the Act of Uniformity. One was absent through illness, and seven for no assignable reason. The Bill was thus opposed by just one more than a third of the whole bench[1]."

Now the Canon's memory seems to me as faulty as the equation $9 + 1 + 7 = 16$. One bishop, he says, was absent through illness, and seven for no assignable reason. Is not imprisonment an assignable reason? Winchester and Lincoln were in gaol because of the

---

[1] *Fortnightly Review*, Oct., 1899, p. 646.

part they played in the Colloquy with the Protestants. St Asaph had received no writ, and had mildly complained that he ought to have been summoned. There is good authority for saying that the Bill was carried by a majority of three[1]. So if Goldwell had been summoned, and White and Watson had been liberated, the Bill might have been lost, and, for anything that I know to the contrary, Mr MacColl and I might be believing in transubstantiation at this day. Then Peterborough had given a proxy to York, London, and Lichfield; Durham to York; Bath to York, London, and Exeter; St David's to York, London, and Peterborough. If these proxies were used, assuredly they were used on the Conservative side. Indeed the solidarity of the English episcopate at this critical moment seems to me as wonderful as it is honourable. That is not the point. What is to the point is, that Mr MacColl's statement of the case can only be saved from a charge of unscrupulous partizanship by a confession that highly important facts were forgotten.

Then I see an argument that bewilders me. Some of the Marian bishops were, we are told, intruders :—

"Now the first step which Elizabeth took in ecclesiastical legislation was to repeal the repealing Acts of Mary, thus reviving the state of things which existed when Mary came to the throne. The effect of this astute policy was to disqualify the Marian bishops to vote either in Parliament or Convocation, and they were thus disqualified when the Act of Uniformity came before them, and had, in fact, subjected themselves to heavy penalties by voting at all....More than

---

[1] 10th May, 1559: Feria to Philip: Kervyn de Lettenhove, *Relations Politiques*, I. 519.

half were disqualified by canonical and statutory law....[And so] their votes [against that Act] were—quite legally and canonically—regarded as null and void."

The author of these sentences must forgive a pedagogue for saying that, had they been written in the hurry of an examination, they would have been regarded as signs of ingenuity—but of indolence also. Coming, as I hope they come, from a comfortable study, I can only wonder at them. As to the disqualification of Marian "intruders," I will say nothing now, though Mr MacColl calls Erastianism what I should have called the highest of high Catholicism. But to his argument, the short answer is, that Elizabeth did not "repeal the repealing Acts of Mary" until after the Act of Uniformity had passed the House of Lords. That House had not done with the Act of Supremacy when it finished its work on the Act of Uniformity. The two Bills received the Royal assent on the same day. But further, the Act of Supremacy expressly said that the Marian Acts were to be repealed "from the last day of this session of Parliament," thus carefully excluding the doctrine of retrospective operation. Furthermore, there was a creditable clause declaring that no one was to suffer under the revived statutes of Henry and Edward for anything done before the end of thirty days next after the end of the session. Why, even the Court of Rome was given sixty days wherein to dispose of some pending appeals! That marvellous clause I have long regarded as the most splendid instance of our English reverence for possession. It is colossal.

Where then is the astuteness? Well, perhaps there

was astuteness; but it was that of the statesman, not that of the pettifogger.   There were hot-headed protestants advising Elizabeth to act much as Mr MacColl thinks that she acted, and to ignore the changes made in Mary's day.   Wisely she at once called a Parliament.   Wisely she sent writs to the Marian bishops. Wisely she treated the Roman Catholic religion as a religion by law established.   Wisely (to mention the small but crowning instance), she allowed Richard Chetwood and Ann his wife to pursue their appeal to the Bishop of Rome.   Wisely she cast her burden on Parliament; and she had her reward.   I do not mean that there was no astuteness of a lower kind.   Bishop Goldwell, it might be said, deserved no writ, as he was in a state of transition between St Asaph and Oxford. Two more voters and two orators were excluded when Watson and White luckily misconducted themselves, and were laid by the heels.   But of any attempt to treat as nullities the votes given by the Marian intruders, there is no sign whatever.

Yes, says Mr MacColl, there is; and now, having shown us his surety of foot, he prepares us for his flight through the void.   In letters patent, dated in 1560, Elizabeth spoke of the Act of Uniformity as one of the statutes that were passed in her first year "by the consent of the three estates of our realm."   Therefore, it is urged, the votes of the Marians must have been ignored, and we must look about us for some other clergymen who will serve as warrantors for the Queen's words about the three estates.

Will the Canon suffer me to strengthen his argument, or does he dread the gifts of the infidels?   The

Act of Supremacy begins with a prayer to the Queen that she will suppress the "foreign usurped power," deliver the nation from "bondage," and repeal the Marian statutes. Who, let us ask, put up this prayer? We shall here find no brief talk of "three estates," but a far more explicit statement; for the petitioners are "the Lords Spiritual and Temporal, and the Commons in this your present Parliament assembled." But this is not all. Canon MacColl can easily find a highly official statement made in the year 1559, to the effect that the two famous and thirty-eight other Acts were passed with the assent of all (yes, all) the Lords Spiritual and Temporal[1]. Clearly, therefore, not only were the votes of the Marian bishops and the Papistical noblemen ignored, but at least two other spiritual lords (shall we say Barlow and Scory?) must have been present in Parliament.

Or else (for there is an alternative) it was already law that two estates of the realm vote as one House, and that the will of the majority of that House is the will of all the Lords Spiritual and Temporal in Parliament assembled. Since then many and many an Act bears on its face the consent of the Lords Spiritual, and yet no bishop voted for it. Are not their votes and defaults registered in a Black Book kept by the Radicals? But, says Mr MacColl, "the spiritual peers constitute the first of the three estates of the Realm, and whatever lawyers may think now, it is unquestionable that, in the time of Elizabeth and previously, an Act of Parliament would have been considered of doubtful authority, if not altogether invalid, [if it were]

---

[1] Heading of the Acts of 1559.

passed in a Parliament where the spiritual state was ignored[1]." To this let us answer, first, that the bishops are not "ignored" whenever a Bill is carried against their votes; secondly, that the judges of Henry VIII's day, holding (rightly or wrongly) that the bishops derived their seats in Parliament from their baronies, declared that a Parliament would be a good Parliament though no bishops had been summoned to it[2]; and, thirdly, that Sir Thomas Smith and Sir Edward Coke knew something about the English law of Elizabeth's day, and clearly teach us that "the Upper House" gives or withholds its assent as one and only one of the three legislating units : to wit, King, Lords, and Commons. Coke treasured, as precedents, two statutes of Richard II's reign. The two archbishops, for the whole clergy of their provinces, made their solemn protestations in open Parliament, that they in no wise meant or would assent to any statute or law in restraint of the Pope's authority; "and yet," says Coke, "both Bills passed by the King, Lords, and Commons." "Whatever lawyers may think now," that is what my Lord Coke thought[3].

I am always unwilling to read lectures on Elizabethan law to Sir Edward Coke, but still he wrote after the great precedent of 1559 had settled the question for ever; and just at this point I am inclined to make a concession to Canon MacColl. In 1559 our rule, that the bishops may all be in the minority and the Act never the worse, was certainly in the making, but I doubt it was already past discussion. The

[1] *Reformation Settlement*, p. 349.
[2] Keilwey's *Reports*, 184 *b*.   [3] *Second Institute*, 587.

Spanish Ambassador, on the 18th of june, says that
"the doctors" (he means the lawyers) are doubting
whether the bishops can be deprived, since the 'Act of
Supremacy was passed in contradiction to the whole
ecclesiastical estate[1]. He adds that the oath has not
been tendered to the judges ; and, I fear, that some of
those judges (Browne and Rastell) were little better
than papists. It is generally known, and Mr Pike has
noted[2], that, just at the critical time, a mysterious
silence falls upon the official journal of the House of
Lords. I do not wish to be uncharitable to Cecil and
Bacon, but cannot help remarking that had Bonner, or
any of his fellows, wished to give proof that the Act
of Supremacy was carried against the voices of the
bishops, there would have been no official document
ready to hand. And Bonner, with the expert Plowden
to guide him, did wish to prove that the Act was
invalid. Mr MacColl speaks as though no contradiction
was offered to Elizabeth's statement about the consent
of the three estates. Bonner flatly contradicted it.
When indicted, he threatened to argue before a jury
that the Act of Supremacy had never received the
assent of the Lords Spiritual and Temporal, and of the
Commons[3]. He was never put upon his trial, but was
left untried in gaol. I have seen the original record on
the rolls of the Queen's Bench. Now, I do not say,
and do not think, that he had a good case, and he
would have had the utmost difficulty in giving a legally

---

[1] Kervyn de Lettenhove, *Relations Politiques*, I. 540.

[2] In the important Preface to his *Constitutional History of the House of Lords.*

[3] Strype, *Annals*, vol. I. pt. 2, p. 4.

acceptable proof of the dissent of the bishops. My humble guess would be that an impartial court (had impartiality been possible) would have decided in favour of our modern doctrine of two estates in one House; and the most that we can say against those who spoke of the Acts of Uniformity and Supremacy as bearing the consent of the Lords Spiritual is, that they gave expression to a constitutional theory which might possibly have been overruled in a court manned by zealous Catholics. Therefore, on this occasion, I do not hear Elizabeth telling a lie. At the very worst, she begs a question—a question that must be begged, if her Anglican settlement is to be maintained.

Mr MacColl noticing the official statement about the three estates, and not noticing the official statements about the Lords Spiritual in Parliament assembled, proceeds to say that "something evidently took place which has escaped the scrutiny of our historians," and he then argues that this something was a second Convocation. But where, we must ask, did he learn that the clergy in Convocation is one of the three estates of the realm? Where did he learn that every Act to which those three estates have assented was laid before a Convocation? Where, above all, did he learn that the assent of Convocation is the assent of the Lords Spiritual in Parliament assembled? Not by a Convocation, real or fictitious, can Elizabeth's accuracy be saved, if it needs saving. Not by a Convocation, real or fictitious, can we dispel the doubts reported by Bishop Quadra. And, by the way, I should like to ask some Spanish scholar whether Sir William Harcourt's "in the teeth of the bishops and clergy" is a very bad translation of this Catholic prelate's "en contradicion de todo el estado ,eclesiastico."

Having persuaded himself that "something evidently took place which has escaped the scrutiny of our historians," Mr MacColl finds the requisite something in a document "discovered" by Mr Wayland Joyce in the State Paper Office[1], and of that document he prints a portion. I will print the whole. It so happens that when I first saw it at the Record Office I did not know that any part of it had been published, nor had I read Mr MacColl's book or article. For a moment I enjoyed the little thrill that comes to us when we fancy that we have unearthed a treasure, and then I said "Rubbish!" and turned the page. Was I wrong?

The document begins thus :—

"Ther returned into England upon Queene Maryes death that had bin bishops in K. Ed. 6 tyme.

" 1. Coverdale.	3. Chenye.
" 2. Scorge.	4. Barlowe.

"Ther remained Bishops for sometyme that were Bishops in Queene Maryes tyme.

"1. Oglethorpe B. of Carleile who crowned Q. Eliz.
"2. Kichin B. of Landafe.

"Ther were Bishops in the Parlament holden primo Eliz. and in the Convocation holden at the same tyme.

"Edmonde B. of London.	Ralph B. of Covent. and Lichfeilde.
"John B. of Wintone.	Thomas B. of Lincolne.
"Richard B. of Wigorne.	James B. of Exon."

---

[1] Joyce, *The Civil Power in its Relations to the Church*, 1869, pp. 135–7.

M. III.

The above is not printed by Mr MacColl. Straight-way upon this there follows what he does print.

"The booke of Common prayer, published primo Eliz., was first resolved upon and established in the Church in the tyme of K. Ed. 6. It was re-examined with some small alterations by the Convocation consistynge of the said [*sic*][1] Bishops and the rest of the Clergy in primo Eliz., which beinge done by the Convocation and Published under the great seal of Englande, ther was an acte of parlament for the same booke which is ordinarily printed in the begininge of the booke; not that a booke was ever subiected to the censure of the parlament, but being aggreed upon and published as afforesaid, a law was made by the parlament for the inflictinge of penalty upon all such as should refuse to use and observe the same; further autority then to [*sic*] is not in the parlament, neyther hath bin in former tymes yealded to the parlament in thinges of that nature but the judgment and determination thereof hath ever bin in the Church, thereto autorised by the kinge, which is that which is yealded to H. 8 in the statute of 25 his raygne."

What shall we say of this stuff? Canon MacColl, knowing only the latter half of it, set himself to guess that a second and unpapistical Convocation was sum-moned to sanction the Prayer Book, the Marian bishops having effaced themselves by opposition. Canon MacColl laboured under the misfortune of knowing something about the votes that these Marians gave in Parliament, and something about a Convoca-tion that upheld the power of the Pope. The writer of our document was not so well informed. Indeed, his mention of "Chenye" (to choose but one blunder) shows that he was recklessly ignorant. Now we must take his story or we must leave it; we cannot pick and choose just what will suit our opinions or our party.

[1] Mr Joyce and Mr MacColl give *same* not *said*.

His Convocation of the year 1559 is held when Parliament is held. In it sit Bonner, White, Pate, Bayne, Watson, and Turberville; and this is the Convocation that approves the Prayer Book. Whether good Father Coverdale was sitting cheek by jowl with bloody Bonner; whether the Rev. Mr Barlow, who, as late as the 1st of March, was out in Germany with Melanchthon, hurried home in time to meet those Holy Confessors White and Watson ere they went to the Tower; whether Cheyney was made bishop for this occasion only; whether Thirlby was still in the Netherlands; all this is not so plain as it might be, and the history of the northern Province is wrapped in its accustomed darkness. But one thing seems perfectly clear, namely, that this writer knows nothing of two Convocations, the earlier of which was all for papal supremacy, while the later enacted the Prayer Book. In his eyes, the Convocation which gives us the Prayer Book is no such select body of divines as that which Mr MacColl has conjured up for us—an assembly which, to my mind, looks little better than a protestant caucus—but the genuine Convocation of the southern Province, in which, for want of an archbishop, Edmund Barker presides.

Is what stands before us a lie? Its audacity seems to crave a more merciful verdict, and I do not know that its writer intended it for publication. One (and probably the later) of the two copies that exist was said by an endorser to be in the hand-writing of Sir Thomas Wilson, who was Keeper of the State Papers under James I[1]. From its presence among the State Papers

[1] Public Record Office, *State Pap. Eliz. Dom.* vol. VII. Nos. 46

no inference can be drawn ; odds and ends of many sorts and kinds are there. Before we acquit its composer of fraud, we have to remember, first, that the tale of the Nag's Head was silly and impudent, and yet generally believed by Roman Catholics. Secondly, that Anglicans, who were twitted about their "parliamentary" church by Romanists, and who resented the Puritanic interference of the House of Commons, were under a temptation to disseminate some such story as this ; and thirdly, that the risk of immediate detection was not very serious, since few documents were in print. However, as at present advised, I incline to a lenient judgment. Perhaps we may see an idle romance that was meant for the fire. Perhaps an attempt to write history *a priori*, and an attempt that did not satisfy its maker. Perhaps an inchoate lie that never got beyond a first draft. These are only guesses ; but, in all seriousness, I venture to counsel Canon MacColl and other honest controversialists to beware of this paper.

The argument from smoke to fire is a favourite with some minds, and, needless to say, it is sometimes legitimate ; but the Roman Catholic champions of the present day have good cause to regret that their predecessors would only surrender bit by bit the story of the Nag's Head, instead of branding it as a good round lie. Even so, Anglicans will run a needless danger if they argue that the paper at the Record Office, though

and 47. The spelling of 47, which is attributed to Wilson, is nearer to modern usage than is that of 46. Canon MacColl talks of Sir Thomas Weston ; but, though the name is ill-written, there can be no doubt that Wilson is meant.

not exactly truthful, must enshrine some core of truth. After all—or perhaps before all—men do endeavour to write history out of their own heads. Here, for example, is Mr MacColl sending into a world in which Jesuits and Erastians live an argument which supposes that the Marian bishops sat and voted in the House of Lords after the Marian Acts had been repealed. We do not say that "there must be some truth" in this. We say that the Canon's arm-chair was comfortable, and that the statute book and the journals of parliament stood just beyond his reach. And if we know ourselves we do not scream at him; so to do would be both unkind and imprudent. We are sinners, all of us. The guess-working spirit is so willing; the verifying flesh is often weary.

It will hardly have escaped the scrutiny of Mr Mac-Coll that the "something" that "escaped the scrutiny of our historians" seems also to have escaped the memory of those who must once have known all about it, and were deeply concerned to tell what they knew. Canon MacColl and Sir William Harcourt, modern though they may be, fill the place of controversialists who long ago went to their rest. Profoundly convinced though I am of Sir William's ability and eminence, I am not sure that he is a more formidable foe than was Dr Nicholas Sanders, especially now that a crisis in the Church is far more likely to end in smoke ("good, strong, thick, stupifying incense smoke") than in the thrust of a dagger aimed at our Queen. Now Sanders' bitter pen touched the point that we have been examining. By three votes, he said, and three only, you subverted the faith of your forefathers, and the bishops,

to a man, were against you. He could not be left
unanswered. Inspired by Parker and Cecil, Bartholomew Clerke took the field. He wrote, what
seems to me, an effective pamphlet ; but Sanders' facts
were not to be denied. As to the victory by three
votes, Clerke says (and with some truth) that immediately after the end of Mary's reign, this was a
marvellously creditable result. As to the bishops (he
adds), well, perhaps they did not resist to a man[1], but
they were a seditious and abusive, yet timid, crew, and
their retreat from the Westminster Colloquy made
them contemptible. Now this will not seem to divine
or lawyer a very appropriate reply. It was, however,
the best that Parker and Cecil could contrive. Why
was not Canon MacColl there to crush the malignant
papist by proof that the votes of the Marian bishops
were "legally and canonically" null, and, by proof, that
the spiritual estate of England was its own reformer ?
But poor Clerke lived too soon. The benighted man
thought that the two parties to the Westminster
Colloquy were rightly called "Papists" and "Protestants" ; and we have changed all that. He lived
before the Oxford movement. Indeed, he lived—but
let us forget it—when a Cambridge movement was in
full flood.

The name of one bishop, and one only, has Canon
MacColl risked, as that of a possible occupant of a
chair in his astutely selected (I had almost said "jerry-
mandered") Convocation. It is the name of Tunstall.
The writer of the paper that lies in Chancery Lane did

---

[1] *Fidelis Servi Responsio*, ed. 1573, sig. L. iiii: "Resistibant itaque
fortasse (ut ais) omnes ad unum episcopi."

not risk this name, probably because he knew that a
bishop of Durham would not be at home in a synod of
the southern Province; and were I in Mr MacColl's
place I would not bring Tunstall away from his states-
manly employment on the Scottish border until after
the Act of Uniformity is secured. Nor would I make
myself a sponsor for his adhesion to the Elizabethan
form of religion. Henricianism he might have accepted.
But we have it from one who was on the spot that,
after the session was over, the moribund old man
journeyed to London in order to persuade the Queen
to abandon the heresies that had been adopted, and to
pay respect to her father's will, even if she could not
accept the Church in its entirety. And laughter, we
are told, was his reward[1]. Now Scory we may hand
over to Canon MacColl. Barlow he may have, and
Coverdale, if he can bring the one from Russia, the
other from Geneva, in time for a meeting, the date of
which is not yet fixed. *Tres faciunt collegium.* Strain-
ing a point, we might admit a suffragan, or even Bale.
Whether an Upper House of Convocation that is thus
concocted would supply the Prayer Book with any
valuable amount of synodical authority, is a question
that I gladly leave to Mr MacColl. Perhaps a wholly
new light might fall on "the ornaments rubric" if we
could be quite sure that it came from the pen of Miles
Coverdale.

As a subsidiary argument, the Canon has argued
that it is not like Elizabeth to ignore the clergy and to

---

[1] Kervyn de Lettenhove, *Relations Politiques*, I. 595: Quadra to
Philip: 13th Aug., 1559. When this letter is read with Tunstall's,
his position seems clear: but "they laughed at him."

allow laymen to settle ecclesiastical affairs. I am not prepared to discuss this matter at any length, but still may suggest that he and others should distinguish between the Queen who has obtained her Act of Uniformity and the young woman who could hardly induce a bishop to anoint her. To me it seems that the Elizabeth of those first few months was wholly unable to dictate to the lords and the beneficed clergy, and was bidding high for the support of the protestants. This is the Elizabeth who made Europe ring by leaving her chapel on Christmas day rather than witness the elevation of the host. When the legal settlement had been made, and the protestants were satisfied, then came the time for an appeal to the moderate, neutral, wavering nucleus of the nation, for hints of crypto-Catholicism, and even for flirtations with the unmarrying bishop of Rome. As to the Prayer Book and the Act of Uniformity, if Canon MacColl will look at the latter—I mean no page in a printed volume, but a sheet of parchment lying at Westminster—he will, so I think, see reason to suspect that the House of Lords amended the Bill and, in effect, erased from the litany that rude prayer for deliverance from the detestable enormities of the Pope. Be that as it may, I would respectfully submit to him that evolving history from half a document when you know that the whole is close at hand, and that you and others have a right to see it, is to expose yourself, your cause, your party, to needless jeopardy. The party to which Canon MacColl belongs has been learned.

CANON LAW IN ENGLAND[1]

A Reply to Dr MacColl.

Some opinions which were stated in a book of mine touching the nature of the law that was administered in the English ecclesiastical courts have lately been disputed by Canon MacColl[2]. As those opinions originally appeared in this *Review*, I crave leave to make in these pages a brief reply to a courteous critic.

1. One of my sentences, when detached from its context, has enabled him to represent my main thesis as being less definite than I meant it to be. " In all probability," so I wrote, "large portions (to say the least) of 'the canon law of Rome' were regarded by the courts Christian in this country as absolutely binding statute law." Had no more than this been said ·I should certainly have laid myself open to the charge of preaching a vague doctrine, and of allowing a judge " to pick and choose *ad libitum* among the decrees of a code[3]." I thought, however, that some

[1] *English Historical Review*, Jan. 1901.
[2] Maitland, *Roman Canon Law in the Church of England*, 1898; MacColl, *The Reformation Settlement*, ed. 8, 1900.
[3] MacColl, p. 760.

immediately subsequent sentences would sufficiently show what was in my mind when I used a phrase so feeble as " large portions (to say the least)."   For reasons that I gave, and think adequate, I proposed to speak of those three law-books which (whatever else we may think of them) were unquestionably issued by popes—namely, the Liber Extra, the Sext, and the Clementines.   I did not propose to discuss "the exact measure of authority that was attributed to the Decretum Gratiani" or the number of those post-Clementine extravagants that made their way into England[1]. Neither of these matters seemed to be of first-rate importance.   On the other hand I hoped to have made it clear that within the three codes there was, in my view, to be no picking and choosing whatsoever, except such as might be involved in the harmonisation of texts that were apparently discrepant or in the rejection of a passage in an older code if a newer code had expressly or impliedly repealed it.   An opinion may be definite although it is diffidently held and deferentially stated.

2.   Then I wrote the two following sentences :—

But if we turn [from the " Decretum "] to the three collections of decretals that were issued by Gregory IX, Boniface VIII, and John XXII, there can surely be no doubt as to the character that they were meant to bear by those who issued them, or as to the character that they bore in the eyes of those who commented upon them.   Each of them was a statute book deriving its force from the pope who published it, and who, being pope, was competent to ordain binding statutes for the catholic church and every part thereof, at all events within those spacious limits that were set even to papal power by the *ius divinum et naturale*[2].

---

[1] Maitland, pp. 3, 9.   [2] Maitland, p. 3.

Perhaps a colon and break should have stood where a full stop stands. I believed that I was attributing a certain doctrine to three popes and to the principal commentators on their decretals, and I was about to argue that the same doctrine prevailed during the later middle ages in the courts of the English church. Canon MacColl, however, having transcribed only the second of these two sentences, makes the following remark :—

> Professor Maitland seems here to exclude the Orthodox Church from "the Catholic Church," for in none of the Oriental Churches was the supremacy of the Pope ever allowed. But his statement does not apply in its integrity even to Catholic countries on the Continent, like France and Austria[1].

I thought and think it evident that my words about the pope's power were an attempt to express an opinion held not by me (it is not like my opinions), but by certain persons, who lived long ago and who knew nothing of modern France or modern Austria. Certainly, however, I did not intend to exclude the Greeks or any other baptised persons either from the catholic church or from the scope of my sentence. My statement might have been bolder than it was. The papal claim to obedience, when at its widest, comprised the whole human race. It comprised Jews, Saracens, and other infidels, and in practice the popes took upon themselves to make laws for Jews, though only among the members of the church could the decrees of these spiritual legislators be directly enforced by what were supposed to be "spiritual" pains and penalties[2]. As

[1] MacColl, p. 755.

[2] See the title *De Iudaeis, Sarracenis et eorum servis*, X. 5, 6,

to the eastern Christians, let it be admitted that "in none of the oriental churches was the supremacy of the pope ever allowed." Considering what happened at Lyons and at Florence, this seems to me somewhat too large a statement; but, albeit I will concede its substantial truth, I cannot perceive its relevance. Dr MacColl does not, I should suppose, suggest that in the eyes of the popes and the leading canonists of the Latin world during the later middle ages (might we not even say from the year 1054 onwards?) the *de facto* independence of the Greek church was anything else than sinful and unlawful schism. Am I called upon to say what Gregory IX[1] or what Raymond of Pennaforte[2] thought about this matter? "According to the emergencies of the church and state" (I quote from Gibbon) "a friendly correspondence was sometimes renewed; the language of charity and concord was sometimes affected; but the Greeks have never recanted their errors; the popes have never repealed their sentence[3]." True it is that there could be no serious project of bringing all the Greeks to trial as notorious criminals. A temporal ruler may be nego-

and Langton's Constitutions, in the appendix to Lyndwood's *Provinciale* (ed. 1679), p. 6. As the ecclesiastical legislator had no direct hold upon the Jew, he was compelled at this point to look for aid to the temporal prince, but seems to have regarded such aid as a matter of right.

[1] See the two letters in Matthew Paris, *Chron. Maiora*, III. 460, 466.

[2] Lea, *History of the Inquisition*, III. 616: "The Greeks were not only schismatics but heretics, for, as St Raymond of Pennaforte proved, schism was heresy."

[3] *Decline and Fall*, ch. lx., speaking of the year 1054.

tiating with insurgents in a remote part of the lands
that he thinks to be his while he is hanging rebels
at home. So the Roman church. Mr Lea has told
us that

the inquisitors of the West were accustomed to lay hold of any
unlucky Greek who might be found in the Mediterranean ports of
France. Their fate (he adds) was doubtless the same in Aragon, for
Eymerich does not hesitate to qualify them as heretics....In 1407
Gregory XII defined that any Greek who reverted to schism after
participating in orthodox sacraments was a relapsed, and he ordered
the inquisitor Elias Petit to punish him as such, calling in, if necessary,
the aid of the secular arm[1].

What was the lawful fate of the "relapsed" we know.

Now if Canon MacColl had shown that in the
thirteenth century or the two next following centuries
the opinion of the English church, or even the opinions
of prominent English divines or prelates, about the
canonical position of the Greeks differed in principle
from that which I am not unwarrantably ascribing to
the issuers of and commentators upon the decretals,
then, so I think, he would have made a good point
against my book, and, what is more important, a
valuable contribution to the discussion of the subject
that lies before us. And far be it from me to say in
my unfeigned ignorance that this point and contribution
will not be made. Meanwhile I observe that Matthew
Paris (to whom I turn because he hated, and, as I
think, righteously hated, many of the doings of his
contemporary popes, and because he thought that the
Greeks were being repelled by the vices of the court
of Rome) could not find short of Lucifer's a rebellious

[1] Lea, III. 620.

pride comparable to that of the schismatics of Constantinople who would make the Greek not a daughter but a sister of the Roman church[1].

3. I gladly pass to a definite issue that has been tendered to me by my critic. Of the case of Nicholas Hereford he writes thus[2]:—

The soundness of a conclusion, like that of a chain, may sometimes be tested by the soundness of a single link. Let us apply this test to the alleged unquestioned acknowledgment of the Pope's unlimited supremacy in the ecclesiastical courts in England. One of Professor Maitland's panegyrists—himself, too[3], claiming to be an

---

[1] Mat. Par. *Chron. Mai.* III. 446–7, ann. 1237 : "Visa igitur tanta malitia et oppressione, erigitur Graeca ecclesia contra Romanam, imperatorem suum expellendo, et soli archiepiscopo suo Constantinopolitano, nomine Germano, obediendo. Qui procaciter Graecorum errores, non tantum veteres, immo novos et adinventos defendens, enormiter a religione catholica delirat. Eorum enim haec est desipientia : asserunt Spiritum Sanctum...Praeterea conficiunt de fermentato...Constituit igitur sedem suam, quasi alter Lucifer, in Aquilone, scilicet in Constantinopoli, Graecorum civitate metropolitana, filius scilicet degener et Antipapa, vocans ecclesiam suam et asserens digniorem, et ecclesiam Romanam sororem eius dicens esse, non matrem." See also *ibid.* VI. 336 : an error of the abbot Joachim. Also the account of the council of Lyons given by Wykes (*Ann. Monast.* IV. 258) : "Graeci...spreta superstitione schismatica qua usque hactenus utebantur...." Walsingham, II. 230, ann. 1399 : the pope orders a collection to be made in England for the defence of Constantinople, "attendens quod licet imperator esset schismaticus, Christianus tamen esset." That Manuel in England and elsewhere was suffered to hear mass according to the Greek rite is, I fear, but poor testimony to the prevalence of tolerant opinions. Compare the privileges that Roman catholic ambassadors enjoyed in later times.

[2] MacColl, p. 755.

[3] I feel fairly sure, from what Mr MacColl is good enough to say

expert on this subject—has cited what he considers a decisive proof of the accuracy of Professor Maitland's views as against Dr Stubbs's. It happens, however, that this test case proves the exact opposite of what the panegyrist intended. It is the case of Nicholas Hereford, who was condemned for heresy by the Archbishop of Canterbury (A.D. 1382). He appealed to Rome, and managed to escape to the Holy City and lodge his appeal in person. The Pope received the appeal; which proves nothing. Every appeal was ostensibly a proof of his universal jurisdiction. So he heard Hereford's appeal and confirmed the English Primate's sentence. But the question is not whether the Pope received Hereford's appeal and reheard his case, but whether the Archbishop of Canterbury admitted Hereford's right of appeal. Any tyro knows that when a right of appeal is recognised the appeal suspends *ad interim* the execution of the judgment of the inferior court[1]. Did it do so in Hereford's case? On the contrary the Archbishop denounced the appeal as "frivolous and pretended" (*frivola et pretensa*), and manifestly illegal in addition (*necnon errorem iuris in se manifestum continentem*). The Pope was too acute to reverse Archbishop Courtney's sentence, and thereby

---

elsewhere, that this "too" does not imply that I claimed to be an expert. My "panegyrist" is, I believe, Mr Round. His opinions are always weighty with me whether they agree with mine or no. But it will be understood that I am not presuming to undertake his defence against Dr MacColl.

[1] It is more than possible that what is known to tyros is unknown to me, but I fancy that at this point the tyro should have a list of exceptions ready. See, for instance, Gul. Durandi, *Speculum Iuris*, 2, 3, de appell. § 11 [ed. Basil. 1574, p. 865]: "De effectu appellationis est videndum. Et quidem effectus is est, ut ea pendente nil innovetur sed omnia in eo statu permaneant in quo erant tempore appellationis emissae....Excipiuntur tamen quidam casus in quibus aliquid innovatur...Primus...Secundus...Tertius...Quartus...Quintus est: nam si excommunicatus appellat a sententia excommunicationis, post appellationem potest denunciari excommunicatus: Extra, de appell. *pastoralis. de hoc.* [c. 53, X. 2, 28]...Sextus...Decimus-sextus...."

invite a rebuff. But the Archbishop of Canterbury not only denounced Hereford's appeal as "frivolous," "pretensed" (to use the old word), and illegal; he proceeded forthwith to execute his own sentence, and excommunicated Hereford for his pains at St Paul's Cathedral on the first day on which "a very large congregation" could be present to witness it. And this striking repudiation of the pope's authority in English ecclesiastical courts is made all the more emphatic by the fact that Archbishop Courtney was in other matters what might be called an Ultramontane....This case alone, it seems to me, suffices to overthrow Professor Maitland's thesis.

If Dr MacColl had said not "overthrow," but "illustrate," I could have agreed with him, for to me it seems that Courtenay did precisely what an archbishop who "was in other matters what might be called an ultramontane" was not merely entitled but bound to do by the canon law of Rome.

First let us set straight the facts[1]. Hereford was not "condemned for heresy." He was sentenced and excommunicated for an utterly different offence—namely, for contumacy, or, in other words, for failing to appear in court. For popular purposes it might be sufficiently true to speak of him as a condemned heretic. The case was going against him: no choice was left to him save that between condemnation for heresy and an acceptance of (among other things) the three decretals which the archbishop had been employing as a standard of eucharistic doctrine[2]. Then he failed to keep his day in court, and was sentenced for his

---

[1] The materials known to me consist of the documents printed by Wilkins, *Concilia*, III. 158 ff., and the story told by Knighton, *Chron.* II. 172–4. See also *Fascic. Zizan.* pp. 319–29.

[2] Namely, *Firmiter credimus*, c. 1, X. 1, 1 ; *Quum Marthae*, c. 6, X. 3, 41 ; and *Si Dominum*, c. un. Clem. 3, 16.

contumacy, and for nothing else. Then he tendered an appeal[1].

Next we ought to set straight the law. That I cannot profess to do. The only advantage that I should at this point claim over Canon MacColl is that, having wetted the soles of my feet on the shore of the mediaeval *oceanus iuris*, I know a little of the profundity and immensity of a flood that exceeds my depth and my gaze. Also I may remark that, so far as I am aware, Hereford's "appeal" (a written document) has not come down to us, and that he may have had more to say for himself—for example, about the fact of contumacy—than we are apt to suppose. But I am well content to accept the archbishop's statement of the case, and to submit to the judgment of those whose judgment is worth having that Archbishop Courtenay (the *iudex a quo*) did what was required of him by the canon law of Rome if he declined to "defer to" but "refuted" as vain, frivolous, and manifestly contrary to law an appeal tendered by a *contumax* from the sentence passed upon him for his contumacy. It may be sufficient for the present if at this point I vouch as my warrantors the Code[1], the

---

[1] *Concilia*, III. 165: "Nos W....archiepiscopus...primas...legatus ...inquisitor...magistros N. H. et P. R. sacrae paginae professores, habentes hos diem et locum ex praefixione nostra ad audiendum decretum nostrum in negotio haereticae pravitatis, praeconizatos, diutius expectatos, et nullo modo comparentes, pronunciamus contumaces: et in poenam huiusmodi contumaciae ipsos et eorum ulrumque excommunicamus in hiis scriptis." This sentence is the act of excommunication. What followed some days after in St Paul's Cathedral was a "denunciation" of an excommunicate.

[2] L. I, C. 7, 65: "Eius qui per contumaciam absens, cum ad

Decretum¹, Speculator², William Lyndwood³, and Dr Paul Hinschius⁴.

If any one has said that the *iudex a quo* (or "judge of the court below") was always bound to defer to an appeal or to "stay execution," I am not he, and I think that he has made a considerable mistake. I see that the Speculator, by jumbling together matters of form and matters of substance, contrives to make above thirty exceptions to the general rule. I see that Dr Hinschius, speaking of criminal causes, mentions

agendam causam vocatus esset, condemnatus est negotio prius summatim perscrutato, appellatio recipi non potest."

¹ c. 41, § 11, C. 2, qu. 6: "Sunt etiam quorum appellationes non recipiuntur. Non enim potest recipi eius appellatio qui per contumaciam absens cum ad agendam causam negotio prius summatim perscrutato vocatus esset, condemnatus est." See also c. 6, C. 24, qu. 3.

² *Spec.* 2, 3, de appell. § 2 [ed. Basil. 1574, p. 830]: "In quibus autem casibus et ex quibus causis appellari possit, et quando appellatio teneat vel non, est videndum. Et quidem in omni causa et ex omni gravamine appellari potest nisi ubi sit prohibita appellatio...Videamus ergo ubi sit prohibita...Primo igitur prohibita est appellatio, quia contumax non auditur appellans...quod verum est in vero contumace, secus in ficto seu praesumptivo...."

³ Lyndwood, de appell. c. *frequens*, gl. ad v. *appellatum* [ed. Oxon. 1679, p. 114]: "Nam 'vere contumax non auditur appellans, et intelligo verum contumacem illum qui inventus et personaliter citatus, cessante impedimento legitimo, non comparet in termino."

⁴ Hinschius, *Kirchenrecht*, VI. 130 [sub tit. "Die Strafgewalt—Geltendes Recht—Appellation—Der Ausschluss der Appellation"]: "Die an sich statthafte Appellation wird demjenigen versagt, welcher in der früheren Instanz trotz ordnungsmässiger Ladung *contumax* gewesen ist." This is a statement of the existing law, but the authorities cited in its support (besides references to Schmalzgrueber, Hergenröther, and a decree of Clement VIII) are mediaeval.

four exceptions of great importance : these are the
case of the *contumax*, the case of one who has been
condemned on his own confession, the case of one who
has been condemned on the ground of "notoriety,"
and the case of a definitive sentence against a heretic[1].
Had a Lollard appealed from a definitive sentence
against him, he would have found that a decretal of
Boniface VIII forbad any deference to his appeal[2], and
in accordance with the canon law of Rome that appeal
might have been stigmatised as frivolous[3]. The pope,
so I understand, was regarded as being competent to
decide appeals in all causes, and, if he heard the
appeal of Nicholas Hereford[4], he did not exceed the
powers which were attributed to him[5]; but none the

[1] Hinschius, *l.c.*

[2] c. 18 in Sexto, 5, 2 : "Non obstantibus appellationibus seu
proclamationibus praedictorum nequitiae filiorum, quum...appel-
lationis et proclamationis beneficium expresse sit haereticis...inter-
dictum."

[3] When Canon MacColl (p. 757) urges that "an appeal on
a question of heresy cannot be described as frivolous" I cannot
agree with him. This was the right word to use in any case in
which the law bade the judge disregard the appeal. See Lyndwood's
gloss on the word "frivole," on p. 115 : "Vel potest dici appellatio
frivola quando nulla causa est expressa, vel non legitima, dato quod
sit vera, vel, licet sit legitima, est tamen manifeste falsa." The
"contumax" and the condemned heretic have no legitimate causes
of appeal.

[4] Knighton's account of the matter is hardly precise enough
to warrant a decision as to the exact nature of the proceedings at
Rome.

[5] Hinschius, *Kirchenrecht*, V. 467, VI. 130, 363, 381. I understand that from an acquittal and from an interlocutory sentence an
appeal was possible. Occasionally even Spanish inquisitors were
deprived of their prey by the pope. See also Lea, *History of the*

less there were important cases in which the duty
of the inferior judge was to "refute" or refuse the
appeal, and to proceed to execution. In the case of
an appeal against a definitive condemnation for obdurate
heresy he would forthwith deliver the appellant to the
secular arm, and death by fire would follow before the
pope heard anything about the matter. The procedure
against the suspects was in the highest degree stringent
and summary; the condemned was allowed no second
chance. If the pope seldom or never revised an
English sentence in a case of heresy, that, so I think,
was due to a cause of which no church should boast—
a deadly determination to root out heresy *sine strepitu
et figura iusticiae*. I see no reason for accusing the
English bishops of inhumanity; but the weapons
which they wielded when they sat as "inquisitors of
heretical pravity" were masterpieces of cruelty.

The mediaeval situation is illustrated by what
Ayliffe understood to be the law of the English church
in the eighteenth century. In a cause of heresy the
archbishop was competent to revise the sentence of
the bishop, but an appeal did not suspend the bishop's
power: he could proceed, unless an inhibition came to
him from above[1]. However, as already said, it was

Inquisition, I. 361, 451; Tanon, *Histoire des tribunaux de l'inquisition*, 1893, pp. 434–8.

[1] Ayliffe, *Parergon*, 1726, p. 77: "In a cause of heresy by the
Canon Law every judge proceeds *appellatione remota*; but if the
person condemn'd of heresy may (on a pretence of an unjust
sentence) appeal from the sentence of the bishop, who is the
ordinary in this case, unto the archbishop, such archbishop may
examine the matter and see whether the sentence of heresy be unjust
or not. Yet this appeal does not suspend the jurisdiction of the

not for heresy that Hereford was condemned by Courtenay. His, to all appearance, was a perfectly plain case falling under an elementary rule of law.

Substantially in the right as I think that the archbishop must have been in declining to defer to the appeal of the contumacious, he proceeded to put himself formally in the right by issuing the document upon which Canon MacColl has commented. That document, as I understand it, is an example of what were known as "refutatory" apostoli[1]. Apostoli of one sort or another the *iudex a quo* was bound to give. If he was deferring to the appeal in the ordinary way, he issued "dimissory" apostoli; he would issue "reverential" apostoli if he deferred merely out of reverence for the *iudex ad quem*, while "refutatory" apostoli were in place if the inferior judge was declining to defer at all[2]. Canon MacColl presses me with another case[3]: a case in which Archbishop Islip "refuted" an appeal made by his suffragan the bishop of Lincoln, and issued refutatory apostoli. Now which of these two English prelates was in the wrong I do not know, nor, so far as I am aware, have' we in

judge *a quo*, unless it be from the time that the judge *ad quem* receiv'd the appeal and sent his inhibition to the judge *a quo*."

[1] Wilkins, *Concilia*, III. 165. Observe the attestatory clause, "In cuius dationis apostolorum testimonium...."

[2] For the practice in this matter see *Spec. Iuris*, 4, 2, de appell. § 3 [ed. cit. pp. 195 ff.]. It will be remembered that apostoli, and indeed the whole scheme of appeals, had been transferred to the ecclesiastical field from the Roman imperial system, in which the "iudex a quo" would be very distinctly the inferior of the "iudex ad quem," and all judges would be the officials of the princeps.

[3] MacColl, p. 757.

printed books nearly sufficient material for deciding
that question. Certainly we must not condemn the
bishop unheard. Also we may notice that this was
one of those cases, common in the middle ages, in
which an ecclesiastical judge had a personal interest in
the validity of his own sentence, and that even impartial judges sometimes make mistakes and sometimes
become irritable when there is talk of an appeal.
However, as I read the documents, the archbishop by
his commissary had pronounced the bishop contumacious, and the bishop in his appeal declared that he
had not been contumacious, as he had never been
properly summoned. Thereupon the archbishop did
what the law required of him : he issued apostoli.
His apostoli were of the refutatory kind, and this was
the proper and, as I understand, the only proper kind
if he was still of opinion that the bishop had been
summoned and was *contumax*[1]. To stop the bishop's
appeal he was utterly powerless, unless he resorted to
lawless force. Professor Tout says that Clement VI

---

[1] For this case see the documents in Wilkins, *Concilia*, III. 3–8,
noting (p. 4) the commissary's judgment that the bishop is "contumax," and the bishop's (p. 6) declaration that he was never
summoned : "ad hoc non vocato aliqualiter vel praemunito, sed
absente non per contumaciam." The archbishop's judgment would
not prevent the bishop contesting the fact of contumacy in the court
above. Hinschius, *Kirchenrecht*, VI. 130, n. 5 : "Wohl aber kann
deswegen appellirt werden, weil das Vorhandensein der *contumacia*
zu Unrecht vom Richter angenommen worden ist." See also Lyndwood, c. *frequens*, tit. de appell. (2, 7), gl. ad v. "appellatum"
(p. 114). For more of this quarrel over the election and confirmation
of a chancellor at Oxford see Wood, *Historia et Antiquitates*, I. 172 ;
Lyte, *Hist. Univ. Oxford*, p. 169 ; Rashdall, *Universities*, II. (2),
446.

decided in Islip's favour[1], and before Canon MacColl suggests the dread of "a rebuff" as a ground for the decision he should consider whether, had the supreme pontiff's judgment been favourable to the bishop, there would have been no room for a hint that the popes were at their old policy of humbling the metropolitan in the eyes of his suffragans. Be this as it may, the appearance of refutatory apostoli will do nothing whatever towards proving the non-Roman character of the law administered by the court of Canterbury unless we see appeals refuted, and systematically refuted, in cases in which "the canon law of Rome," or, as I prefer to say, the *ius commune* of the catholic church, commanded their acceptance. As it is, I cannot think that Canon MacColl's efforts have been felicitous.

4. "In the year 1414 the University of Oxford," so Dr MacColl says[2], "presented to King Henry V certain articles for the reformation of the universal church[3]." He is right in adding that the seventh of these articles protested "against the reservation of firstfruits, *authorised by no written law*," and he may be right in giving to a remarkable phrase the prominence of italic type. But when without argument he assumes that by the term *ius scriptum* the university meant some "national law" of England he seems to me to be hasty. Why, we may ask, did these learned doctors and masters use this phrase of one of those many grievances proceeding from Rome of which they

---

[1] *Dict. Nat. Biogr.* XXIX. 76.
[2] MacColl, p. 758.
[3] Wilkins, *Concilia*, III. 360–5.

complained? Was it not because in the set of books which already had gained the name of "Corpus Iuris Canonici" there was no law reserving the firstfruits, or, in other words, no law prescribing the payment of annates[1]? It seems to me that this was the point that they desired to make, and in 1414, when the council of Constance was meeting, it was an effective point that others were making. This petition proceeded, as we may see if we read it, from reformers of a very moderate kind, and in the matter of papal "reservations" a return to the *ius scriptum* or *corpus iuris* had become the project of a moderate party which would be content with changes that were not radical[2]. No doubt, as has been remarked by historians, this use of the term *ius scriptum* implied an opinion that uncodified extravagants did not stand upon one level with the three old codes. I hope that I have said nothing implying that such an opinion was not entertained by many Englishmen in the early years of the fifteenth century, when the conciliar movement was strong and hopeful, though I believe that a short time afterwards

---

[1] Besides art. 7 the term "ius scriptum" occurs in art. 24 (relating to the excessive fees demanded by bishops) and in art. 25 (relating to the excessive retinues of archdeacons). In the last of these instances I see an allusion to c. 6, X. 3, 39, which was treated as law in one of Langton's constitutions: Lyndwood, p. 220, gl. ad v. "evectionis numerum." I admit, however, that neither of these two instances is decisive. For a contemporary use of the term by Archbishop Arundel see Lyndwood, p. 289, and the gl. ad v. "limitata in eo."

[2] Hübler, *Die Constanzer Reformation*, 1867, pp. 49 ff., 82 ff.; Schulte, *Geschichte der Quellen und Literatur des canonischen Rechts*, II. 56.

Lyndwood would have rejected the distinction. Indeed I feel in no way concerned to dispute the interpretation that Dr MacColl has put upon the text, for the whole scheme of papal "reservations" was opposed not only to the unwritten law of the English temporal courts, but to written statutes of the English parliament[1]; nevertheless I venture to think that not this but something else was in the minds of the petitioners at Oxford who desired a conciliar reformation of the universal church. The way in which they thought of ecclesiastical law may be illustrated by their expressed desire for a settlement of the controversy between the seculars and the friars as to whether "the statute of the lord Clement, cap. 'Dudum,' or the statute of the lord John, cap. 'Vas electionis,' had derogated from the ancient statute 'Omnis utriusque sexus[2].'"

5. "And how would Professor Maitland reconcile the deposing power claimed and exercised by the popes with his theory[3]?" Very easily. As the deposition of a king was not, at least obviously, a spiritual punishment, and as the substitution of one prince for another was not, at least obviously, an act of ecclesiastical jurisdiction, even those men who made the pope a monarch within the church were logically free to say that neither by laws nor by judgments

---

[1] Maitland, *Roman Canon Law*, pp. 62–73.

[2] In other words, what is the relation between c. 12, X. 5, 38 (a decree of Conc. Lat. IV.), and c. 2, Clem. 3, 7 (a decree of the Council of Vienne), and c. 2, Extrav. Comm. 5, 3 (an extravagant of John XXII)? Compare the heretical opinions of Henry Crompe, *Fascic. Zizan.* 343 ff.

[3] MacColl, p. 759.

could popes or ecclesiastical councils dispose of temporal lordships.   Those two questions should be kept apart : the question touching the delimitation of the fields of worldly and spiritual affairs, and the question touching the pope's power within the spiritual domain.   Then I am challenged to say what I think of those famous words in what Lyndwood knew and often cited as the canon " Excommunicamus[1]," those words, translated by Canon MacColl, which threaten that the pope will discharge from their oath of fealty the subjects of a prince who does not purge his land of heresy.   Surely (so my adversary seems to argue) the English church was never committed to this nonsense.   My answer can be short.   I am not persuaded that the words in question would have been regarded by the generality of Englishmen in the fourteenth and fifteenth centuries as a valid part of the law of the church.   It is even possible that some Englishmen, without risk of condemnation, would have said that this clause infringed the law of God, since the *regnum* proceeded *immediate a Deo*.   The question lay outside the domain of practicable law, and even beyond the limit of easily imaginable events.   But at the same time we ought to be very cautious at this point.   If the low-church theory (so we might call it) which co-ordinates the state with the church was known in England, the high-church theory[2] which concedes to the pope *utrumque gladium* was also known in a country which had given to the world not only William of Ockham, but

[1] c. 13, X. 5, 7.

[2] For the two theories see Gierke, *Genossenschaftsrecht,* III. 519 ff.

John of Salisbury. And heresy was still hideous. I do not feel sure of Lyndwood, who was very familiar with the useful parts of "Excommunicamus"; I do not feel sure of Arundel[1]. And, turning from the clergy to the laity, I fear that Chief Justice Sir John Fortescue, that apostle of English constitutionalism, held extravagantly papalistic opinions concerning the subservience of temporal princes, and would have allowed that if (*per impossibile*) the English king failed to deal faithfully with heretics the pope might punish him and legitimately declare that the contract of fealty was dissolved[2].

[1] Surely it were difficult to find in the middle ages a much stronger statement of the papal supremacy over the church than the following: "Christ ordained St Peter the apostle to be his vicar here in earth; whose see is the church of Rome; ordaining and granting the same power that he gave to Peter should succeed to all Peter's successors, the which we call now popes of Rome. By whose power in churches particular, special been ordained prelates, as archbishops, bishops, curates, and other degrees, to whom Christian men ought to obey after the laws of the church of Rome. This is the determination of holy church." Yet this comes in writing from Archbishop Arundel on a solemn occasion when he is trying Oldcastle (*Fascic. Zizan.* p. 442, spelling modernised). See also Lyndwood, p. 292, gl. ad v. "declarentur": "Nam omnino censetur haereticus qui non tenet id quod docet Sancta Romana Ecclesia....Dicitur etiam haereticus qui ex contemptu Romanae Ecclesiae contemnit servare ea quae Romana Ecclesia statuit."

[2] Fortescue, *Works*, ed. Clermont, p. 535: "All kings and princes are subjects to the pope in their persons as in their temporalities. He ought to punish them for their negligence and defaults. Thus have popes punished emperors and kings when they have misruled their subjects, as we read in the chronicles of old days. Christ is King of all kings, and Lord of all the world, having in the hands of the pope, his vicar, both swords, for which he is called 'Rex et

Nor must it be forgotten that the canon "Excommunicamus" was not merely a chapter in the decretals of Gregory IX. A professional canonist might perhaps say that when once it stood in that statute book its earlier history became unimportant. But we, if we wish to know whether its issue shocked mankind, must remember that it was a decree of the Lateran council of 1215. Not only were hundreds of patriarchs, primates, archbishops, bishops, and other prelates assembled, some from England, some even from the orient, but an eastern emperor, a western emperor elect, and the kings of France, England, Hungary, Aragon, Sicily, Cyprus, and Jerusalem were represented. I fear that "Excommunicamus" when it appeared did not shock the short-sighted princes of the world. Perhaps by that time nothing that the church could have done would have shocked Count Raymond or the hunted heretics.

Sacerdos,' and compelleth all princes, as well spiritual as temporal, to come to his great councils." See also Mr Plummer's remarks in his edition of Fortescue's *Governance of England*, p. 103. Fortescue seems to have held in germ that combination of opinions which, so I am told, is characteristic of some of the great Jesuits: the king derives his power from the people; the pope derives from God a power which in principle hardly falls short of omnipotence, though in temporal matters it should only be exercised upon extraordinary occasions.

ELIZABETHAN GLEANINGS[1]

I. "DEFENDER OF THE FAITH, AND SO FORTH."

FOR nearly two hundred and fifty years the solemn style and title of the king or queen of this country ended with the words "and so forth," or in Latin *et caetera*. On the first day of the nineteenth century a change was made. Queen Victoria's grandfather became king of a "United Kingdom" of Great Britain and Ireland. He ceased to be king of France. He also ceased to be "and so forth."

Had this phrase always been meaningless? I venture to suggest that it had its origin in a happy thought, a stroke of genius.

If we look at the book to which we naturally turn when we would study the styles and titles of our English kings, if we look at Sir Thomas Hardy's Introduction to the Charter Rolls, we shall observe that the first sovereign who bears an "&c." is Queen Elizabeth. Now let us for a moment place ourselves in the first days of her reign. Shall we not be eager to know what this new queen will call herself, for will not her style be a presage of her policy? No doubt she is by the Grace of God of England, France, and

[1] *English Historical Review*, 1900.

Ireland Queen. No doubt she is Defender of the Faith, though we cannot be sure what faith she will defend. But is that all? Is she or is she not Supreme Head upon earth of the Church of England and Ireland?

The full difficulty of the question which this young lady had to face so soon as she was safely queen may not be justly appreciated by our modern minds. We say, perhaps, that acts of parliament had bestowed a certain title, and had since been repealed by other acts of parliament. But to this bald statement we must make two additions. In the first place, one at least of the Henrician statutes had declared that the headship of the church was annexed to the kingship by a bond stronger and holier than any act of parliament: to wit, by the very word of God[1]. In the second place, one of the Marian statutes had rushed to the opposite limit. It had in effect declared that Henry's ecclesiastical supremacy had all along been a nullity. It had indeed excused Queen Mary's temporary assumption of a title that was not rightfully hers, and documents in which the obnoxious phrase occurred were not for that reason to be invalid; but it applauded Mary for having seen the error of her ways, and having of her own motion rejected a title which no parliament could lawfully confer[2].

It was a difficult problem. On both sides there were men with extreme opinions, who, however, agreed in holding that the solution of the question was not to be found in any earthly statute book. That question

---

[1] Stat. 37 Hen. VIII, c. 17.
[2] Stat. 1 & 2 P. et M. c. 8, secs. 42, 43.

had been answered for good and all in one sense or the other by the *ius divinum*, by the word of God. We know that Elizabeth was urged to treat the Marian statutes as void or voidable, because passed by a parliament whose being was unlawful, since it was summoned by a queen who had unlawfully abdicated her God-given headship of the church[1]. This, if in our British and Calvinian way we make too free with the Greek version of Thomas Lüber's name, we may call the opinion of the immoderate Erastians:—what God has joined together man attempts to put asunder "under pain of nullity." At the opposite pole stood a more composite body, for those who would talk of the vanity of all attempts to rob Christ's vicar of his vicariate were being reinforced by strange allies from Geneva, where Calvin had spoken ill of Henricianism. Then between these extremes there was room for many shades of doctrine, and in particular for that which would preach the omnicompetence of parliament.

Then a happy thought occurs. Let her highness etceterate herself. This will leave her hands free, and then afterwards she can explain the etceteration as occasion shall require. Suppose that sooner or later she must submit to the pope, she can still say that she has done no wrong. She can plead that, at least in some of his documents, King Philip, the catholic king, etceterates himself. There are always, so it might be said, some odds and ends that might conveniently be packed up in "and so forth." What of the Channel

[1] See the oration of John Hales in Fox, *Acts and Monuments*, ann. 1558.

Islands, for example? They are not parts of England, and they are hardly parts of France. Besides, even Paul IV would be insaner than we think him, if, when securing so grand a prize as England, he boggled over an &c. And then, on the other hand, if her grace finds it advisable, as perhaps it will be, to declare that the Marian statutes are null, she cannot be reproached with having been as bad as her sister, for we shall say that no reasonable man, considering all that has happened, can have doubted that the "&c." signified that portion of King Henry's title and King Edward's title which, for the sake of brevity, was not written in full. Lastly, suppose that the parliament which is now to be summoned is willing to go great lengths in an Erastian and protestant direction, no harm will have been done. Indeed, hereafter the queen's highness in her exercise of her ecclesiastical supremacy may find it advisable to assert that this supremacy was in being before any parliament recognised its existence, and therefore is not to be controlled even by the estates of the realm. Therefore let her be "defender of the faith, and so forth." He who knows what faith is "the" faith will be able to make a good guess touching the import of " and so forth."

And now it must be allowed that, though, so far as I am aware, Elizabeth is the first sovereign of this country who is solemnly etceterated, there may seem to be evidence to the contrary. It had been usual in certain classes of records to abbreviate the king's style. A king whose full style was Henry, by the Grace of God King of England, Lord of Ireland, Duke of Normandy and Aquitaine, and Count of Anjou, might well become upon a roll *H. d. g. Rex Angl. &c.* What I believe to be new in Elizabeth's reign is the addition of "&c." to an unabbreviated style. When she has called herself Queen of England, France, and Ireland, and Defender of the Faith, she has given herself all the titles that were borne by her father and brother, save one only, and in the place of that one she puts "&c." The change is the more remarkable because of all people who have ever reigned in England her immediate predecessors had the best excuse for an etceteration. But no: whatever King Philip's Spanish chancery may have done, King Philip and Queen Mary are not etcetered in solemn English documents. The whole wearisome story must be told: Jerusalem must not be forgotten, nor Tyrol. Even the town-clerk at Cambridge, when he is writing out the borough accounts, will write of Flanders and Milan. Then comes Elizabeth with her conveniently short title, with no duchies, archduchies, and counties to be enumerated; and yet she must be &c.

Now let us discover, if we can, the moment of time at which the etceteration began. So to do is the more important because I am not in a position to contend that this addition to the royal style is to be found in every place in which, if my theory be true, it ought to occur. In particular, any one who relied only on the officially printed volumes of statutes might infer that the change took place before the parliament of 1563, but after the parliament of 1559. On the other hand, we may see the little syllable in a writ of 21 Jan. 1559 which prorogued parliament from the 23rd to the 25th of that month. Occasionally a clerk will make a slip, an omissive slip: especially by leaving unmodified an old formula which he ought to modify. So let us look at the very first document in which Queen Elizabeth announced her royal will and pleasure. In Humfrey Dyson's collection at the British Museum lies the proclamation, "imprynted at London by Richard Jugge," which tells us how it hath pleased Almighty God to call to his mercy out of this mortal life, to our great grief, "our deerest suster of noble memory," and how the kingdoms of England, France, and Ireland, "with all maner titles and rights there-unto in any wise apperteyning," have come to Us, " Elizabeth, by the grace of God Queene of Englande Fraunce and Ireland defendour of the fayth. &c.[1]"

A little later Mary's body was borne to the grave, and there was heraldic display, of which an apparently official account is extant[2]. Heralds are bound to be careful of titles. The late queen had a lengthy title, but it must be recited at full length. Then, when the dirge has been chanted and the crowd is questioning whether many more dirges will be chanted in England, comes the demand for a loyal shout for a new queen, whose title is brief, but who is something that her sister was not: for she is &c.

Then we know that parliament had hardly as-sembled (25 Jan.) before the commons appointed (30 Jan.) a committee to consider the validity of the

---

[1] Brit. Mus., Grenville 6463. I refer to this precious volume because, as I understand, what is there to be seen is one of the very papers that came from Jugge's office.

[2] *State Papers, Domestic*, vol. I. no. 32 (MS.); see *Foreign Calendar* for 1559–60, p. cxxviii.

summons which had called them together, and of the writs by virtue whereof some of Mary's last parliaments were holden. The committee reported (3 Feb.) that the omission of the words *Supremum Caput* was no cause of nullity. I should suppose that Elizabeth's ministers had by this time decided—and surely it was a wise decision—that whatever ecclesiastical changes were to be made should be made in a straightforward manner by repeal, and should not be attempted by means of a theory which Roman Catholics and Calvinists would accuse of blasphemy and the plain man would charge with chicane. It may be, therefore, that they never had to rely on their "&c."; but some of us would gladly have been present at the deliberations of that committee.

Some years later certain English members of the Roman church were consulting some high authority—not the pope himself, but some high authority—touching the course of conduct that they ought to pursue towards a queen whom Pius V had denounced as excommunicate and deposed. Their questions and the answers that were given thereto were published by Dr Creighton in this *Review*[1]. These scrupulous persons desire to know whether Elizabeth may be called Queen of England, and, if so, whether the "&c." may be added. Question and answer run as follows :—

Cum Elizabetha in forma titulorum adiungat in fine "et caetera," quo intelligitur esse ecclesiae supremum caput, quoniam eo excepto omnes alii tituli expresse nominantur, an catholici hoc intelligentes

---

[1] *English Historical Review*, VII. 81.

possunt salva fidei professione etiam illam particulam "et caetera" adiungere?

Licet haeretici per illam vocem "et caetera" intelligant caput ecclesiae Anglicanae, non coguntur tamen catholici ita eam intelligere: ea enim vox indifferens est ad alia multa: immo vox est quae ut plurimum apponi solet in titulis aliorum regum.

If, then, we see significance in this "&c.," we are only seeing what was seen by some at least of Elizabeth's subjects, and the brain to which *illa particula* occurred seems to deserve credit for its ingenuity. Catholic and Calvinist can say that this is a *vox indifferens* common in regal styles. On the other hand the champions of a divinely instituted caesaro-papalism will observe that all Elizabeth's possible titles, except one, have been expressly named.

For all this we might fear that we were making much ado about nothing, and discovering deep policy in some clerk's flourish, were it not for a piece of evidence that remains to be mentioned. At the Record Office is preserved a paper on which Cecil has scribbled memoranda[1]. It is ascribed to 18 Nov. 1558, the second day of Elizabeth's reign. Apparently the secretary is taking his mistress's pleasure about a great variety of matters, and, as he does so, he jots down notes which will aid his memory. Ambassadors must be sent to foreign princes; a new great seal must be engraved; a preacher must be selected to fill the pulpit at Paul's Cross next Sunday. Then, among these notes—which should be photographed, for no print could represent them—we find the following:—

> A commission to make out wryttes for yᵉ parlement
> touchyng &c. in yᵉ style of wryttes.

---

[1] *State Papers, Domestic,* vol. I. no. 3.

This seems to me proof positive that "&c. in the style of writs" was the outcome, not of chance but of deliberation that took place at the first moment of the reign in the highest of high quarters.

So we might expand the symbol thus :—

&c. = and (if future events shall so decide, but not further or otherwise) of the Church of England and also of Ireland upon earth the Supreme Head.

II. Queen Elizabeth and Paul IV.

A well-known story about Elizabeth and Paul IV was told by Sarpi[1], endorsed by Pallavicino[2], and believed by Ranke[3]. Lingard[4], after accepting, saw cause to reject it, and his example has been very generally followed by English historians, though often they manifest their disbelief rather by silence than by contradiction. Still the tale is not quite dead, and I do not know that the evidence which disproves it has ever been fully stated, albeit that evidence lies in obvious places. It is concerned with an important matter—namely, the immediate causes of those ecclesiastical changes which were heralded by the death of Mary Tudor.

It runs thus in Sarpi's history. Elizabeth began her reign with hesitation. She was hurried into decisive measures by the insensate arrogance of the

---

[1] *Hist. Conc. Trid.* ed. 1620, p. 333; transl. Le Courayer, II. 53.

[2] *Vera Conc. Trid. Hist.* II. 532.

[3] *Englische Geschichte,* I. 301.

[4] *Hist. Engl.* ed. 1823, v. 146; ed. 1854, VI. 3.

pope. Sir Edward Carne was residing at Rome as Mary's ambassador. The new queen sent him letters of credence, and bade him announce to the pope her accession to the throne. Thereupon Paul broke into reproach and menace. She was a bastard, England was a papal fief, and her assumption of the crown was insolent usurpation. Nevertheless, if she would submit herself to his discretion, he would do in her favour all that was compatible with the dignity of the holy see. Many people, says Sarpi, thought that this rude reception of Elizabeth's advances was due not only to Paul's imperious temper, but also to the solicitations of the French, who were concerned to prevent a marriage between the queen of England and the king of Spain. Then, having suffered this rebuff, Elizabeth decided to have no more to do with Rome, and allowed the English protestants to have their way.

Pallavicino accepted Sarpi's facts, but defended the pope's conduct. Rude Paul might have been, and tactless; but Elizabeth was a hypocrite, and substantially the pope was in the right. Lingard at one time apologetically told his readers that "it was the misfortune of Paul, who had passed his eightieth year, that he adopted opinions with the credulity and maintained them with the pertinacity of old age." Afterwards the catholic doctor found reason to withdraw his well-turned sentence.

Now this was a lifelike story. Had it not been lifelike, Sarpi would not have told, Pallavicino would not have endorsed, Ranke would not have believed it. There was a real danger that Pope Paul would do just what he is said to have done. This danger was evident to Feria in England. A week after Elizabeth's accession he wrote thus to his master, King Philip:—

I am very much afraid that if the queen do not send her obedience to the pope, or delay doing so, or if he should take it into his head to recall matters concerning the divorce of King Henry, there may be a defect in the queen's title, which, more than anything else, will upset the present state of affairs in this country[1].

Paul was imprudent enough for anything. Even if Elizabeth did all that a catholic sovereign should do, it was quite possible that the hot-headed old man would fling her bastardy in her face, and declare that England was a fief moving from St Peter. At the moment he was asserting that, without his sanction, Charles V's abdication of the empire was a nullity, and he was doing all that mortal pope could do to drive the patient Ferdinand into Lutheranism.

Perhaps it was just this that prevented some such explosion as that which Sarpi has recorded. Paul had one great quarrel on his hands, and even he—for he was human—could hardly afford another. As a matter of fact during the months that will concern us he was showing some desire to stand well with the Spanish while he denounced the Austrian Hapsburg, and a declaration in favour of Mary Stuart's claim to the English crown would have been very much like a declaration of war against Philip. Little good had come to Pope Paul of his alliance with France; and

[1] *Spanish Cal.* 1558–67, p. 6 ; Kervyn de Lettenhove, *Relations Politiques*, I. 309.

the ascendency of his nephew Carlo Caraffa, whom we shall see as the French advocate, was almost at an end.

Be all this as it may, Sarpi's story cannot be true.

Let us remember that Elizabeth became queen on 17 Nov. 1558. Now it is apparent in notes written by Cecil during the first hours of the new reign that no sooner was Mary dead than he was thinking of the embassies that must be sent to foreign potentates. Not only was the pope included in his list, but, having mentioned the emperor before the pope, the exact minister was at pains to correct his mistake and to give the accustomed precedence to the holy father[1]. These notes may have been written before Cecil had met his young mistress. Then it is apparent from other notes that this project was abandoned or suspended[2]. Envoys were to go to Ferdinand and Philip and some other friendly powers; but seemingly there was to be no mission to Rome.

To the first weeks of the new reign we must attribute the remarkable paper of advice tendered by Richard Goodrich[3]. Some part of the counsel that he gave was rejected. It was extremely cautious counsel. He did not believe that the parliament which was being summoned could be induced to abolish the papal and restore the royal supremacy over the church. What the estates of the realm actually did a few months afterwards was, in his eyes,

---

[1] *Domestic*, vol. I. no. 2 (MS.).

[2] Nothing of the pope in the paper ascribed to 18 Nov.: *Domestic*, vol. I. no. 3 (MS.).

[3] *Domestic*, vol. I. no. 68 (MS.). Froude made good use of this discourse, but has not referred to the portion that will concern us.

something too good to be expected. This estimate of affairs, made by an able man who lived in their midst, should be weighed by those, if such there be, who think that Elizabeth's revolt from Rome was an inevitable concession to an irresistible demand. But one part of Goodrich's advice seems to have been taken, that, namely, which is given in the following words :—

I would also...have letters sent to the agent there [i.e. at Rome] to continue his residence, and to advertise as occasion shall be given without desire of any audience, and, if he should be sent for, that he should signify that he understood from hence that there was a great embassy either despatched or ready to be despatched for the affairs, whose despatch I would should be published with the persons' names, and yet treated so as it should pass for the most part of next summer, and in the meantime to have good consultation what is to be done at home, and do it, and thereafter send.

The plan is that Carne is to have no new letters of credence, but is to remain at Rome as an "intelligencer," and, if pressed by inquiries, is to say that a grand embassy is coming. The mission of that embassy can be delayed until the parliament is over, and meanwhile Elizabeth can make her own arrangements untroubled by an embarrassing correspondence with his holiness.

The rest of the story can be told by notes of letters and events.

1 *Dec.* 1558.—A letter is sent to Carne at Rome, telling him that, "as he was theretofore placed there as a public person by reason of his ambassade," he is not to act as solicitor in a certain matrimonial suit that is depending before the curia[1].

[1] *Foreign*, 1558–9, no. 56.

17 *or* 18 *Dec.*—Carne has just heard of Elizabeth's accession, and writes to congratulate her[1].

20 *Dec.*—Probably a letter is sent to Carne in the sense advised by Goodrich—namely, to the effect that, if asked about this matter, he may say that a grand embassy is being prepared. The contents of this letter, which does not seem to be forthcoming, we learn in a manner that will be explained hereafter[2].

25 *Dec. Carne to Elizabeth.*—He sends some Italian news, and also informs her that the pope intends to depose the three Lutheran electors and give their dominions to catholic princes[3].

25 *Dec.*—Elizabeth refuses to witness the elevation of the host, and thus chooses a great festival of the church for an act which must, at this moment, be regarded as a display of unequivocal protestantism.

25 *Dec. The Bishop of Angoulême to the King of France.*—With great difficulty the bishop has obtained an audience of the pope. Paul cannot believe that Elizabeth will wish to marry Philip, but will not promise to refuse a dispensation[4]. It seems quite clear from this interesting letter that Paul had not pronounced, and was not prepared to pronounce, against Elizabeth's title to the throne. The French ambassador did not, according to his own account, say a word about bastardy or about the hereditary right of the dauphiness. He contented himself with the endeavour to prevent a marriage between Elizabeth

---

[1] *Foreign,* 1558–9, nos. 123, 162.
[2] See below under 16 Feb.
[3] *Foreign,* 1558–9, no. 123.
[4] Ribier, *Mémoires,* II. 776.

and her brother-in-law, and even in this modest enterprise was not very successful, for the pope would make no definite promise. Also it seems clear that at this moment Paul did not suspect—and indeed he had little reason for suspecting—that the English queen was joining the number of the schismatical and heretical princes. He talked kindly of her, and could not believe that she was foolish enough to marry a Spaniard.

31 *Dec. Carne to Elizabeth.*—A mutilated letter which was thus summarised in England :—

> Sir Edward Carne (ambassador resident at Rome from Queen Mary, and after by a letter from her majesty continued) writeth unto her that the ambassador of France laboureth the Pope to declare the queen illegitimate. Cardinal Caraffa is their instrument. The French likewise labour to withdraw the king of Spain, if they can, from affecting the queen of England[1].

31 *Dec. Carne to Cecil.*—He offers his services to the queen, though he would like to be recalled. He desires to know the queen's pleasure, as his old commission has expired. [He has not as yet received the letter of 20 Dec.[2]]

25 *Jan.* 1559.—The English parliament meets, and by this time it is abundantly plain in England that the queen means to abolish the papal supremacy. Any further dissimulation at Rome would be useless.

1 *Feb. Resolution of the Queen's Council.*—A letter is to be sent to Carne telling him that he is to come home, as there is no cause why he should remain at Rome[3]. On 4 Feb. the letter is sent[4].

---

[1] *Foreign*, 1558–9, nos. 160, 161. [2] *Ibid.* no. 162.
[3] *Ibid.* no. 299. [4] *Ibid.* no. 474.

15 *Feb. Bull "Cum ex Apostolatus,"* declaring that heretical princes are deposed by the mere fact of heresy[1].

16 *Feb. Carne to the Queen.*—He had written on the 11th. The French here can obtain nothing from the pope against her ; "he [Paul] has such respect to herself and her realm that he will attempt nothing against either unless occasion be given therehence [i.e. from England]." The pope means to send a nuncio, but waits until an ambassador shall come from Elizabeth[2].

An abstract of the last-mentioned letter runs thus : "A nuncio intended for England, but stayeth until the queen first sendeth to the pope, according to the message he [Carne] had delivered by the queen's directions by her letters of 20 Dec.[3]" It is thus that we learn of the letter of 20 Dec. and of the attempt to keep the pope quiet by talk of a coming embassy.

10 *March.*—Carne receives the letter of 4 Feb. which recalls him. He then tries to obtain from the pope licence to leave Rome, giving various excuses— for example, that he wants to see his wife and children and will soon return. He learns, however, from Cardinal Trani that Paul knows of the recall.

21 *March.*—Trani tells Carne that the pope is "sore moved" and will not hear of Carne's departure.

27 *March.*—Trani tells Carne that the pope forbids his departure, since Elizabeth and her realm have revolted from obedience to the Roman see.

---

[1] *Magnum Bullarium* (Luxemb. 1727), I. 846.
[2] *Foreign*, 1558-9, no. 331.   [3] *Ibid.* no. 333.

1 *April. Carne to Elizabeth.*—He tells of his detention. From this letter are derived the facts stated in our last three paragraphs. That Carne reports them accurately must not be assumed[1].

3 *April. Carne to Elizabeth.*—Again he tells how he is detained and is compelled by the pope to take charge of the English hospital at Rome. "He perceives the French have obtained somewhat of their purpose the month before, but in what particular he cannot learn[2]."

24 *April. Philip to Feria.*—As Elizabeth has refused the title of "supreme head" when it was offered to her, there may still be some hope. Seeing this, and seeing how damaging it would be if the pope were to declare her a bastard, which he might decide to do, "since I am not to marry her," I have endeavoured to stay his hand by assuring him that there are hopes of her amendment[3].

30 *May. Throckmorton to Cecil.*—He has heard from the Venetian ambassador at the court of France that Carne was a willing prisoner at Rome, and thankfully accepted the charge of the hospital[4].

Now from all this it seems plain enough that Sarpi's story is radically untrue, and Pallavicino's defence unnecessary. Whether Paul ever made any attack against Elizabeth on the score of her base birth is very doubtful. That he never made any public and solemn attack against her on that score, or even on

---

[1] *Foreign*, no. 474.   [2] *Ibid.* no. 492.
[3] *Spanish Cal.* 1558-67, p. 60; Kervyn de Lettenhove, *Relations Politiques*, I. 508.
[4] *Foreign*, 1558-9, no. 789.

the score of heresy and schism, is fairly certain : many would have preserved copies of a bull that denounced her, whether as heretic or as usurper. But at least it should be indubitable that she was not driven into protestantism by his insults. Apparently he did and said nothing against her until he learnt that she was withdrawing her minister from his court, and that her talk of sending an embassy had been deceitful.

Whether she was one of the people who were in his mind when the bull that is dated on 15 February was being prepared would be a delicate question. Primarily he was thinking of the three protestant electors who had dared to take part in the choice of an emperor. In the background may have stood Maximilian, who was leaning towards Luther, and Anthony, who was leaning towards Calvin. We should suppose that by the middle of February Paul had heard of a scene enacted in a royal chapel on Christmas Day by a young actress, who planned her scenes with admirable art. Still even at the date of the bull Carne was saying that the pope was Elizabeth's friend, and to find a reason why the ambassador should lie about this matter would not be easy. Not until later would the pope have serious cause to doubt the truth of Philip's repeated assurances that all would go well in England, and already the miserable man had on his hands his own scandalous nephews, besides a wrongfully elected emperor. But even if it were in some sort true that "Cum ex Apostolatus" was aimed at Elizabeth as well as some other people, still no names were named in it, and if, according to canonical reckoning, her reign ends in the spring of 1559, that is not because King John held England of Pope Innocent, nor because King Henry and Queen Anne were adulterers, but because Elizabeth, as she had frankly admitted, was a heretic : *porque era erege*[1]. Sometimes truth speaks through truthless lips.

When did Elizabeth's reign end ? I do not know. English historians, so far as I have observed, say nothing of Paul's bull, and I gather from the *Bullarium* that it may not have been "published" in the technical sense of that term[2]. At a later date the English catholics were told that the question whether an heretical prince was *privatus lata sententia* or merely *privandus sententia ferenda* was a somewhat doubtful question, and therefore it was somewhat doubtful whether Elizabeth was queen until Pius V denounced her. According to a "probable opinion" his denunciation merely declared to the world an effect which her heresies had produced without the aid of any sentence ; but the contrary was said to be "the commoner opinion[3]." Be that as it may (and with such subtleties we had better not meddle), we have little reason for accusing Paul V of striking Elizabeth before, or even after, he was stricken.

Who started the story that Sarpi told? There were times when Elizabeth explained to the right people—to Spanish ambassadors and the like—that in the early days of her reign she had been forced

---

[1] *Spanish Cal.* 1558–67, p. 37 ; Kervyn de Lettenhove, *Relations Politiques*, I. 475.

[2] It was confirmed in 1566 by a bull of Pius V—*Inter multiplices* (*Bullarium*, II. 214 ; Hinschius, *Kirchenrecht*, v. 682).

[3] *Eng. Hist. Rev.* VII. 87 (Answer to Question 14).

to seem less catholic, more protestant, than really she
was. Whatever else she may have been, she was a
great storyteller, and I am not sure that this lifelike
legend of a reasonable young woman and an impracticable old pope would have been unworthy of
her genius.

By way of appendix to a paper which perhaps has
repeated too much that is generally known, I will add
an account of Elizabeth's Christmas escapade which is
lying among the " Roman Transcripts " at the Record
Office. At this moment I am not able to describe the
source whence this extract was taken, but apparently
we learn that the news of Elizabeth's unfinished mass
and of her almost contemporary edict touching epistle
and gospel soon reached Rome. As we should expect,
the story was improved by transmission ; but to me it
seems that very fairly might the as yet uncrowned
queen be charged at Rome with having openly declared herself a heretic (or in the Italian of the time
a Lutheran) if, rather than witness the elevation of
the host, she ostentatiously quitted her chapel[1].

Corsini 38 *F* 6. *Diario Pontificum.* 1327–1561.

1559.

La Regina d' Inghilterra finalmente di questo mese (Gennaro) si
dichiara Luterana, e fece un decreto che non se douesse predicar

---

[1] The evidence is good. See Feria's letter, *Spanish Cal.* 1558–
67, p. 17 ; Kervyn de Lettenhove, *Relations Politiques*, I. 365 ;
ll Schifanoya's letter, *Venetian*, 1558–80, p. 2 ; Letter of Sir W.
Fitzwilliam, Ellis, *Orig. Letters*, sec. ser. II. 262 ; extracts printed in
Bridgett and Knox, *Queen Elizabeth and the Catholic Hierarchy*,
p. 65.

altro che l' Evangelio e l' Epistola di San Paolo, et essendo alla messa non uolse stare a ueder consecrare, anzi uolse impedire il uescouo che non consecrasse, e permise a ciascuno di uiuere a suo modo sin tanto che ella dichiaraua per decreto il [*sic*] Parlamento che si hauesse da uiuere nella uera e pura fede, qual intendeua, secondo che dicono i Luterani.

Il Re Filippo fece intendere alla detta regina, che poi ch' ella non uoleua uiuere catolicamente, ch' egli le protestaua, che non uoleua hauerla piu per confederata, ne tener conto delle cose di quel regno d' Inghilterra.

7 Marzo.

Le cose della religione in Inghilterra andauano di male in peggio, et haueuano fatti Inquisition contra Papistam [*sic*] che cosi si chiamauano questi heretici.

III. Pius IV and the English Church Service.

It has long been known that Pope Pius IV did something in the way of prohibiting those Englishmen who were likely to attend to papal commands from participating in the worship of the English church. I am not aware, however, that the document in which he spoke his mind has been printed, though a copy of it is lying very close to our hands among the transcripts which Froude brought from Simancas[1]. My attention was drawn to this copy by a short note contained in Major Hume's *Calendar of Spanish Papers*, who apparently thought that its subject-matter was of too little interest to deserve any but the briefest notice. Yet I think that the following "Case and

[1] Brit. Mus. Add. MS. 26,056, pp. 182, 185.

Opinion" are none too well known even among professed students of ecclesiastical history[1].

On 7 Aug. 1562, Alvaro de Quadra, the Spanish ambassador in England, wrote to Francesco de Vargas, the Spanish ambassador at Rome, -to the following effect :—

The enclosed paper has been given to me on behalf of the catholics of this realm. They desired that it should be sent to Trent, but I think that you had better lay it before his holiness, for he is more perfectly informed about the circumstances of the case than those at Trent are likely to be. The case is novel and unusual; it is very different from an ordinary case of communicating with excommunicates. The question *Si est metus aut coactio?* cannot be seriously raised; the coercion is absolute, for capital punishment is imposed on every one who will not live as a heretic. Also in this instance we have only to do with presence at what are called "common prayers," and these contain no impiety or false doctrine, for they consist of Scripture and prayers taken from the catholic church, though what concerns the merits and intercession of saints has been omitted. Moreover we have not to deal with the communion, which is celebrated only at Easter and other great festivals. The question is solely as to presence at these "common prayers."

The writer adds that he has been chary of giving advice to those who have consulted him, since he

---

[1] *Spanish Calendar*, 1558–67, p. 258. "Sends an address from the English catholics asking for an authoritative decision as to the legality of their attending the reformed- services. Sets forth the arguments in favour of their being allowed to do so."

wished neither to condemn the feeble nor to damp
the ardour of the strong. As I understand him, he
doubts whether any general rule will adequately meet
all possible cases[1].

The question that was submitted to the pope and
the answer that he gave to it—the answer seems to
have been dated on 2 Oct.—run in the following
words :—

Casus est :—

Quidam principatus lege et statutis prohibuit sub poena capitali
ne aliquis sit catholicus, sed omnes vitam hereticam agant, et inter-
sint psalmis eorum more lingua vulgari decantandis, et lectionibus
ex Bibliis lingua item populari depromptis, nec non concionibus
quae ad eorum dogmata aprobanda apud populum frequentius
habentur, commemorantur et fiant.

Quaestio :—

An subditi fideles et catholici sine periculo damnationis aeternae
animae suae supradictis interesse possint.

Ad casum respondemus quod neque vitam catholicam relinquere, ·
nec hereticam ducere, neque eorum psalmis, lectionibus et concionibus interesse licet: cum in casu proposito non esset cum hereticis
comunicare et cum eis participare sed vitam et errores illorum
protestari, cum non velint aliam ob causam interesse nisi ut tanquam
heretici reputati poenas catholicis impositas effugiant; et scriptum est
Obedire oportet Deo dicenti Qui me erubuerit et meos sermones[2],
quanquam hominibus vitam et ritus Deo et ecclesiae contrarios
precipientibus, et eo magis cum nobiles et magnates non sine
pusillorum scandalo supradictis interesse possint.

It seems pretty clear that those who "settled this
case for opinion" desired an answer very different

---

[1] This covering letter is in Spanish. The "Case and Opinion"
are, I think, in Froude's own handwriting. I will give them as they
stand ; some small emendations will occur to the reader.

[2] Here, I suppose, an *etc.* should mark the end of an unfinished
text.

from that which they received. We can hardly acquit them of grossly exaggerating their woes. To listen to them one would think that non-attendance at church was a capital crime, instead of being cause for a twelvepenny fine. Quadra is guilty of a similar mis-representation when he says *siendo prohibido aqui por ley el ser catolico y puestas penas capitales a quien no viviere como herege,* unless indeed every one is living as a heretic if he refrains from actively pro-claiming the papal supremacy. At any rate we must allow that the very utmost that could be done to induce a soft answer was done by those who thus brought capital punishment into contact with absence from church. Moreover they do not ask for any counsel of perfection. All that they want to know is whether church-going is deadly sin. And, again, Quadra makes it quite plain that there is no talk of any participation in the Lord's Supper—the devilish supper, as even moderate English catholics could call it[1]—and in favour of "the common prayers" he seems to say all that could fairly be said by a prelate who was in communion with Rome. But no, Pius, the conciliatory Pius, will have none of it. If the choice lies between church and gallows the gallows must be chosen.

IV. THOMAS SACKVILLE'S MESSAGE FROM ROME.

Pius IV, though he had serious thoughts of de-nouncing Elizabeth as an excommunicate heretic and deposed queen, made at least four attempts to secure

[1] See *English Historical Review,* VII. 85.

her conversion. A good deal is generally known about the mission of Vincent Parpaglia in 1560 and the mission of Martinengo in 1561. Something also is easily discoverable about the efforts made by the cardinal of Ferrara in 1562, and they were sanctioned by Pius, though by this time he was no longer hopeful[1]. Then we may learn a little of an episode in which Thomas Sackville was the principal actor. He is the Thomas Sackville who wrote poetry that is admired, and became Lord Buckhurst and earl of Dorset.

In the winter of 1563-4 he was in Rome and was arrested as a spy; but he was soon liberated, and held converse with some illustrious people. In January Cecil was anxious about his fate; Cecil's Italian "intelligencers" were to find out what had happened. Then from a letter written in February we may gather that Cecil did not know whether Sackville had or had not a commission from the queen[2]. Then in November Guzman de Silva, the Spanish ambassador in England, had something to tell King Philip about Sackville's proceedings. The pope, so the Spaniard said, had conversed with Sackville, and had assured him that if what was preventing Elizabeth from making dutiful submission was the fear that she would be deposed as illegitimate, or the fear that she would not be allowed to marry whom she pleased, she might set her mind at rest. The ambassador added that Sackville, having journeyed from Rome to Flanders, thence wrote to

---

[1] Among the Roman transcripts are two letters of 3 Jan. and 15 March 1562 about this negotiation.

[2] *Foreign Calendar*, 1564-5, nos. 109, 113, 159.

the queen, who wrote in reply without the knowledge
of Cecil or Cecil's friends.   Despite this secrecy Silva
did not believe that Elizabeth was in earnest.   He
suspected, and so may we, that she was endeavouring
to keep the catholics quiet by the semblance of a
confidential correspondence with his holiness[1].

Among the Roman transcripts at the Record Office
are two which bear upon this story.   The first is
a curious document signed by Goldwell, bishop of
St Asaph, and others of the English refugees at
Rome.   It is dated on 19 Jan. 1564 at the English
hospital.   In effect it is a certificate of respectability
given by these refugees in Sackville's favour.   Richard
Sackville is the queen's cousin, one of her councillors,
and a very wealthy man.   Thomas is his son and heir
apparent.   Moreover Thomas is a man of good behaviour and of such pleasant discourse that many of
the nobles take great delight in his conversation[2].

Then there is a paper dated at Rome on 3 May
1564.   At its end the writer calls himself " Vincentius
Parpaglia Abbas S. Solutoris Turini."   It sets forth
what Thomas Sackville may report to Elizabeth as
having been heard by him from the mouth of Pius IV
on two different occasions when the pope gave him
audience.   In the final and attestatory clause Parpaglia
states that he was present at these interviews, as well
as at others which Sackville had with Cardinals
Boromeo and Morone.   To be brief, Sackville may
say that the pope expressed surprise at Elizabeth's
refusal to admit into England the nuncios (first

[1] *Spanish Calendar*, p. 390.
[2] This document is printed in Brady, *Episcopal Succession*, I. 87.

Parpaglia and then Martinengo) who had been sent
to her. Pius, however, had been given to understand
that two causes had weighed with Elizabeth—first the
divorce of her parents, and secondly the alienation of
church property.

Ad quae sua Sanctitas hunc in modum responsum dedit : se non
velle ullo modo tantam rationem et curam rerum temporalium et
humanarum haberi ut animarum salus impediatur : atque ideo si
quando serenissima regina ad unionem ecclesiae et obedientiam
huius sanctae sedis reverti voluerit, sua Sanctitas pollicetur se paterno
affectu et quanto amore desiderari possit eam recepturam ; et illis
difficultatibus quas supradixi[1] ea remedia adhibituram quae reginae
maiestas, parlamentum generale et totius regni consensus indicaverit
ad coronam stabiliendam et pacem atque quietem totius populi
confirmandam esse aptissima, et in omni re quod iustum piumque
iudicabitur confirmaturam.

Sackville was to beg Elizabeth to be merciful to the
bishops and other catholics in her realm, and was to
add that if she publicly or privately sent an envoy to
Rome he would be honourably treated, and an endeavour would be made to satisfy all pious and honest
demands that he might make.

It would hardly, I think, be too much to say that
Elizabeth was once more told that if she would enter
the catholic fold she might be as legitimate as the pope
could make her, and that there would be no trouble
about the spoils of the monasteries. On the other
hand, no hint is given of any approval of her prayer
book or any compromise in matters of faith or
worship.

What seems to be an allusion to this episode occurs
in the semi-official answer to Nicholas Sanders which

---

[1] Parpaglia is speaking.

was published in 1573, and is ascribed to the pen of Bartholomew Clerk. Seven years ago, he says, it happened that a noble Englishman was at the court of Rome and had converse with Pius IV. The pope professed his inability to understand how a wise and literate queen could fall away from the faith. He suspected, so he said, that Elizabeth's defection was due to the holy see's condemnation of her mother's marriage, and added that were that so he was prepared to reverse the sentence if his primacy were recognised. Then Clerk, having told this tale, exclaims to Sanders, " If you doubt me there are extant among us the articles written by the hand of the abbot of S. Salute, and there are extant the letters of Cardinal Morone, in which he strenuously exhorts the nobleman in question earnestly to solicit our queen in this matter[1]."

It has been suggested that Clerk's nobleman was the earl of Arundel. It has been suggested also that the boast about the existence of articles in Parpaglia's handwriting was untrue[2]. There can now—so I submit—be little doubt that Sackville was the man whom Clerk had in mind, and the document that has been described above looks as if it were the articles to which Sanders was rhetorically referred[3].

Parpaglia's signature enables us to identify the abbey of which he was the titular head. Too long

---

[1] *Fidelis Servi Subdito Infideli Responsio*, Lond., Jo. Daye, 1573, sig. k, II.

[2] Estcourt, *Question of Anglican Orders*, pp. 361, 366.

[3] In 1573 nine, rather than seven, years would have elapsed since the Sackville episode.

he has figured as abbot of San Saluto, San Salute, San Salvatore, Saint Sauveur, St Saviour's, and so forth. Really the abbey was that of SS. Solutore, Avventore ed Ottavio de Sangano at Turin ; it seems to have been suppressed in 1536, and in 1570 its revenues were given to the Jesuits[1].

V. SUPREMACY AND UNIFORMITY.

It may seem rash to suppose that about those two famous statutes of the first year of Elizabeth anything remains to be said. They have been approached by innumerable writers from almost every conceivable point. Still I am not sure that "diplomatic" has yet said its say about them, or, to use a less lofty and therefore a more becoming phrase, I am not sure that any one has had the curiosity to examine those acts in the hope of learning something from the external aspect of the parchment and the work that has been done thereon by pens and knives. But, whatever else an act of parliament may be, it is a piece of parchment. It is preserved in the palace at Westminster. It can be inspected by the public. It may tell tales, and such tales as an official editor of the statutes of the realm is not authorised to repeat. Having seen enough to persuade me that in this manner a few grains of information might be gleaned, I asked my friend Mr H. C. Barker to make a careful inspection of the acts in question, with an eye to all marks of

---

[1] Döllinger, *Beiträge zur Geschichte der sechs letzten Jahrhunderte*, II. 238.

erasure, cancellation, and interlineation. The results of his labours may, so I think, be of some interest to others besides myself. But before I state them two or three prefatory words should be said.

A bill, as we all know, had to pass through both houses of parliament. Before the first house (that is, the house in which it originated) had done with it, it was engrossed. From that time forward there was a piece of parchment which was the bill. If then we find that the text which was written on that piece of parchment shows signs of erasure, cancellation, and interlineation, we are entitled as a general rule to the inference that amendments were made either in the second house or else at a late stage in the transit of the measure through the first house[1]. In a given case this inference may be wrong. It may happen that the engrossing clerk, while he is at his work, makes a mistake and then corrects it with knife and pen. The two acts of which we are speaking show a considerable number of instances in which two or three letters of a word seem to be written over an erasure, while the rest of the word stands on parchment that to all appearance has not felt the knife. We have, therefore, to exercise a little common sense in endeavouring to distinguish between corrected slips of the pen and amendments made in parliament after the text has been engrossed[2].

---

[1] Smith, *Commonwealth*, ed. 1635, p. 89. A bill may be committed and amended before it is engrossed, "yea, and some time after."

[2] Such amendments were said to be "made at the table." I take it that the actual erasing and so forth was done in the view of the assembled members.

For example, if we see that on many occasions the phrase "the last day of this session of parliament" is so written that the first part of it stands over an erasure and the second part of it is interlined, we shall hardly talk of clerical error, but we shall infer that an amendment was moved and carried. In the following remarks no notice will be taken of what clearly seem to be slips of the pen and the correction of such slips. For instance, we will not record that in the word "metropolitan" two or three of the middle letters seem to stand upon an erasure. All that may be significant we will mention.

What lies before me as I write is a copy of Dr Prothero's *Statutes and Constitutional Documents*, annotated by Mr Barker. As that book is deservedly in common use and very handy, I will refer to its pages and lines, but will in every instance give words enough to enable a reader to find in any other collection of statutes the passage which is the subject of remark. Dr Prothero spells words in modern fashion, and in this we will follow him. Words that are written over an erasure will be printed in italics. Words that are interlined will be printed within square brackets. An erasure over which nothing has been written will be indicated by three asterisks. As to the length of such an erasure, a word will be said in a footnote. The number of words in a line of the manuscript is a varying number; but when it is said that a line is erased this will mean that some twenty words have disappeared. It will be understood that when we speak of erasure we speak of the work done by a knife. If words are struck through by a pen, we shall say that they are, not erased, but cancelled[1].

1. *The Act of Supremacy* (1 *Eliz. c.* 1).

The roll consists of three skins, fastened end to end, and affixed to the last are four small "schedules" or "followers." These are fastened to the left-hand side of the roll by a narrow strip of parchment. The words which express the royal assent are easily legible. The top right-hand corner of the roll is soiled and creased, and this makes the direction for delivery to the second house difficult to read. A crease has run along the line of words which express the assent of the second house and has defaced the inscription. Perhaps, were there any lack of other evidence, we could just discern that in this instance the second house was the house of lords. We should also see that the bill went to the second house with two provisos annexed and received that house's assent with four provisos annexed.

We may now proceed to the work of annotation.

Sec. i. (Prothero, p. 2, ll. 24–5): "may from *the last day* [of this session of parliament] by authority . . ." Of this and similar indications of a change affecting the commencement of the act we shall speak below.

Sec. ii. (p. 3, ll. 1–5): "and one other act * * *[2] made in the

---

[1] It will be remembered that on the roll the sections are not numbered and that the numeration is not authoritative; also that the text in the official edition was taken, not from the original act, but from the clean transcript enrolled in the chancery.

[2] An erasure of the length of three or four letters.

twenty-fifth [year of the said late king, concerning restraint of payment of annates and firstfruits of archbishoprics and bishoprics to the see of Rome and one other act in the said twenty-fifth] year . . ." This may be the correction of a clerk's blunder occasioned by the recurrence of "twenty-fifth year"; or the draftsman may have forgotten that there were two acts about annates which required mention.

Sec. ii. (p. 3, ll. 23–4): "all times *after the last day of this* [session of parliament] shall be revived . . ."

Sec. iv. (p. 4, ll. 14–20): "all other laws and statutes and the branches and clauses of any act or statute repealed and made void by the said act of repeal made in the time of the said late King Philip and Queen Mary * * *[1] and *not* in this present act especially mentioned and revived, shall stand, remain, and be repealed and void in such like manner and form as they were before the making of this act . . ." Here we find an extensive alteration made at an important point; but we can hardly guess the cause. This section prevents the revival of certain Henrician statutes by the repeal of Mary's repealing act. The erased words may have been of the exceptive sort, and may have been struck out by the conservatives in the house of lords. To speculate about this matter would, however, be dangerous.

Sec. v. (p. 4, ll. 25–8): "an act against such persons as shall unreverendly speak against the sacrament of the body and blood of Christ, commonly * * *[2] called the sacrament of the altar, and for receiving thereof *under* both kinds . . ." It seems possible that there was some hesitation between "under" and "in." In the body of the Edwardian act that was being revived we see "under both kinds," while the title of that act on the chancery roll has "in both kinds[3]."

Sec. v. (p. 4, ll. 30–1): "from *the last day* [of this session of parliament] be revived, and from *th*enceforth . . ."

Sec. vi. (p. 5, ll. 8–9): "from the *last day of this* [session of parliament] deemed . . ."

---

[1] An erasure of just two lines, equal to the space between "all" and "Mary."

[2] An erasure of one or two letters.

[3] *Statutes of the Realm*, IV. 1–3.

Sec. vii. (p. 5, ll. 18–9): "any time *after the last day* [of this session of parliament] use . . ."

Sec. vii. (p. 5, ll. 23–4): "but fro*m t*henceforth the same shall . . ."

Sec. ix. (p. 7, ll. 9–10): "as well in all spiritual [or ecclesiastical] things or causes as temporal . . ." This occurs in the oath of supremacy. If the interpolated words are an amendment we have at first sight some little difficulty in imagining the motives of those who desired it; but perhaps they thought that "or ecclesiastical" would so explain "spiritual" that any claim to jurisdiction *in foro conscientiae* would be excluded.

Sec. x. (p. 7, l. 24): "archbishop, bishop, or other ecclesiastical *officer* or minister." Possibly "officer" took the place of "person[1]."

Sec. xi. (p. 8, ll. 24–6): "shall presently be judged disabled in the law to receive, take, or have *the same* promotion spiritual or ecclesiastical, *the same* * * *[2] temporal office, ministry, or service . . ." An amendment narrowing the scope of a disabling clause seems a possible cause of these alterations.

Sec. xiii. (p. 9, ll. 22–3): "the said refusal, *and shall and may use and exercise the said office in such manner and form*[3] . . ."

Sec. xiv. (p. 9, l. 27), "and for *the more* [sure] observation of this act . . ."

Sec. xiv. (p. 10, l. 3): "of your highness, or * * *[4] shall advisedly . . ."

Sec. xiv. (p. 10, ll. 30–1): "or do the said offences or any of them [in manner and form aforesaid] and be thereof duly convicted . . ."

Sec. xiv. (p. 11, ll. 1–2): "or any of them [in manner and form aforesaid] and be thereof duly convicted . . ." This and the last amendment seem to come from those who would have the definitions of the offences strictly construed.

---

[1] See § ix.

[2] An erasure of the length of "the same."

[3] The parchment seems to have been scraped, but it is not clear that any writing was erased.

[4] An erasure of 14 to 16 letters.

Sec. xv.   In this section the phrase "one half-year next" occurs twice.   On the. second, but not on the first, occurrence, the "half" is interlined.   The context seems to show that this is, only the correction of a blunder.

Sec. xv.   At the end of this section occur seven lines of writing that are cancelled by a pen.   Of them we shall speak below.

Sec. xviii.   (p. 12, ll. 5–6): "for any offence that is *revived* [or made premunire or] treason by this act . . ."

Sec. xviii.   At the end of this section occur six and a half lines of writing which are cancelled by a pen.   Of them we shall speak below.

Here the roll ends.   We pass to the schedules.

The first schedule is marked with a direction for delivery to the lords.   It therefore originates in the commons.   It contains the proviso which is printed as sec. xix.   It is a curious proviso, coming apparently from the reforming side, to the effect that nothing done by this present parliament shall hereafter be judged heresy or schism.   Not a very useful proviso, one would think, if ever the conservative party returned to power.

The second schedule contains three provisos which are printed as sections xx., xxi., xxii.   These originated in the house of lords, for on the schedule stand the order for delivery to the commons, and a note that the commons have assented.

Sec. xx.   This section says that the persons, whom for the sake of brevity we may call the high commissioners, "shall not in any wise have authority or power to order, determine, or adjudge any matter or cause to be heresy, but only such as heretofore have been determined, ordered, or adjudged to be heresy [by the authority of the canonical Scriptures or by the first four general councils or any of them, or by any other general council wherein the same was declared heresy by the express and plain words of the said canonical Scriptures][1], or such as hereafter shall be ordered, judged, or determined to be heresy by the high court of parliament of this

---

[1] Interlined in very small letters.

realm with the assent of the clergy in their convocation; anything in this act contained to the contrary notwithstanding." .

The two portions of this section seem to proceed from different parties, and, whether we have here a clause added by the lords and amended by the commons, or a clause proposed in the upper house (perhaps by the committees) and altered in that house, we have reason to infer the occurrence of an interesting episode. It strikes the conservatives in the upper house that, unless something be said to the contrary, these royal commissioners may soon be adjudging heretical many of the old beliefs—for example, a belief in transubstantiation. So a limit must be set, and it takes a very conservative form: only what has been adjudged heresy in the past is to be adjudged heresy in the future, unless convocation, which has lately shown its conservatism, consents to a change. But this adoption of the old standard, though only in a one-sided fashion, would hardly suit the reforming party. A clause is inserted which expresses a certain theory about ecclesiastical history, and even if we cannot call that theory definitely protestant it is opposed to traditional teaching. It draws a line among the general councils of the church. The result makes for toleration. To put the matter briefly and roughly, none of the old beliefs, nor any of those new beliefs that are held by decent people, are to be heretical; but we may think it lucky for the reformers that this section was not administered by the conservatives, for have not councils which called themselves general seen a good deal that protestants cannot see "in the express and plain words of the said canonical Scriptures?" At any rate, however, we have warrant for saying that the lords materially modified the bill in a conservative and also a tolerant sense.

Sec. xxi. This proviso is substituted for a clause which stood at the end of sec. xv. and which has been cancelled. They both aim at the requirement of two witnesses if any one is to be convicted for an offence against the act, but the cancelled words were singularly clumsy. The house of lords seems to have desired to make perfectly clear a rule favourable to accused conservatives.

Sec. xxii. This proviso is substituted for a clause which stood at the end of sec. xviii. In this instance it may be well to print the text in such wise that the action of the lords in protecting the accused may be plainly seen.

Original Version.

Provided always and be it enacted by the authority aforesaid that if any person or persons shall hereafter happen to give any relief, aid, or comfort, or in any wise to[1] be aiding, helping, or comforting[2] the person or persons of any that shall hereafter [3]offend[3] in any matter or case of premunire[4] revived or made by this act [5]not knowing of such offence to be committed or done by the same person or persons at the time of such relief, aid, or comfort, that every such relief, aid, or comfort shall not in any wise be judged or taken to be any offence[5], any thing in this act[6] to the contrary notwithstanding.

Amended Version.

[1] *Omit* to.
[2] *Insert* to.

[3-3] *Substitute* happen to be any offender.
[4] *Insert* or treason.
[5-5] *Substitute* that then such relief, aid, or comfort given shall not be judged or taken to be any offence, unless there be two sufficient witnesses at the least that can and will openly testify and declare that the person or persons that so gave such relief, aid, or comfort had notice and knowledge of such offence committed and done by the said offender at the time of such relief, aid, or comfort so to him given or ministered.
[6] *Insert* contained or any other matter or cause.

Sec. xxiii. This curious section touching the pending cause of Richard Chetwood, Esq., stands on the third schedule. It evidently proceeds from the commons. A direction for delivery to the lords and a notice of the lords' assent are endorsed upon it.

Sec. xxiv. is on the fourth schedule, and this also represents the work of the lower house. It is concerned with the case of Robert Harecourt.

It will be noticed that in sec. i., which repeals an act of Philip and Mary, and in sec. ii., which revives certain acts of Henry VIII, and in sec. v., which

revives an act of Edward VI, and in sec. vi., which
repeals an act of Philip and Mary, and in sec. vii.,
which declares that no foreign prince, &c., shall exercise jurisdiction, &c., the phrase "the last day of this
session of parliament" has been substituted for some
other and much shorter phrase. Apparently that phrase
was "henceforth" or something equivalent thereto.   In
sec. v. and again in sec. vii. we may see a "henceforth" changed into "thenceforth."   Also in sec. iii.,
which revives certain earlier acts, the word "henceforth" still stands: the revival is to take place immediately.   Perhaps we may ascribe to mere carelessness
the fact that the change made in sec. i., ii., v., vi., and
vii. was not made in sec. iii.   The cause of the alteration we may probably find in the rule that "all acts of
parliament relate to the first day of parliament, if it be
not otherwise provided by the act[1]."   It may occur to
us that a certain retrospectivity had been desired by
those who drew the bill.   But I do not think that such
a wish can be laid to their charge.   When the bill was
first engrossed it already contained sec. xvii., which
explicitly says that the act is not to extend to any
offence against any of the revived acts if that offence
is committed "before the end of thirty days next after
the end of the session of the present parliament."
Moreover sec. xiv., which creates the offence of advisedly maintaining the authority of a foreign prelate,
was careful to allow a similar immunity until "after the
end of thirty days next after the determination of this
session of this present parliament."   I think therefore
that we may fairly absolve the framers of the measure

[1] Coke, *Fourth Institute*, p. 25.

of any intent to punish men for doing what was no offence at the time when it was done. The change, however, that was made in five sections may in the eyes of the conservatives have been worth making. Awkward consequences might flow from retrospective revivals and repeals, even though those consequences did not extend to the infliction of punishment on men who had broken no existing law.

At this point I may be allowed to say that I am by no means so willing as some commentators are to apply to the historical interpretation of an act of 1559 the well-known rule about the "relation" of statutes to the first day of the session. We know that rule well, because it stands in the Fourth Institute; but in 1559 Edward Coke was yet a little boy. I have never minutely explored the history of the rule, but I fancy that at the beginning of Elizabeth's reign the amount of written authority at its back consisted of a single dictum of a certain clerk of parliament which is found in the Year Book of 1455[1]. From the nature of the case it was a rule that could only come into play on extremely rare occasions, and I much doubt whether we ought to construct lofty edifices on the assumption that this canon of interpretation was generally known to laymen or even to lawyers before it found a place in the works of our great dogmatist. And so (to revert

---

[1] Y. B. 33 Hen. VI f. 17 (Pasch. pl. 8). The rule, however, passed into Broke's *Abridgement*, "Exposicion de certein parolx," pl. 33. Broke died in 1558; the *Abridgement* was published in 1568. In the medieval period the Statute Roll shows no date except that of the first day of the parliament, so interpreters would hardly have any choice.

to our starting point) the substitution of a reference to the end of the session for some such word as "henceforth" may be regarded rather as the removal of an ambiguity than as anything of greater significance.

We may now consider how the information that we have obtained by the contemplation of this parchment accords with what we may learn from other sources.

Apparently the long session of 1559 saw three attempts to deal with the question of ecclesiastical supremacy. Bill No. 1 was introduced into the lower house, read a first time on 9 Feb., read a second time on the 13th, debated on the 14th, committed on the 15th, and then to all appearance withdrawn or abandoned. Bill No. 2[1] was read a first time on the 21st, read a second time and ordered to be engrossed on the 22nd, read a third time on the 25th, with two provisos relating respectively to Richard Chetwood and Robert Harecourt. It was sent up to the lords on the 27th, read a first time on the 28th, and read a second time (after a fortnight's interval) on 13 March, and then committed to the Duke of Norfolk, the bishops of Exeter and Carlisle, and Lords Winchester, Westmoreland, Shrewsbury, Rutland, Sussex, Pembroke, Montagu, Clinton, Morley, Rich, Willoughby, and North. It was read a third time, with certain provisos added by the lords and sundry other amendments on 18 March. On that day it was carried to the commons, who read it (or the new matter in it) a first time on the 20th, a second time on the 21st, and a third time on the 22nd. Then it, with a new proviso annexed by the commons, was read thrice in the upper house on

---

[1] Expressly marked as *nova* in the *Commons' Journal.*

the 22nd. To that bill the royal assent was not given. The Easter recess and the Colloquy of Westminster here intervene.

Bill No. 3 was read a first time in the commons on 10 April. It was read a second time and ordered to be engrossed on the 12th, and it was read a third time on the 13th. Therefore I take it that the now existing engrossment was made between the session of the 12th and the session of the 13th. Then it was delivered to the lords on the 14th, and a note upon it tells that two schedules went with it. These will be the third and fourth concerning Chetwood and Harecourt, and they are represented in modern editions by secs. xxiii., xxiv.[1] The bill was read a first time in the lords on the 15th[2]. On the 17th it was read a second time and committed to the bishops of Ely and Carlisle, the Duke of Norfolk, Lords Arundel, Shrewsbury, Worcester, Rutland, Sussex, Bedford, Montagu, Clinton, Howard of Effingham, Rich, Hastings, and St John. On the 25th[3] a proviso to be annexed to the bill was read thrice and ordered to be engrossed. This I take to be the second schedule, containing secs. xx., xxi., xxii. Then the bill was read a third time and returned to the commons on the 26th. On the 27th it was returned with a new proviso to the lords, who seem to have read that proviso thrice on

---

[1] We have seen that similar or perhaps the very same schedules were annexed to Bill No. 2.

[2] The existing journal records no sitting between the 13th and the 17th.

[3] Here we become dependent on Dewes and the material that he had before him.

the 29th. This proviso I take to be the first schedule, or in other words sec. xix.

On the whole, then, as fairly certain conclusions, we may hold (1) that the commons send up a measure consisting of secs. i.–xviii., xxii., and xxiv.; (2) that the lords add sec. xx. (restriction of the scope of heresy), sec. xxi. (requirement of two witnesses), and sec. xxii. (aiding and comforting offenders), and at the same time cancel certain parts of secs. xv. and xviii., which the new clauses have made unnecessary; and (3) that the commons at the last moment add sec. xix., declaring that no act in this present parliament shall be adjudged to be "any error, heresy, schism, or schismatical opinion."

Other inferences must be much less certain. In particular we cannot tell how those interesting words about the first four councils forced their way into a section which as originally drawn seems to have been meant merely to protect the adherents of the old learning. Unfortunately erasure was permitted where we would rather have seen cancellation. However, in a given context a free use of the knife may not be insignificant.

Without making this paper too long I may be suffered to refer to the interesting question why that supremacy bill—"No. 2," as I call it—which had with great difficulty been forced through all its stages before Easter, was abandoned, so that a new bill had to be introduced. It seems to me that Froude, having access to Feria's letters, really solved a problem which had perplexed his predecessors; but, having a soul above parliamentary detail, he hardly made his solution sufficiently plain. There can, I think, be little doubt that Bill No. 2 declared that Elizabeth was supreme head of the church of England, though perhaps in its ultimate form, when the lords had amended it, she was given an embarrassing option of saying whether she was supreme head or not. And further there can, I think, be little doubt that at the last moment, and when the bill, having passed both houses, was no longer amendable, she decided (or for the first time published her decision) that she would not assume the irritating title.

Thus we obtain an explanation of a speech delivered by Archbishop Heath which, as many observers have seen, was a foolish, irrelevant speech if the bill that he was opposing did not profess to bestow or to acknowledge a supreme headship[1]. Then we have Feria's despatches. On 19 March[2] he relates how he has recently (since the 6th) had an interview with Sir Thomas Parry, who came, with Elizabeth's knowledge, to speak with him in private, and at the outset gave a promise that she would not take the title "head

---

[1] Dixon, *History of the Church of England*, v. 67, note: "A great part of Heath's speech is fired against 'supreme head,' but 'supreme head' was not in the bill. Hence nearly half of Heath's speech was thrown away." If Canon Dixon had attended to Froude he would not have said so confidently that "supreme head" was not in the bill. Dr Gee (*The Elizabethan Prayer Book*, p. 100) has come to another conclusion. Froude's only mistake, so it seems to me, is that he speaks as if after Easter "a variation of phrase was all that was necessary," and as if the bill was at once "conclusively passed." Really a new bill was necessary, was opposed in the house of lords, amended and reamended, before it became law.

[2] Kervyn de Lettenhove, *Relations Politiques*, I. p. 475.

of the church." The ambassador further says that
since then Elizabeth had by her own mouth made
him the same promise. On the 15th, so Feria adds,
"these heretics" had moderated their original proposal
and were providing that the queen might take the title
if she pleased. (On the 13th, we may observe, the bill
was before the lords and had been sent to a committee
on which conservatives and waverers were well represented.) Then on the 24th[1] Feria tells how he had by
letter begged Elizabeth not to confirm what parliament
had been doing until she had seen him after the Easter
recess. He then states that Elizabeth sent for him,
that he saw her at nine o'clock in the morning of the
24th (Good Friday), that she had resolved to go to
parliament that day at one o'clock after dinner for the
purpose of giving her assent to what had been done,
but that she had postponed her going until Monday,
3 April, and that the heretics were downcast. On
11 April[2] Feria takes credit to himself for this change
in the queen's intentions : on Good Friday she was
resolved to confirm what parliament had done, but
almost miraculously the blow had been averted. He
proceeds to say that the queen has declared in parliament (this might be by a minister) that she does not
wish to be called head of the church, also that on the
10th (the day on which Bill No. 3 makes its first
appearance in the journals) Cecil went to the lower
house and explained that, though the queen was
grateful for the offered title, she, out of humility,
would not assume it, but desired that some other form

[1] Kervyn de Lettenhove, *Relations Politiques*, I. p. 481.
[2] *Ibid.*, p. 493.

of words concerning supremacy or primacy might be devised.. Thereupon, so the Spaniard asserts, Cecil was told that what he was doing was contrary to the word of God, and that honourable members were surprised at his coming every day to the house with some new scheme. Then on the 15th Feria can inform his master that *cabeza* is changed into *gobernadora*.

This tale seems consistent with itself and with what we read in the journals of the two houses. Moreover it seems to let in light upon a very puzzling episode. Bill No. 2 passed its last stage on 22 March (Wednesday in Holy Week), and, if it ever became law, it would revive the Edwardian act touching the reception of the communion in both kinds. Now by a proclamation dated the 22nd[1] the queen says that in "the present last session" of parliament she, with the assent of lords and commons, "made" a statute reviving this act of her brother's reign, which statute, however, cannot be printed and published abroad in time for the Easter festival, being of great length; and that therefore the queen, by the advice of sundry of her nobility and commons "lately" assembled in parliament, declares to all her subjects that the Edwardian act is revived and in force. With some confidence we may infer that the man who drafted this proclamation believed that before it was issued the supremacy bill would have received the royal assent, and seemingly he also believed that parliament would have been dissolved or prorogued ; and then Feria explains to us

[1] Gee, *Elizabethan Prayer Book*, p. 255, from Dyson's *Proclamations*.

that almost by a miracle the queen determined at the very last moment to withhold her approbation[1].

And then Elizabeth reaped her reward. She rarely acted without consideration; and by "consideration" we mean what the lawyers mean. On 24 April Philip tells Feria that, as she has refused the supreme headship when it was offered to her, he has told the pope that there are hopes of her amendment and has en-

---

[1] Since the above sentences were in type I have seen the article in the *Dublin Review* (January 1903) in which Father J. H. Pollen has forestalled what I had to say of Bill No. 2 and the proclamation of 22 March. It was with great pleasure that I read what he had written. I thought of suppressing this part of my note, but will leave it standing, as he and I have approached the matter from different points. His surmise that the proclamation, of which we have an apparently unique copy, may never have been issued seems by no means improbable. He also remarks that Supremacy Bill No. 2 seems to have contained clauses concerning public worship, so that had the royal assent been given to it no Act of Uniformity would have been necessary and parliament might have been dissolved before Easter. When Mr Alfred Harrison was courteously showing to me the original of the lords' journal, he pointed out to me that already the clerk who wrote it had been confused by the plurality of Supremacy Bills. At the end of the session there is a list of the acts that have been passed. The twenty-fourth item in it is "An Act for restoring the Supremacy of the Imperial Crown of this Realm and repealing divers Acts of Parliament made to the contrary." The thirty-second item is (or was, for it has been cancelled) "An Act restoring to the Crown the ancient Jurisdiction over the State Ecclesiastical and Spiritual and abolishing all Foreign Power repugnant to the same." Then one of these two items having to be cancelled, the clerk struck his pen through the wrong one—namely, that which accurately gives the title of our Act of Uniformity. In the printed journal (vol. I. p. 579) the cancelled passage is simply omitted. Editors should know that cancelled passages sometimes tell interesting tales.

deavoured to prevent the issue of any decree concerning her bastardy[1]. What King Philip and the count of Feria were too orthodox and too haughty to know was that the amendment in Elizabeth's conduct, which they ascribed to the fear of Spain and of Rome, was ascribed by despicable heretics to the persuasive words of the godly Mr Lever. She was an economical woman and thought one stone enough for two birds[2].

But Romanists and Calvinists were not the only people to be considered. What of the Cæsaro-papalists: of the people who were for holding that the Marian statutes were void, because Mary had abandoned her divine office[3]: the people who talked about the word of God when Cecil came after Easter and explained that there must be a new bill? Perhaps these men saw in the new bill something that was sufficiently satisfactory. At any rate we ought to notice a fact too little noticed in recent books, namely, that Elizabeth's parliament certainly did not make it clear that the king of England is not supreme head of the church of England. It expressly revived what must have seemed both to catholics and Calvinists, if they looked

[1] Kervyn de Lettenhove, *Relations Politiques*, I. p. 508.

[2] Sandys to Parker, 30 April 1559, Parker's *Correspondence*, p. 66: "The bill of supreme government, of both the temporality and clergy, passeth with a proviso that nothing shall be judged heresy which is not condemned by the canonical Scriptures and four general councils. Mr Lever wisely put such a scruple in the queen's head that she would not take the title of supreme head." Sandys would hardly be telling Parker this at the end of April if all along it had been clear that Elizabeth was only to be supreme governor.

[3] See *Engl. Hist. Rev.* xv. 121–3.

into the matter, the most offensive of all King Henry's statutes, that concerning the doctors of the civil law (37 Hen. VIII, c. 17). That act states that Henry's "most royal majesty is and hath always been, by the word of God, supreme head in earth of the church of England, and hath full power and authority to correct, punish, and repress all manner of heresies . . . and to exercise all other manner of jurisdiction commonly called ecclesiastical jurisdiction." It also states that his majesty "is the only and undoubted supreme head of the church of England, and also of Ireland, to whom by Holy Scripture all authority and power is wholly given to hear and determine all manner of causes ecclesiastical." These words were revived in 1559, and, as I understand, remained on our statute book until 1863, when they were repealed by one of the Statute Law Revision Acts, which said, however, that the repeal was not to affect "any principle or rule of law[1]." This declaration, which we well might call the *Unam sanctam* of the royal supremacy, since it bases that supremacy upon the very Word of God, was statute law in the reign of Elizabeth, and, unless repealed by implication, was statute law in the reign of Victoria. But we must return to our parchments.

2. *The Act of Uniformity* (1 *Eliz. c.* 2).

The roll, which consists of two skins without any schedules, shows an order for delivery to the lords, the assent of the lords, and the assent of the queen.

[1] Stat. 26-27 Vict. c. 125.

Sec. i. (p. 14, l. 9): "the feast of *the Nativity* [of St John Baptist] next coming . . ."

Sec. i. (p. 14, ll. 13–4): "the said feast of *the Nativity* [of St John Baptist] in full force . . ." This at first sight would seem to point to a change in, and probably to a postponement of, the date fixed for the commencement of the act. But "the feast of the Nativity of St John Baptist" occurs twice in sec. ii., twice in sec. iii., once in sec. iv., and twice in sec. vii., and in none of these instances are there signs of interpolation. It does not seem likely that the different sections were to take effect at different times. The alteration in the text of the first two sections may be traceable to some general change of dates which was made in the bill while it was in the lower house, and to a change that was insufficiently obvious on the paper document that lay before the engrossing clerk.

Sec. ii. (p. 14, ll. 28–32): "with one alteration or addition of certain lessons to be used on every Sunday in the year [and the form of the litany altered and corrected,] and two sentences only added in the delivery of the sacrament to the communicants, and none other or otherwise . . ." This is an interesting interpolation. It looks like a lords' amendment. We may well imagine that there were some temporal peers who, though willing to vote for the Prayer Book as a whole, yet scrupled to use hard words of the bishop of Rome. However, there seems to be a little evidence that the offensive phrase had already disappeared out of "the Letanye used in the Quenes Maiesties Chappel, according to the tenor of the Proclamation[1]." Also those who are versed *in re diplomatica* will notice the recurrent "and" as a possible source of mischief. On the other side we may note that if there is not a change of hand there certainly seems to be a change of ink.

Sec. ii. (p. 14, ll. 33–4): "and that if any manner of *parson*, vicar or other whatsoever . . ."

Sec. ii. (p. 15, ll. 2–10): "or shall wilfully or obstinately (standing in the same) use * * *[2] any other rite, ceremony, order, form or manner of celebrating of the Lord's Supper openly or privily, or

---

[1] Clay, *Liturgies set forth in the Reign of Queen Elizabeth* (Parker Soc.), pp. x–xii, 12.

[2] Erasure of three letters.

Matins, Evensong, administration of the sacraments, or other open prayers *than is mentioned and set forth in the said book* (¹*open prayer in and throughout this act is meant that prayer which is for other* [to come unto or hear] either in common churches or private chapels or oratories, commonly called the service of the church), or shall preach, declare . . ." Here the change is extensive, but possibly represents what we should call a draftsman's amendment. Even as it is we find an "interpretation clause" let into the middle of the enactment, and perhaps the original text was yet clumsier.

Sec. ii. (p. 15, ll. 27–30): "it shall be lawful to all patrons or donors of all and singular the same spiritual promotions *or of any of them to present or collate to the same as though the persons so offending were dead*; and that if . . ."

Sec. ii. (p. 15, ll. 33–5): "the person so offending and convicted the third time [shall be deprived *ipso facto* of all his spiritual promotions, and also] shall suffer imprisonment during his life . . ." The repetition of "shall" may have caused a careless omission. If this be not so a penalty is increased. It is not, perhaps, uncharitable to suppose that some wavering noblemen may have been reconciled to the bill by thoughts of patronage. Nothing, it will be remembered, is being said that will deprive of his rights a patron who adheres to the old creed. That is a remarkable feature in the settlement; there is no test for patrons.

Sec. xiii. (p. 20, ll. 12–5): "such ornaments of the church and of the ministers thereof shall be retained and be in use as w*as*² in this³ church of England . . ." Unless some one thought fit deliberately to substitute "as was" for the "as were" which we nowadays expect, we seem to have here only the correction of some slip of the pen. In the many commentaries that have been written on this famous clause has it ever been noticed that the term "the metropolitan of this realm" is very curious? There never was any such person. If Archbishop Heath had been a kindly critic of the bill he would not have protested against a phrase which in the eyes of the uninstructed

---

¹ Dr Prothero, for the convenience of modern readers, inserts "[by]."

² The writing just fills the erasure.

³ So the act. The official edition gives "the."

might seem to give an undue preeminence to Canterbury. In the face of this trace of hasty draftsmanship we can hardly make the common assumption that the words "by the authority of parliament in the second year of the reign of King Edward VI" must have had some one precise meaning for all the then members of parliament. Few indeed are the critics of documents who have made allowance enough for mere carelessness and forgetfulness.

If there is anything significant in the somewhat unusual form of the enacting clause in this act—"be it enacted by the queen's highness with the assent of the lords and commons in this present parliament"—we can say with some certainty that this form had been chosen before the bill had left the house of commons, for the parchment shows no alteration at this point. It is possible that the bishops' dissent was discounted by the framers of the original bill; but it is not impossible that the omission of "spiritual and temporal" was an accident[1]. The Act of Supremacy has the usual words, and on the face of that act "the lords spiritual and temporal" are party to the abolition of the papal jurisdiction and the repeal of the Marian statutes. Also the general heading of the chancery roll for the session proclaims the assent *omnium dominorum tam spiritualium quam temporalium* to, among other acts, this Act of Uniformity[2].

What we see upon the parchment agrees with what we read elsewhere. The bill was introduced in the lower house, had its three readings on the 18th, 19th, and 20th of April, and when read the second time was ordered to be engrossed. It was brought in before the lords on the 25th, and had its three readings on the 26th, 27th, and 28th. Apparently it was not again

[1] See Pike, *Const. Hist. of the House of Lords*, p. viii.
[2] *Statutes of the Realm*, IV. 9.

sent to the commons; but from this fact we are not, I believe, entitled to infer that the lords made no amendments. The theory of the time seems to have required a return of the bill to the first house if the second house amended it in such a way that it would do more than the first house originally intended, but no return was necessary if the amendment made by the second house was of such a kind that it reduced the amount of work that the bill would do—for example, if the second house struck out one of a series of clauses which aimed at the creation of new offences. This is a matter about which further information is desirable. Some day we ought to have of these and some others of our acts of parliament a "diplomatic" edition such as Frenchmen or Germans would have made long ago.

It is well known that the *Journal of the House of Lords* becomes suddenly silent at the most exciting moment of this momentous session. It leaps from Saturday, 22 April, to Monday, 1 May : in other words, it leaps over the days on which the Supremacy Bill (No. 3) and the Uniformity Bill were receiving the assent of the house of lords. Is this due to accident or is it due to fraud? This question springs to our lips, for we have every reason to believe that the journal ought to have recorded the fact that not one lord spiritual voted for these bills and that every prelate who was present voted against them. This fact might indeed be notorious; but notoriety is not evidence, and in the then state of constitutional doctrine the queen's ministers may have wished to deprive their adversaries of the means of "averring by matter of record" that the first estate of the realm was no party to the religious settlement. With some slight hope that the handwriting might be more eloquent than print I obtained permission to see the original journal. It made no disclosure. In the first place, the work is so neat and regular that it looks, not like a journal kept day by day, but like a fair text made at the end of the session from notes that had been taken as the session proceeded. In the second place, the practice was to devote one page—or rather one side of a page—to every day, whether there was much or little to record. The session of Saturday, 22 April, is described on the back of a page and ends with an adjournment to the next Tuesday; the session of Monday, 1 May, is described on the front of the next page. Even if the book were unbound it would, I fear, reveal no more; for, as we apparently have to deal with a clean text made at the end of the session, any inference that we might be disposed to draw from the distribution of quires and sheets would be highly precarious, and "This may or may not have been an accident" would have to be our last word. There is, I may add, another omission which has not attracted so much attention. There is no record of the house having sat on 14 and 15 April. That it did sit on these days we know. The third Supremacy Bill was brought to it on the 14th, and read a first time on the 15th. Whether or not this increases the probability that the more serious omission was the result of mere carelessness is not very plain. We are dealing with a problem in which one of the quantities—the co-efficient of negligence, we might call it—is very much unknown.

THE CORPORATION SOLE[1]

PERSONS are either natural or artificial. The only natural persons are men. The only artificial persons are corporations. Corporations are either aggregate or sole.

This, I take it, would be an orthodox beginning for a chapter on the English Law of Persons, and such it would have been at any time since the days of Sir Edward Coke[2]. It makes use, however, of one very odd term which seems to approach self-contradiction, namely, the term "corporation sole," and the question may be raised, and indeed has been raised, whether our corporation sole is a person, and whether we do well in endeavouring to co-ordinate it with the corporation aggregate and the individual man. A courageous paragraph in Sir William Markby's *Elements of Law*[3] begins with the words, "There is a curious thing which we meet with in English law called a corporation sole," and Sir William then maintains that we have no better reason for giving this name to a rector or to the king than we have for giving it to an executor. Some little debating of this question will do no harm, and may perhaps do some good, for it is in some sort prejudicial to other and more important questions.

[1] *Law Quarterly Review*, Oct. 1900.
[2] Co. Lit. 2 a, 250 a.   [3] Markby, *Elements of Law*, § 145.

A better statement of what we may regard as the theory of corporations that is prevalent in England could hardly be found than that which occurs in Sir Frederick Pollock's book on Contract[1]. He speaks of "the Roman invention, adopted and largely developed in modern systems of law, of constituting the official character of the holders for the time being of the same office, or the common interest of the persons who for the time being are adventurers in the same undertaking, into an artificial person or ideal subject of legal capacities and duties." There follows a comparison which is luminous, even though some would say that it suggests doubts touching the soundness of the theory that is being expounded. "If it is allowable to illustrate one fiction by another, we may say that the artificial person is a fictitious substance conceived as supporting legal attributes."

It will not be news to readers of this journal that there are nowadays many who think that the personality of the corporation aggregate is in no sense and no sort artificial or fictitious, but is every whit as real and natural as is the personality of a man. This opinion, if it was at one time distinctive of a certain school of Germanists, has now been adopted by some learned Romanists, and also has found champions in France and Italy. Hereafter I may be allowed to say a little about it[2]. Its advocates, if they troubled themselves with our affairs, would claim many rules of English law as evidence that favours their doctrine and as protests against what they call "the Fiction Theory." They

---

[1] Pollock, *Contract*, ed. 6, p. 107.
[2] Dr Otto Gierke, of Berlin, has been its principal upholder.

would also tell us that a good deal of harm was done when, at the end of the Middle Ages, our comm n lawyers took over that theory from the canonists and tried, though often in a half-hearted way, to impose it upon the traditional English materials.

In England we are within a measurable distance of the statement that the only persons known to our law are men and certain organized groups of men which are known as corporations aggregate. Could we make that statement, then we might discuss the question whether the organized group of men has not a will of its own—a real, not a fictitious, will of its own— which is really distinct from the several wills of its members. As it is, however, the corporation sole stops, or seems to stop, the way. It prejudices us in favour of the Fiction Theory. We suppose that we personify offices.

Blackstone, having told us that "the honour of inventing" corporations "entirely belongs to the Romans," complacently adds that "our laws have considerably refined and improved upon the invention, according to the usual genius of the English nation: particularly with regard to sole corporations, consisting of one person only, of which the Roman lawyers had no notion[1]." If this be so, we might like to pay honour where honour is due, and to name the name of the man who was the first and true inventor of the corporation sole.

Sir Richard Broke died in 1558, and left behind him a Grand Abridgement, which was published in 1568. Now I dare not say that he was the father of "the corporation sole"; indeed I do not know that he

[1] 1 Comm. 469.

ever used precisely that phrase; but more than once he
called a parson a "corporation," and, after some little
search, I am inclined to believe that this was an unusual statement.   Let us look at what he says:

Corporations et Capacities, pl. 41 : Vide Trespas in fine ann. 7 E. 4
fo. 12 per Danby : one can give land to a parson and to his successors,
and so this is a corporation by the common law, and elsewhere it is
agreed that this is mortmain.

Corporations et Capacities, pl. 68 : Vide tithe *Encumbent* 14, that
a parson of a church is a corporation in succession to prescribe, to
take land in fee, and the like, 39 H. 6, 14 and 7 E. 4, 12.

Encumbent et Glebe, pl. 14 [Marginal note: *Corporacion en le
person*:] a parson can prescribe in himself and his predecessor, 39 H.
6, fo. 14; and per Danby a man may give land to a parson and his
successors, 7 E. 4, fo. 12; and the same per Littleton in his chapter
of Frankalmoin.

The books that Broke vouches will warrant his law,
but they will not warrant his language.   In the case of
Henry VI's reign[1] an action for an annuity is maintained against a parson on the ground that he and all
his predecessors have paid it; but no word is said of his
being a corporation.   In the case of Edward IV's reign
we may find Danby's dictum[2].   He says that land may
be given to a parson and his successors, and that when
the parson dies the donor shall not enter; but there is
no talk of the parson's corporateness.   So again we
may learn from Littleton's chapter on frankalmoin[3]
that land may be given to a parson and his successors;
but again there is no talk of the parson's corporateness.
There is, it is true, another passage in what at first
sight looks like Littleton's text which seems to imply

[1]   39 Hen. VI, f. 13 (Mich. pl. 17).
[2]   7 Edw. IV, f. 12 (Trin. pl. 2).   [3]   Lit. sec. 134.

that a parson is a body politic, and Coke took occasion of this passage to explain that every corporation is either "sole or aggregate of many," and by so doing drew for future times one of the main outlines of our Law of Persons[1]. However, Butler has duly noted the fact that just the words that are important to us at the present moment are not in the earliest editions of the Tenures, and I believe that we should be very rash if we ascribed them to Littleton[2].

Still the most that I should claim for Broke would be that by applying the term "corporation" to a parson, he suggested that a very large number of corporations sole existed in England, and so prepared the way for Coke's dogmatic classification of persons. Apparently for some little time past lawyers had occasionally spoken of the chantry priest as a corporation. So early as 1448 a writ is brought in the name of "John Chaplain of the Chantry of B. Mary of Dale"; objection is taken to the omission of his surname; and to this it is replied that the name in which he sues may be that by which he is corporate[3]. Then it would appear that in 1842 Bryan C. j. and Choke j. supposed the existence of a corpora-

---

[1] Lit. sec. 413; Co. Lit. 250 a. Other classical passages are Co. Lit. 2 a; *Sutton's Hospital* case, 10 Rep. 29 b.

[2] Littleton is telling us that no dying seised tolls an entry if the lands pass by "succession." He is supposed to add: "Come de prelates, abbates, priours, deans, ou parson desglyse [ou dauter corps politike]." But the words that are here bracketed are not in the Cambridge MS.; nor in the edition by Lettou and Machlinia; nor in the Rouen edition; nor in Pynson's. On the other hand they stand in one, at least, of Redman's editions.

[3] 27 Hen. VI, f. 3 (Mich. pl. 24): "poet estre entende que il est corporate par tiel nom."

tion in a case in which an endowment was created for a single chantry priest. Fitzherbert, seemingly on the authority of an unprinted Year Book, represents them as saying that "if the king grants me licence to make a chantry for a priest to sing in a certain place, and to give to him and his successors lands to the value of a certain sum, and I do this, that is a good corporation without further words[1]." Five years later some serjeants, if I understand them rightly, were condemning as void just such licences as those which Bryan and Catesby had discussed, and thereby were proposing to provide the lately crowned Henry VII with a rich crop of forfeitures. Keble opines that such a licence does not create a corporation (apparently because the king cannot delegate his corporation-making power), and further opines that the permission to give land to a corporation that does not already exist must be invalid[2]. Whether more came of this threat—for such it seems to be—I do not know[3]. Bullying the chantries was not a new practice in the days of Henry VII's son and grandson. In 1454 Romayn's Chantry, which had been confirmed by Edward III and Richard II, stood in need of a private Act of Parliament because a new generation of lawyers was not content with documents which had satisfied their less ingenious predecessors[4].

[1] Fitz. Abr. Graunt, pl. 30, citing T. 22 Edw. IV and M. 21 Edw. IV, 56. The earlier part of the case stands in Y. B. 21 Edw. IV, f. 55 (Mich. pl. 28). The case concerned the municipal corporation of Norwich, and the dictum must have been gratuitous.

[2] 2 Hen. VII, f. 13 (Hil. pl. 16).

[3] 20 Hen. VII, f. 7 (Mich. pl. 17): Rede J. seems to say that such a licence would make a corporation.

[4] Rot. Parl. v. 258. It had been supposed for a hundred and

Now cases relating to endowed chantry priests were just the cases which might suggest an extension of the idea of corporateness beyond the sphere in which organized groups of men are active. Though in truth it was the law of mortmain, and not any law touching the creation of fictitious personality, which originally sent the founders of chantries to seek the king's licence, still the king was by this time using somewhat the same language about the single chantry priest that he had slowly learned to use about bodies of burgesses and others. The king, so the phrase went, was enabling the priest to hold land to himself and his successors. An investigation of licences for the formation of chantries might lead to some good results. At present, however, I cannot easily believe that, even when the doom of the chantries was not far distant, English lawyers were agreed that the king could make, and sometimes did make, a corporation out of a single man or out of that man's official character. So late as the year 1522, the year after Richard Broke took his degree at Oxford, Fineux, C. J. B. R., was, if I catch the sense of his words, declaring that a corporation sole would be an absurdity, a nonentity. "It is argued," he said, "that the Master and his Brethren cannot make a gift to the Master, since he is the head of the corporation. Therefore let us see what a corporation is and what kinds of corporations there are. A corporation is an aggregation of head and body: not a head

twenty years that there had been a chantry sufficiently founded in law and to have stood stable in perpetuity "which for certain diminution of the form of making used in the law at these days is not held sufficient."

by itself, nor a body by itself; and it must be consonant to reason, for otherwise it is worth nought. For albeit the king desires to make a corporation of J. S., that is not good, for common reason tells us that it is not a permanent thing and cannot have successors[1]." The Chief Justice goes on to speak of the Parliament of King, Lords, and Commons as a corporation by the common law. He seems to find the essence of corporateness in the permanent existence of the organized group, the "body" of "members," which remains the same body though its particles change, and he denies that this phenomenon can exist where only one man is concerned. This is no permanence. The man dies and, if there is office or benefice in the case, he will have no successor until time has elapsed and a successor has been appointed. That is what had made the parson's case a difficult case for English lawyers. Fineux was against feigning corporateness where none really existed. At any rate, a good deal of his judgment seems incompatible with the supposition that "corporation sole" was in 1522 a term in current use.

That term would never have made its fortune had it not been applied to a class much wider and much less exposed to destructive criticism than was the class of permanently endowed chantry priests. That in all

---

[1] 14 Hen. VIII, f. 3 (Mich. pl. 2): "Car coment que le roy veut faire corporacion a J. S. ceo n'est bon, pur ceo que comon reson dit que n'est chose permanente et ne peut aver successor." Considering the context, I do not think that I translate this unfairly, though the words "faire corporacion a J. S." may not be exactly rendered or renderable. The king, we may say, cannot make a corporation which shall have J. S. for its basis. ["Grant to J. S. to be a corporation" seems the most plausible version.—Ed.]

the Year Books a parochial rector is never called a
corporation I certainly dare not say. Still, as a note
at the end of this paper may serve to show, I have
unsuccessfully sought the word in a large number of
places where it seemed likely to be found if ever it was
to be found at all. Such places are by no means rare.
Not unfrequently the courts were compelled to consider
what a parson could do and could not do, what leases
he could grant, what charges he could create, what sort
of estate he had in his glebe. Even in Coke's time
what we may call the theoretical construction of the
parson's relation to the glebe had hardly ceased to be
matter of debate. " In whom the fee simple of the
glebe is," said the great dogmatist, " is a question in
our books[1]." Over the glebe, over the parson's freehold, the parson's fee, the parson's power of burdening
his church or his successors with pensions or annuities,
there had been a great deal of controversy; but I
cannot find that into this controversy the term " corporation" was introduced before the days of Richard
Broke.

If now we turn from the phrase to the legal phenomena which it is supposed to describe, we must look
for them in the ecclesiastical sphere. Coke knew two
corporations sole that were not ecclesiastical, and I
cannot find that he knew more. They were a strange
pair: the king[2] and the chamberlain of the city of
London[3]. As to the civic officer, a case from 1468
shows us a chamberlain suing on a bond given to a

---

[1] Co. Lit. 340 b, 341 a.
[2] *Sutton's Hospital* case, 10 Rep. 29 b.
[3] *Fulwood's* case, 4 Rep. 65 a.

previous chamberlain "and his successors." The lawyers who take part in the argument say nothing of any corporation sole, and seem to think thát obligations could be created in favour of the Treasurer of England and his successors or the Chief Justice and his successors[1]. As to the king, I strongly suspect that Coke himself was living when men first called the king a corporation sole, though many had called him the head of a corporation. But of this at another time. The centre of sole corporateness, if we may so speak, obviously lies among ecclesiastical institutions. If there are any, there are thousands of corporations sole within the province of church property law.

But further, we must concentrate our attention upon the parish parson. We may find the Elizabethan and Jacobean lawyers applying the new term to bishops, deans, and prebendaries; also retrospectively to abbots and priors. Their cases, however, differed in what had been a most important respect from the case of the parochial rector. They were members, in most instances they were heads, of corporations aggregate. As is well known, a disintegrating process had long been at work within the ecclesiastical groups, more especially within the cathedral groups[2]. Already when the Year Books began their tale this process had gone far. The bishop has lands that are severed from the lands of the cathedral chapter or cathedral monastery; the dean has lands, the prebendary has lands or other sources of revenue. These partitions

[1] 8 Edw. IV, f. 18 (Mich. pl. 29).
[2] Lib. Ass. f. 117, ann. 25, pl. 8: "All the cathedral churches and their possessions were at one time a gross."

have ceased to be merely matters of internal economy; they have an external validity which the temporal courts recognize[1]. Still, throughout the Middle Ages it is never forgotten that the bishop who as bishop holds lands severed from the lands of the chapter or the convent holds those lands as head of a corporation of which canons or monks are members. This is of great theoretical importance, for it obviates a difficulty which our lawyers have to meet when they consider the situation of the parochial rector. In the case of the bishop a permanent "body" exists in which the ownership, the full fee simple, of lands can be reposed. "For," as Littleton says, "a bishop may have a writ of right of the tenements of the right of his church, for that the right is in his chapter, and the fee simple abideth in him and in his chapter[2]." The application of the term "corporation sole" to bishops, deans, and prebendaries marked the end of the long disintegrating process, and did some harm to our legal theories. If the episcopal lands belong to the bishop as a "corporation sole," why, we may ask, does he require the consent of the chapter if he is to alienate them? The "enabling statute" of Henry VIII and the "disabling statutes" of Elizabeth deprived this question of most of its practical importance. Thenceforward in the way of grants or leases the bishop could

---

[1] For instance, *Chapter* v. *Dean of Lincoln*, 9 Edw. III, f. 18 (Trin. pl. 3) and f. 33 (Mich. pl. 33).

[2] Lit. sec. 645. 6 Edw. III, f. 10, 11 (Hil. pl. 28), it is said in argument, "The right of the church [of York] abides rather in the dean and chapter than in the archbishop, car ceo ne mourt pas." This case is continued in 6 Edw. III, f. 50 (Mich. pl. 50).

do little with that he could not do without the chapter's consent[1]. It is also to be remembered that an abbot's powers were exceedingly large; he ruled over a body of men who were dead in the law, and the property of his "house" or "church" was very much like his own property. Even if without the chapter's consent he alienated land, he was regarded, at least by the temporal courts, much rather as one who was attempting to wrong his successors than as one who was wronging that body of "incapables" of which he was the head. It is to be remembered also that in England many of the cathedrals were monastic. This gave our medieval lawyers some thoughts about the heads of corporations aggregate and about the powerlessness of headless bodies which seem strange to us. A man might easily slip from the statement that the abbey is a corporation into the statement that the abbot is a corporation, and I am far from saying that the latter phrase was never used so long as England had abbots in it[2]; but, so far as I can see, the "corporation sole" makes its entry into the cathedral along with the royal supremacy and other novelties. Our interest lies in the parish church[3].

[1] See Coke's exposition, Co. Lit. 44 a, ff; and Blackstone's 2 Com. 319.

[2] Apparently in 1487 (3 Hen. VII, f. 11, Mich. pl. 1), Vavasor J. said "chescun abbe est corps politique, car il ne poet rien prendre forsque al use del Meason."

[3] Is the idea of the incapacity of a headless corporation capable of doing harm at the present day? Grant, *Corporations*, 110, says that "if a master of a college devise lands to the college, they cannot take, because at the moment of his death they are an incomplete body." His latest authority is Dalison, 31. In 1863 Dr Whewell or

Of the parish church there is a long story to be
told. Dr Stutz is telling it in a most interesting
manner[1]. Our own Selden, however, was on the true
track; he knew that the patron had once been more
than a patron[2], and we need go no further than Blackstone's Commentaries to learn that Alexander III did
something memorable in this matter[3]. To be brief: in
the twelfth century we may regard the patron as one
who has been the owner of church and glebe and
tithe, but an owner from whom ecclesiastical law has
gradually been sucking his ownership. It has been
insisting with varying success that he is not to make
such profit out of his church as his heathen ancestor
would have made out of a god-house. He must
demise the church and an appurtenant manse to an
ordained clerk approved by the bishop. The ecclesiastical "benefice" is the old Frankish *beneficium*, the
old land-loan of which we read in all histories of

his legal adviser was careful about this matter. A devise was made
"unto the Master, Fellows, and Scholars of Trinity College aforesaid
and their successors for ever, or, in case that devise would fail of
effect in consequence of there being no Master of the said College at
my death, then to the persons who shall be the Senior Fellows of the
said College at my decease and their heirs until the appointment of a
Master of such College, and from and after such appointment (being
within twenty-one years after my death) to the Master, Fellows, and
Scholars of the said College and their successors for ever." Thus
international law was endowed while homage was paid to the law of
England. But perhaps I do wrong in attracting attention to a rule
that should be, if it is not, obsolete.

   [1] Ulrich Stutz, *Geschichte des kirchlichen Benefizialwesens.* Only
the first part has yet appeared, but Dr Stutz sketched his programme
in *Die Eigenkirche*, Berlin, 1895.

   [2] *History of Tithes*, c. 12.   [3] 2 Bl. Com. 23.

feudalism[1]. In the eleventh century occurred the world-shaking quarrel about investitures. Emperors and princes had been endeavouring to treat even ancient cathedrals as their "owned churches." It was over the investiture of bishops that the main struggle took place; nevertheless, the principle which the Hildebrandine papacy asserted was the broad principle, "No investiture by the lay-hand." Slowly in the twelfth century, when the more famous dispute had been settled, the new rule was made good by constant pressure against the patrons or owners of the ordinary churches. Then a great lawyer, Alexander III (1159–81), succeeded, so we are told, in finding a new "juristic basis" for that right of selecting a clerk which could not be taken away from the patron. That right was to be conceived no longer as an offshoot of ownership, but as an outcome of the Church's gratitude towards a pious founder. Thus was laid the groundwork of the classical law of the Catholic Church about the *ius patronatus*; and, as Dr Stutz says, the Church was left free to show itself less and less grateful as time went on.

One part of Pope Alexander's scheme took no effect in England. Investiture by the lay hand could be suppressed. The parson was to be instituted and inducted by his ecclesiastical superiors. Thus his rights in church and glebe and tithe would no longer appear as rights derived out of the patron's ownership, and the patron's rights, if they were to be conceived— and in England they certainly would be conceived—as

---

[1] Stutz, "Lehen und Pfründe," *Zeitschrift der Savigny-Stiftung*, Germ. Abt. xx. 213.

rights of a proprietary kind, would be rights in an incorporeal thing, an "objectified" advowson.   But with successful tenacity Henry II and his successors asserted on behalf of the temporal forum no merely concurrent, but an absolutely exclusive jurisdiction over all disputes, whether possessory or petitory, that touched the advowson.   One consequence of this most important assertion was that the English law about this matter strayed away from the jurisprudence of the Catholic Church.   If we compare what we have learned as to the old English law of advowsons with the *ius commune* of the Catholic Church as it is stated by Dr Hinschius we shall see remarkable differences, and in all cases it is the law of England that is the more favourable to patronage[1].   Also in England we read of survivals which tell us that the old notion of the patron's ownership of the church died hard[2].

[1] *Kirchenrecht*, vol. III., p. 1 ff. In particular, English law regards patronage as normal.   When the ordinary freely chooses the clerk, this is regarded as an exercise of patronage; and so we come by the idea of a "collative advowson."   On the other hand, the catholic canonist should, so I understand, look upon patronage as abnormal, should say that when the bishop selects a clerk this is an exercise not of patronage but of "jurisdiction," and should add that the case in which a bishop as bishop is patron of a benefice within his own diocese, though not impossible, is extremely rare (Hinschius, op. cit. pp. 35-7).   To a king who was going to exercise the "patronage" annexed to vacant bishoprics, but could not claim spiritual jurisdiction, this difference was of high importance.

[2] See Pike, "Feoffment and Livery of Incorporeal Hereditaments," *Law Quarterly Review*, v. 29, 35 ff.   43 Edw. III, f. 1 (Hil. pl. 4): advowson conveyed by feoffment at church door.   7 Edw. III, f. 5 (Hil. pl. 7): Herle's dictum that not long ago men did not know what an advowson was, but granted churches.   11 Hen. VI, f. 4 (Mich. pl. 8):

But here we are speaking of persons. If the patron is not, who then is the owner of the church and glebe? The canonist will "subjectify" the church. The church (subject) owns the church (object). Thus he obtains temporary relief[1]. There remains the question how this owning church is to be conceived; and a troublesome question it is. What is the relation of the *ecclesia particularis* (church of Ely or of Trumpington) to the universal church? Are we to think of a *persona ficta*, or of a patron saint, or of the Bride of Christ, or of that vast corporation aggregate the *congregatio omnium fidelium*, or of Christ's vicar at Rome, or of Christ's poor throughout the world; or shall we say that walls are capable of retaining possession? Mystical theories break down: persons who can never be in the wrong are useless in a court of law. Much might be and much was written about these matters, and we may observe that the extreme theory which places the ownership of all church property in the pope was taught by at least one English canonist[2]. Within or behind a subjectified church lay problems which English lawyers might well endeavour to avoid.

On the whole it seems to me that a church is no

per Martin, an advowson will pass by livery, and in a writ of right of advowson the summons must be made upon the glebe. 38 Edw. III, f. 4 (scire facias): per Finchden, perhaps in old time the law was that patron without parson could charge the glebe. 9 Hen. VI, f. 52 (Mich. pl. 35): the advowson of a church is assets, for it is an advantage to advance one's blood or one's friend. 5 Hen. VII, f. 37 (Trin. pl. 3): per Vavasour and Danvers, an advowson lies in tenure, and one may distrain [for the services] in the churchyard.

[1] See Gierke, *Genossenschaftsrecht*, vol. III. *passim.*

[2] J. de Athon (ed. 1679), p. 76, gl. ad v. *summorum pontificum.*

person in the English temporal law of the later Middle Ages. I do not mean that our lawyers maintain one consistent strain of language. That is not so. They occasionally feel the attraction of a system which would make the parson a guardian or curator of an ideal ward. *Ecclesia fungitur vice minoris* is sometimes on their lips[1]. The thought that the " parson " of a church was or bore the " person " of the church was probably less distant from them than it is from us, for the two words long remained one word for the eye and for the ear. Coke, in a theoretical moment, can teach that in the person of the parson the church may sue for and maintain " her " right[2]. Again, it seems that conveyances were sometimes made to a parish church without mention of the parson[3], and when an action for land is brought against a rector he will sometimes say, " I found my church seised of this land, and therefore pray aid of patron and ordinary[3]."

We may, however, remember at this point that in modern judgments and in Acts of Parliament lands are often spoken of as belonging to "a charity." Still, our books do not teach us that charities are persons. Lands that belong to a charity are owned, if not by a corporation, then by some man or men. Now we must not press this analogy between medieval churches and modern charities very far, for medieval lawyers were but slowly elaborating that idea of a trust which bears heavy weights in modern times and enables all religious

---

[1] Pollock and Maitland, *Hist. Eng. Law*, ed. 2, i. 503.

[2] Co. Lit. 300 b.

[3] 11 Hen. IV, f. 84 (Trin. pl. 34). But see 8 Hen. V, f. 4 (Hil. pl. 15).

bodies, except one old-fashioned body, to conduct their affairs conveniently enough without an apparatus of corporations sole. Still, in the main, church and charity seem alike. Neither ever sues, neither is ever sued. The parson holds land "in right of his church." So the king can hold land or claim a wardship or a presentation, sometimes "in right of his crown," but sometimes "in right of" an escheated honour or a vacant bishopric. So too medieval lawyers were learning to say that an executor will own some goods in his own right and others *en autre droit*.

The failure of the church to become a person for English temporal lawyers is best seen in a rule of law which can be traced from Bracton's day to Coke's through the length of the Year Books. A bishop or an abbot can bring a writ of right, a parson cannot. The parson requires a special action, the *iurata utrum*; it is a *singulare beneficium*[1] provided to suit his peculiar needs. The difficulty that had to be met was this :— You can conceive ownership, a full fee simple, vested in a man "and his heirs," or in an organized body of men such as a bishop and chapter, or abbot and convent, but you cannot conceive it reposing in the series, the intermittent series, of parsons. True, that the *iurata utrum* will be set to inquire whether a field belongs (*pertinet*) to the plaintiff's "church." But the necessity for a special action shows us that the *pertinet* of the writ is thought of as the *pertinet* of appurtenancy, and not as the *pertinet* of ownership. As a garden belongs to a house, as a stopper belongs to a bottle,

[1] Bracton, f. 286 b.

not as house and bottle belong to a man, so the glebe belongs to the church.

If we have to think of "subjectification" we have to think of "objectification" also. Some highly complex "things" were made by medieval habit and perceived by medieval law. One such thing was the manor; another such thing was the church. Our ⸝pious ancestors talked of their churches much as they talked of their manors. They took esplees of the one and esplees of the other; they exploited the manor and exploited the church. True, that the total sum of right, valuable right, of which the church was the object might generally be split between parson, patron, and ordinary. Usually the claimant of an advowson would have to say that the necessary exploitation of the church had been performed, not by himself, but by his presentee. But let us suppose the church impropriated by a religious house, and listen to the head of that house declaring how to his own proper use he has taken esplees in oblations and obventions, great tithes, small tithes, and other manner of tithes[1]. Or let us see him letting a church to farm for a term of years at an annual rent[2]. The church was in many contexts a complex thing, and by no means *extra commercium*. I doubt if it is generally known how much was done in the way of charging "churches" with annuities or pensions in the days of Catholicism. On an average every year seems to produce one law-suit that is worthy to be reported and has its origin in this practice. In the Year Books the church's objectivity

[1] 5 Edw. III, f. 18 (Pasch. pl. 18).
[2] 9 Hen. V, f. 8 (Mich. pl. 1).

as the core of an exploitable and enjoyable mass of wealth is, to say the least, far more prominent than its subjectivity[1].

"If," said Rolfe Serj., in 1421, "a man gives or devises land to God and the church of St Peter of Westminster, his gift is good, for the church is not the house nor the walls, but is to be understood as the *ecclesia spiritualis*, to wit, the abbot and convent, and because the abbot and convent can receive a gift, the gift is good ... but a parish church can only be understood as a house made of stones and walls and roof which cannot take a gift or feoffment[2]."

We observe that God and St Peter are impracticable feoffees, and that the learned serjeant's "spiritual church" is a body of men at Westminster. It seems

---

[1] Sometimes the thing that is let to farm is called, not the church, but the rectory. This, however, does not mean merely the rectory house. 21 Hen. VII, f. 21 (Pasch. pl. 11): "The church, the churchyard, and the tithe make the rectory, and under the name of rectory they pass by parol." See *Greenslade* v. *Darby*, L. R. 3 Q. B. 421: The lay impropriator's right to the herbage of the churchyard maintained against a perpetual curate: a learned judgment by Blackburn J. See also Lyndwood, *Provinciale*, pp. 154 ff, as to the practice of letting churches. 30 Edw. III, f. 1: Action of account against bailiff of the plaintiff's church; unsuccessful objection that defendant should be called bailiff, not of the church, but of a rectory: car esglise est a les parochiens, et nemy le soen [the parson's]. This is the only instance that I have noticed in the Year Books of any phrase which would seem to attribute to the parishioners any sort of proprietary right in the church.

[2] 8 Hen. V, f. 4 (Hil. pl. 15). I omit some words expressing the often recurring theory that the conventual church cannot accept a gift made when there is no abbot. Headless bodies cannot act, but they can retain a right.

to me that throughout the Middle Ages there was far more doubt than we should expect to find as to the validity of a gift made to "the [parish] church of X," or to "the parson of X and his successors," and that Broke was not performing a needless task when he vouched Littleton and Danby to warrant a gift that took the latter of these forms. Not much land was, I take it, being conveyed to parish churches or parish parsons, while for the old glebe the parson could have shown no title deeds. It had been acquired at a remote time by a slow expropriation of the patron.

The patron's claim upon it was never quite forgotten. Unless I have misread the books, a tendency to speak of the church as a person grows much weaker as time goes on. There is more of it in Bracton than in Littleton or Fitzherbert[1]. English lawyers were no longer learning from civilians and canonists, and were constructing their grand scheme of estates in land. It is with their heads full of "estates" that they approach the problem of the glebe, and difficult they find it. At least with the consent of patron and ordinary, the parson can do much that a tenant for life cannot do[2];

---

[1] 21 Edw. IV, f. 61 (Mich. pl. 32): per Pigot, fines were formerly received which purported to convey *Deo et ecclesiae*, but the judges of those days were ignorant of the law. 9 Hen. VII, f. 11 (Mich. pl. 6): conveyances to God and the church are still held valid if made in old time; they would not be valid if made at the present day.

[2] Even without the active concurrence of patron and ordinary, who perhaps would make default when prayed in aid, the parson could do a good deal in the way of diminishing his successor's revenue by suffering collusive actions. See e.g. 4 Hen. VII, f. 2 (Hil. fol. 4), where the justices in Cam. Scac. were divided, four against three.

and, on the other hand, he cannot do all that can be done by a tenant in fee simple. It is hard to find a niche for the rector in our system of tenancies. But let us observe that this difficulty only exists for men who are not going to personify churches or offices.

There is an interesting discussion in 1430[1]. The plaintiff's ancestor had recovered land from a parson, the predecessor of the defendant, by writ of *Cessavit*; he now sues by *Scire facias*, and the defendant prays aid of the patron; the question is whether the aid prayer is to be allowed.

Cottesmore J. says :—

"I know well that a parson has only an estate for the term of his life; and it may be that the plaintiff after the judgment released to the patron, and such a release would be good enough, for the reversion of the church is in him [the patron], and this release the parson cannot plead unless he has aid. And I put the case that a man holds land of me for the term of his life, the reversion being in me; then if one who has right in the land releases to me who am in reversion, is not that release good? So in this case."

Paston J. takes the contrary view :—

"I learnt for law that if *Praecipe quod reddat* is brought against an abbot or a parson, they shall never have aid, for they have a fee simple in the land, for the land is given to them and their successors, so that no reversion is reserved upon the gift....If a writ of right is brought against them they shall join the mise upon the *mere droit*, and that proves that they have a better estate than for term of life. And I have never seen an estate for life with the reversion in no one; for if the parson dies the freehold of the glebe is not in the patron, and no writ for that land is maintainable against any one until there is another parson. So it seems to me that aid should not be granted."

---

[1] 8 Hen. VI, f. 24 (Hil. pl. 10).

Then speaks Babington C. J., and, having put an ingenious case in which, so he says, there is a life estate without a reversion, he proceeds to distinguish the case of the abbot from that of the parson :—

"When an abbot dies seised the freehold always remains in the house (*meason*) and the house cannot be void...but if a parson dies, then the church is empty and the freehold in right is in the patron, notwithstanding that the patron can take no advantage of the land; and if a recovery were good when the patron was not made party, then the patronage would be diminished, which would be against reason. So it seems to me that [the defendant] shall have aid."

Two other judges, Strangways and Martin, are against the aid prayer ; Martin rejects the theory that the parson is tenant for life, and brings into the discussion a tenant in tail after possibility of issue extinct. On the whole the case is unfavourable to the theory which would make the parson tenant for life and the patron reversioner, but that this theory was held in 1430 by a Chief Justice of the Common Pleas seems plain and is very remarkable. The weak point in the doctrine is the admission that the patron does not take the profits of the vacant church. These, it seems settled, go to the ordinary[1], so that the patron's "reversion" (if any) looks like a very nude right. But the Chief Justice's refusal to repose a right in an empty "church," while he will place one in a "house" that has some monks in it, should not escape attention.

Nearly a century later, in 1520, a somewhat similar

---

[1] 11 Hen. VI, f. 4 (Mich. pl. 8): per Danby, the ordinary shall have the occupation and all the profit. 9 Hen. V, f. 14 (Mich. pl. 19) accord. See Stat. 28 Hen. VIII, c. 11, which gives the profits to the succeeding parson.

case came before the court[1], and we still see the same diversity of opinion. Broke J. (not Broke of Abridgement) said that the parson had the fee simple of the glebe *in iure ecclesiae*.

"It seems to me," said Pollard J., "that the fee simple is in the patron ; for [the parson] has no inheritance in the benefice and the fee cannot be in suspense, and it must be in the patron, for the ordinary only has power to admit a clerk. And although all parsons are made by the act of the ordinary, there is nothing in the case that can properly be called succession. For if land be given to a parson and his successor, that is not good, for he [the parson] has no capacity to take this ; but if land be given *Priori et Ecclesiae* that is good, because there is a corporation....And if the parson creates a charge, that will be good only so long as he is parson, for if he dies or resigns, his successor shall hold the land discharged; and this proves that the parson has not the fee simple. But if in time of vacation patron and ordinary charge the land, the successor shall hold it charged, for they [patron and ordinary] had at the time the whole interest[2]."

Eliot J. then started a middle opinion :—

"It seems to me that the parson has the fee *in iure ecclesiae*, and not the patron—as one is seised in fee *in iure uxoris suae*—and yet for some purposes he is only tenant for life. So tenant in tail has a fee tail, and yet he has only for the term of his life, for if he makes a lease or grants a rent charge, that will be only for the term of his life....As to what my brother Pollard says, namely, that in time of vacation patron and ordinary can create a charge, that is not so."

Then Brudenel C. J. was certain that the parson has a fee simple :—

"He has a fee simple by succession, as an heir [has one] by inheritance, and neither the ordinary nor the patron gives this to the parson."

---

[1] 12 Hen. VIII, f. 7 (Mich. pl. 1).

[2] Apparently Belknap J. had said that such a charge would be good : Fitz. Abr. Annuitie, pl. 53 (8 Ric. II).

Pollard's opinion was belated ; but we observe that on the eve of the Reformation it was still possible for an English judge to hold that the ownership, the fee simple, of the church is in the patron. And at this point it will not be impertinent to remember that even at the present day timber felled on the glebe is said to belong to the patron[1].

In the interval between these two cases Littleton had written. He rejected the theory which would place the fee simple in the patron; but he also rejected that which would place it in the parson. Of any theory which would subjectify the church or the parson's office or dignity he said nothing ; and nothing of any corporation sole. Let us follow his argument.

He is discussing "discontinuance" and has to start with this, that if a parson or vicar grants land which is of the right of his church and then dies or resigns, his successor may enter[2]. In other words, there has been no discontinuance. "And," he says, "I take the cause to be for that the parson or vicar that is seised as in right of his church hath no right of the fee simple in the tenements, and the right of the fee simple doth not[3] abide in another person." That, he explains, is the difference between the case of the parson and

---

[1] *Sowerby* v. *Fryer* (1869), L. R. 8 Eq. 417, 423 : James V. C. : "I never could understand why a vicar who has wrongfully cut timber should not be called to account for the proceeds after he has turned it into money, in order that they may be invested for the benefit of the advowson ; *it being conceded that the patron is entitled to the specific timber.*"

[2] Litt. sec. 643.

[3] There are various readings, but the argument seems plainly to require this "not."

the case of a bishop, abbot, dean, or master of a hospital; their alienations may be discontinuances, his cannot; "for a bishop may have a writ of right of the tenements of the right of the church, for that the right is in his chapter, and the fee simple abideth in him and his chapter....And a master of a hospital may have a writ of right because the right remaineth in him and in his *confreres*, &c.; and so in other like cases. But a parson or vicar cannot have a writ of right, &c." A discontinuance, if I rightly understand the matter, involves the alienation of that in which the alienor has some right, but some right is vested in another person. In the one case the bishop alienates what belongs to him and his chapter; in the other case the parson alienates what belongs to no one else.

Then we are told[1] that the highest writ that a parson or vicar can have is the *Utrum*, and that this "is a great proof that the right of fee is not in them, nor in others. But the right of the fee simple is in abeyance; that is to say, that it is only in the remembrance, intendment, and consideration of law, for it seemeth to me that such a thing and such a right which is said in divers books to be in abeyance is as much as to say in Latin, Talis res, vel tale rectum, quae vel quod non est in homine adtunc superstite, sed tantummodo est et consistit in consideratione et intelligentia legis, et, quod alii dixerunt, talem rem aut tale rectum fore in nubibus." Yes, rather than have any dealings with fictitious persons, subjectified churches, personified dignities, corporations that are not bodies,

[1] Lit. sec. 646.

we will have a subjectless right, a fee simple in the clouds[1].

Then in a very curious section Littleton[2] has to face the fact that the parson with the assent of patron and ordinary can charge the glebe of the parsonage perpetually. Thence, so he says, some will argue that these three persons, or two or one of them, must have a fee simple. Littleton must answer this argument. Now this is one of those points at which a little fiction might give us temporary relief. We might place the fee simple in a fictitious person, whose lawfully appointed guardians give a charge on the property of their imaginary ward. We might refer to the case of a town council which sets the common seal to a conveyance of land which belongs to the town. But, rather than do anything of the kind, Littleton has recourse to a wholly different principle.

The charge has been granted by parson, patron, and ordinary, and then the parson dies. His successor cannot come to the church but by the presentment of the patron and institution of the ordinary, "and for this cause he ought to hold himself content and agree to that which his patron and the ordinary have lawfully done before." In other words, the parson is debarred by decency and gratitude from examining the mouth of the gift horse. No one compelled him to accept the benefice. Perhaps we might say that by his own act he is estopped from quarrelling with the past acts

[1] Apparently the talk about a fee simple *in nubibus* began in debates over contingent remainders: 11 Hen. IV, f. 74 (Trin. pl. 14).

[2] Lit. sec. 648.

of his benefactors. Such a piece of reasoning would surely be impossible to any one who thought of the church or the rector's office as a person capable of sustaining proprietary rights.

Before Littleton's Tenures came to Coke's hands, Broke or some one else had started the suggestion that a parson was a corporation, or might be likened to a corporation. Apparently that suggestion was first offered by way of explaining how it came about that a gift could be made to a parson and his successors. Now it seems to me that a speculative jurist might have taken advantage of this phrase in order to reconstruct the theory of the parson's relation to the glebe. He might have said that in this case, as in the case of the corporation aggregate, we have a *persona ficta*, an ideal subject of rights, in which a fee simple may repose; that the affairs of this person are administered by a single man, in the same way in which the affairs of certain other fictitious persons are administered by groups of men; and that the rector therefore must be conceived not as a proprietor but as a guardian, though his powers of administration are large, and may often be used for his own advantage. And Coke, in his more speculative moments, showed some inclination to tread this path. Especially is this the case when he contrasts " persons natural created of God, as J. S., J. N., &c., and persons incorporate and politic created by the policy of man," and then adds that the latter are " of two sorts, viz. aggregate or sole[1]." But to carry that theory through would have necessitated a breach with traditional ideas of the

[1] Co. Litt. 2 a.

parson's estate and a distinct declaration that Littleton's way of thinking had become antiquated[1]. As it is, when the critical point is reached and we are perhaps hoping that the new-found corporation sole will be of some real use, we see that it gives and can give Coke no help at all, for, after all, Coke's corporation sole is a man : a man who fills an office and can hold land "to himself and his successors," but a mortal man.

When that man dies the freehold is in abeyance. Littleton had said that this happened "if a parson of a church dieth." Coke adds[2] : "So it is of a bishop, abbot, dean, archdeacon, prebend, vicar, and of every other sole corporation or body politic, presentative, elective, or donative, which inheritances put in abeyance are by some called *haereditates iacentes.*" So here we catch our corporation sole *in articulo mortis.* If God did not create him, then neither the inferior not yet the superior clergy are God's creatures.

So much as to the state of affairs when there is no parson : the freehold is in abeyance, and "the fee and right is in abeyance." On the other hand, when there is a parson, then, says Coke[3], "for the benefit of the church and of his successor he is in some cases esteemed in law to have a fee qualified ; but, to do anything to the prejudice of his successor, in many cases the law adjudgeth him to have in effect but an estate for life." And again, "It is evident that to many purposes a parson hath but in effect an estate for life, and to many

---

[1] In *Wythers* v. *Iseham*, Dyer, f. 70 (pl. 43), the case of the parson had been noticed as the only exception to the rule that the freehold could not be in abeyance.

[2] Co. Litt. 342 b.   [3] *Ibid.* 341 a.

a qualified fee simple, but the entire fee and right is not in him."

This account of the matter seems to have been accepted as final. Just at this time the Elizabethan statutes were giving a new complexion to the practical law. The parson, even with the consent of patron and ordinary, could no longer alienate or charge the glebe, and had only a modest power of granting leases. Moreover, as the old real actions gave place to the action of ejectment, a great deal of the old learning fell into oblivion. Lawyers had no longer to discuss the parson's aid prayer or his ability or inability to join the mise on the *mere droit*, and it was around such topics as these that the old indecisive battles had been fought. Coke's theory, though it might not be neat, was flexible : for some purposes the parson has an estate for life, for others a qualified fee. And is not this the orthodoxy of the present day ? The abeyance of the freehold during the vacancy of the benefice has the approval of Mr Challis[1]; the "fee simple qualified" appears in Sir H. Elphinstone's edition of Mr Goodeve's book[2].

Thus, so it seems to me, our corporation sole refuses to perform just the first service that we should require at the hands of any reasonably useful *persona ficta*. He or it refuses to act as the bearer of a right which threatens to fall into abeyance or dissipate itself among the clouds for want of a "natural" custodian. I say

---

[1] Challis, *Real Property*, ed. 2, p. 91.

[2] Goodeve, *Real Property*, ed. 4, pp. 85, 133. See the remarks of Jessel M. R. in *Mulliner* v. *Midland Railway Co.*, 11 Ch. D. 622.

"he or it "; but which ought we to say ?   Is a beneficed
clergyman—for instance, the Rev. John Styles—a
corporation sole, or is he merely the administrator or
representative of a corporation sole ?   Our Statute
Book is not very consistent.   When it was decreeing
the Disestablishment of the Irish Church it declared
that on January 1, 1871, every ecclesiastical corporation
in Ireland, whether sole or aggregate, should be dissolved[1], and it were needless to say that this edict
did not contemplate a summary dissolution of worthy
divines.   But turn to a carefully worded Statute of
Limitations.   " It shall be lawful for any archbishop,
bishop, dean, prebendary, parson, master of a hospital,
or other spiritual or eleemosynary corporation sole to
make an entry or distress, or to bring an action or suit
to recover any land or rent within such period as
hereinafter is mentioned next after the time at which
the right of such corporation sole or of his predecessor...
shall have first accrued[2]."   Unquestionably for the
draftsman of this section the corporation sole was,
as he was for Coke, a man, a mortal man.

If our corporation sole really were an artificial
person created by the policy of man we ought to
marvel at its incompetence.   Unless custom or statute
aids it, it cannot (so we are told) own a chattel, not
even a chattel real[3].   A different and an equally
inelegant device was adopted to provide an owning
"subject" for the ornaments of the church and the
minister thereof—adopted at the end of the Middle

[1]   32 & 33 Vict. c. 42, sec. 13.
[2]   3 & 4 Will. IV, c. 27, sec. 29.
[3]   *Fulwood's* case, 4 Rep. 65 a ; *Arundel's* case, Hob. 64.

Ages by lawyers who held themselves debarred by the theory of corporations from frankly saying that the body of parishioners is a corporation aggregate. And then we are also told that in all probability a corporation sole "cannot enter into a contract except with statutory authority or as incidental to an interest in land[1]." What then can this miserable being do? It cannot even hold its glebe tenaciously enough to prevent the freehold falling into abeyance whenever a parson dies.

When we turn from this mere ghost of a fiction to a true corporation, a corporation aggregate, surely the main phenomenon that requires explanation, that sets us talking of personality and, it may be, of fictitious personality, is this, that we can conceive and do conceive that legal transactions, or acts in the law, can take place and do often take place between the corporation of the one part and some or all of the corporators of the other part. A beautiful modern example[2] shows us eight men conveying a colliery to a company of which they are the only members; and the Court of Appeal construes this as a "sale" by eight persons to a ninth person, though the price consists not in cash, but in the whole share capital of the newly formed corporation. But to all appearance there can be no legal transaction, no act in the law, between the corporation sole and the natural man who is the one and only corporator. We are told, for example, that "a sole corporation, as a bishop or a parson, cannot

---

[1] Pollock, *Contract*, ed. 6, p. 109. The principal modern authority is *Howley* v. *Knight*, 14 Q. B. 240.

[2] *Foster & Son, Lim.* v. *Com. of Inland Rev.* [1894] 1 Q. B. 156.

make a lease to himself, because he cannot be both lessor and lessee[1]." We are told that "if a bishop hath lands in both capacities he cannot give or take to or from himself[2]." Those who use such phrases as these show plainly enough that in their opinion there is no second "person" involved in the cases of which they speak : "he" is "himself," and there is an end of the matter[3]. I can find no case in which the natural man has sued the corporation sole or the corporation sole has sued the natural man.

When a man is executor, administrator, trustee, bailee, or agent, we do not feel it necessary to speak of corporateness or artificial personality, and I fail to see why we should do this when a man is a beneficed clerk. Whatever the Romans may have done—and about this there have been disputes enough—we have made no person of the *hereditas iacens*. On an intestate's death we stopped the gap with no figment, but with a real live bishop, and in later days with the Judge of the Probate Court : English law has liked its persons to be real. Our only excuse for making a fuss over the parson is that, owing to the slow expropriation of the patron, the parson has an estate in church and glebe which refuses to fit into any of the ordinary categories of our real property law ; but, as we have already seen, our talk of corporations sole has failed to

---

[1] *Salter* v. *Grosvenor*, 8 Mod. 303, 304.

[2] *Wood* v. *Mayor, &c., of London*, Salk. 396, 398. See also Grant, *Corporations*, 635.

[3] The matter was well stated by Broke J. in 14 Hen. VIII, f. 30 (Pasch. pl. 8) : a parson cannot grant unto or enfeoff himself, "car comment il ad deux respects uncore il est mesme le person."

solve or even to evade the difficulty. No one at the present day would dream of introducing for the first time the scheme of church property law that has come down to us, and I think it not rash to predict that, whether the Church of England remains established or no, churches and glebes will some day find their owners in a corporation aggregate or in many corporations aggregate[1]. Be that as it may, the ecclesiastical corporation sole is no "juristic person"; he or it is either natural man or juristic abortion.

The worst of his or its doings we have not yet considered. He or it has persuaded us to think clumsy thoughts or to speak clumsy words about King and Commonwealth[2].

[1] See *Eccl. Com.* v. *Pinney* [1899] 1 Ch. 99, a case prophetic of the ultimate fate of the glebe.

[2] In looking through the Year Books for the corporation sole, I took note of a large number of cases in which this term is not used, but might well have been used had it been current. I thought at one time of printing a list of these cases, but forbear, as it would fill valuable space and only points to a negative result. The discussion of the parson's rights in F. N. B. 109–112 is one of the places to which we naturally turn, but turn in vain.

THE CROWN AS CORPORATION[1]

"THE greatest of artificial persons, politically speaking, is the State. But it depends on the legal institutions and forms of every commonwealth whether and how far the State or its titular head is officially treated as an artificial person. In England we now say that the Crown is a corporation: it was certainly not so when the king's peace died with him, and 'every man that could forthwith robbed another[2].'"

I quote these words from Sir F. Pollock's *First Book of Jurisprudence*. They may serve to attract a little interest to that curious freak of English law, the corporation sole. In a previous paper I have written something concerning its history[3]. I endeavoured to show that this strange conceit originated in the sixteenth century and within the domain of what we may call "church property law." It held out a hope, which proved to be vain, that it would provide a permanent "subject" in which could be reposed that fee simple of the parochial glebe which had been slowly abstracted from the patron and was not comfortable in those clouds to which Littleton had banished it. Then, following in the steps of Sir William Markby, I ventured to say

---

[1] *Law Quarterly Review*, April 1901.
[2] Pollock, *First Book of Jurisprudence*, p. 113.
[3] *L. Q. R.* XVI. 335.

that this corporation sole has shown itself to be no "juristic person," but is either a natural man or a juristic abortion.

If the corporation sole had never trespassed beyond the ecclesiastical province in which it was native, it would nowadays be very unimportant. Clearly it would have no future before it, and the honour of writing its epitaph would hardly be worth the trouble. Unfortunately, however, the thought occurred to Coke—or perhaps in the first instance to some other lawyer of Coke's day—that the King of England ought to be brought into one class with the parson : both were to be artificial persons and both were to be corporations sole.

Whether the State should be personified, or whether the State, being really and naturally a person, can be personified, these may be very interesting questions. What we see in England, at least what we see if we look only at the surface, is, not that the State is personified or that the State's personality is openly acknowledged, but (I must borrow from one of Mr Gilbert's operas) that the king is "parsonified." Since that feat was performed, we have been, more or less explicitly, trying to persuade ourselves that our law does not recognize the personality or corporate character of the State or Nation or Commonwealth, and has no need to do anything of the sort if only it will admit that the king, or, yet worse, the Crown, is not unlike a parson.

It would be long to tell the whole story of this co-ordination of king and parson, for it would take us deep into the legal and political thoughts of the

Middle Ages. Only two or three remarks can here be hazarded[1].

The medieval king was every inch a king, but just for this reason he was every inch a man and you did not talk nonsense about him. You did not ascribe to him immortality or ubiquity or such powers as no mortal can wield. If you said that he was Christ's Vicar, you meant what you said, and you might add that he would become the servant of the devil if he declined towards tyranny. And there was little cause for ascribing to him more than one capacity. Now and then it was necessary to distinguish between lands that he held in right of his crown and lands which had come to him in right of an escheated barony or vacant bishopric. But in the main all his lands were his lands, and we must be careful not to read a trusteeship for the nation into our medieval documents. The oft-repeated demand that the king should "live of his own" implied this view of the situation. I do not mean that this was at any time a complete view. We may, for example, find the lawyers of Edward II's day catching up a notion that the canonists had propagated, declaring that the king's crown is always under age, and so co-ordinating the *corona* with the *ecclesia*[2]. But English lawyers were not good at work of this kind; they liked their persons to be real, and what we have seen of the parochial glebe has shown us that even the church (*ecclesia particularis*) was not for them

[1] The theme of this paper was suggested by Dr Gierke's *Genossenschaftsrecht*, a portion of which I have lately published in English : *Political Theories of the Middle Age.* Cambridge, 1900.

[2] *Placit. Abbrev.* p. 339 (15 Edw. II).

a person[1]. As to the king, in all the Year Books I have seen very little said of him that was not meant to be strictly and literally true of a man, of an Edward or a Henry.

Then, on the other hand, medieval thought conceived the nation as a community and pictured it as a body of which the king was the head. It resembled those smaller bodies which it comprised and of which it was in some sort composed. What we should regard as the contrast between State and Corporation was hardly visible. The "commune of the realm" differed rather in size and power than in essence from the commune of a county or the commune of a borough. And as the *comitatus* or county took visible form in the *comitatus* or county court, so the realm took visible form in a parliament. "Every one," said Thorpe C. J. in 1365, "is bound to know at once what is done in Parliament, for Parliament represents the body of the whole realm[2]." For a time it seems very possible, as we read the Year Books, that so soon as lawyers begin to argue about the nature of corporations or bodies politic and clearly to sever the Borough, for example, from the sum of burgesses, they will definitely grasp and formulate the very sound thought that the realm is "a corporation aggregate of many." In 1522 Fineux C. J., after telling how some corporations are made by the king, others by the pope, others by both king and pope, adds that there are corporations by the common law, for, says he, "the parliament of the king and the lords and the commons are a corporation[3]."

---

[1] *L. Q. R.* XVI. 344.   [2] Y. B. 39 Edw. III, f. 7.
[3] Y. B. 14 Hen. VIII, f. 3 (Mich. pl. 2).

What is still lacking is the admission that the corporate realm, besides being the wielder of public power, may also be the "subject" of private rights, the owner of lands and chattels.   And this is the step that we have never yet formally taken[1].

The portrait that Henry VIII painted of the body politic of which he was the sovereign head will not be forgotten[2]:

"Where by divers sundry old authentic histories and chronicles it is manifestly declared and expressed that this realm of England is an Empire, and so hath been accepted in the world, governed by One supreme Head and King, having the dignity and royal estate of the Imperial Crown of the same, unto whom a Body Politick, compact of all sorts and degrees of people and by names of Spirituality and Temporalty been bounden, and owen to bear, next to God, a natural and humble obedience...."

It is stately stuff into which old thoughts and new are woven.   "The body spiritual" is henceforth to be conceived as "part of the said body politick" which culminates in King Henry.   The medieval dualism of Church and State is at length transcended by the majestic lord who broke the bonds of Rome. The frontispiece of the Leviathan is already before our eyes.   But, as for Hobbes, so also for King Henry, the personality of the corporate body is concentrated in and absorbed by the personality of its monarchical head.   His reign was not the time when the king's lands could be severed from the nation's

---

[1] The mistake, so I think, of Allen's memorable treatise on the Royal Prerogative consists in the supposition that already in very old days the Folk could be and was clearly conceived as a person : a single 'subject' of ownership and other rights.

[2] 25 Hen. VIII, c. 12 (For the Restraint of Appeals).

lands, the king's wealth from the common wealth, or even the king's power from the power of the State. The idea of a corporation sole which was being prepared in the ecclesiastical sphere might do good service here. Were not all Englishmen incorporated in King Henry? Were not his acts and deeds the acts and deeds of that body politic which was both Realm and Church?

A certain amount of disputation there was sure to be over land acquired by the king in divers ways. Edward VI, not being yet of the age of twenty-one years, purported to alienate land which formed part of the duchy of Lancaster. Did this act fall within the doctrine that the king can convey while he is an infant? Land had been conveyed to Henry VII "and the heirs male of his body lawfully begotten." Did this give him an estate tail or a fee simple conditional? Could the head of a body politic beget heirs? A few cases of this kind came before the Court soon after the middle of the sixteenth century. In Plowden's reports of these cases we may find much curious argumentation about the king's two "bodies," and I do not know where to look in the whole series of our law books for so marvellous a display of metaphysical—or we might say metaphysiological—nonsense[1]. Whether this sort of talk was really new about the year 1550, or whether it had gone unreported until Plowden arose, it were not easy to say ; but the Year Books have not prepared us for it. Two sentences may be enough to illustrate what I mean :

[1] *Case of the Duchy of Lancaster*, Plowden, 212; *Willion* v. *Berkley, Ib.* 223; *Sir Thomas Wroth's* case, *Ib.* 452.

"So that he [the king] has a body natural adorned and invested with the estate and dignity royal, and he has not a body natural distinct and divided by itself from the office and dignity royal, but a body natural and a body politic together indivisible, and these two bodies are incorporated in one person and make one body and not divers, that is, the body corporate in the body natural *et e contra* the body natural in the body corporate. So that the body natural by the conjunction of the body politic to it (which body politic contains the office, government and majesty royal) is magnified and by the said consolidation hath in it the body politic[1]."

"Which faith," we are inclined to add, "except every man keep whole and undefiled, without doubt he shall perish everlastingly." However, a gleam of light seems sometimes to penetrate the darkness. The thought that in one of his two capacities the king is only the "head" of a corporation has not been wholly suppressed.

"The king has two capacities, for he has two bodies, the one whereof is a body natural...the other is a body politic, and the members thereof are his subjects, and he and his subjects together compose the corporation, as Southcote said, and he is incorporated with them and they with him, and he is the head and they are the members, and he has the sole government of them[2]."

Again, in that strange debate occasioned by the too sudden death of Sir James Hales, Brown J. says that suicide is an offence not only against God and Nature, but against the King, for "he, being the Head, has lost one of his mystical members[3]." But, for reasons that lie for the more part outside the history of law, this thought fell into the background. The king was left with "two bodies"; one of them was natural, the other non-natural. Of this last body

---

[1] Plowden, 213.   [2] *Ib.* 234.   [3] *Ib.* 261.

we can say little; but it is "politic," whatever "politic" may mean.

Meanwhile the concept of a corporation sole was being fashioned in order to explain, if this were possible, the parson's relation to the glebe. Then came Coke and in his masterful fashion classified Persons for the coming ages. They are natural or artificial. Kings and parsons are artificial persons, corporations sole, created not by God but by the policy of man[1].

Abortive as I think the attempt to bring the parson into line with corporations aggregate—abortive, for the freehold of the glebe persists in falling into abeyance whenever a parson dies—the attempt to play the same trick with the king seems to me still more abortive and infinitely more mischievous. In the first place, the theory is never logically formulated even by those who are its inventors. We are taught that the king is two "persons," only to be taught that though he has "two bodies" and "two capacities" he "hath but one person[2]." Any real and consistent severance of the two personalities would naturally have led to "the damnable and damned opinion," productive of "execrable and detestable consequences," that allegiance is due to the corporation sole and not to the mortal man[3]. In the second place, we are plunged into talk about kings who do not die, who are never under age, who are ubiquitous, who do no wrong and (says Blackstone[4]) think no wrong; and such talk has

---

[1] Co. Lit. 2 a, 250 a ; *Sutton's Hospital* case, 10 Rep. 26 b.
[2] *Calvin's* case, 7 Rep. 10 a.   [3] *Ib.* 11 a, b.
[4] 1 Comm. 246.

not been innocuous.   Readers of Kinglake's *Crimea*
will not have forgotten the instructive and amusing
account of "the two kings" who shared between them
control of the British army: "the personal king" and
"his constitutional rival."   But in the third place, the
theory of the two kings or two persons stubbornly
refuses to do any real work in the cause of jurisprudence.

We might have thought that it would at least have
led to a separation of the land that the king held as
king from the land that he held as man, and to a legal
severance of the money that was in the Exchequer
from the money that was in the king's pocket.   It did
nothing of the sort.   All had to be done by statute,
and very slowly and clumsily it was done.   After the
king's lands had been made inalienable, George III
had to go to Parliament for permission to hold some
land as a man and not as a king, for he had been
denied rights that were not denied to "any of His
Majesty's subjects[1]."   A deal of legislation, extending
into Queen Victoria's reign, has been required in order
to secure "private estates" for the king.   "Whereas
it is doubtful," says an Act of 1862[2].   "And whereas
it may be doubtful," says an Act of 1873[3].   Many
things may be doubtful if we try to make two persons
of one man, or to provide one person with two bodies.

The purely natural way in which the king was regarded in the Middle Ages is well illustrated by the
terrible consequences of what we now call a demise
of the Crown, but what seemed to our ancestors the

[1] 39 & 40 Geo. III, c. 88.   [2] 25 & 26 Vict. c. 37.
[3] 36 & 37 Vict. c. 61.

death of a man who had delegated many of his powers
to judges and others. At the delegator's death the
delegation ceased. All litigation not only came to a
stop but had to be begun over again. We might have
thought that the introduction of phrases which gave
the king an immortal as well as a mortal body would
have transformed this part of the law. But no. The
consequences of the old principle had to be picked off
one after another by statute[1]. At the beginning of
Queen Victoria's reign it was discovered that "great
inconvenience had arisen on occasion of the demise
of the Crown from the necessity of renewing all
military commissions under the royal sign manual[2]."
When on a demise of the Crown we see all the wheels
of the State stopping or even running backwards, it
seems an idle jest to say that the king never dies.

But the worst of it is that we are compelled to
introduce into our legal thinking a person whose
personality our law does not formally or explicitly
recognize. We cannot get on without the State, or
the Nation, or the Commonwealth, or the Public, or
some similar entity, and yet that is what we are pro-
fessing to do. In the days when Queen Elizabeth
was our Prince—more often Prince than Princess—her
secretary might write in Latin *De republica Anglorum,*
and in English *Of the Commonwealth of England*:
Prince and Republic were not yet incompatible. A
little later Guy Fawkes and others, so said the Statute
Book, had attempted the destruction of His Majesty
and "the overthrow of the whole State and Common

---

[1] 1 Edw. VI, begins the process.

[2] 7 Will. IV & 1 Vict. c. 31.

wealth[1]." In 1623 the Exchequer Chamber could speak of the inconvenience that "remote limitations" had introduced "in the republic[2]." But the great struggle that followed had the effect of depriving us of two useful words. "Republic" and "Commonwealth" implied kinglessness and therefore treason. As to "the State," it was a late comer—but little known until after 1600—and though it might govern political thought, and on rare occasions make its way into the preamble of a statute, it was slow to find a home in English law-books. There is wonderfully little of the State in Blackstone's Commentaries[3]. It is true that "The people" exists, and "the liberties of the People" must be set over against "the prerogatives of the King"; but just because the King is no part of the People, the People cannot be the State or Commonwealth.

But "the Publick" might be useful. And those who watch the doings of this Publick in the Statute Book of the eighteenth century may feel inclined to say that it has dropped a first syllable. After the rebellion of 1715 an Act of Parliament declared that the estates of certain traitors were to be vested in the king "to the use of the Publick[4]." Whether this is the first appearance of "the Publick" as *cestui que trust* of a part of those lands of which the king is owner I do not know; but it is an early example.

---

[1] 3 Jac. I, c. 3, pr.   [2] *Child* v. *Baylie*, Palm. 335, 336.

[3] Such phrases as "when the danger of the state is great" (1, 135) are occasionally used.

[4] 1 Geo. I, stat. 2, c. 50. We must distinguish this Public from the Public (*quilibet de populo*) to whom a highway is dedicated.

Then we come upon an amusing little story which illustrates the curious qualities of our royal corporation sole. One of the attainted traitors was Lord Derwentwater, and the tenants of his barony of Langley had been accustomed to pay a fine when their lord died :—such a custom was, I believe, commoner elsewhere than in England. But, says an Act of 1738, the said premises "being vested in His Majesty, his heirs and successors in his politick capacity, which in consideration of law never dies, it may create a doubt whether the tenants of the said estates ought...to pay such fines...on the death of His present Majesty (whom God long preserve for the benefit of his People) or on the death of any future King or Queen." So the tenants are to pay as they would have paid "in case such King or Queen so dying was considered as a private person only and not in his or her politick capacity[1]." Thus that artificial person, the king in his politick capacity, who is a trustee for the Publick, must be deemed to die now and then for the benefit of *cestui que trust*.

But it was of "the Publick" that we were speaking, and I believe that "the Publick" first becomes prominent in connexion with the National Debt. Though much might be done for us by a slightly denaturalized king, he could not do all that was requisite. Some proceedings of one of his predecessors, who closed the Exchequer and ruined the goldsmiths, had made our king no good borrower. So the Publick had to take his place. The money might be "advanced to His Majesty," but the Publick

---

[1] 11 Geo. II, c. 30, pr. and sec. 1.

had to owe it. This idea could not be kept off the statute book. "Whereas," said an Act of 1786, "the Publick stands indebted to" the East India Company in a sum of four millions and more[1].

What is the Publick which owes the National Debt? We try to evade that question. We try to think of that debt not as a debt owed by a person, but as a sum charged upon a pledged or mortgaged thing, upon the Consolidated Fund. This is natural, for we may, if we will, trace the beginnings of a national debt back to days when a king borrows money and charges the repayment of it upon a specific tax; perhaps he will even appoint his creditor to collect that tax, and so enable him to repay himself. Then there was the long transitional stage in which annuities were charged on the Aggregate Fund, the General Fund, the South Sea Fund, and so forth. And now we have the Consolidated Fund; but even the most licentious "objectification" (or, as Dr James Ward says, "reification") can hardly make that Fund "a thing" for jurisprudence. On the one hand, we do not conceive that the holders of Consols would have the slightest right to complain if the present taxes were swept away and new taxes invented, and, on the other hand, we conceive that if the present taxes will not suffice to pay the interest of the debt more taxes must be imposed. Then we speak of "the security of an Act of Parliament," as if the Act were a profit-bearing thing that could be pledged. Or we introduce "the Government" as a debtor. But what, we may ask, is this Government? Surely not the group of

[1] 26 Geo. III, c. 62.

Ministers, not the Government which can be contrasted with Parliament. I am happy to think that no words of mine can affect the price of Bank Annuities, but it seems to me that the national debt is not a "secured debt" in any other than that loose sense in which we speak of "personal security," and that the creditor has nothing to trust to but the honesty and solvency of that honest and solvent community of which the King is the head and "Government" and Parliament are organs.

One of our subterfuges has been that of making the king a trustee (*vel quasi*) for unincorporated groups. Another of our subterfuges has been that of slowly substituting "the Crown" for King or Queen. Now the use which has been made in different ages of the crown—a chattel now lying in the Tower and partaking (so it is said[1]) of the nature of an heirloom—might be made the matter of a long essay. I believe, however, that an habitual and perfectly unambiguous personification of the Crown—in particular, the attribution of acts to the Crown—is much more modern than most people would believe. It seems to me that in fully half the cases in which Sir William Anson writes "Crown," Blackstone would have written "King." In strictness, however, "the Crown" is not, I take it, among the persons known to our law, unless it is merely another name for the King. The Crown, by that name, never sues, never prosecutes, never issues writs or letters patent. On the face of formal records the King or Queen does it all. I would not, if I could, stop the process which is making "the Crown" one of

[1] Co. Lit. 18 b.

the names of a certain organized community; but in
the meantime that term is being used in three or four
different, though closely related, senses. "We all know
that the Crown is an abstraction," said Lord Penzance[1].
I do not feel quite sure of knowing even this[2].

The suggestion that "the Crown" is very often a
suppressed or partially recognized corporation aggregate is forced upon us so soon as we begin to attend
with care to the language which is used by judges
when they are freely reasoning about modern matters
and are not feeling the pressure of old theories. Let us
listen, for example, to Blackburn J., when in a famous
opinion he was explaining why it is that the Postmaster-General or the captain of a man-of-war cannot
be made to answer in a civil action for the negligence
of his subordinates. "These cases were decided upon
the ground that *the government* was the principal and
the defendant merely the servant...All that is decided
by this class of cases is that the liability of a servant
of *the public* is no greater than that of the servant of
any other principal, though the recourse against the
principal, *the public*, cannot be by an action[3]." So here
the Government and the Public are identified, or else
the one is an organ or agent of the other. But the
Postmaster-General or the captain of a man-of-war is

---

[1] *Dixon* v. *London Small Arms Co.*, L. R. 1 App. Cas. 632,
at 652.

[2] The Acts which enable the king to hold "private estates" are
officially indexed under "Crown Private Estates." It is hard to
defend this use of the word unless the Crown is to give garden
parties.

[3] *Mersey Docks Trustees* v. *Gibbs*, L. R. 1 H. L. 93, 111. The
italics, it need hardly be said, are mine.

assuredly a servant of the Crown, and yet he does not serve two masters. A statute of 1887 tells us that "the expressions 'permanent civil service of the State,' 'permanent civil service of Her Majesty,' and 'permanent civil service of the Crown,' are hereby declared to have the same meaning[1]." Now as it is evident that King Edward is not (though Louis XIV may have been) the State, we seem to have statutory authority for the holding that the State is "His Majesty." The way out of this mess, for mess it is, lies in a perception of the fact, for fact it is, that our sovereign lord is not a "corporation sole," but is the head of a complex and highly organized "corporation aggregate of many"— of very many. I see no great harm in calling this corporation a Crown. But a better word has lately returned to the statute book. That word is Commonwealth.

Even if the king would have served as a satisfactory debtor for the national debt, some new questions would have been raised in the course of that process which has been called the expansion of England; for colonies came into being which had public debts of their own. At this point it is well for us to remember that three colonies which were exceptionally important on account of their antiquity and activity, namely Massachusetts, Rhode Island, and Connecticut, were corporations duly created by charter with a sufficiency of operative and inoperative words. Also we may notice that the king was no more a corporator of Rhode Island than he was a corporator of the city of Norwich or of the East India Company, and that the Governor of Connecticut

[1] Pensions (Colonial Service) Act, 1887, 50 & 51 Vict. c. 13, s. 8.

was as little a deputy of the king as was the Governor
of the Bank of England. But even where there was
a royal governor, and where there was no solemnly
created corporation, there was a "subject" capable of
borrowing money and contracting debts. At least as
early as 1709, and I know not how much earlier, bills
of credit were being emitted which ran in this form :—

"This indented bill of —— shillings due from the Colony of New
York to the possessor thereof shall be in value equal to money and
shall be accepted accordingly by the Treasurer of this Colony for the
time being in all public payments and for any fund at any time in
the Treasury. Dated, New York the first of November, 1709, by
order of the Lieutenant Governor, Council and General Assembly of
the said Colony[1]."

In 1714 the Governor, Council and General Assembly of New York passed a long Act "for the paying
and discharging the several debts and sums of money
claimed as debts of this Colony." A preamble stated
that some of the debts of the Colony had not been
paid because the Governors had misapplied and extravagantly expended "the revenue given by the loyal
subjects aforesaid to Her Majesty and Her Royal
Predecessors, Kings and Queens of England, sufficient
for the honourable as well as necessary support of their
Government here." "This Colony," the preamble
added, "in strict justice is in no manner of way
obliged to pay many of the said claims"; however,
in order "to restore the Publick Credit," they were to
be paid[2]. Here we have a Colony which can be
bound even in strict justice to pay money. What the

[1] Act of 12 Nov. 1709 (8 Anne).
[2] Act of 1714 (13 Anne).

great colonies did the small colonies did also. In 1697 an Act was passed at Montserrat "for raising a Levy or Tax for defraying the Publick Debts of this His Majesty's Island."

The Colonial Assemblies imitated the Parliament of England. They voted supplies to "His Majesty"; but they also appropriated those supplies. In Colonial Acts coming from what we may call an ancient date and from places which still form parts of the British Empire, we may see a good deal of care taken that whatever is given to the king shall be marked with a trust. For instance, in the Bermudas, when in 1698 a penalty is imposed, half of it is given to the informer, "and the remainder to His Majesty, His Heirs and Successors, to be imployed for and towards the support of the Government of these Islands and the contingent charges thereof[1]." If "the old house and kitchen belonging to their Majesties [William and Mary] and formerly inhabited by the Governors of these Islands" is to be sold, then the price is to be paid "into the Publick Stock or Revenue for the Publick Uses of these Islands and the same to be paid out by Order of the Governor, Council and a Committee of Assembly[2]." It would, I believe, be found that in some colonies in which there was no ancestral tradition of republicanism, the Assemblies were not far behind the House of

[1] Act of 11 Nov. 1698. Acts of the British Parliament (e.g. 6 Geo. II, c. 13, s. 3) sometimes give a penalty to the use of the king "to be applied for the support of the government of the colony or plantation in which the same shall be recovered." See Palfrey, *New England*, IV. 302. Apparently it was over a clause of this kind that James Otis first came to the front in Massachusetts.

[2] Act of 29 Sept. 1693.

Commons in controlling the expenditure of whatever money was voted to the king. In 1753 the Assembly of Jamaica resolved "that it is the inherent and un-doubted right of the Representatives of the People to raise and apply monies for the services and exigencies of government and to appoint such person or persons for the receiving and issuing thereof as they shall think proper, which right this House hath exerted and will always exert in such manner as they shall judge most conducive to the service of His Majesty and the interest of his People." In many or most of the colonies the treasurer was appointed, not by the Governor but by an Act of Assembly; sometimes he was appointed by a mere resolution of the House of Representatives. In the matter of finance, "respon-sible government" (as we now call it) or "a tendency of the legislature to encroach upon the proper functions of the executive" (as some modern Americans call it) is no new thing in an English colony[1].

We deny nowadays that a Colony is a corporation. The three unquestionably incorporated colonies have gone their own way and are forgotten of lawyers. James L. J. once said that it seemed to him an abuse of language to speak of the Governor and Government of New Zealand as a corporation[2]. So be it, and I should not wish to see a "Governor" or a "Government" in-corporated. But can we—do we really and not merely in words—avoid an admission that the Colony of New

---

[1] See Mr E. B. Greene's very interesting book on the Provincial Governor, Harvard Historical Series; especially p. 177 ff. The Jamaican resolution stands on p. 172.

[2] *Sloman* v. *Government of New Zealand*, 1 C. P. D. 563.

Zealand is a person? In the case that was before the Court a contract for the conveyance of emigrants had professedly been made between " Her Majesty the Queen for and on behalf of the Colony of New Zealand " of the first part, Mr Featherston, "the agent-general in England for the Government of New Zealand," of the second part, and Sloman & Co. of the third part. Now when in a legal document we see those words "for and on behalf of" we generally expect that they will be followed by the name of a person; and I cannot help thinking that they were so followed in this case. I gather that some of the colonies have abandoned the policy of compelling those who have aught against them to pursue the ancient, if royal, road of a petition of right. Perhaps we may not think wholly satisfactory the Australian device of a "nominal defendant" appointed to resist an action in which a claim is made "against the Colonial Government," for there is no need for "nominal" parties to actions where real parties (such, for example, as a Colony or State) are forthcoming [1]. But it is a wholesome sight to see "the Crown" sued [2] and answering for its torts [3]. If the field that sends cases to the Judicial Committee is not narrowed, a good many old superstitions will be put upon their trial.

In the British North America Act, 1867, there are courageous words [4]. " Canada shall be liable for the

---

[1] *Farnell* v. *Bowman*, 12 App. Cas. 643 (N. S. Wales).

[2] *Hettihewage Siman Appu* v. *The Queen's Advocate*, 9 App. Cas. 571 (Ceylon).

[3] *A.-G. of the Straits Settlement* v. *Wemyss*, 13 App. Cas. 192 (Penang).

[4] 30 Vict. c. 3, ss. 110–125.

debts and liabilities of each Province existing at the Union. Ontario and Quebec conjointly shall be liable to Canada...The assets enumerated in the fourth schedule...shall be the property of Ontario and Quebec conjointly. Nova Scotia shall be liable to Canada...New Brunswick shall be liable to Canada... The several Provinces shall retain all their respective public property...New Brunswick shall receive from Canada...The right of New Brunswick to levy the lumber duties...No lands or property belonging to Canada or any Province shall be liable to taxation..." This is the language of statesmanship; of the statute book, and of daily life. But then comes the lawyer with theories in his head, and begins by placing a legal estate in what he calls the Crown or Her Majesty. "In construing these enactments, it must always be kept in view that wherever public land with its incidents is described as 'the property of' or as 'belonging to' the Dominion or a Province, these expressions merely import that the right to its beneficial use, or to its proceeds, has been appropriated to the Dominion or the Province, as the case may be, and is subject to the control of its legislature, the land itself being vested in the Crown[1]." And so we have to distinguish the lands vested in the Crown "for" or "in right of" Canada from the lands vested in the Crown "for" or "in right of" Quebec or Ontario or British Columbia,

---

[1] *St Catharine's Milling and Lumber Co.* v. *The Queen*, 14 App. Cas. 46. esp. p. 56; *A.-G. of Brit. Columbia* v. *A.-G. of Canada*, 14 App. Cas. 295; *A.-G. of Ontario* v. *Mercer*, 8 App. Cas. 767; *A.-G. of Canada* v. *As.-Gs. of Ontario, Quebec, Nova Scotia* [1898], App. Cas. 700.

or between lands "vested in the Crown as represented
by the Dominion" and lands "vested in the Crown as
represented by a Province." Apparently "Canada"
or "Nova Scotia" is person enough to be the Crown's
cestui que trust and at the same time the Crown's
representative, but is not person enough to hold a
legal estate. It is a funny jumble, which becomes
funnier still if we insist that the Crown is a legal
fiction.

"Although the Secretary of State [for India] is a
body corporate, or in the nature of a body corporate,
for the purpose of contracts, and of suing and being
sued, yet he is not a body corporate for the purpose of
holding property. Such property as formerly vested,
or would have vested, in the East India Company now
vests in the Crown[1]." So we sue Person No. 1, who
has not and cannot have any property, in order that we
may get at a certain part of the property that is owned
by Person No. 2. It is a strange result; but not perhaps one at which we ought to stand amazed, if we
really believe that both these Persons, however august,
are fictitious: fictitious like the common vouchee and
the casual ejector[2].

---

[1] Ilbert, *Government of India*, p. 173.

[2] In *Kinlock* v. *Secretary of State for India in Council*, 15 Ch. D.
1, 8, James L. J. said that "there really is in point of law, no such
person or body politic whatever as the Secretary of State for India in
Council." Apparently in his view this is only a name by which "the
Government of India" is to sue and be sued. But this only has the
effect of making "the Government of India" a person, real or fictitious.
[The report of the final appeal to the House of Lords, 7 App. Cas.
619, adds nothing on this head.]

We are not surprised when we read the following passage in an American treatise :

"Each one of the United States in its organized political capacity, although it is not in the proper use of the term a corporation, yet it has many of the essential faculties of a corporation, a distinct name, indefinite succession, private rights, power to sue, and the like. Corporations, however, as the term is used in our jurisprudence, do not include States, but only derivative creations, owing their existence and powers to the State, acting through its legislative department. Like corporations, however, a State, as it can make contracts and suffer wrongs, so it may, for this reason and without express provision, maintain in its corporate name actions to enforce its rights and redress its injuries[1]."

There are some phrases in this passage which imply a disputable theory. However, the main point is that the American State is, to say the least, very like a corporation : it has private rights, power to sue and the like. This seems to me the result to which English law would naturally have come, had not that foolish parson led it astray. There is nothing in this idea that is incompatible with hereditary kingship. "The king and his subjects together compose the corporation, and he is incorporated with them and they with him, and he is the head and they are the members[2]."

There is no cause for despair when "the people of New South Wales, Victoria, South Australia, Queensland and Tasmania, humbly relying on the blessing of Almighty God, have agreed to unite in one indissoluble Federal Commonwealth under the Crown of the United Kingdom of Great Britain and Ireland."

---

[1] Dillon, *Municipal Corporations*, ed. 4, § 31.
[2] Plowden, p. 234.

We may miss the old words that were used of Connecticut and Rhode Island : "one body corporate and politic in fact and name"; but "united in a Federal Commonwealth under the name of the Commonwealth of Australia" seems amply to fill their place[1]. And a body politic may be a member of another body politic.

But we must return from an expanding Empire, or rather Commonwealth, to that thin little thought the corporation sole, and we may inquire whether it has struck root, whether it has flourished, whether it is doing us any good.

Were there at the beginning of the nineteenth century more than two corporations sole that were not ecclesiastical? Coke had coupled the Chamberlain of the City of London with the King[2]. But the class of corporations sole was slow to grow, and this seems to me a sure proof that the idea was sterile and unprofitable. It is but too likely that I have missed some instances[3], but provisionally I will claim the third place in the list for the Postmaster-General. In 1840 the Postmaster-General and his successors "is and are" made "a body corporate" for the purpose of holding and taking conveyances and leases of lands and hereditaments for the service of the Post Office. From the Act that effected this incorporation we may learn that the Postmaster as a mere individual had

---

[1] 63 & 64 Vict. c. 12.   [2] *Fulwood's* case, 4 Rep. 64 b.

[3] The Master of the Rolls (who, however, as a matter of history, was not quite free from an ecclesiastical taint) must have been not unlike a corporation sole, for he held land in right of his office. 12 Car. II, c. 36 ; 20 Geo. II, c. 34 (Sir J. Jekyll granted leases to a trustee for himself).

been holding land in trust for the Crown[1]. One of the main reasons, I take it, for erecting some new corporations sole was that our " Crown," being more or less identifiable with the King, it was difficult to make the Crown a Ieaseholder or copyholder in a direct and simple fashion. The Treasurer of Public Charities was made a corporation sole in 1853[2]. Then in 1855 the Secretary of State intrusted with the seals of the War Department was enabled to hold land as a corporation sole[3]. Perhaps if there were a Lord High Admiral he would be a corporation sole *vel quasi*[4]. The Solicitor to the Treasury was made a corporation sole in 1876, and this corporation sole can hold " real and personal property of every description[5]." All this—and there is more to be said of Boards such as the Board of Trade and the Board of Agriculture and so forth—seems to me to be the outcome of an awkward endeavour to ignore the personality of the greatest body corporate and politic that has ever existed. And after all, we must ask whether this device does its work. The throne, it is true, is never vacant, for the kingship is entailed and inherited. But we have yet to be taught that the Solicitor to the Treasury never dies. When a Post-master-General dies, what becomes of the freehold of countless post offices ? If we pursue the ecclesiastical analogy—and it is the only analogy—we must let the freehold fall into abeyance, for, when all is said, our corporation sole is a man who dies[6].

---

[1] 3 & 4 Vict. c. 96, s. 67.　　　[2] 16 & 17 Vict. c. 137, s. 47.
[3] 18 & 19 Vict. c. 117, s. 2.　　[4] 27 & 28 Vict. c. 57, s. 9.
[5] 39 & 40 Vict. c. 18, s. 1.　　　[6] See *L. Q. R.* XVI. 352.

Suppose that a prisoner is indicted for stealing a letter being the proper goods of "the Postmaster-General," and suppose that he objects that at the time in question there was no Postmaster-General, he can be silenced ; but this is so, not because the Postmaster is a corporation sole, but because a statute seems to have said with sufficient clearness that the indictment is good[1]. So long as the State is not seen to be a person, we must either make an unwarrantably free use of the King's name, or else we must for ever be laboriously stopping holes through which a criminal might glide. A critical question would be whether the man who is Postmaster for the time being could be indicted for stealing the goods of the Postmaster, or whether the Solicitor to the Treasury could sue the man who happened to be the Treasury's Solicitor. Not until some such questions have been answered in the affirmative have we any reason for saying that the corporation sole is one person and the natural man another[2].

I am aware of only one instance in which a general law, as distinguished from *privilegia* for this or that officer of the central government, has conferred the quality of sole-corporateness or corporate-soleness upon a class of office-holders. The exceptional case is that of the clerks of the peace[3]. This arrangement, made in 1858, was convenient because we did not and

[1] 7 Will. IV & 1 Vict. c. 36, s. 40; and see 11 & 12 Vict. c. 88, s. 5.

[2] See *L. Q. R.* XVI. 355.

[3] 21 & 22 Vict. c. 92. But this Act does not use the term *corporation sole.*

do not regard the justices of the peace as a corporation. But then so soon as the affairs of the counties were placed upon a modern footing by the Act of 1888, a corporation aggregate took the place of the corporation sole, and what had been vested in the clerk of the peace became vested in the county council. Such is the destined fate of all corporations sole[1].

[1] 51 & 52 Vict. c. 41, s. 64. We do not find it necessary to use mysterious language about the corporateness of every public accountant. But when such an accountant dies the balance to his credit at the bank where the public account is kept is not "in any manner subject to the control of his legal representative." See 29 & 30 Vict. c. 39, s. 18.

THE UNINCORPORATE BODY[1]

OF the Taff Vale Case we are likely to hear a good deal for some time to come. The trade unions are not content; there will be agitation; perhaps there will be legislation.

To one reader of English history and of English law it seems that certain broad principles of justice and jurisprudence are involved in and may be evolved from the debate: certain broad principles which extend far beyond the special interests of masters and workmen. Will he be able to persuade others that this is so? Can he assign to this Taff Vale Case its place in a long story?

Of late years under American teaching we have learned to couple together the two terms "corporations" and "trusts." In the light of history we may see this as a most instructive conjunction. And yet an apprentice of English law might well ask what the law of trusts has to do with the law of corporations. Could two topics stand farther apart from each other in an hypothetical code? Could two law-books have less in common than Grant on Corporations and Lewin on Trusts?

[1] Read to the Eranus Club.

To such questions English history replies that, none the less, a branch of the law of trusts became a supplement for the law of corporations, and some day when English history is adequately written one of the most interesting and curious tales that it will have to tell will be that which brings trust and corporation into intimate connexion with each other.

A few words about the general law of trusts may not be impertinent even though they say nothing that is new. The idea of a trust is so familiar to us all that we never wonder at it. And yet surely we ought to wonder. If we were asked what is the greatest and most distinctive achievement performed by Englishmen in the field of jurisprudence I cannot think that we should have any better answer to give than this, namely, the development from century to century of the trust idea.

"I do not understand your trust," these words have been seen in a letter written by a very learned German historian familiar with law of all sorts and kinds.

Where lies the difficulty ? In the terms of a so-called "general jurisprudence" it seems to lie here :— A right which in ultimate analysis appears to be *ius in personam* (the benefit of an obligation) has been so treated that for practical purposes it has become equivalent to *ius in rem* and is habitually thought of as a kind of ownership, "equitable ownership." Or put it thus :— If we are to arrange English law as German law is arranged in the new code we must present to our law of trust a dilemma : it must place itself under one of two rubrics ; it must belong to the Law of Obligations or to the Law of Things. In sight of this dilemma it reluctates and recalcitrates. It was made by men who had no Roman law as explained by medieval commentators in the innermost fibres of their minds.

To say much of the old feoffment to uses would be needless. Only we will note that for a long time the only and for a longer time the typical subject-matter of a trust is a piece of land or some incorporeal thing, such as an advowson, which is likened to a piece of land. For trusts of movable goods there was no great need. The common law about bailments was sufficient. We may indeed see these two legal concepts deriving from one source : the source that is indicated in Latin by *ad opus*, in old French by *al oes*, in English by "to the use." In the one case however a channel is cut by the Courts of Common Law and the somewhat vague *al oes* explicates itself in a law of bailments and agency, while in the other the destined channel must be cut, if at all, by a new court since the law of rights in land has already attained a relatively high stage of development and finds its expression in an elaborate scheme of writs and formal actions. For the purposes of comparative jurisprudence it is of some importance to observe that though for a long time past our trust idea—the idea of a trust strictly and technically so called—has been extended to things of all sorts and kinds, still were it not for trusts of land we should hardly have come by trusts of other things. The ideas of bailment, agency, guardianship, might have shown themselves capable of performing all that was reasonably necessary. Foreigners manage to live without trusts. They must.

In the fourteenth century when feoffments to uses were becoming common, the most common of all instances seems to have been the feoffment to the feoffor's own use. The landowner enfeoffed some of his friends as joint tenants hoping for one thing that by keeping the legal ownership in joint tenants and placing new feoffees in vacant gaps no demand could ever be made by the feudal lord for wardship or marriage, relief or escheat, and hoping for another thing that the feoffees would observe his last will and that so in effect he might acquire that testamentary power which the law denied him and which the eternal interest of his sinful soul made an object of keen desire.

Now between feoffor and feoffee in such a case there is agreement. We have only to say that there is contract and then the highly peculiar character of our trust will soon display itself. For let us suppose that we treat this relationship as a contract and ask what will follow.

Well (1) as between feoffor and feoffee how shall we enforce that contract? Shall we just give damages if and when the contract is broken or shall we decree specific performance on pain of imprisonment? Perhaps this difficulty was hardly felt, for it can, so I think, be amply shown that the idea of compelling a man specifically to perform a contract relating to land was old, and that what was new was the effectual pressure of threatened imprisonment. But (2) think of the relationship as contractual and how are we to conceive the right of the feoffor? It is the benefit of a contract. It is a chose in action at a time when a chose in action is inalienable. Also if we held tight by this conception there would be much to be said for holding that the use or trust is in all cases personal property. Then (3) there is great difficulty in holding that a contract can give rights to a third person. We in England feel that difficulty now-a-days. Foreign lawyers and legislatures are surmounting it. We should have had to surmount it, had it not been for our trust. But from an early time, we find that the action, or rather the suit, is given to the destinatory, the beneficiary, the *cestui que use* as we call him, and indeed if the trustor can enforce the trust this will only be so because in the particular case he is the destinatory. And then (4) arises the all important question as to the validity of the beneficiary's right against purchasers from the trustee and against the trustee's creditors. Think steadily of that right as the benefit of a contract and you will find it hard to say why it should be enforced against one who was no party to the contract.

We know what happened. No sooner has the Chancellor got to work than he seems bent on making these "equitable" rights as unlike mere *iura in personam* and as like *iura in rem* as he can possibly make them. The ideas that he employs for this purpose are not many; they are English; certainly they are not derived from any knowledge of Roman law with which we may think fit to equip him. On the one hand as regards what we might call the internal character of these rights, the analogies of the common law are to be strictly pursued. A few concessions may be made in favour of greater "flexibility" but on the whole there is to be a law of equitable estates in land which is a mere replica of the law of legal estates. There are to be estates in fee simple, estates in fee tail, terms of years, remainders, reversions and the rest of it : the equitable estate tail (this is a good example) is to be barred by an equitable recovery. Then as regards the external side of the matter, "good conscience" becomes the active principle ; a conscience that can be opposed to strict law. The trust is to be enforced against all whose conscience is to be "affected" by it. Class after class of persons is brought within the range of this idea. The purchaser who for value obtains ownership from the trustee must himself become a trustee if at the time of the purchase he knew of the trust; for it is unconscionable to buy what you know to be another's "in equity." Then the purchaser who did not know of the trust must be bound by it if he ought to have known of it : that is to say, if he would have known of it had he made such investigation of his vendor's title as a prudent purchaser makes in his own interest. It remains to screw up this standard of diligence higher and higher, until the purchaser who has obtained a legal estate *bona fide* for value and without notice, express or implied, of the equitable right, is an extremely rare and extremely lucky person. And apparently he is now the only person who can hold the land and yet ignore the trust. It was not so always. The lord who came to the land by escheat came to it with a clear conscience. Also we read in our old books that a use cannot be enforced against a corporation because a corporation has no conscience. But in the one case a statute has come to the rescue and in the other we have rejected the logical consequence of a certain speculative theory of corporations to which we still do lip-service. The broad result is that we habitually think of the beneficiary's right as practically equivalent to full ownership, and the instances of rare occurrence in which a purchaser can ignore it seem almost anomalous. And in passing it may be noticed that such danger as there is falls to absolute zero in a class of cases of which we are to speak hereafter. No one will ever be heard to say that he has purchased without notice of a trust a building that was vested in trustees but was fitted up as a club-house, a Jewish synagogue, a Roman catholic cathedral.

Even that is not quite all. Even when the Court of Equity could not give the *cestui que trust* the very thing that was the original subject-matter of the trust it has struggled hard to prevent its darling from falling into the ruck of unsecured creditors of a defaulting trustee. It has allowed him to pursue a " reified " trust-fund from investment to investment : in other words, to try to find some thing for which the original thing has been exchanged by means of a longer or shorter series of exchanges. That idea of the trust-fund which is dressed up (invested) now as land and now as current coin, now as shares and now as debentures seems to me one of the most remarkable ideas developed by modern English jurisprudence. How we have worked that metaphor! May not one have a vested interest in a fund that is vested in trustees who have invested it in railway shares. Even a Philosophy of Clothes stands aghast. However, the main point is that *cestui que trust* is magnificently protected.

Now I cannot but think that there is one large part of this long story of the trust that ordinarily goes untold. The student is expected to learn something about feoffments to uses and the objects that were gained thereby, something about the Chancellor's interposition, something about the ambitious statute that added three words to a conveyance; but no sooner is King Henry outwitted, no sooner is the Chancellor enforcing the secondary use, than the law of uses and trusts becomes a highly technical matter having for its focus the family settlement with its trustees to preserve contingent remainders, its name and arms clauses, its attendant terms and so forth. Very curious and excellent learning it all is, and in some sort still necessary to be known at least in outline; still we are free to say that some of the exploits that the trust performed in this quarter are not admirable in modern eyes, and at any rate it seems to me a misfortune that certain other and much less questionable exploits pass unnoticed by those books whence beginners obtain their first and their most permanent notions of legal history.

First and last the trust has been a most powerful instrument of social experimentation. To name some well-known instances:—It (in effect) enabled the land-owner to devise his land by will until at length the legislature had to give way, though not until a rebellion had been caused and crushed. It (in effect) enabled a married woman to have property that was all her own until at length the legislature had to give way. It (in effect) enabled men to form joint-stock companies with limited liability, until at length the legislature had to give way. The case of the married woman is specially instructive. We see a prolonged experiment. It is deemed a great success. And at last it becomes impossible to maintain (in effect) one law for the poor and another for the rich, since, at least in general estimation, the tried and well-known "separate use" has been working well. Then on the other hand let us observe how impossible it would have been for the most courageous Court of Common Law to make or to suffer any experimentation in this quarter.

Just to illustrate the potency of the trust in unexpected quarters we might mention an employment of it which at one time threatened radically to change the character of the national church. Why should not an advowson be vested in trustees upon trust to present such clerk as the parishioners shall choose? As a matter of fact this was done in a not inconsiderable number of cases and we may even see Queen Elizabeth herself taking part in such a transaction[1]. Had a desire for ministers elected by their congregations become general among conformists, the law was perfectly ready to carry out their wishes. The fact that parishioners are no corporation raised no difficulty.

But there are two achievements of the trust which in social importance and juristic interest seem to eclipse all the rest. The trust has given us a liberal substitute for a law about personified institutions. The trust has given us a liberal supplement for a necessarily meagre law of corporations. The social importance of these movements will appear by and by. The juristic

---

[1] *In re* St Stephen, Coleman Street, 39 Ch. Div. 492.

interest might perhaps escape us if we could not look abroad.

We in England say that persons are natural or artificial, and that artificial persons are corporations aggregate or corporations sole. A foreign lawyer would probably tell us that such a classification of persons will hardly cover the whole ground that in these days has to be covered : at all events he would tell us this if he knew how little good we get out of our corporation sole—a queer creature that is always turning out to be a mere mortal man just when we have need of an immortal person. We should be asked by a German friend where we kept our *Anstalt* or *Stiftung*, our Institution or Foundation. And then we should be told that, though in particular cases it may be difficult to draw the line between the corporation and the institute, we certainly in modern times require some second class of juristic persons. This necessity we should see if, abolishing in thought our law of trusts, we asked what was to become of our countless "charities." Unless some feat of personification can be performed they must perish. Let the "charitable" purpose of Mr Styles be, for example, the distribution of annual doles among the deserving poor of Pedlington, an incorporation of the deserving poor is obviously out of the question, and therefore we must either tell Mr Styles that he cannot do what he wants to do or else we must definitely admit " Styles's Charity" into the circle of "persons known to the law." In the latter case what will follow ? What is likely to follow among men who have been taught the orthodox and cosmopolitan lore of the fictitious person ? Surely this, that without the cooperation of the State no charitable institution can be created. And this doctrine is likely to endure even in days when the State is relaxing its hold over the making of corporations and learned men are doubting the fictitiousness of the corporation's personality. Hear the new German Code :—"Zur Entstehung einer rechtsfähigen Stiftung ist ausser dem Stiftungsgeschäfte die Genehmigung des Bundesstaats erforderlich, in dessen Gebiete die Stiftung ihren Sitz haben soll." Translate that into English and suppose it to have been always law in England. How the face of England is changed!

Our way of escape was the trust. Vest the lands, vest the goods in some man or men. The demand for personality is satisfied. The lands, the goods, have an owner : an owner to defend them and recover them : an owner behind whom a Court of Common Law will never look. All else is mere equity.

Apparently we slid quite easily into our doctrine of charitable trusts. We may represent the process as gradual ; we might call it the evanescence of *cestui que trust*. Observe the following series of directions given to trustees of land :—(1) to sell and divide the proceeds among the twelve poorest women of the parish : (2) to sell and divide the proceeds among the twelve women of the parish who in the opinion of my trustees shall be the most deserving : (3) annually to divide the rents and profits among the twelve poorest for the time being : (4) annually to divide the rents and profits among the twelve who are most deserving in the opinion of the trustees. The bodily "owners in equity" who are apparent enough in the first of these cases seem to fade out of sight as small changes are made in the wording of the trust. When they disappear from view, what, let us ask, do they leave behind them?

Well, they leave "a charity" and perhaps no more need be said. If we must have a theory I do not think that any good will come of introducing the Crown or the Attorney-General, the State or the Public, for, although it be established in course of time that the Attorney-General is a necessary party to suits concerning the administration of the trust, still we do not think of Crown or Attorney-General, State or Public as "beneficial owner" of the lands that are vested in the trustees of Nokes's charity, and trustees are not to be multiplied *praeter necessitatem*. Nor do I think that we personify the "charity": it cannot sue or be sued. Apparently our thought would be best expressed by saying that in these cases there is no "equitable owner" and that the accomplishment of a purpose has taken the place of *cestui que trust*. Our rule that the place of *cestui que trust* cannot be taken by a "non-charitable" purpose—a rule that has not been always rigorously observed[1]—has not acted as a very serious restraint upon the desires of reasonable persons, so exceedingly wide from first to last has been our idea of "charity."

Now no doubt our free foundation of charitable

---

[1] See *In re* Dean, 41 Ch. Div. 559: a trust for the comfortable maintenance of specific dogs and horses adjudged valid, though not charitable and not enforceable by any one. See however an article by J. C. Gray, 15 *Harv. L. Rev.* 509 on "Gifts for a non-charitable purpose."

institutions has had its dark side, and no doubt we discovered that some supervision by the State of the administration of charitable trust funds had become necessary, but let us observe that Englishmen in one generation after another have had open to them a field of social experimentation such as could not possibly have been theirs, had not the trustee met the law's imperious demand for a definite owner. Even if we held the extreme opinion that endowed charities have done more harm than good, it might well be said of us that we have learned this lesson in the only way it could be learnt.

And so we came by our English *Anstalt* or *Stiftung* without troubling the State to concede or deny the mysterious boon of personality. That was not an inconsiderable feat of jurisprudence. But a greater than that was performed. In truth and in deed we made corporations without troubling king or parliament though perhaps we said that we were doing nothing of the kind.

Probably as far back as we can trace in England any distinct theory of the corporation's personality or any assertion that this personality must needs have its origin in some act of sovereign power, we might trace also the existence of an unincorporated group to whose use land is held by feoffees. At any rate a memorable and misunderstood statute tells us that this was a common case in 1532. "Where by reason of feoffments...and assurances made of trusts of manors... and hereditaments to the use of parish churches, chapels, church-wardens, guilds, fraternities, comminalties, companies or brotherhoods erected or made of devotion or by common assent of the people without any corporation...there groweth and issueth to the King our Sovereign Lord, and to other lords and subjects of this realm the same like losses and inconveniences, and is [*sic*] as much prejudicial to them as doth and is in case where lands be aliened into mortmain." Upon this recital follows a declaration that "all and every such uses, intents and purposes" that shall be declared or ordained after the 1st of March in 28 Henry VIII shall be utterly void in law if they extend beyond a term of twenty years. We know how Elizabethan lawyers construed this statute. They said that it struck at uses that were superstitious and not at such as were good and godly. We are better able than they are to trace the evolution of King Henry's abhorrence of superstition. In 1532 he was beginning to threaten the pope with a retention of annates, but he was no heretic and not even a schismatic ; and indeed this very statute clearly contemplates the continued creation of obits provided that the trust does not exceed the limit of twenty years. The voice that speaks to us is not that of the Supreme Head upon earth of a purified church but that of a supreme landlord who is being done out of escheats and other commodities. I will not' say but that there were some words in the Act which in the eyes of good and godly lawyers might confine its effect within narrow limits, but I also think that good and godly lawyers belonging as they did to certain already ancient and honourable societies for which lands were held in trust must have felt that this statute had whistled very near their ears.

THE BODY POLITIC[1]

I HOPE that you will forgive me for choosing a subject which lies very near to that which Sidgwick discussed at our last meeting. I had thought of it before I heard his paper, and though to my great delight he said some things which I had long wanted to hear said, his object was not quite that which I have in view. He spoke of the means, the very inadequate means, that we have of foretelling the future of bodies politic, I wish to speak of the means, the very inadequate means as some people seem to think them, that we have of filling up the gaps that at present exist in our knowledge of the past history of these political organisms. The two processes, that of predicting the future and that of reconstructing the past are essentially similar, both are processes of inference and generalization. Of course when the historian tells us a single fact, for example, gives the date of a battle, inference and generalization are already at work. He has got this supposed fact from (let us say) some chronicler or some tombstone, and he has come to the conclusion that about such a

---

[1] Read to the Eranus Club.

matter this chronicler's or this tombstone's word may be trusted. But when he goes on to represent as usual or rare some habit or custom or mode of thought or of conduct he is very obviously drawing general conclusions from particular instances, and is, if I may so say, predicting the past.

Sidgwick drew a distinction between empirical and scientific predictions. I will apply this distinction to postdictions. I did not gather from him that he meant to draw a hard and accurate line between the empirical and the scientific. Certainly for my purpose I could not draw it with a firm hand. But still though we have before us a matter of degree the distinction is real and important. The historian of the old-fashioned type who does not talk about scientific method or laws of nature is drawing inferences and making generalizations, but these do not as a general rule go far outside the country and the time that he is studying. We may compare him to the chancellor of the exchequer who is estimating the produce of next year's taxes. Sometimes the two procedures are very strictly comparable, as when the historian who thinks that he has examined enough accounts ventures on a general statement about the revenue of Henry II or George III. Now in a certain sense it is true that the method employed in these cases ought to be a scientific method, that is to say, it ought to be the method best adapted to the purpose in hand. Still it is only scientific in the sense in which the method of a Sherlock Holmes would be scientific. The end of it all is a story, a causally connected story tested and proved at every point. Also it must I think be allowed that history of this old-fashioned kind is successfully standing one of those tests of a science that Sidgwick mentioned last time. No historian dreams of beginning the work all over again. Even if he has a taste for paradox and a quarrelsome temper he accepts what is after all the great bulk of his predecessor's results. Men are disputing now whether the forged decretals were concocted in the east or in the west of France, whether they shall be dated a little after or a little before 850; the man who attributed them to the popes whose names they bear would be in much the same position as that which is assigned to the man who says that the world is flat; he would be taking up arms against an organized body of knowledge. I should doubt whether books about the most rapidly advancing of the physical sciences become antiquated more rapidly than those books about history which do not belong to the very first class.

Now to this progress I do not think that we can set any narrow limits. During the present century there has been a rapid acceleration. Tracts which were dark are now fairly well lit and neglected and remote pieces of the story are being systematically explored. Of course I am including under the name of history what some people call archaeology; for to my mind an archaeology that is not history is somewhat less than nothing, and a Special Board for History and Archaeology is like a Special Board for Mathematics and the Rule of Three. Whether we fix our eyes on the east or the west, on ancient or modern times, we see that new truths are being brought in and secured, and this in that gradual fashion in which a healthy body of knowledge grows, the new truth generally turning out to be but a quarter-truth and yet one which must modify the whole tale.

But this process, rapid as it seems to me (for I am comparing it with the growth of historical knowledge in the last century), seems far too slow to some who compare it with the exploits of the natural sciences. They want to have a science of history comparable to some of those sciences, and, for choice, to biology. A desire of this kind there has been for a long time past; in our own day it has become very prominent and there are many writers and readers who seem to think that we are within a measurable distance of a sociology or an inductive political science which shall take no shame when set beside the older sciences. Having a science of the body natural we are at last to have a similar science of the body politic. The comparison of a state or nation to a living body is of course ancient enough. The Herbert Spencer of the twelfth century worked it out with grotesque medieval detail; the John of Salisbury of our own century teaches us that the comparison is just about to become strictly scientific since we have at last an evolutionary biology. Now the suggestions derived from this comparison have been of inestimable value to mankind at large and to historians in particular. I wish once for all to make a very large admission about this matter. But for this comparison, the vocabulary of the historian and of the political theorist would be exceedingly meagre, and I need not say that a rich, flexible, delicate vocabulary is necessary if there is to be accurate thinking and precise description. For the presentation—nay, for the perception—of unfamiliar truth we have need of all the metaphors that we can command, and any source of new and apt metaphors is a source of new knowledge. The language of any and every science must be in the eyes of the etymologist a mass of metaphors and of very mixed metaphors. I am also very far from denying that every advance of biological science, but more especially any popularization of its results, will supply the historian and the political theorist with new thoughts, and with new phrases which will make old thoughts truer. I can conceive that a century hence political events will be currently described in a language which I could not understand so full will it be of terms borrowed from biology, or, for this also is possible, from some science of which no one has yet laid the first stone. But I think that at present the man studying history will do well not to hand himself over body and soul to the professor of any one science; that if in one sentence he has spoken of political germs or embryos or organisms, he will not be ashamed to speak in the next of political machinery and checks and balances. He may write of the decay, death, dissolution of the Roman empire, but at times he will not contemn the classical decline and fall.

But I ought to be speaking not of metaphor but of method. Now were there to be any talk of scientific biology I would at once end this paper with a confession of blank ignorance, but my contention is that we ought not to believe ourselves to be within sight of such talk. To me it seems that if we start with the comparison suggested by such phrases as "body politic" or "social organism" we are not within sight of that sort of knowledge that every old woman in a village has and has long had of the human body. She knows truths about the span of life, about the growth of children, about their teething, about gray hairs, old age and death, the like of which we do not know, and so far as I can see are not going to know about the parallel social phenomena, if any such parallel phenomena there be. In effect she judges from time to time that some child is not in a normal condition, though she does not use the word "normal." She sends for the doctor, or, may be, living in Devonshire, she sends for the seventh son of a seventh son. No matter what she does, no matter how absurd may be the remedies that she tries, she knows that normally a baby's body is not covered with scarlet blotches. Have we brought, are we likely to bring our inductive political science up to this high level?

Take the best known truth about the life of man, the old major premiss, "All men are mortal." Take a generalization which aims at greater precision, "The days of our years are three score years and ten." Now among our sociologists I seem to see a great unwillingness to grapple with this somewhat elementary question. Are all states or nations mortal? Have you any phenomenon which is parallel to natural, as contrasted with violent death? Sidgwick touched this point last time, mentioning the case of the Roman empire. Now I should agree with him that if in this context we are to speak of death at all, it must be of violent death; "she died in silence biting hard among the dying hounds." But biting and struggling in the strangest fashion so that when the turmoil is over we hardly know which is dead, the Roman wolf or the German wolf-hound. If really we are to apply this metaphor of death to the events of the fifth century we shall I think have to eke out the vocabulary of biology with that of psychical research. After a while we see, to use Hobbes's splendid phrase, "the ghost of old Rome sitting crowned upon the ruins thereof." But when did the ghost become a ghost? Of course we must not ask the sociologist for anything so unscientific as a precise date. I don't want to pin him to 476 or to 1453 or to 1806, besides the question seems to me a foolish one. That a historian may now and again find it well to speak of the Empire perishing or dying in the fifth century I would not deny—though the contemporary history of what has once been even if it is not still the Eastern half of a single body politic will warn him that this analogy has difficulties before it—but I am sure that he will not ride his metaphor very far without a fall, and I don't think that biology is going to dictate a peace to the scholars who are quarrelling bitterly as to the revival of Roman organization in Merovingian Gaul.

I suppose that sometimes a political organism of a low kind, some tribe or horde does cease to exist in a fashion that we can with no great strain of language compare to a natural death; but I cannot think of any instance in which this figure of speech could be consistently elaborated for the purpose of describing the disappearance of a political organism of a high type, and I see no reason whatever for the belief that the bodies politic which we know as France, Germany and so forth must grow feeble and die if they are not destroyed from without.

There are many other questions that I should like to ask. How are we to picture some such historical events as the partition of Poland, the transfer backwards and forwards between France and Germany of lands which in a neutral language are called Alsatia and Lotharingia, the peopling of North America by men of many different races. Poland we say is torn to pieces and devoured. Yes but for a long time the undigested fragments of it which lie in three separate stomachs are striving to be one again. The Irish in North America have a for us most unfortunate habit of regarding themselves as part of the Irish nation. This cross organization, if I may so call it, is one of the great difficulties. The man who is an Englishman if you please but first a Catholic bids us pause, for surely we are sticking in the very bark of our social science and becoming the slaves of that militancy that Mr Spencer detests if we will have no organisms except such as are defined for us by international lawyers. Of course the history the Catholic church gives us is by far the grandest instance of a super-national or extra-national organization. But we have not seen the last of phenomena which in one respect we may call similar. We have not I fear seen the last of a super-national or infra-national organization of anarchists, whose doings are likely to produce remarkable changes in the police organization of various countries. We see too the beginnings of many societies which aim, it may be at the spread of science and learning, it may be at the encouragement of sport, but which neglect national boundaries. If we have a long peace before us all this may become of great importance. We may be destined to hear "An Englishman if you please but first a professor of sociology in the University of Man."

Now that complication and interdependence of all human affairs of which we find a by no means solitary example in this cross-organization gives as one of the reasons why we are not bringing our generalizations about social organisms up to that standard of precision that the old woman has attained when she speaks to us of life and death and the teeth of babies. It seems to me that those who are talking most hopefully about sociology are constantly forgetting the greatest lesson that Auguste Comte taught, though I cannot say that his practice came up to his preaching. I mean the interdependence of human affairs, for example the interdependence of political, religious and economic phenomena. It seems to me that the people who have learnt that lesson are not the sociologists but the historians. If I may make a guess, and it is here that they would find their defence against a criticism which, if I remember rightly, Sidgwick passed upon them, namely that in their keen hunt for new discoveries they neglect what after all are the important matters. They would I think say—We do not yet know except in the roughest way what are the important, the causally important matters, only this we know for certain that they were neglected by even the greatest of our predecessors. Even if you only wish to study political organization (giving to political its

narrowest sense), you are perforce compelled to study
a great many other phenomena in order that you may
put the political into their right places in a meshwork
of cause and effect.　You may for instance write a
political or constitutional history which says very little
of religion, or of rents and prices.　Life is short ;
history is the longest of all the arts ; a minute division
of labour is necessary.　No one man will ever write of
even a short period of that full history which should
be written if we are to see in all completeness the
play of those many forces which shape the life of man,
even of man regarded as a political animal.　And
therefore I think it is that some of the best because
the truest history books are those which are professedly
fragmentary, those which by their every page impress
upon the reader that he has only got before him a
small part of the whole tale.　That is the reason why,
though history may be an art, it is falling out of the
list of fine arts and will not be restored thereto for a
long time to come.　It must aim at producing not
aesthetic satisfaction but intellectual hunger.

All this by the way.　The fault, so it seems to me,
of the would-be scientific procedure of our sociologists
lies in the too frequent attempt to obtain a set of
"laws" by the study of only one class of phenomena,
the attempt for example encouraged by this University
to fashion an inductive political science.　Too often it
seems to be thought that you can detach one kind of
social phenomena from all other kinds and obtain by
induction a law for the phenomena of that class.　For
example it seems to be assumed that *the* history of *the*
family can be written and that it will come out in some

such form as this :—We start with promiscuity, the next stage is " mother right," the next " father right," and so forth. Or again take the history of property— land is owned first by the tribe or horde, then by the house-community, then by the village-community, then by the individual.

Now I will not utterly deny the possibility of some such science of the very early stages in human progress. I know too little about the materials to do that. But even in this region I think it plain that our scientific people have been far too hasty with their laws. When this evidence about barbarians gets into the hands of men who have been trained in a severe school of history and who have been taught by experience to look upon all the social phenomena as interdependent it begins to prove far less than it used to prove. Each case begins to look very unique and a law which deduces that " mother right " cannot come after " father right," or that "father right" cannot come after "mother right," or which would establish any other similar sequence of "states" begins to look exceedingly improbable. Our cases, all told, are not many and very rarely indeed have we any direct evidence of the passage of a barbarous nation from one state to another. My own belief is that by and by anthropology will have the choice between being history and being nothing.

If we climb a little higher the outlook for science is far more hopeless. If the creator of the universe had chosen to make a world full of compartments divided by walls touching the heavens, had put into each of those cells a savage race—if at some future time the progress of science had enabled men to scale these walls—I won't say but that this would have been an interesting world. We imagine the inquirer passing from cell to cell, examining the present state of its inmates, exploring their past history as recorded by documents which range from the chipped flint to the printed book. After a while he begins to know what he will find in the next box—"Ah! I thought so, promiscuity, group-marriage, exogamy,—fetishism, polytheism, monotheism, positivism—picture writing, ideogram, phonogram, ink, block-books, movable type, —the old tale." After a while he has got a law—What, no evidence of a polytheistic stage in this country. I supply that stage with certainty; the evidence must have been lost. He comes to a more puzzling case where twist the evidence how he will it breaks his law. But by this time he is justified in using such terms as "morbid," "abnormal," "retrogression"—here is a diseased community and he will investigate the climate of the cell and so forth in order to get at the cause of the disease. There remain many compartments with walls so high that they are still insurmountable. "Considering my many thousands of observations," he says, "I feel entitled to make a scientific prediction as to what is behind these barriers—in some cases I shall be wrong and to details I will not commit myself— but in general I shall be right."

A very interesting world this would be, but exceedingly unlike the world in which we live. In the real world the political organisms have been and are so few and the history of each of them has been so unique that we have no materials apt for an induction of this sort, we have no means of forming the idea of the *normal* life of a body politic. Not to speak of the biologist's materials we are not within sight of materials of that kind where our villagers have drawn their rude laws of life. We do not know, if I may so put it, that Siamese twins are abnormal. A funny comparative anatomy we should have had if the only living things that the men of science had seen were those collected in the booth of a fair—the two-headed nightingale, the pig-faced lady, and the five-legged donkey. Of course I am exaggerating if I take the monstrous assembly as a fair representative of the family of nations. Nations have much in common, but then a very great part, an indeterminately great part of what they have in common is the outcome of deliberate imitation. Of course I am aware that human beings imitate each other and that within limits they can modify the structure of their bodies by this imitative conduct—but I do not think that those who know about this matter will contradict me if I say that these modifications are trivial when compared with the changes produced in bodies politic by the analogous process. Mr Leslie Stephen has compared the acquisition by a state of a new kind of artillery to the acquisition by an animal of new and stronger teeth. The modern state says, "Go to! I will have strong teeth because another state has got them"—and straightway within a year the teeth are there. A superficial change, we may say, is to be compared with the acquisition of artificial teeth. Yes, but what a series of social changes a new weapon may set up. I read, and I suppose this to be a plausible theory, that one of the most decisive steps in that process which we call the feudalization of Gaul, and therefore of western Europe, was the outcome of an effort to obtain a cavalry able to cope with the Saracen horsemen and is it not trite that the invention of gunpowder has profoundly modified our social and political organization.

I will take an example of imitation. Near the end of the last century England had a criminal procedure that was all her own, trial by jury. I believe that I am right in saying that there was then nothing that resembled it in any country, at all events in any country that was at all likely to be taken as a model by other states. The difference was great ; the whole civilized world was against us. Our procedure was public, accusatory, contradictory, theirs was secret, inquisitory and relied on torture—the same procedure in all its main features was common to all states in the western half of Europe. And then country after country copied, deliberately and professedly copied us. Now I am very ready to allow that if England had never existed the continental procedure which was stupid and cruel would sooner or later have been destroyed, but I do not see the remotest probability that a jury or anything resembling a jury would have been introduced. I am not praising the constitution of ours ; I am not at all certain that foreigners might not have done better if they had not copied it ; but copy it they did and at first in minute detail. I am also very ready to admit that deliberately copied institutions rarely produce in their new home all the good that is expected of them and often turn out to be failures. I am quite willing to believe, for example, that this pretty new constitution of Japan will break down—I do not mind saying, though I know little that entitles me to say, that the Japanese have tried to skip too many stages—but of one thing I feel moderately certain, namely that they can never return to the place where they were in 1850, and that the great attempt to be European will for a very long time to come give shape and colour to the whole history of Japan. To what changes in the body natural can we liken these changes.

And this sort of thing has been going on since the remotest past. How pleasant it would be to have a natural history of one of the chief of those instruments which have modelled the body politic. I mean the alphabet. How nice to say you start with pictures, you pass to ideograms, to phonograms, to letters. Have we four instances of the completed process, have we three, have we two? I do not know, but the number of alphabets which were regarded as independent has been decreasing very fast of late—and now I suppose it to be established that the Egyptian alphabet is the mother of a very numerous family. Would the Greeks have evolved an alphabet if they had not borrowed from borrowers—and what changes must we not introduce in Greek political thought and political practice—and therefore in the political thought and practice of the whole western world in later times— if we deprive Greek thinkers of the alphabet.

For this reason if we are to talk of organisms at all it seems to me expedient that we should very often regard the whole progressive body of mankind as a single organism—I feel inclined to add: and as one infected by that strange, that unique disease called civilization which is running through all its organs, always breaking out in fresh places, and the end whereof no man has seen. And for this reason it is that I have a special dread of those theorists who are trying to fill up the dark ages of medieval history with laws collected from the barbarian tribes that have been observed in modern days. This procedure urges me to ask, If these tribes of which you speak are on the normal high-road of progress why have they not by this time gone further along it? If I see a set of trucks standing on a railway line from week to week, I do not say, This is the main up line to London, I say, This must be a siding. The traveller who has studied the uncorrupted savage can often tell the historian of medieval Europe what to look for, never what to find, for the German or the Slav hardly appears upon the scene before he is tainted by the subtlest of all poisons.

For one last illustration may I return to criminal procedure. Perhaps I exaggerate its importance but on the whole I think that if some fairy gave me the power of seeing a scene of one and the same kind in every age of the history of every race, the kind of scene that I would choose would be a trial for murder, because I think that it would give me so many hints as to a multitude of matters of the first importance. Well, are we to have some law as to the normal development of judicial organization in its higher stage, if so which piece of history are you going to treat as typical for that stage of progress which our modern nations covered between let me say 1100 and 1789? Is it to be the English or French, they are radically different. If we regard the mere number of persons or the mere number of nations that stand on the two sides, there can be no doubt that we must decide in favour of the French. I believe that a certain amount of generalization is possible here—that the current of changes in Italy, Spain, Germany and the Low Countries flows in the same direction as the current of changes in France, though France leads the way, and there is a great deal of deliberate imitation of French institutions. A very careful French historian with this problem before him has pointed to a course of divergence and I have little doubt that he has pointed in the right direction. Of all these countries at the critical time, say between 1150 and 1300, Britain was the only one in which there was no persecution of heretics, in which there were no heretics to persecute. Everywhere else the inquisitory process fashioned by Innocent III for the trial of heretics becomes a model for the temporal courts. I do not think that this is the full answer. If I were to say more I should have to speak of the causes which made the England of the twelfth century the most governable and the most governed of all European countries, for if a Tocqueville had visited us in 1200 he would have gone home to talk to his fellow-countrymen of English civilization and English bureaucracy. However there can I think be no doubt that we have laid our finger on one extremely important cause of divergence when we have mentioned the Catharan heresy. Behind that stand Bulgarian monks and so we go back to Manes. Or if we ask why this faith becomes endemic in the south of France we have to explore the political and

economic causes which had made Languedoc a fertile
seed-bed for any germs of heresy which might be
blown thither from any quarter.　Now the question
that I have proposed seems to me one which cannot
be answered and should not be asked.　The history
of judicial procedure in England seems to me to be
exactly as normal as the history of judicial procedure
in France or in Germany, or (to put it another way)
the idea of normalness is in this context an inappropriate and a delusive idea ; it implies a comparison
that we cannot make.　What I have said about
judicial procedure might I think be said also, with the
proper variations, about governmental and legislative
organization.　The history of the parliament of Westminster is neither more nor less normal than the history
of the parliament of Paris.　But a science of bodies
politic which knows nothing of the normal or the
abnormal—which cannot apply either of these adjec-
tives to the process which made a Louis XIV the
absolute king that he was, or the process which subjected William III to the control of a house of commons
—seems to me a science falsely so called and one which
must expect to hear from the other sciences—" Well
you don't know much and that's a fact."

That is the reason why when I see a good set of
examination questions headed by the words " Political
Science" I regret not the questions but the title.　Each
question if anything more than the loosest, vaguest,
baldest answer is expected is really a question about
some specific piece of history, and I regret the suggestion that names and dates may properly be omitted.
For example a question about the causes of feudalism

seems to me to be a question about a certain specific
piece of Frankish history, though no doubt a full
answer would say something about the causes which
prepared other nations to receive willingly or unwil-
lingly certain Frankish institutions. The answer
would not be the worse for saying a word about Japan
—but so far as I can learn from some commended
book on Japanese history I think it should say that
of the origin of the so-called feudalism of Japan next
to nothing is known and that men who profess to know
what is known say nothing about that precarious tenure
of land by warriors which I had thought to be the
very essence of Frankish and therefore of European
feudalism in its first stage. I do not regret the questions—on the contrary it seems to me very desirable
that under whatever name youths should be taught
as much history as possible—but I do regret the suggestion that at the present time the student of history
should hope for and aim at ever wider and wider
generalizations.

MORAL PERSONALITY AND LEGAL PERSONALITY[1]

THE memory of Henry Sidgwick is not yet in need of revival. It lives a natural life among us, and will live so long as those who saw and heard him draw breath. Still the generations, as generations must be reckoned in this place, succeed each other rapidly, and already I may be informing, rather than reminding, some of you when I say that among his many generous acts was the endowment of a readership in English Law, of which one of his pupils was fortunate enough to be the first holder. If that pupil ventures to speak here this afternoon, it will not be unnatural that he should choose his theme from the borderland where ethical speculation marches with jurisprudence.

Ethics and Jurisprudence.—That such a border-land exists all would allow, and, as usually happens in such cases, each of the neighbouring powers is wont to assert, in practice, if not in theory, its right to define the scientific frontier. We, being English, are, so I fancy, best acquainted with the claims of ethical speculation, and in some sort prejudiced in their favour. We are proud of a long line of moralists,

---

[1] The Sidgwick Lecture for 1903, delivered at Newnham College.

which has not ended in Sidgwick and Martineau and Green, in Herbert Spencer and Leslie Stephen, and we conceive that the "jurist," if indeed such an animal exists, plays, and of right ought to play, a subordinate, if not subservient, part in the delimitation of whatever moral sciences there may happen to be. I am not sure, however, that the poor lawyer with antiquarian tastes might not take his revenge by endeavouring to explain the moral philosopher as a legal phenomenon, and by classing our specifically English addiction to ethics as a by-product of the specifically English history of English law. That statement, if it be more than the mere turning of the downtrodden worm, is obviously too large, as it is too insolent, a text for an hour's lecture. What I shall attempt will be to indicate one problem of a speculative sort, which (so it seems to me) does not get the attention that it deserves from speculative Englishmen, and does not get that attention because it is shrouded from their view by certain peculiarities of the legal system in which they live.

The Natural Person and the Corporation.— Texts, however, I will have. My first is taken from Mr Balfour. Lately in the House of Commons the Prime Minister spoke of trade unions as corporations. Perhaps, for he is an accomplished debater, he anticipated an interruption. At any rate, a distinguished lawyer on the Opposition benches interrupted him with "The trade unions are not corporations." "I know that," retorted Mr Balfour, "I am talking English, not law." A long story was packed into that admirable reply[1].

[1] The *Standard*, April 23, 1904. *Mr Balfour:* "The mere fact

And my second text is taken from Mr Dicey, who delivered the Sidgwick lecture last year. "When," he said, "a body of twenty, or two thousand, or two hundred thousand men bind themselves together to act in a particular way for some common purpose, they create a body, which by no fiction of law, but by the very nature of things, differs from the individuals of whom it is constituted[1]." I have been waiting a long while for an English lawyer of Professor Dicey's eminence to say what he said—to talk so much "English." Let me repeat a few of his words with the stress where I should like it to lie: "they create a body, which *by no fiction of law, but by the very nature of things,* differs from the individuals of whom it is constituted." So says Blackstone's successor. Blackstone himself would, I think, have inverted that phrase, and would have ascribed to a fiction of law that phenomenon—or whatever we are to call it—which Mr Dicey ascribes to the very nature of things.

Now for a long time past the existence of this phenomenon has been recognised by lawyers, and the orthodox manner of describing it has been somewhat of this kind. Besides men or "natural persons," law knows persons of another kind. In particular it knows the corporation, and for a multitude of purposes it treats

that funds can be used, or are principally used, for benefit purposes, is surely not of itself a sufficient reason for saying that trade unions, and trade unions alone, out of all the corporations in the country, commercial——" *Sir R. Reid:* "The trade unions are not corporations." *Mr Balfour:* "I know; I am talking English, not law" (*cheers and laughter*).

[1] Professor Dicey's lecture on the Combination Laws is printed in *Harvard Law Review*, xvii. 511. See p. 513.

the corporation very much as it treats the man. Like the man, the corporation is (forgive this compound adjective) a right-and-duty-bearing unit. Not all the legal propositions that are true of a man will be true of a corporation. For example, it can neither marry nor be given in marriage ; but in a vast number of cases you can make a legal statement about x and y which will hold good whether these symbols stand for two men or for two corporations, or for a corporation and a man. The University can buy land from Downing, or hire the gildhall from the Town, or borrow money from the London Assurance ; and we may say that *exceptis excipiendis* a court of law can treat these transactions, these acts in the law, as if they took place between two men, between Styles and Nokes. But further, we have to allow that the corporation is in some sense composed of men, and yet between the corporation and one of its members there may exist many, perhaps most, of those legal relationships which can exist between two human beings. I can contract with the University : the University can contract with me. You can contract with the Great Northern Company as you can with the Great Eastern, though you happen to be a shareholder in the one and not in the other. In either case there stands opposite to you another right-and-duty-bearing unit—might I not say another individual ?—a single " not-yourself " that can pay damages or exact them. You expect results of this character, and, if you did not get them, you would think ill of law and lawyers. Indeed, I should say that, the less we know of law, the more confidently we Englishmen expect that the organised group, whether called a corporation or not, will be treated as person : that is, as right-and-duty-bearing unit.

Legal Orthodoxy and the Fictitious Person. —Perhaps I can make the point clearer by referring to an old case. We are told that in Edward IV's day the mayor and commonalty—or, as we might be tempted to say, the municipal corporation—of Newcastle gave a bond to the man who happened to be mayor, he being named by his personal name, and that the bond was held to be void because a man cannot be bound to himself[1]. The argument that is implicit in those few words seems to us quaint, if not sophistical. But the case does not stand alone ; far from it. If our business is with medieval history and our aim is to re-think it before we re-present it, here lies one of our most serious difficulties. Can we allow the group—gild, town, village, nation—to stand over against each and all of its members as a distinct person ? To be concrete, look at Midsummer Common. It belongs, and, so far as we know, has always in some sense belonged, to the burgesses of Cambridge. But in what sense ? Were they co-proprietors ? were they corporators ? Neither —both ?

I would not trouble you with medievalism. Only this by the way : If once you become interested in the sort of history that tries to unravel these and similar problems, you will think some other sorts of history

---

[1] Year Book, 21 Edw. IV, f. 68 : "Come fuit ajudgé en le cas del Maior de Newcastle ou le Maior et le Cominalty fist un obligation a mesme le person que fuit Maior par son propre nosme, et pur ceo que il mesme fuit Maior, et ne puit faire obligation a luy mesme, il [=l'obligation] fuit tenus voide."

rather superficial. Perhaps you will go the length of saying that much the most interesting person that you ever knew was *persona ficta*. But my hour flies.

To steer a clear or any course is hard, for controversial rocks abound. Still, with some security we may say that at the end of the Middle Age a great change in men's thoughts about groups of men was taking place, and that the main agent in the transmutation was Roman Law. Now just how the classical jurists of Rome conceived their *corpora* and *universitates* became in the nineteenth century a much debated question. The profane outsider says of the Digest what some one said of another book :

> Hic liber est in quo quaerit sua dogmata quisque
> Invenit et pariter dogmata quisque sua.

Where people have tried to make antique texts do modern work, the natural result is what Mr Buckland has happily called "Wardour Street Roman Law[1]." Still, of this I suppose there can be no doubt, that there could, without undue pressure, be obtained from the Corpus Juris a doctrine of corporations, which, so far as some main outlines are concerned, is the doctrine which has ruled the modern world. Nor would it be disputed that this work was done by the legists and canonists of the Middle Age, the canonists leading the way. The group can be a person : co-ordinated, equiparated, with the man, with the natural person.

With the "natural" person—for the personality of

---

[1] Buckland, "Wardour Street Roman Law," *Law Quarterly Review*, XVII, 179.

the *universitas*, of the corporation, is not natural—it is fictitious. This is a very important part of the canonical doctrine, first clearly proclaimed, so we are told, by the greatest lawyer that ever sat upon the chair of St Peter, Pope Innocent IV. You will recall Mr Dicey's words : "not by fiction of law, but by the very nature of things." Invert those words, and you will have a dogma that works like leaven in the transformation of medieval society.

If the personality of the corporation is a legal fiction, it is the gift of the prince. It is not for you and me to feign and to force our fictions upon our neighbours. "Solus princeps fingit quod in rei veritate non est[1]." An argument drawn from the very nature of fictions thus came to the aid of less questionably Roman doctrines about the illicitness of all associations, the existence of which the prince has not authorised. I would not exaggerate the importance of a dogma, theological or legal. A dogma is of no importance unless and until there is some great desire within it. But what was understood to be the Roman doctrine of corporations was an apt lever for those forces which were transforming the medieval nation into the modern State. The federalistic structure of medieval society is threatened. No longer can we see the body politic as *communitas communitatum*, a system of groups, each of which in its turn is a system of groups. All that stands between the State and the individual has but a derivative and precarious existence.

Do not let us at once think of England.   English

---

[1] Lucas de Penna, cited in Gierke, *Das deutsche Genossenschafts-recht*, iii, 371.

history can never be an elementary subject : we are not logical enough to be elementary. If we must think of England, then let us remember that we are in the presence of a doctrine which in Charles II's day condemns all—yes, all—of the citizens of London to prison for "presuming to act as a corporation." We may remember also how corporations appear to our absolutist Hobbes as troublesome entozoa. But it is always best to begin with France, and there, I take it, we may see the pulverising, macadamising tendency in all its glory, working from century to century, reducing to impotence, and then to nullity, all that intervenes between Man and State.

The State and the Corporation.—In this, as in some other instances, the work of the monarchy issues in the work of the revolutionary assemblies. It issues in the famous declaration of August 18, 1792 : "A State that is truly free ought not to suffer within its bosom any corporation, not even such as, being dedicated to public instruction, have merited well of the country[1]." That was one of the mottoes of modern absolutism: the absolute State faced the absolute individual. An appreciable part of the interest of the French Revolution seems to me to be open only to those who will be at pains to give a little thought to the theory of corporations. Take, for example, those memorable debates touching ecclesiastical property. To whom belong these broad lands when you have pushed fictions aside, when you have become a

---

[1] "Considérant qu'un État vraiment libre ne doit souffrir dans son sein aucune corporation, pas même celles qui, vouées à l'enseignement public, ont bien mérité de la patrie."

truly philosophical jurist with a craving for the natural? To the nation, which has stepped into the shoes of the prince. That is at least a plausible answer, though an uncomfortable suspicion that the State itself is but a questionably real person may not be easily dispelled. And as with the churches, the universities, the trade-gilds, and the like, so also with the communes, the towns and villages. Village property—there was a great deal of village property in France—was exposed to the dilemma : it belongs to the State, or else it belongs to the now existing villagers. I doubt we Englishmen, who never clean our slates, generally know how clean the French slate was to be.

Associations in France.—Was to be, I say. Looking back now, French lawyers can regard the nineteenth century as the century of association, and, if there is to be association, if there is to be group-formation, the problem of personality cannot be evaded, at any rate if we are a logical people. Not to mislead, I must in one sentence say, that even the revolutionary legislators spared what we call partnership, and that for a long time past French law has afforded comfortable quarters for various kinds of groups, provided (but notice this) that the group's one and only object was the making of pecuniary gain. Recent writers have noticed it as a paradox that the State saw no harm in the selfish people who wanted dividends, while it had an intense dread of the comparatively unselfish people who would combine with some religious, charitable, literary, scientific, artistic purpose in view. I cannot within my few minutes be precise, but at the beginning of this twentieth century it was still a misdemeanour to belong to any unauthorised *association* having more than twenty members. A licence from the prefect, which might be obtained with some ease, made the *association* non-criminal, made it licit ; but personality—"civil personality," as they say in France—was only to be acquired with difficulty as the gift of the central government.

Now I suppose it to be notorious that during the last years of the nineteenth century law so unfavourable to liberty of association was still being maintained, chiefly, if not solely, because prominent, typically prominent, among the *associations* known to Frenchmen stood the *congrégations*—religious houses, religious orders. The question how these were to be treated divided the nation, and at last, in 1901, when a new and very important law was made about "the contract of association," a firm line was drawn between the non-religious sheep and the religious goats. With the step then taken and the subsequent woes of the congregations I have here no concern ; but the manner in which religious and other groups had previously been treated by French jurisprudence seems to me exceedingly instructive. It seems to me to prove so clearly that in a country where people take their legal theories seriously, a country where a Prime Minister will often talk law without ceasing to talk agreeable French, the question whether the group is to be, as we say, "a person in the eye of the law" is the question whether the group as group can enjoy more than an uncomfortable and precarious existence. I am not thinking of attacks directed against it by the State. I am thinking of collisions between it and private persons. It lives at the mercy of its neighbours, for a law-suit will dissolve it into its constituent atoms.   Nor is that all. Sometimes its neighbours will have cause to complain of its legal impersonality.   They will have been thinking of it as a responsible right-and-duty-bearing unit, while at the touch of law it becomes a mere many, and a practically, if not theoretically, irresponsible many.

Group-Personality.—During the nineteenth century (so I understand the case) a vast mass of experience, French, German, Belgian, Italian, and Spanish (and I might add, though the atmosphere is hazier, English and American), has been making for a result which might be stated in more than one way.   (1) If the law allows men to form permanently organised groups, those groups will be for common opinion right-and-duty-bearing units; and if the law-giver will not openly treat them as such, he will misrepresent, or, as the French say, he will "denature" the facts: in other words, he will make a mess and call it law.   (2) Group-personality is no purely legal phenomenon.   The law-giver may say that it does not exist, where, as a matter of moral sentiment, it does exist.   When that happens, he incurs the penalty ordained for those who ignorantly or wilfully say the thing that is not.   If he wishes to smash a group, let him smash it, send the policeman, raid the rooms, impound the minute-book, fine, and imprison; but if he is going to tolerate the group, he must recognise its personality, for otherwise he will be dealing wild blows which may fall on those who stand outside the group as well as those who stand within it.   (3) For the morality of common sense the group is person, is right-and-duty-bearing unit. Let the moral philosopher explain this, let him explain it as illusion, let him explain it away; but he ought not to leave it unexplained, nor, I think, will he be able to say that it is an illusion which is losing power, for, on the contrary, it seems to me to be persistently and progressively triumphing over certain philosophical and theological prejudices.

You know that classical distribution of Private Law under three grand rubrics—Persons, Things, Actions. Half a century ago the first of these three titles seemed to be almost vanishing from civilised jurisprudence. No longer was there much, if anything, to be said of exceptional classes, of nobles, clerics, monks, serfs, slaves, excommunicates or outlaws. Children there might always be, and lunatics; but women had been freed from tutelage. ⌐The march of the progressive societies was, as we all know, from status to contract.¬ And now? And now that forlorn old title is wont to introduce us to ever new species and new genera of persons, to vivacious controversy, to teeming life; and there are many to tell us that the line of advance is no longer from status to contract, but through contract to something that contract cannot explain, and for which our best, if an inadequate, name is the personality of the organised group. \

Fact or Fiction ?—Theorising, of course, there has been. I need not say so, nor that until lately it was almost exclusively German. Our neighbours' conception of the province of jurisprudence has its advantages as well as its disadvantages. On the one hand, ethical speculation (as we might call it) of a very interesting kind was until these last days too often

presented in the unattractive guise of Wardour Street
Roman Law, or else, raising the Germanistic cry of
"Loose from Rome!" it plunged into an exposition
of medieval charters.   On the other hand, the theorising is often done by men who have that close grasp
of concrete modern fact which comes of a minute
and practical study of legal systems.   Happily it is no
longer necessary to go straight to Germany.   That
struggle over "the contract of association" to which
I have alluded, those woes of the "congregations" of
which all have heard, invoked foreign learning across
the border, and now we may read in lucid French of
the various German theories.   Good reading I think
it; and what interests me especially is that the French
lawyer, with all his orthodoxy (legal orthodoxy) and
conservatism, with all his love of clarity and abhorrence
of mysticism, is often compelled to admit that the traditional dogmas of the law-school have broken down.
Much disinclined though he may be to allow the group
a real will of its own, just as really real as the will of a
man, still he has to admit that if n men unite themselves
in an organised body, jurisprudence, unless it wishes to
pulverise the group, must see $n + 1$ persons.   And that
for the mere lawyer should I think be enough.   "Of
heaven and hell he has no power to sing," and he might
content himself with a phenomenal reality—such reality,
for example, as the lamp-post has for the idealistic on-
tologist.   Still, we do not like to be told that we are
dealing in fiction, even if it be added that we needs
must feign, and the thought will occur to us that a
fiction that we needs must feign is somehow or another
very like the simple truth.

Why we English people are not interested in a problem that is being seriously discussed in many other
lands, that is a question to which I have tried to provide
some sort of answer elsewhere[1]. It is a long, and you
would think it a very dreary, story about the most
specifically English of all our legal institutes; I mean
the trust. All that I can say here is that the device
of building a wall of trustees enabled us to construct
bodies which were not technically corporations and
which yet would be sufficiently protected from the
assaults of individualistic theory. The personality of
such bodies—so I should put it—though explicitly
denied by lawyers, was on the whole pretty well recognised in practice. That something of this sort
happened you might learn from one simple fact.
For some time past we have had upon our statute
book the term "unincorporate body." Suppose that
a Frenchman saw it, what would he say? "Unincorporate body: inanimate soul! No wonder your Prime
Minister, who is a philosopher, finds it hard to talk
English and talk law at the same time."

One result of this was, so I fancy, that the speculative Englishman could not readily believe that in
this quarter there was anything to be explored except
some legal trickery unworthy of exploration. The
lawyer assured him that it was so, and he saw around
him great and ancient, flourishing and wealthy groups
—the Inns of Court at their head—which, so the
lawyer said, were not persons. To have cross-examined

[1] Maitland, "Trust und Korporation," Wien, 1904 (from *Grünhut's
Zeitschrift für das Privat- und Öffentliche-Recht*, vol. xxxii). See
below, p. 321.

the lawyer over the bodiliness of his "unincorporate body" might have brought out some curious results; but such a course was hardly open to those who shared our wholesome English contempt for legal technique.

The Ultimate Moral Unit.—Well, I must finish; and yet perhaps I have not succeeded in raising just the question that I wanted to ask. Can I do that in two or three last sentences? It is a moral question, and therefore I will choose my hypothetical case from a region in which our moral sentiments are not likely to be perplexed by legal technique. My organised group shall be a sovereign state. Let us call it Nusquamia. Like many other sovereign states, it owes money, and I will suppose that you are one of its creditors. You are not receiving the expected interest and there is talk of repudiation. That being so, I believe that you will be, and indeed I think that you ought to be, indignant, morally, righteously indignant. Now the question that I want to raise is this: Who is it that really owes you money? Nusquamia. Granted, but can you convert the proposition that Nusquamia owes you money into a series of propositions imposing duties on certain human beings that are now in existence? The task will not be easy. Clearly you do not think that every Nusquamian owes you some aliquot share of the debt. No one thinks in that way. The debt of Venezuela is not owed by Fulano y Zutano and the rest of them. Nor, I think, shall we get much good out of the word "collectively," which is the smudgiest word in the English language, for the largest "collection" of zeros is only zero. I do not wish to say that I have suggested an impossible task, and that the right-and-duty-bearing group must be for the philosopher an ultimate and unanalysable moral unit: as ultimate and unanalysable, I mean, as is the man. Only if that task can be performed, I think that in the interests of jurisprudence and of moral philosophy it is eminently worthy of circumspect performance. As to our national law, it has sound instincts, and muddles along with semi-personality and demi-semi-personality towards convenient conclusions. Still, I cannot think that Parliament's timid treatment of the trade unions has been other than a warning, or that it was a brilliant day in our legal annals when the affairs of the Free Church of Scotland were brought before the House of Lords, and the dead hand fell with a resounding slap upon the living body. As to philosophy, that is no affair of mine. I speak with conscious ignorance and unfeigned humility; only of this I feel moderately sure, that those who are to tell us of the very nature of things and the very nature of persons will not be discharging their duties to the full unless they come to close terms with that triumphant fiction, if fiction it be, of which I have said in your view more than too much, and in my own view less than too little[1].

[1] In the following list will be found the titles of a few French books which (by way of historical retrospect or legal exposition or juristic speculation or political controversy) illustrate competing theories of legal personality and bring them into close relation with a recent and interesting chapter of French history, namely the campaign against the *congrégations*. Some of these works (see especially M. Michoud's articles) will also serve as an introduction to German speculation.

J. Brissaud, *Manuel d'histoire du droit français*, pp. 1769—1785:

Paris, 1899. M. Planiol, *Traité élémentaire de droit civil*, t. i, pp. 259—290 (*Les personnes fictives*); t. ii, pp. 618—623 (*Association*): Paris, 1901. G. Trouillot et F. Chapsal, *Du contrat d'association —Commentaire de la Loi du* 1ᵉʳ *Juillet* 1901: Paris, 1902. M. Vauthier, *Études sur les personnes morales*: Bruxelles et Paris, 1887. Le Comte de Vareilles-Sommières, *Du contrat d'association, ou, La loi française permet-elle aux associations non reconnues de posséder?* Paris, 1903. Le Marquis de Vareilles-Sommières, *Les personnes morales*: Paris, 1902. L. Michoud, "La notion de personnalité morale" (*Revue du droit public et de la science politique*, t. xi, pp. 1, 193: Paris, 1899). A. Mestre, *Les personnes morales et le problème de leur responsabilité pénale*: Paris, 1899. M. Hauriou, "De la personnalité comme élément de la réalité sociale" (*Revue générale du droit, de la législation et de la jurisprudence*, t. xxii, pp. 1, 119: Paris, 1898). D. Négulesco, *Le problème juridique de la personnalité morale et son application aux sociétés civiles et commerciales*: Paris, 1900. A. Gouffre de Lapradelle, *Théorie et pratique des fondations perpétuelles*: Paris, 1895. F. Garcin, *La mainmorte,—de* 1749 *à* 1901. Paris et Lyon, 1903. J. Imbart de Latour, *Des biens communaux*: Paris, 1899. P. M. Waldeck-Rousseau, *Associations et congrégations*: Paris, 1901. E. Combes, *Une campagne laïque* (1902—1903), Préface par Anatole France: Paris, 1904.

TRUST AND CORPORATION [1]

NOT very long ago, in the pages of this Review, Dr Redlich, whose book on English Local Government we in England are admiring, did me the honour of referring to some words that I had written concerning our English Corporations and our English Trusts [2]. I have obtained permission to say with his assistance a few more words upon the same matter, in the hope that I may thereby invite attention to a part of our English legal history which, so far as my knowledge goes, has not attracted all the notice that it deserves.

Perhaps I need hardly say that we on this side of the sea are profoundly grateful to those foreign explorers who have been at pains to investigate our insular arrangements. Looking at us from the outside, it has been possible for them to teach us much about ourselves. Still we cannot but know that it is not merely for the sake of England that English law, both ancient and modern, has been examined. Is it not true that England has played a conspicuous, if a passive, part in that development of historical jurisprudence which was one of the most remarkable

---

[1] *Grünhut's Zeitschrift für das Privat- und Öffentliche Recht*, Bd. xxxii.

[2] *Ibid.*, Bd. xxx, S. 167.

scientific achievements of the nineteenth century? Over and over again it has happened that our island has been able to supply just that piece of evidence, just that link in the chain of proof, which the Germanist wanted but could not find at home. Should I go too far if I said that no Germanistic theory is beyond dispute until it has been tested upon our English material?

Now I know of nothing English that is likely to be more instructive to students of legal history, and in particular to those who are concerned with Germanic law, than that *Rechtsinstitut* of ours which Dr Redlich described in the following well chosen words: "das Rechtsinstitut des Trust, das ursprünglich für gewisse Bedürfnisse des englischen Grundeigenthumsrechtes enstanden, nach und nach zu einem allgemeinen Rechtsinstitute ausgebildet worden ist und auf allen Gebieten des Rechtslebens praktische Bedeutung und eine ausserordentlich verfeinerte juristische Ausbildung erlangt hat."

It is a big affair our Trust. This must be evident to anyone who knows—and who does not know?—that out in America the mightiest trading corporations that the world has ever seen are known by the name of "Trusts." And this is only the Trust's last exploit. Dr Redlich is right when he speaks of it as an "allgemeine Rechtsinstitut." It has all the generality, all the elasticity of Contract. Anyone who wishes to know England, even though he has no care for the detail of Private Law, should know a little of our Trust.

We may imagine an English lawyer who was

unfamiliar with the outlines of foreign law taking up the new Civil Code of Germany. "This," he would say, "seems a very admirable piece of work, worthy in every way of the high reputation of German jurists. But surely it is not a complete statement of German private law. Surely there is a large gap in it. I have looked for the Trust, but I cannot find it; and to omit the Trust is, I should have thought, almost as bad as to omit Contract." And then he would look at his book-shelves and would see stout volumes entitled " Law of Trusts," and he would open his " Reports " and would see trust everywhere, and he would remember how he was a trustee and how almost every man that he knew was a trustee.

Is it too bold of me to guess the sort of answer that he would receive from some German friend who had not studied England ? " Well, before you blame us, you might tell us what sort of thing is this wonderful Trust of yours. You might at least point out the place where the supposed omission occurs. See, here is our general scheme of Private Law. Are we to place this precious *Rechtsinstitut* under the title *Sachenrecht* or should it stand under *Recht der Schuldverhältnisse*, or, to use a term which may be more familiar, *Obligationen-recht* ? "

To this elementary question I know of no reply which would be given at once and as a matter of course by every English lawyer. We are told in one of our old books that in the year 1348 a certain English lawyer found himself face to face with the words *contra inhibitionem novi operis*, and therefore said, "en ceux parolx il n'y ad pas d'entendment."

I am not at all sure that some men very learned in
our law would not be inclined to give a similar answer
if they were required to bring our Trust under any
one of those rubrics which divide the German Code.

"Das englische Recht," says Dr Redlich, "kennt
keine Unterscheidung von öffentlichem und privatem
Recht." In the sense in which he wrote that
sentence it is, I think, very true. Now-a-days young
men who are beginning to study our law are expected
to read books in which there is talk about this distinction : the distinction between Private Law and
Public Law. Perhaps I might say that we regard
those terms as potential rubrics. We think, or many
of us think, that if all our law were put into a code
that pair of terms might conveniently appear in very
large letters. But they are not technical terms. If
I saw in an English newspaper that Mr A. B. had
written a book on "Public Law," my first guess would
be that he had been writing about International Law.
If an English newspaper called Mr C. D. a "publicist,"
I should think that he wrote articles in newspapers
and magazines about political questions.

In the same sense it might be said that English
Law knows no distinction between *Sachenrecht* and
Obligationenrecht. It is needless to say that in England
as elsewhere there is a great difference between owning
a hundred gold coins and being owed a hundred pounds,
and of course one of the first lessons that any be-
ginner must learn is the apprehension of this difference.
And then he will read in more or less speculative
books—books of "General Jurisprudence"—about *iura
in rem* and *iura in personam,* and perhaps will be

taught that if English law were put into a Code, this distinction would appear very prominently. But here again we have much rather potential rubrics than technical terms. The technical concepts with which the English lawyer will have to operate, the tools of his trade (if I may so speak), are of a different kind.

I have said this because, so it seems to me, the Trust could hardly have been evolved among a people who had clearly formulated the distinction between a right *in personam* and a right *in rem*, and had made that distinction one of the main outlines of their legal system. I am aware that the question how far this distinction was grasped in medieval Germany has been debated by distinguished Germanists, and I would not even appear to be intervening between Dr Laband and Dr Heusler. Still I cannot doubt who it is that has said the words that will satisfy the student of English legal history. In the thirteenth century Englishmen find a distinction between the *actio in rem* and the *actio in personam* in those Roman books which they regard as the representatives of enlightened jurisprudence. They try to put their own actions— and they have a large number of separate actions, each with its own name, each with his own procedure— under these cosmopolitan rubrics. And what is the result? Very soon the result is that which Dr Laband has admirably stated :

" Die Klage characterisirt sich nach dem, was der Kläger fordert, wozu ihm der Richter verhelfen soll, nicht nach dem Grunde, aus welchem er es fordert... Dagegen vermisst man in den Quellen des Mittelalters eine Characterisirung der Klagen nach dem zu Grunde liegenden Rechtsverhältniss und insbesondere der Unterscheidung dinglicher und persönlicher Klagen. Der der römischen Bezeichnung *actio in rem* scheinbar entsprechende Ausdruck *clage up gut* [in England *real action*] hat gar keinen Zusammenhang mit der juristischen Natur des Rechts des Klägers, sondern er bezieht sich nur darauf, dass das bezeichnete Gut vom Kläger in Anspruch genommen wird[1]."

To this very day we are incumbered with those terms "real property" and "personal property" which serve us as approximate equivalents for *Liegenschaft* and *Fahrnis*. The reason is that in the Middle Age, and indeed until 1854, the claimant of a movable could only obtain a judgment which gave his adversary a choice between giving up that thing and paying its value. And so, said we, there is no *actio realis* for a horse or a book. Such things are not "realty"; they are not "real property." Whether this use of words is creditable to English lawyers who are living in the twentieth century is not here the question ; but it seems to me exceedingly instructive.

For my own part if a foreign friend asked me to tell him in one word whether the right of the English *Destinatär* (the person for whom property is held in trust) is *dinglich* or *obligatorisch*, I should be inclined to say : "No, I cannot do that. If I said *dinglich*, that would be untrue. If I said *obligatorisch*, I should suggest what is false. In ultimate analysis the right may be *obligatorisch* ; but for many practical purposes of great importance it has been treated as though it were *dinglich*, and indeed people habitually speak and think of it as a kind of *Eigenthum*."

This, then, is the first point to which I would ask

---

[1] Laband, *Die Vermögensrechtlichen Klagen*, S. 5—7.

attention; and I do so because, so far as my knowledge goes, this point is hardly to be seen upon the surface of those books about English law that a foreign student is most likely to read[1].

I.

Before going further I should like to transcribe some sentences from an essay in legal history which has interested me deeply: I mean "Die langobardische Treuhand und ihre Umbildung zur Testamentsvollstreckung" by Dr Alfred Schultze[2]. I think that we may see what is at the root the same *Rechtsinstitut* taking two different shapes in different ages and different lands, and perhaps a German observer will find our Trust the easier after a short excursion into Lombardy.

To be brief, the Lombard cannot make a genuine testament. He therefore transfers the whole or some part of his property to a *Treuhänder*, who is to carry out his instructions. Such instructions may leave greater or less liberty of action to the *Treuhänder*. He may only have to transfer the things to some named person or some particular church, or, at the other extreme, he may have an unlimited choice among

---

[1] Heymann in the sketch of English law that is included in the new edition of Holtzendorff's *Encyklopädie* has declined to place our Trust under "Das Sachenrecht" or under "Forderungsrecht." It seems to me that in this as in many other instances he has shown a true insight into the structure of our system.

[2] Gierke's *Untersuchungen*, 1895.

the various means by which the soul of a dead man can be benefited. And now we will listen to Dr Schultze.

"Das Treuhandverhältnis wird regelmässig begründet durch Vertrag zwischen dem letztwillig Verfügenden und dem von ihm zum Treuhänder Erkorenen. Dieser Vertrag stellt sich da, wo dem Treuhänder eine unmittelbare Gewalt über körperliche Sachen zugewiesen wird, häufig schon durch seine äussere Erscheinung als dinglicher Vertrag dar. Jene Sachen werden ihm *per cartam* zu dem gewollten Zweck übertragen. Dabei ist ausdrücklich von 'tradere res' die Rede....Einzelne Urkunden des Regesto di Farfa aus dem 11. Jahrhundert sprechen von der Investitur, die der Schenker dem Treuhänder ertheilt hat. Der Schenker tradirt an den Treuhänder nicht blos das fragliche Grundstück, sondern auch, wie das nach einer langobardischen Rechtssitte bei Uebertragung dinglicher Rechte zu geschehen pflegt, seine eigene Erwerbsurkunde und diejenigen seiner Vorgänger, soweit sie sich in seinem Besitze befinden. Er wendet, wenn er ein Franke ist, die fränkischen Investitur-symbole, festuca notata, Messer, Scholle, Zweig und Handschuh, an."

That is what I should have expected, an English reader would say. The land is conveyed to the trustee. Of course he has *ein dingliches Recht*. He has *Eigenthum*. In the Middle Age he will be *feoffatus, vestitus et seisitus; feffé, vestu et seisi*. And naturally *die Erwerbsurkunden*, "the title deeds," are handed over to him. But we must return to Dr Schultze's exposition.

"Der Treuhänder hat, wie soeben nachgewiesen ist, kraft Rechtsnachfolge ein eigenes dingliches Recht an den ihm zugewiesenen körperlichen Sachen. Welcher Art ist dieses Recht?

Wir haben zunächst einige Urkunden herauszuheben die keinen Zweifel daran lassen, dass hier der Treuhänder volles Eigenthum hat und in der Nutzniessung und Verfügung weder dinglich noch obligatorisch beschränkt ist. Es sind sämmtlich Fälle, in denen der Geber die Sachen im Interesse seines Seelenheils nach freier Bestimmung des Treuhänders verwendet wissen will, sodass der letztere die Rolle des Dispensators im eigentlichen Sinne hat."

This, however, was not the common case. Generally what the *Treuhänder* has is not

"die volle, freie Verfügungsmacht, sondern ein in bestimmte Schranken gebanntes Veräusserungsrecht." "Er nimmt hier im Verhältnis zu der oben geschilderten Rechtsstellung des Dispensators *optimo jure* eine Minderstellung ein. Aber worin besteht die Minderung? Es kann an dieser Stelle noch unerörtert bleiben, ob hier der Treuhänder obligatorisch beschränkt, dem Geber oder dessen Erben oder sonst jemandem kraft Privatrechts obligatorisch verpflichtet ist. Es handelt sich hier vielmehr um die Frage, ob sein Recht ein dinglich gemindertes ist. Diese Frage ist zu bejahen."

Dr Schultze then proceeds to expound the *Treuhänder's* right as

"Eigenthum, aber Eigenthum unter auflösender Bedingung, resolutiv bedingtes Eigenthum." "Die Bedingung wurde existent wenn das Vergabungsobject dem gesetzten Zweck entfremdet oder der Zweck aus irgend einem Grunde unerfüllbar wurde. Die Folge war, dass das Eigenthum auf Seiten des Treuhänders erlosch und ohne jede Rücktradition dem Geber oder seinen Erben anfiel, die nun mit der dinglichen Klage (Eigenthumsklage) das Gut wieder in ihren Besitz bringen konnten."

Now that is not true of the English trustee. His right is not "resolutiv bedingtes Eigenthum." I cite it, however, because of what follows. And what follows is highly instructive to those who would study English "equity": indeed some of Dr Schultze's sentences might have been written about the England of the fourteenth or the England of the twentieth century.

"Die in der schwebenden Resolutivbedingung liegende dingliche Beschränkung des Eigenthums zu treuer Hand konnte gegen Drittererwerber Wirkung haben....Diese Wirkung gegen Dritte setzte

Offenkundigkeit (Publizität) jener dinglichen Beschränkung voraus, ein solches Mass von Offenkundigkeit, dass jeder Dritter-werber ohne Härte der Beschränkung unterworfen werden konnte, gleichgültig ob er im einzelnen Falle wirklich davon wusste oder nicht. Nun mögen auch die Langobarden in Bezug auf Grund-stücke früher eine volksrechtliche Form der Rechtsveränderung gekannt haben, welche den Act selbst im Augenblick seiner Vornahme den Volksgenossen in genügendem Masse kundthat (Vornahme auf dem Grundstück, in mallo). In der hier interessi-renden Zeit war aber bei weitem vorherrschend und wurde jedenfalls bei den ordentlichen Vergabungen auf den Todesfall, auch denjenigen zu treuer Hand, ausschliesslich angewendet die Form der *traditio cartae.*...Jede Rechtsveränderung die vermittelst traditio cartae stattgefunden hatte, war damit erschöpfend beurkundet....Wer ein Grundstück in derivativer Weise erwerben wollte, erlangte daher über das Recht seines Auktors dadurch sichere Auskunft, dass er sich die carta vorweisen liess, die seinerzeit für den Auktor von dessen Vorgänger ausgestellt worden war. Es wurde sogar schon frühe üblich diese carta zur dauernden Sicherung der Legitimation sich mit dem Grundstück zusammen übereignen zu lassen. Und— das war nur eine selbstverständliche Folgerung—nicht blos die Erwerbsurkunde des Auktors, sondern auch die in dessen Hand befindlichen sämmtlichen Erwerbsurkunden seiner Vorgänger.... Wer also von einem Treuhànder ein Grundstück erwerben wollte, erkannte sofort bei Prüfung der bis zu diesem herabreichenden Urkunden die Treuhänder-Eigenschaft des Gegenparts, die Bedingt-heit seines Eigenthums. Kümmerte er sich aber der Rechtssitte zuwider nicht um die Erwerbsurkunden, so lag dann darin, dass die Bedingung, unvorhergesehen, auch gegen ihn ihre Wirksamkeit entfaltete, keine Härte; der ihm etwa daraus erwachsende Schade traf ihn nicht unverschuldet."

But what have we here?—an Englishman might say—why, it is our "doctrine of constructive notice," the key-stone which holds together the lofty edifice of trusts that we have raised. These Lombards, he would add, seem to have gone a little too far, and with a "resolutiv bedingtes Eigenthum" we have not to do.

But of course the *Eigenthum* of a piece of land is conveyed *per traditionem cartae*. And of course every prudent buyer of land will expect to see *die Erwerbs-urkunden* which are in his Auktor's hand and to have them handed over to himself when the sale is completed. "Kümmerte er sich aber der Rechtssitte zuwider nicht um die Erwerbsurkunden," then there is no hardship if he is treated as knowing all that he would have discovered had he behaved as reasonable men behave. He has "constructive notice" of it all. "Der ihm etwa daraus erwachsende Schade trifft ihn nicht unverschuldet."

We must make one other excerpt before we leave Lombardy.

"Indessen dies galt nur für Liegenschaften. Dem Fahrnis-verkehr fehlten, ebenso wie in den übrigen germanischen Rechten, Vorkehrungen, die einem die Uebereignung beschränkenden Geding Publizität im Verhältnis zu Dritten verschafft hätten....Gewiss war der letztwillige Treuhänder auch in Ansehung der Mobilien durch die Zweckbestimmung rechtlich gebunden. Gewiss war er ding-lich gebunden und hatte, wie an Grundstücken, nur resolutiv bedingtes Eigenthum....Hatte er die Mobilien aber bereits an die falsche Adresse befördert, so konnten die Erben des Donators gegen die dritten Besitzer, selbst wenn sie beim Erwerb die Sachlage überschaut hatten, nichts ausrichten. Der Grund, weswegen bei Liegenschaften alle Dritten der Wirkung des Gedings unterworfen wurden, war hier nicht gegeben...Waren die dem Treuhander anvertrauten Mobilien durch Veruntreuung aus seinem Besitz gelangt und daher mit der dinglichen Rückforderungsklage 'Malo ordine possides' nicht erreichbar, so trat an die Stelle eine persönliche Schadenersatzklage."

That does not go quite far enough, the English critic might say. If it could be proved that *der dritte Besitzer* actually knew of the "trust," it does not seem

to me equitable that he should be able to disregard it.
Also it does not seem to me clear that if the movables
can no longer be pursued, the claim of the *Destinatär*
must of necessity be a mere *persönliche · Schadenersatzklage* against the *Treuhänder*. But it is most
remarkable to see our cousins the Lombards in these
very ancient days seizing a distinction that is very
familiar to us. The doctrine of "constructive notice"
is not to be extended from land to movables[1].

II.

We may now turn to the England of the fourteenth century, and in the first place I may be suffered
to recall a few general traits of the English law of
that time, which, though they may be well enough
known, should be had in memory.

A deep and wide gulf lies between *Liegenschaft*
and *Fahrnis*. It is deeper and wider in England than
elsewhere. This is due in part to our rigorous primo-
geniture, and in part to the successful efforts of the
Church to claim as her own an exclusive jurisdiction
over the movables of a dead man, whether he has
made a last will or whether he has died intestate.
One offshoot of the ancient Germanic *Treuhandschaft*
is already a well established and flourishing institute.
The English last will is a will with executors. If

---

[1] I am aware that Schultze's construction of the right of the
Lombard *Treuhänder* as "resolutiv bedingtes Eigenthum" is open
to dispute. See, for example, Caillemer, *Exécution Testamentaire*,
Lyon (1901), 351. A great deal of what M. Caillemer says about
England in this excellent book seems to be both new and true.

there is no will or no executor, an "administrator" appointed by the bishop fills the vacant place. This will is no longer a *donatio post obitum* of the old kind, but under canonical influence has assumed a truly testamentary character. The process which makes the executor into the "personal representative" of the dead man, his representative as-regards all but his *Liegenschaft*, is already far advanced. It is a process which in course of time makes the English executor not unlike a Roman *haeres*. In later days when the Trust, strictly so called, had been developed, these two institutes, which indeed had a common root, began to influence each other. We began to think of the executor as being for many purposes very like a trustee. However, the Trust, properly so called, makes its appearance on the legal stage at a time when the Englishman can already make a true testament of his movables, and at a time when the relationship between the executor and the legatees is a matter with which the secular courts have no concern.

As to dealings with movables *inter vivos*, we cannot say that there is any great need for a new *Rechtsinstitut*. It is true that in the fourteenth century this part of our law is not highly developed. Still it meets the main wants of a community that knows little of commerce. We will notice in passing that the current language is often using a term which, when used in another context, will indicate the germ of the true Trust: namely the term that in Latin is *ad opus*, and in French *al oes*. Often it is said that one man holds goods or receives money *ad opus alterius*. But the

Common Law is gradually acquiring such categories as deposit, mandate and so forth, which will adequately meet these cases. This part of our law is young and it can grow.

On the other hand, the land law is highly developed, and at every point it is stiffened by a complicated system of actions and writs (*brevia*). A wonderful scheme of "estates"—I know not whether that word can be translated—has been elaborated: "estates in fee simple, estates in fee tail, estates for life, estates in remainder, estates in reversion, etc."; and each "estate" is protected by its corresponding writ (*breve*). The judges, even if they were less conservative than they are, would find it difficult to introduce a new figure into this crowded scene. In particular we may notice that a "resolutiv bedingtes Eigenthum," which Dr Schultze finds in Lombardy, is very well known and is doing very hard work. All our *Pfandrecht* is governed by this concept. More work than it is doing it could hardly do.

Then in the second half of the fourteenth century we see a new Court struggling for existence. It is that Court of Chancery whose name is to be inseverably connected with the Trust. The old idea that when ordinary justice fails, there is a reserve of extraordinary justice which the king can exercise is bearing new fruit. In civil (*privatrechtliche*) causes men make their way to the king's Chancellor begging him in piteous terms to intervene "for the love of God and in the way of charity." It is not of any defect in the material law that they complain; but somehow or another they cannot get justice. They are poor and helpless; their adversaries are rich and powerful. Sheriffs are partial; jurors are corrupt. But, whatever may be the case with penal justice, it is by no means clear that in civil suits there can be any room for a formless, extraordinary jurisdiction. Complaints against interference with the ordinary course of law were becoming loud, when something was found for the Chancellor to do, and something that he could do with general approval. I think it might be said that if the Court of Chancery saved the Trust, the Trust saved the Court of Chancery.

And now we come to the origin of the Trust. The Englishman cannot leave his land by will. In the case of land every germ of testamentary power has been ruthlessly stamped out in the twelfth century. But the Englishman would like to leave his land by will. He would like to provide for the weal of his sinful soul, and he would like to provide for his daughters and younger sons. That is the root of the matter[1]. But further, it is to be observed that the law is hard upon him at the hour of death, more especially if he is one of the great. If he leaves an heir of full age, there is a *relevium* to be paid to the lord. If he leaves an heir under age, the lord may take the profits of the land, perhaps for twenty years, and may sell the marriage of the heir. And then if there is no heir, the land falls back ("escheats") to the lord for good and all.

Once more recourse is had to the *Treuhänder*. The landowner conveys his land to some friends.

---

[1] I do not wish to deny that there were other causes for trusts; but comparatively they were of little importance.

They are to hold it "to his use (*a son oes*)." They will let him enjoy it while he lives, and he can tell them what they are to do with it after his death.

I say that he conveys his land, not to a friend, but to some friends. This is a point of some importance. If there were a single owner, a single *feoffatus*, he might die, and then the lord would claim the ordinary rights of a lord ; *relevium, custodia haeredis, maritagium haeredis, escaeta*, all would follow as a matter of course. But here the Germanic *Gesammt-handschaft* comes to our help. Enfeoff five or perhaps ten friends *zu gesammter Hand* ("as joint tenants"). When one of them dies there is no inheritance ; there is merely accrescence. The lord can claim nothing. If the number of the *feoffati* is running low, then indeed it will be prudent to introduce some new ones, and this can be done by some transferring and retransferring. But, if a little care be taken about this matter, the lord's chance of getting anything is very small.

Here is a principle that has served us well in the past and is serving us well in the present. The "Gesammthandprincip" enables us to erect (if I may so speak) a wall of trustees which will not be always in need of repair. Some of those "charitable" trusts of which I am to speak hereafter will start with numerous trustees, and many years may pass away before any new documents are necessary. Two may die, three may die ; but there is no inheritance ; there is merely accrescence ; what was owned by ten men, is now owned by eight or by seven ; that is all[1].

¹ Our "joint ownership" is not a very strong form of *Gesammt-*

In a land in which Roman law has long been seriously studied it would be needless, I should imagine, for me to say that it is not in Roman books that Englishmen of the fourteenth century have discovered this device ; but it may be well to remark that any talk of *fides, fiducia, fideicommissum* is singularly absent from the earliest documents in which our new *Rechtsinstitut* appears. The same may be said of the English word "trust." All is being done under the cover of *ad opus.* In Old French this becomes *al oes, al ues* or the like. In the degraded French of Stratford-atte-Bow we see many varieties of spelling. It is not unusual for learned persons to restore the Latin *p* and to write *oeps* or *eops.* Finally in English mouths (which do not easily pronounce a French *u*) this word becomes entangled with the French *use.* The English for "ad opus meum" is "to my use."

It is always interesting, if we can, to detect the point at which a new institute or new concept enters the field of law. Hitherto the early history of our "feoffments to uses" has been but too little explored : I fear that the credit of thoroughly exploring it is reserved for some French or German scholar. However, there can be little doubt that the new practice first makes its appearance in the highest and noblest circles of society. I will mention one early example. The "feoffor" in this case is John of Gaunt, son of a King of England and himself at one time titular King of Castile. Among the persons who are to

handschaft. One of several "joint owners" has a share that he can alienate *inter vivos* ; but he has nothing to give by testament.

profit by the trust is his son Henry who will be our King Henry IV.

On the 3rd of February, 1399, "old John of Gaunt, time-honoured Lancaster" makes his testament[1]. Thereby he disposes of his movables and he appoints seventeen executors, among whom are two bishops and three earls. To this instrument he annexes a "Codicillus" (as he calls it) which begins thus :—

Item, la ou jeo Johan filz du Roy d'Engleterre, Duc de Lancastre, ay purchacez et fait purchacer a mon eops diverses seigneuries, manoirs, terres, tenementz, rentz, services, possessions, reversions et advoesons des benefices de seynt esglises, ove leur apurtenances... si ay je fait faire cest cedule annexee a cest mon testament, contenant ma darrein et entier volenté touchant les suisdites seigneuries, manoirs, terres, tenementz, rentz, services, possessions, reversions, avoesons ove leur appurtenances.

He then says what is to be done with these lands. Thus for example :—

Item je vueille que mon trescher batchelor Robert Nevill, William Gascoigne, mes treschers esquiers Thomas de Radeclyff et William Keteryng, et mon trescher clerk Thomas de Longley, qi de ma ordennance sont enfeffez en [le] manoir de Bernolswyk en [le] Counté d'Everwyk facent annuelement paier a mes executours...

To be brief, certain sums of money are to be paid to the executors, who will apply them for pious purposes, and

adonques soit estat fait du dit manoir a mon trezaimé filz ainé

---

[1] *Testamenta Eboracensia* (Surtees Society), vol. i. p. 223. In the same volume (p. 113) an earlier example will be found, the will of William, Lord Latimer (13 April, 1381). See also the will of the Earl of Pembroke (5 May, 1372), and the will of the Earl of Arundel (4 March, 1392-3) in J. Nichols, *Royal Wills* (1870), pp. 91, 120.

Henry duc de Hereford et a ses heirs de son corps, et par defaute d'issue du ditz Henry la remeindre[1] a mez droiz heirs.

Then at the end stand these words :—

Item je vueille que toutz autres seigneuries, manoirs, terrez... ove leurs appurtenances a mon eops purchasez et remaignantz uncore es mains des enfeffez par moi a ce ordennez, soient après ma mort (si je ne face autre ordenance en ma vie) donnez a l'avantdit Thomas mon filz a avoir a lui et a ses heirs de son corps issantz; et par defaute d'issue de son corps, la remeindre a l'avantdit Johan son frere et a sez heirs de son corps issantz; et par defaute d'issue de dit Johan, la remeindre a la susdite Johanne leur seur et a ses heirs de son corps issantz; et par defaute d'issue de la dite Johanne, la remeindre a mez drois heirs qui serront heirs del heritage de Lancastre : veuillantz toutez voies que toutes icestes mes volentees, ordenances et devys en ceste cedule compris, soient tout accomplez par ceulx q'en averont l'estat et poveir, et par l'avys, ordenance et conseil de gentz de loy en la plus sure manere que en se purra ordenner.

We see what the situation is. The Duke has transferred various lands to various parties of friends and dependants. When he feels that death is approaching, he declares what his wishes are, and they fall under two heads. He desires to increase the funds which his executors are to expend for the good of his soul, and he desires also to make some provision for his younger and (so it happens) illegitimate children.

Apparently the new fashion spread with great rapidity. We have not in print so many collections of wills as we ought to have ; but in such as have been published the mention of land held to the testator's "use" begins to appear somewhat suddenly in the last years of the fourteenth century and thence-

---

[1] This is an *Anwartschaft*.

forward it is common. We are obliged to suppose that the practice had existed for some time before it found legal protection. But that time seems to have been short. Between 1396 and 1403 the Chancellor's intervention had been demanded[1].

It would have been very difficult for the old Courts, "the Courts of Common Law," to give any aid. As already said, the system of our land law had become prematurely osseous. The introduction without Act of Parliament of a new *dingliches Recht*, some new modification of *Eigenthum*, would have been impossible. In our documents we see no attempt to meet the new case by an adaptation of the terms that are employed when there is to be a "resolutiv bedingtes Eigenthum[2]." And on the other hand we see a remarkable absence of those phrases which are currently used when an *obligatorischer Vertrag* is being made. No care is taken to exact from the *Treuhänder* a formal promise that the trust shall be observed. From the first men seem to feel that a contract binding the trustees to the author of the trust, binding the *feoffati* to the *feoffator*, is not what is wanted.

Moreover, it was probably felt, though perhaps but dimly felt, that if once the old Courts began to take notice of these arrangements a great question of policy would have to be faced. The minds of the

---

[1] *Select Cases in Chancery* (Selden Society), p. 69.

[2] This is not quite true. A few attempts were made to attain the end by means of "conditions," and Edward III himself made, so it seems, some attempt of this kind. But the mechanism of a "condition" would have been very awkward.

magnates were in all probability much divided. They wanted to make wills. But they were "lords," and it was not to their advantage that their "tenants" should make wills. And then there was one person in England who had much to gain and little to lose by a total suppression of this novelty. That person was the King, for he was always "lord" and never "tenant." An open debate about this matter would have made it evident that if landowners, and more especially the magnates, were to make wills, the King would have a fair claim for compensation. Even medieval Englishmen must have seen that if the King could not "live of his own," he must live by taxes. The State must have a revenue. Perhaps we may say, therefore, that the kindest thing that the old Courts could do for the nascent Trust was to look the other way. Certain it is that from a very early time some of our great lawyers were deeply engaged in the new practice. We have seen a certain William Gascoigne as a *Treuhänder* for John of Gaunt. He was already a distinguished lawyer. He was going to be Chief Justice of England and will be known to all Shakespeare's readers. Thomas Littleton (ob. 1481) when he expounds the English land law in a very famous book will have hardly a word to say about "feoffments to uses"; but when he makes his own will he will say, "Also I wulle that the feoffees to myn use [of certain lands] make a sure estate unto Richard Lyttelton my sonne, and to the heirs of his bodie."

When we consider where the king's interest lay, it is somewhat surprising that the important step should be taken by his first minister, the Chancellor. It seems very possible, however, that the step was taken without any calculation of loss and gain[1]. We may suppose a scandalous case. Certain persons have been guilty of a flagrant act of dishonesty, condemned by all decent people. Here is an opportunity for the intervention of a Court which has been taught that it is not to intervene where the old Courts of Common Law offer a remedy. And as with politics, so with jurisprudence. I doubt whether in the first instance our Chancellor troubled his head about the "juristic nature" of the new *Rechtsinstitut* or asked himself whether the new chapter of English law that he was beginning to write would fall under the title *Sachenrecht* or under the title *Obligationenrecht*. In some scandalous case he compelled the trustees to do what honesty required. Men often act first and think afterwards.

For some time we see hesitation at important points. For example, we hear a doubt whether the trust could be enforced against the heir of a sole trustee. As already said, efforts were generally made to prevent this question arising : to prevent the land coming to the hands of one man. So long as the wall was properly repaired, there would be no inheriting. But on the whole our new *Rechtsinstitut*

---

[1] It may have been of decisive importance that at some critical moment the King himself wanted to leave some land by will. Edward III had tried ineffectually to do this. In 1417 King Henry V had a great mass of land in the hands of feoffees (including four bishops, a duke and three earls) and made a will in favour of his brothers. See Nichols, *Royal Wills*, 236.

seems soon to find the line of least resistance and to move irresistibly forward towards an appointed goal.

III.

We are to speak of the rights of the *Destinatär*, or in our jargon *cestui que trust*[1]. Postponing the question against whom those rights will be valid, we may ask how those rights are treated within the sphere of their validity. And we soon see that within that sphere they are treated as *Eigenthum* or as some of those modalities of *Eigenthum* in which our medieval land law is so rich. The *Destinatär* has an "estate," not in the land, but in "the use." This may be "an estate in fee simple, an estate for life, an estate in remainder," and so forth. We might say that "the use" is turned into an incorporeal thing, an incorporeal piece of land; and in this incorporeal thing you may have all those rights, those "estates," which you could have in a real, tangible piece of land. And then in course of time movable goods and mere *Forderungen* are held in trust, and we get, as it were, a second edition of our whole *Vermögensrecht*: a second and in some respects an amended edition. About all such matters as inheritance and alienation, the Chancellor's Equity, so we say, is to follow the Common Law.

Another point was settled at an early date. The earliest trust is in the first instance a trust for the author of the trust; he is not only the author of the

---

[1] At starting the phrase would be *cestui a qui oes le feffement fut fait*. This degenerates into *cestui que use*; and then *cestui que trust* is made.

trust but he is the *Destinatär*. But it is as *Destinatär* and not as contracting party that he obtains the Chancellor's assistance. The notion of contract is not that with which the Chancellor works in these cases : perhaps because the old Courts profess to enforce contracts. It is the destinatory who has the action, and he may be a person who was unborn when the trust was created. This is of importance for, curiously enough, after some vacillation our Courts of Common Law have adopted the rule that in the case of a "pactum in favorem tertii" the *tertius* has no action.

But a true ownership, a truly *dingliches Recht*, the destinatory cannot have. In the common case a full and free and unconditioned ownership has been given to the trustees. Were the Chancellor to attempt to give the destinatory a truly *dingliches Recht*, the new Court would not be supplementing the work of the old Courts, but undoing it.

This brings us to the vital question, " Against whom can the destinatory's right be enforced ? " We see it enforced against the original trustees. Then after a little while we see it enforced against the heir of a trustee who has inherited the land ; and, to speak more generally, we see it enforced against all those who by succession on death fill the place of a trustee. But what of a person to whom in breach of trust the trustee conveys the land ? Such a person, so far as the old Courts can see, acquires ownership: full and free ownership: nothing less. The question is whether, although he be owner, he can be compelled to hold the land in trust for the destinatory. We soon learn that all is to depend upon the state of his "conscience" at the time when he acquired the ownership. It is to be a question of "notice." This we are told already in 1471. "If my trustee conveys the land to a third person who well knows that the trustee holds for my use, I shall have a remedy in the Chancery against both of them : as well against the buyer as against the trustee : for in conscience he buys my land[1]."

That is a basis upon which a lofty structure is reared. The concept with which the Chancellor commences his operations is that of a guilty conscience. If any one knowing that the land is held upon trust for me obtains the ownership of it, he does what is unconscientious and must be treated as a trustee for me. In conscience the land is "ma terre."

This being established, no lawyer will be surprised to hear that the words " if he knew " are after a while followed by the words " or ought to have known," or that a certain degree of negligence is coordinated with fraud. By the side of "actual notice " is placed constructive notice."

And now we may refer once more to what Dr Schultze has said of the Lombards :

Nun mögen auch die Langobarden in Bezug auf Grundstücke früher eine volksrechtliche Form der Rechtsveränderung gekannt haben, welche den Act selbst im Augenblick seiner Vornahme den Volksgenossen in genügenden Masse kundthat. In der hier interessirenden Zeit war aber bei weitem vorherrschend und wurde jedenfalls

---

[1] Year Book, 11 Edward IV, folio 8 : Si mon feoffee de trust etc. enfeoffe un autre, que conust bien que le feoffor rien ad forsque a mon use, subpoena girra vers ambideux : scil. auxibien vers le feoffee come vers le feoffor...pur ceo que en conscience il purchase ma terre.

bei den ordentlichen Vergabungen auf den Todesfall, auch denjenigen zu treuer Hand, ausschliesslich angewendet die Form der *traditio
cartae*.

With some modifications, which it would be long to
explain and which for our purpose are not very important, these words are true of the England in which
the Trust was born and are yet truer of modern
England. The buyer before he pays the price and
obtains the land will investigate the seller's title. He
will ask for and examine the *Urkunden* (" deeds ")
which prove that the seller is owner, and unless the
contract is specially worded, the seller of land is under
a very onerous duty of demonstrating his ownership.
This *Rechtssitte*, as Dr Schultze calls it, enabled the
Chancery to set up an external and objective standard
of diligence for purchasers of land: namely the conduct
of a prudent purchaser. The man who took a conveyance of land might be supposed to know (and he
had "constructive notice") of all such rights of destinatories as would have come to his knowledge if he had
acted as a prudent purchaser would in his own interest
have acted " Kümmerte er sich aber der Rechtssitte
zuwider nicht um die Erwerbsurkunden...der ihm etwa
daraus erwachsende Schade traf ihn nicht unverschuldet." Quite so. Such a purchaser himself became
a trustee. We might say that he became a trustee *ex
delicto vel quasi*. If not guilty of *dolus*, he was guilty
of that sort of negligence which is equivalent to *dolus*.
He had shut his eyes in order that he might not see.
A truly *dingliches Recht* the Chancellor could not
create. The trustee is owner. It had to be admitted
that if the purchaser who acquired ownership from the

trustee was, not only ignorant, but excusably ignorant of the rights of the destinatory, then he must be left to enjoy the ownership that he had obtained. If he had acted as a prudent purchaser, as the reasonable man, behaves, then "his conscience was unaffected" and the Chancellor's Equity had no hold upon him. But the Court of Chancery screwed up the standard of diligence ever higher and higher. The judges who sat in that Court were experts in the creation of trusts. We might say that they could smell a trust a long way off, and they were apt to attribute to every reasonable man their own keen scent. They were apt to attribute to him a constructive notice of all those facts which he would have discovered if he had followed up every trail that was suggested by those *Erwerbsurkunden* that he had seen or ought to have seen.

Of late years there has been some reaction in favour of purchasers. The standard, we are told, is not to be raised yet higher and perhaps it is being slightly lowered. Still it is very hard for any man to acquire land in England without acquiring "constructive notice" of every trust that affects that land. I might almost say that this never happens except when some trustee has committed the grave crime of forgery.

It remains to be observed that a strong line was drawn in this as in other respects between the *entgeltliche* and the *unentgeltliche Handlung*. A man who acquired the land from the trustee without giving "value" for it was bound by the trust, even if at the time of acquisition he had no notice of it. It would be "against conscience" for him to retain the gift after he knew that it had been made in breach of trust. It was only the "purchaser for value" who could disregard the claims of the destinatory.

Also we see it established that the creditors of the trustee cannot exact payment of their debts out of the property that he holds in trust. And on the other hand the creditors of the destinatory can regard that property as part of his wealth. If we suppose that there is bankruptcy on both sides, this property will be divided, not among the creditors of the trustee but among the creditors of the destinatory. This, it need hardly be said, is an important point.

To produce all these results took a long time. The *Billigkeitsrecht* of the new Court moved slowly forward from precedent to precedent : but always towards one goal : namely, the strengthening at every point of the right of the destinatory. In our present context it may, for example, be interesting to notice that at one time it was currently said that the right of the destinatory could not be enforced against a corporation which had acquired the land, for a corporation has no conscience, and conscience is the basis of the equitable jurisdiction. But this precious deduction from the foreign *Fiktionstheorie* was long ago ignored, and it is the commonest thing to see a corporation as *Treuhänder*.

But perhaps the evolution of this *Rechtsinstitut* may be best seen in another quarter. To a modern Englishman it would seem plainly unjust and indeed intolerable that, if a sole trustee died intestate and without an heir, the rights of the destinatory should perish. And on the other hand it might seem to him unnatural that if the destinatory, "the owner in equity," of this land died intestate and without an heir, the trustee should thenceforward hold the land for his own benefit. But the Court, working merely with the idea of good conscience, could not attain what we now regard as the right result. In the first case (trustee's death) the land fell back (escheat) to the King or to some other feudal lord. He did not claim any right through the trustee or through the creator of the trust, and equity had no hold upon him, for his conscience was clean[1]. In the second case (destinatory's death), the trust was at an end. The trustee was owner, and there was no more to be said. The King or the feudal lord was not a destinatory. In both respects, however, modern legislation has reversed these old rules.

Thus we come by the idea of an "equitable ownership" or "ownership in equity." Supposing that a man is in equity the owner ("tenant in fee simple") of a piece of land, it makes very little difference to him that he is not also "owner at law" and that, as we say, "the legal ownership is outstanding in trustees." The only serious danger that he is incurring is that this "legal ownership" may come to a person who acquires it *bona fide*, for value, and without actual or constructive notice of his rights. And that is an uncommon event. It is an event of which practical lawyers must often be thinking when they give advice or compose documents ; but still it is an uncommon event. I believe that for the ordinary thought of Englishmen "equitable ownership" is just ownership pure and simple, though it is subject to a peculiar,

[1] The law about this matter had become somewhat doubtful before Parliament intervened.

technical and not very intelligible rule in favour of *bona fide* purchasers. A professor of law will tell his pupils that they must not think, or at any rate must not begin by thinking, in this manner. He may tell them that the destinatory's rights are in history and in ultimate analysis not *dinglich* but *obligatorisch* : that they are valid only against those who for some special reason are bound to respect them. But let the Herr Professor say what he likes, so many persons are bound to respect these rights that practically they are almost as valuable as if they were *dominium*[1].

This is not all. Let us suppose that the thing that is held upon trust passes into the hands of one against whom the trust cannot be enforced. This may happen with land ; it may more easily happen in the case of movables, because (for the reason that Dr Schultze has given) the Court could not extend its doctrine of constructive notice to traffic in movables. Now can we do no more for our destinatory than give him a mere *Schadenersatzklage* against the dishonest trustee? That will not always be a very effectual remedy. Dishonest people are often impecunious, insolvent people.

The Court of Chancery managed to do something more for its darling. What it did I cannot well describe in abstract terms, but perhaps I may say that it

---

[1] Some writers even in theoretical discussion have allowed themselves to speak of the destinatory as "the real owner," and of the trustee's ownership as "nominal" and "fictitious." See Salmond, *Jurisprudence*, p. 278. But I think it is better and safer to say with a great American teacher that "Equity could not create rights *in rem* if it would, and would not if it could." See Langdell, *Harvard Law Review*, vol. I, p. 60.

converted the "trust fund" into an incorporeal thing, capable of being "invested" in different ways. Observe that metaphor of "investment." We conceive that the "trust fund" can change its dress, but maintain its identity. To-day it appears as a piece of land; to-morrow it may be some gold coins in a purse; then it will be a sum of Consols; then it will be shares in a Railway Company, and then Peruvian Bonds. When all is going well, changes of investment may often be made; the trustees have been given power to make them. All along the "trust fund" retains its identity. "Pretium succedit in locum rei," we might say, "et res succedit in locum pretii." But the same idea is applied even when all is not going well. Suppose that a trustee sells land meaning to misappropriate the price. The price is paid to him in the shape of a bank-note which is now in his pocket. That bank-note belongs "in equity" to the destinatories. He pays it away as the price of shares in a company; those shares belong "in equity" to the destinatories. He becomes bankrupt; those shares will not be part of the property that is divisible among his creditors; they will belong to the destinatories. And then, again, if the trustee mixes "trust money" with his own money, we are taught to say that, so long as this is possible, we must suppose him to be an honest man and to be spending, not other people's money, but his own. This idea of a "trust fund" that can be traced from investment to investment does not always work very easily, and for my own part I think it does scanty justice to the claims of the trustee's creditors. But it is an important part of our system. The Court of

Chancery struggled hard to prevent its darling, the destinatory, from falling to the level of a mere creditor. And it should be understood that he may often have more than one remedy. He may be able both to pursue a piece of land and to attack the trustee who alienated it. It is not for others to say in what order he shall use his rights, so long as he has not got what he lost or an equivalent for it.

To complete the picture we must add that a very high degree not only of honesty but of diligence has been required of trustees. In common opinion it has been too high, and of late our legislature, without definitely lowering it, has given the courts a discretionary power of dealing mercifully with honest men who have made mistakes or acted unwisely. The honest man brought to ruin by the commission of "a technical breach of trust," brought to ruin at the suit of his friend's children, has in the past been only too common a figure in English life. On the other hand, it was not until lately that the dishonest trustee who misappropriated money or other movables could be treated as a criminal. Naturally there was a difficulty here, for "at law" the trustee was owner, and a man cannot be guilty of stealing what he both owns and possesses. But for half a century we have known the criminal breach of trust, and, though we do not call it theft, it can be severely punished.

Altogether it is certainly not of inadequate protection that a foreign jurist would speak if he examined the position of our destinatory. Rather I should suppose that he would say that this lucky being, the spoilt child of English jurisprudence, has been favoured at the expense of principles and distinctions that ought to have been held sacred. At any rate, those who would understand how our "unincorporate bodies" have lived and flourished behind a hedge of trustees should understand that the right of the destinatory, though we must not call it a true *dominium rei*, is something far better than the mere benefit of a promise.

IV.

To describe even in outline the various uses to which our Trust has been put would require many pages. As we all know, when once a *Rechtsinstitut* has been established, it does not perish or become atrophied merely because its original function becomes unnecessary. Trusts may be instituted because land-owners want to make testaments but cannot make testaments. A statute gives them the power to make testaments; but by this time the trust has found other work to do and does not die. There is a long and very difficult story to be told about the action of Henry VIII. He was losing his feudal revenue and struck a blow which did a good deal of harm, and harm which we feel at the present day. But in such a survey as the present what he did looks like an ineffectual attempt to dam a mighty current. The stream sweeps onward, carrying some rubbish with it.

Soon the Trust became very busy. For a while its chief employment was "the family settlement." Of "the family settlement" I must say no word, except this, that the trust thus entered the service of a wealthy and powerful class: the class of great landowners who could command the best legal advice and the highest technical skill. Whether we like the result or not, we must confess that skill of a very high order was applied to the construction of these "settlements" of great landed estates. Everything that foresight could do was done to define the duties of the trustees. Sometimes they would be, as in the early cases, the mere depositaries of a nude *dominium*, bound only to keep it until it was asked for. At other times they would have many and complex duties to perform and wide discretionary powers. And then, if I may so speak, the "settlement" descended from above: descended from the landed aristocracy to the rising monied class, until at last it was quite uncommon for any man or woman of any considerable wealth to marry without a "marriage settlement." Trusts of money or of invested funds became as usual as trusts of land. It may be worthy of notice that this was, at least in part, the effect of an extreme degree of testamentary freedom. Our law had got rid of the *Pflichttheil* altogether, and trusts in favour of the children of the projected marriage were a sort of substitute for it. However, in this region, what we have here to notice is that the trust became one of the commonest institutes of English law. Almost every well-to-do man was a trustee; and though the usual trusts might fall under a few great headings, still all the details (which had to be punctually observed) were to be found in lengthy documents; and a large liberty of constructing unusual trusts was both conceded in law and exercised in fact. To classify trusts is like classifying contracts.

I am well aware that all this has its dark side, and I do not claim admiration for it. But it should not escape us that a very wide field was secured for what I may call social experimentation. Let me give one example. In 1882 a revolutionary change was made in our *eheliches Güterrecht*. But this was no leap in the dark. It had been preceded by a prolonged course of experimentation. Our law about this matter had become osseous at an early time, and, especially as regards *Fahrnis*, was extremely unfavourable to the wife. There was no *Gemeinschaft*. The bride's movables became the husband's; if the wife acquired, she acquired for her husband. Now *eheliches Güterrecht*, when once it has taken a definite shape, will not easily be altered. Legislators are not easily persuaded to touch so vital a point, and we cannot readily conceive that large changes can be gradually made by the practice of the courts. You cannot transfer ownership from the husband to the wife by slow degrees.

But here the Trust comes to our help. We are not now talking of ownership strictly so called. Some trustees are to be owners. We are only going to speak of their duties. What is to prevent us, if we use words enough, from binding them to pay the income of a fund into the very hands of the wife and to take her written receipt for, it? But the wedge was in, and it could be driven home. It was a long process; but one successful experiment followed another. At length the time came when four well-tested words ("for her separate use") would give a married woman a *Vermögen* of which she was the complete mistress "in equity"; and if there was no other trustee appointed, her husband had to be trustee. Then, rightly or wrongly we came to the conclusion that all this experimentation had led to satisfactory results. Our law of husband and wife was revolutionized. But great as was the change, it was in fact little more than the extension to all marriages of rules which had long been applied to the marriages of the well-to-do.

But the liberty of action and experimentation that has been secured to us by the Trust is best seen in the freedom with which from a remote time until the present day *Anstalten* and *Stiftungen* of all sorts and kinds had been created by Englishmen.

Whether our law knows or ever has known what foreign lawyers would call a *selbstständige Anstalt* might be a vexed question among us, if we had—but we have not—any turn for juristic speculation. For some centuries we have kept among our technical notions that of a "corporation sole." Applied in the first instance to the parson of a parish church (*rector ecclesiae parochialis*) we have since the Reformation applied it also to bishops and to certain other ecclesiastical dignitaries. We have endeavoured to apply it also—much to our own disadvantage, so I think,—to our King or to the Crown; and in modern times we have been told by *Gesetz* that we ought to apply it to a few officers of the central government, *e.g.* the Post Master General. It seems to me a most unhappy notion: an attempt at personification that has not succeeded. Upon examination, our "corporation sole" turns out to be either a natural man or a juristic abortion: a sort of hybrid between *Anstalt* and

Mensch. Our medieval lawyers were staunch realists. They would attribute the ownership of land to a man or to a body of men, but they would not attribute it to anything so unsubstantial as a personified *ecclesia* or a personified *dignitas*. Rather they would say that when the rector of a parish church died there was an interval during which the *gleba ecclesiae* was *herrenlos*. The *Eigenthum*, they said, was "in nubibus," or "in gremio legis"; it existed only "en abéance"; that is "in spe." And I do not think that an English lawyer is entitled to say that this is not our orthodox theory at the present day. Practically the question is of no importance. For a long time past this part of our law has ceased to grow, and I hope that we are not destined to see any new "corporations sole[1]."

We have had no need to cultivate the idea of a *selbstständige Anstalt*, because with us the *unselbstständige Anstalt* has long been a highly-developed and flourishing *Rechtsinstitut*. I believe that the English term which most closely corresponds to the *Anstalt* or the *Stiftung* of German legal literature is "a charity." It is very possible that our concept of "a charity" would not cover every *Anstalt* or *Stiftung* that is known to German lawyers : but it is and from a remote time has been enormously wide. For example, one of our courts had lately to decide that the mere encouragement of sport is not "charity." The annual giving of a prize to be competed for in a yacht-race is not a "charitable" purpose. On the other hand, "the total suppression of vivisection" is a charitable purpose, though it implies the repeal of an

[1] See above, pp. 210—270.

Act of Parliament, and though the judge who decides this question may be fully persuaded that this so-called "charity" will do much more harm than good. English judges have carefully refrained from any exact definition of a "charity"; but perhaps we may say that any *Zweck* which any reasonable person could regard as directly beneficial to the public or to some large and indefinite class of men is a "charitable" purpose. Some exception should be made of trusts which would fly in the face of morality or religion; but judges who were themselves stout adherents of the State Church have had to uphold as "charitable," trusts which involved the maintenance of Catholicism, Presbyterianism, Judaism.

To the enforcement of charitable trusts we came in a very natural way and at an early date. A trust for persons shades off, we might say, into a trust for a *Zweck*. We are not, it will be remembered, speaking of true ownership. Ownership supposes an owner. We cannot put ownership into an indefinite mass of men; and, according to our English ideas, we cannot put ownership into a *Zweck*. I should say that there are vast masses of *Zweckvermögen* in England, but the owner is always man or corporation. As regards the trust, however, transitions are easy. You may start with a trust for the education of my son and for his education in a particular manner. It is easy to pass from this by slow degrees to the education of the boys of the neighbourhood, though in the process of transition the definite destinatory may disappear and leave only a *Zweck* behind him[1].

[1] In the oldest cases the Court of Chancery seems to enforce the

At any rate, in 1601 there was already a vast mass of *Zweckvermögen* in the country; a very large number of *unselbstständige Stiftungen* had come into existence. A famous *Gesetz* of that year became the basis of our law of Charitable Trusts, and their creation was directly encouraged. There being no problem about personality to be solved, the courts for a long while showed every favour to the authors of "charitable" trusts. In particular, it was settled that where there was a "charitable" *Zweck* there was to be no trouble about "perpetuity." The exact import of this remark could not be explained in two or three words. But, as might be supposed, even the Englishman, when he is making a trust of the ordinary private kind, finds that the law sets some limits to his power of bestowing benefits upon a long series of unborn destinatories; and these limits are formulated in what we know as "the rule against perpetuities." Well, it was settled that where there is "charity," there can be no trouble about "perpetuity[1]."

It will occur to my readers that it must have been necessary for English lawyers to make or to find some juristic person in whom the benefit of the "charitable" trust would inhere and who would be the destinatory. But that is not true. It will be understood that in external litigation—*e.g.* if there were an adverse claim to a piece of land held by the trustees—the interests of the trust would be fully represented by the "charitable" trust upon the complaint of anyone who is interested, without requiring the presence of any representative of the State.

[1] An Englishman might say that § 2109 of the B.G.B. contains the German "rule against perpetuities" and that it is considerably more severe than is the English.

trustees. Then if it were necessary to take proceedings against the trustees to compel them to observe the trust, the *Reichsanwalt* (Attorney-General) would appear. We find it said long ago that it is for the King "ut parens patriae" to intervene for this purpose. But we have stopped far short of any theory which would make the State into the true destinatory (*cestui que trust*) of all charitable trusts. Catholics, Wesleyans, jews would certainly be surprised if they were told that their cathedrals, chapels, synagogues were in any sense *Staatsvermögen*. We are not good at making juristic theories, but of the various concepts that seem to be offered to us by German books, it seems to me that *Zweckvermögen* is that which most nearly corresponds to our way of thinking about our "charities."

That great abuses took place in this matter of charitable trusts is undeniable. Slowly we were convinced by sad experience that in the way of supervision something more was necessary than the mere administration of the law (technically of "equity") at the instance of a *Staatsanwalt* who was casually set in motion by some person who happened to see that the trustees were not doing their duty. Since 1853 such supervision has been supplied by a central *Behörde* (the Charity Commissioners); but it is much rather supervision than control, and, so far from any check being placed on the creation of new *Stiftungen*, we in 1891 repealed a law which since 1736 had prevented men from giving land to "charity" by testament[1].

---

[1] In some cases the land will have to be sold, but the "charity" will get the price.

I understand that in the case of an *unselbstständige Stiftung* German legal doctrine knows a *Treuhänder* or *Fiduziar*, who in many respects would resemble our trustee, and I think that I might bring to light an important point by quoting some words that I read in Dr Regelsberger's *Pandekten* :

"Es hat ferner die Ansicht gute Gründe für sich, dass das Zweckvermögen dem Zugriff von Gläubigern des Fiduziars entrückt ist, deren Ansprüche nicht aus dem Zweckvermögen erwachsen sind, dass ferner im Konkurs des Fiduziars oder bei Verhängung einer Vermögenseinziehung für das Zweckvermögen ein Aussonderungsrecht in Anspruch genommen werden kann, da der Empfänger zwar Rechtsträger, aber nur im fremden Interesse ist[1]."

Now in England these would not be probable opinions: they would be obvious and elementary truths. The trustee's creditors have nothing whatever to do with the trust property. Our *unselbstständige Anstalt* lives behind a wall that was erected in the interests of the richest and most powerful class of Englishmen: it is as safe as the duke and the millionaire.

But the wall will need repairs.

"Das Rechtssubject, dem bei einer unselbstständigen Gründung das Zweckvermögen zugewendet wird, ist (says Dr Regelsberger) in der Regel eine juristische Person, denn nur sie bietet einen dauernden Stützpunkt[2]."

We have not found that to be true. Doubtless a corporation is, because of its permanence, a convenient trustee. But it is a matter of convenience. By means of the Germanic *Gesammthandschaft* and of a power given to the surviving trustees—or perhaps to some destinatories, or perhaps to other people (*e.g.* the

---

[1] *Pandekten*, 442.   [2] Ibid. 341.

catholic bishop of the diocese for the time being)—of appointing new trustees, a great deal of permanence can be obtained at a cost that is not serious if the property is of any considerable value. Extreme cases, such as that of a sole trustee who is wandering about in Central Africa with the ownership of some English land in his nomadic person, can be met by an order of the Court ("a vesting order") taking the ownership out of him and putting it in some more accessible receptacle. We have spent a great deal of pains over this matter. I am far from saying that all our devices are elegant. On juristic elegance we do not pride ourselves, but we know how to keep the roof weather-tight.

And here it should be observed that many reformers of our "charities" have deliberately preferred that "charitable trusts" should be confided, not to corporations, but to "natural persons." It is said—and appeal is made to long experience—that men are more conscientious when they are doing acts in their own names than when they are using the name of a corporation. In consequence of this prevailing opinion, all sorts of expedients have been devised by Parliament for simplifying and cheapening those transitions of *Eigenthum* which are inevitable where mortal men are the *Stützpunkt* of an *unselbstständige Stiftung*. Some of these would shock a theorist. In the case of certain places of worship, we may see the *dominium* taken out of one set of men and put into another set of men by the mere vote of an assembly—an unincorporated congregation of Nonconformists[1]. Of course no rules of merely private

[1] Trustees Appointment Acts, 1850–69—90.

law can explain this; but that does not trouble us.

This brings us to a point at which the Trust performed a signal service. All that we English people mean by "religious liberty" has been intimately connected with the making of trusts. When the time for a little toleration had come, there was the Trust ready to provide all that was needed by the barely tolerated sects. All that they had to ask from the State was that the open preaching of their doctrines should not be unlawful.

By way of contrast I may be allowed to cite a few words written by Dr Hinschius[1]:—

Das frühere Staatskirchenthum konnte, als es in Folge der veränderten Verhältnisse neben der herrschenden Kirche noch einzelne andere Religionsgesellschaften zu dulden anfing, diese nicht als reine Privatvereine gelten lassen, da es die Religion als Staatssache ansah. Vielmehr musste es aus diesem Grunde zu dem Standpunkte gelangen, solche Genossenschaften in gewissem Umfange als Korporationen mit öffentlichen Rechten zu behandeln, sie aber andererseits weitgehenden staatlichen Kontrollen und staatlichen Eingriffen zu unterwerfen.

But just what, according to Dr Hinschius, could not be done, was in England the easy and obvious thing to do. If in 1688 the choice had lain between conceding no toleration at all and forming corporations of Nonconformists, and even "Korporationen mit öffentlichen Rechten," there can be little doubt that "das herrschende Staatskirchenthum" would have left them untolerated for a long time to come, for in England, as elsewhere, incorporation meant privilege and exceptional favour. And, on the other hand,

[1] Marquardsen's *Handbuch des Öffentlichen Rechts*, B. i, S. 367.

there were among the Nonconformists many who
would have thought that even toleration was dearly
purchased if their religious affairs were subjected to
State control. But if the State could be persuaded
to do the very minimum, to repeal a few persecuting
laws, to say "You shall not be punished for not going
to the parish church, and you shall not be punished
for going to your meeting-house," that was all that was
requisite. Trust would do the rest, and the State and
das Staatskirchenthum could not be accused of any
active participation in heresy and schism. Trust soon
did the rest. I have been told that some of the
earliest trust deeds of Nonconformist "meeting-
houses" say what is to be done with the buildings if
the Toleration Act be repealed. After a little hesitation, the courts enforced these trusts, and even held
that they were "charitable."

And now we have in England Jewish synagogues
and Catholic cathedrals and the churches and chapels
of countless sects. They are owned by natural
persons. They are owned by trustees.

Now I know very well that our way of dealing
with all the churches, except that which is "by law
established" (and in America and the great English
colonies even that exception need not be made), looks
grotesque to some of those who see it from the outside.
They are surprised when they learn that such an
"historic organism" as the Church of Rome, "einem
Privatverein, einer Ballspielgesellschaft rechtlich gleich-
steht[1]." But when they have done laughing at us, the

---

[1] Hinschius, op. cit. S. 222—4.

upshot of their complaint or their warning is, not that
we have not made this historic organism comfortable
enough, but that we have made it too comfortable.

I have spoken of our "charity" as an *Anstalt* or
Stiftung; but, as might be expected in a land where
men have been very free to create such "charitable
trusts" as they pleased, *anstaltliche* and *genossenschaftliche* threads have been interwoven in every
conceivable fashion. And this has been so from the
very first. In dealing with charitable trusts one by
one, our Courts have not been compelled to make any
severe classification. *Anstalt* or *Genossenschaft* was
not a dilemma which every trust had to face, though I
suppose that what would be called an *anstaltliches
Element* is implicit in our notion of a charity. This
seems particularly noticeable in the ecclesiastical
region. There is a piece of ground with a building
on it which is used as a place of worship. Who or
what is it that in this instance stands behind the
trustees? Shall we say *Anstalt* or shall we say
Verein?

No general answer could be given. We must
look at the "trust deed." We may find that as a
matter of fact the trustees are little better than
automata whose springs are controlled by the catholic
bishop, or by the central council ("Conference") of the
Wesleyans; or we may find that the trustees themselves have wide discretionary powers. A certain
amount of *Zweck* there must be, for otherwise the
trust would not be "charitable." But this demand
is satisfied by the fact that the building is to be used
for public worship. If, however, we raise the question

who shall preach here, what shall he preach, who shall appoint, who shall dismiss him, then we are face to face with almost every conceivable type of organization from centralized and absolute monarchy to decentralized democracy and the autonomy of the independent congregation. To say nothing of the Catholics, it is well known that our Protestant Nonconformists have differed from each other much rather about Church government than about theological dogma : but all of them have found satisfaction for their various ideals of ecclesiastical polity under the shadow of our trusts.

V.

This brings us to our "unincorporated bodies," and by way of a first example I should like to mention the Wesleyans. They have a very elaborate and a highly centralized constitution, the primary outlines of which are to be found in an *Urkunde* to which John Wesley set his seal in 1784. Thereby he declared the trusts upon which he was holding certain lands and buildings that had been conveyed to him in various parts of England. Now-a-days we see Wesleyan chapels in all our towns and in many of our villages. Generally every chapel has its separate set of trustees, but the trust deeds all follow one model, devised by a famous lawyer in 1832—the printed copy that lies before me fills more than forty pages—and these deeds institute a form of government so centralized that Rome might be proud of it, though the central organ is no pope, but a council.

But we must not dwell any longer on cases in which there is a "charitable trust," for, as already said, there is in these cases no pressing demand for a personal destinatory. We can, if we please, think of the charitable *Zweck* as filling the place that is filled by a person in the ordinary private trust. When, however, we leave behind us the province, the wide province, of "charity," then—so we might argue *a priori*—a question about personality must arise. There will here be no *Zweck* that is protected as being "beneficial to the public." There will here be no intervention of a *Staatsanwalt* who represents the "parens patriae." Must there not therefore be some destinatory who is either a natural or else a juristic person? Can we have a trust for a *Genossenschaft*, unless it is endowed with personality, or unless it is steadily regarded as being a mere collective name for certain natural persons? I believe that our answer should be that in theory we cannot, but that in practice we can.

If then we ask how there can be this divergence between theory and practice, we come upon what has to my mind been the chief merit of the Trust. It has served to protect the unincorporated *Genossenschaft* against the attacks of inadequate and individualistic theories.

We should all agree that, if an *Anstalt* or a *Genossenschaft* is to live and thrive, it must be efficiently defended by law against external enemies. On the other hand, experience seems to show that it can live and thrive, although the only theories that lawyers hold about its internal affairs are inadequate.

Let me dwell for a moment on both of these truths.

Our *Anstalt*, or our *Genossenschaft*, or whatever it may be, has to live in a wicked world: a world full of thieves and rogues and other bad people. And apart from wickedness, there will be unfounded claims to be resisted: claims made by neighbours, claims made by the State. This sensitive being must have a hard, exterior shell. Now our Trust provides this hard, exterior shell for whatever lies within. If there is theft, the thief will be accused of stealing the goods of Mr A. B. and Mr C. D., and not one word will be said of the trust. If there is a dispute about a boundary, Mr A. B. and Mr C. D. will bring or defend the action. It is here to be remembered that during the age in which the Trust was taking shape all this external litigation went on before courts where nothing could be said about trusts. The judges in those courts, if I may so say, could only see the wall of trustees and could see nothing that lay beyond it. Thus in a conflict with an external foe no question about personality could arise. A great deal of ingenuity had been spent in bringing about this result.

But if there be this hard exterior shell, then there is no longer any pressing demand for juristic theory. Years may pass by, decades, even centuries, before jurisprudence is called upon to decide exactly what it is that lies within the shell. And if what lies within is some *Genossenschaft*, it may slowly and silently change its shape many times before it is compelled to explain its constitution to a public tribunal. Disputes there will be; but the disputants will be very unwilling to call in the policeman. This unwillingness may reach its highest point in the case of religious bodies. Englishmen are a litigious race, and religious people have always plenty to quarrel about. Still they are very reluctant to seek the judgment seat of Gallio. As is well known, our "Law Reports," beginning in the day of Edward I, are a mountainous mass. Almost every side of English life is revealed in them. But if you search them through in the hope of discovering the organization of our churches and sects (other than the established church) you will find only a few widely scattered hints. And what is true of religious bodies, is hardly less true of many other *Vereine*, such as our "clubs." Even the "kampflustige Engländer," whom Ihering admired, would, as we say, think once, twice, thrice, before he appealed to a court of law against the decision of the committee or the general meeting. I say "appealed," and believe that this is the word that he would use, for the thought of a "jurisdiction" inherent in the *Genossenschaft* is strong in us, and I believe that it is at its strongest where there is no formal corporation. And so, the external wall being kept in good repair, our English legal *Dogmatik* may have no theory or a wholly inadequate and antiquated theory of what goes on behind. And to some of us that seems a desirable state of affairs. Shameful though it may be to say this, we fear the petrifying action of juristic theory.

And now may I name a few typical instances of "unincorporated bodies" that have lived behind the trustee wall?

I imagine a foreign tourist, with Bädeker in hand,

visiting one of our "Inns of Court": let us say Lincoln's Inn[1]. He sees the chapel and the library and the dining-hall; he sees the external gates that are shut at night. It is in many respects much like such colleges as he may see at Oxford and Cambridge. On inquiry he hears of an ancient constitution that had taken shape before 1422, and we know not how much earlier. He learns that something in the way of legal education is being done by these Inns of Court, and that for this purpose a federal organ, a Council of Legal Education, has been established. He learns that no man can practise as an advocate in any of the higher courts who is not a member of one of the four Inns and who has not there received the degree of "barrister-at-law." He would learn that these Inns have been very free to dictate the terms upon which this degree is given. He would learn that the Inn has in its hands a terrible, if rarely exercised, power of expelling ("disbarring") a member for dishonourable or unprofessional conduct, of excluding him from the courts in which he has been making his living, of ruining him and disgracing him. He would learn that in such a case there might be an appeal to the judges of our High Court: but not to them as a public tribunal: to them as "visitors" and as constituting, we might say, a second instance of the domestic forum.

Well, he might say, apparently we have some curious hybrid—and we must expect such things in England—between an *Anstalt des öffentlichen Rechtes*

---

[1] In Latin documents the word corresponding to our *inn* is *hospitium*.

and a *privilegierte Korporation.* Nothing of the sort, an English friend would reply; you have here a *Privatverein* which has not even juristic personality. It might—such at least our theory has been—dissolve itself tomorrow, and its members might divide the property that is held for them by trustees. And indeed there was until lately an Inn of a somewhat similar character, the ancient Inn of the " Serjeants at Law," and, as there were to be no more serjeants, its members dissolved the *Verein* and divided their property. Many people thought that this dissolution of an ancient society was to be regretted ; there was a little war in the newspapers about it ; but as to the legal right we were told that there was no doubt.

It need hardly be said that the case of these Inns of Court is in a certain sense anomalous. Such powers as they wield could not be acquired at the present day by any *Privatverein*, and it would not be too much to say that we do not exactly know how or when those powers were acquired, for the beginning of these societies of lawyers was very humble and is very dark. But, before we leave them, let us remember that the English judges who received and repeated a great deal of the canonistic learning about corporations, *Fiktions-theorie, Concessionstheorie* and so forth, were to a man members of these *Körperschaften* and had never found that the want of juristic personality was a serious mis-fortune. Our lawyers were rich and influential people. They could easily have obtained incorporation had they desired it. They did not desire it.

But let us come to modern cases. To-day German ships and Austrian ships are carrying into all the seas

the name of the keeper of a coffee-house, the name
of Edward Lloyd.   At the end of the seventeenth
century he kept a coffee-house in the City of London,
which was frequented by "underwriters" or marine
insurers.   Now from 1720 onwards these men had to
do their business in the most purely individualistic
fashion.   In order to protect two privileged corporations, which had lent money to the State, even a
simple *Gesellschaft* among underwriters was forbidden.
Every insurer had to act for himself and for himself
only.   We might not expect to see such individualistic
units coalescing so as to form a compactly organized
body—and this too not in the middle age but in the
eighteenth century.   However, these men had common
interests : an interest in obtaining information, an
interest in exposing fraud and resisting fraudulent
claims.   There was a subscription ; there was a small
"trust fund" ; the exclusive use of the "coffee house"
was obtained.   The *Verein* grew and grew.   During
the great wars of the Napoleonic age, "the Committee
for regulating the affairs of Lloyd's Coffee House"
became a great power.   But the organization was still
very loose until 1811, when a trust deed was executed
and bore more than eleven hundred signatures.   I
must not attempt to tell all that "Lloyd's" has done
for England. The story should be the better known
in Germany, because the hero of it, J. J. Angerstein,
though he came to us from Russia, was of German
parentage.   But until 1871 Lloyd's was an unincorporated *Verein* without the least trace (at least so we
said) of juristic personality about it.   And when
incorporation came in 1871, the chief reason for the

change was to be found in no ordinary event, but in the recovery from the bottom of the Zuyder Zee of a large mass of treasure which had been lying there since 1799, and which belonged—well, owing to the destruction of records by an accidental fire, no one could exactly say to whom it belonged. In the life of such a *Verein* "incorporation" appears as a mere event. We could not even compare it to the attainment of full age. Rather it is as if a "natural person" bought a type-writing machine or took lessons in stenography[1].

Even more instructive is the story of the London Stock Exchange[2]. Here also we see small beginnings. In the eighteenth century the men who deal in stocks frequent certain coffee-houses: in particular "Jonathan's." They begin to form a club. They pay the owner an annual sum to exclude those whom they have not elected into their society. In 1773 they moved to more commodious rooms. Those who used the rooms paid sixpence a day. In 1802 a costly site was bought, a costly building erected, and an elaborate constitution was formulated in a "deed of settlement." There was a capital of £20,000 divided into 400 shares. Behind the trustees stood a body of "proprietors," who had found the money; and behind the "proprietors" stood a much larger body of "members," whose subscriptions formed the income that was divided among the "proprietors." And then there was building and always more building. In 1876 there was a new "deed of settlement"; in 1882 large

[1] F. Martin, *History of Lloyd's*, 1876.
[2] C. Duguid, *Story of the Stock Exchange*, 1901.

changes were made in it; there was a capital of
£240,000 divided into 20,000 shares.

Into details we must not enter. Suffice it that
the organization is of a high type. It might, for
example, strike one at first that the shares of the
"proprietors" would, by the natural operation of
private law, be often passing into the hands of people
who were in no wise interested in the sort of business
that is done on the Stock Exchange, and that thus the
genossenschaftliche character of the constitution would
be destroyed. But that danger could be obviated.
There was nothing to prevent the original subscribers
from agreeing that the shares could only be sold to
members of the Stock Exchange, and that, if by
inheritance a share came to other hands, it must be
sold within a twelvemonth. Such regulations have
not prevented the shares from being valuable.

In 1877 a Royal Commission was appointed to
consider the Stock Exchange. It heard evidence; it
issued a report; it made recommendations. A majority
of its members recommended that the Stock Exchange
should be incorporated by royal charter or Act of
Parliament.

And so the Stock Exchange was incorporated?
Certainly not. In England you cannot incorporate
people who do not want incorporation, and the
members of the Stock Exchange did not want it.
Something had been said about the submission of the
"bye-laws" of the corporation to the approval of a
central *Behörde*, the Board of Trade. That was the
cloven hoof. *Ex pede diabolum*[1].

[1] London Stock Exchange Commission, *Parliamentary Papers*,
1878, vol. XIX.

Now, unless we have regard to what an Englishman would call "mere technicalities," it would not, I think, be easy to find anything that a corporation could do and that is not being done by this *nicht rechtsfähige Verein*. It legislates profusely. Its representative among the Royal Commissioners did not scruple to speak of "legislation." And then he told how it did justice and enforced a higher standard of morality than the law can reach. And a terrible justice it is. Expulsion brings with it disgrace and ruin, and minor punishments are inflicted. In current language the committee is said to "pronounce a sentence" of suspension for a year, or two years or five years.

The "quasi-judicial" power of the body over its members—*quasi* is one of the few Latin words that English lawyers really love—is made to look all the more judicial by the manner in which it is treated by our courts of law. A man who is expelled from one of our clubs,—or (to use a delicate phrase) whose name is removed from the list of members—will sometimes complain to a public court. That court will insist on a strict observance of any procedure that is formulated in the written or printed "rules" of the club ; but also there may be talk of "natural justice." Thereby is meant an observance of those forms which should secure for every accused person a full and fair trial. In particular, a definite accusation should be definitely made, and the accused should have a sufficient opportunity of meeting it. Whatever the printed rules may say, it is not easy to be supposed that a man has placed his rights beyond that protection which should be afforded to all men by "natural justice." Theoretically the "rules," written or unwritten, may only be the terms of a contract, still the thought that this man is complaining that justice has been denied to him by those who were bound to do it, often finds practical expression. The dread of a *Vereinsherrschaft* is hardly represented among us.

I believe that in the eyes of a large number of my fellow-countrymen the most important and august tribunal in England is not the House of Lords but the Jockey Club; and in this case we might see "jurisdiction"—they would use that word—exercised by the *Verein* over those who stand outside it. I must not aspire to tell this story. But the beginning of it seems to be that some gentlemen form a club, buy a race-course, the famous Newmarket Heath, which is conveyed to trustees for them, and then they can say who shall and who shall not be admitted to it. I fancy, however, that some men who have been excluded from this sacred heath ("warned off Newmarket Heath" is our phrase) would have much preferred the major excommunication of that "historic organism" the Church of Rome.

It will have been observed that I have been choosing examples from the eighteenth century: a time when, if I am not mistaken, corporation theory sat heavy upon mankind in other countries. And we had a theory in England too, and it was of a very orthodox pattern; but it did not crush the spirit of association. So much could be done behind a trust, and the beginnings might be so very humble. All this tended to make our English jurisprudence disorderly, but also gave to it something of the character of an experimental science, and that I hope it will never lose.

But surely, it will be said, you must have some juristic theory about the constitution of the *Privatverein* : some theory, for example, about your clubs and those luxurious club-houses which we see in Pall Mall.

Yes, we have, and it is a purely individualistic theory. This it must necessarily be. As there is no "charity" in the case, the trust must be a trust for persons, and any attempt to make it a trust for unascertained persons (future members) would soon come into collision with that "rule against perpetuities" which keeps the *Familienfideicommiss* within moderate bounds. So really we have no tools to work with except such as are well known to all lawyers. Behind the wall of trustees we have *Miteigenthum* and *Vertrag*. We say that "in equity" the original members were the only destinatories : they were *Miteigenthümer* with *Gesammthandschaft* ; but at the same time they contracted to observe certain rules.

I do not think that the result is satisfactory. The "ownership in equity" that the member of the club has in land, buildings, furniture, books etc. is of a very strange kind. (1) Practically it is inalienable. (2) Practically his creditors cannot touch it by execution. (3) Practically, if he is bankrupt, there is nothing for them[1]. (4) It ceases if he does not pay his annual

---

[1] In a conceivable case the prospective right to an aliquot part of the property of a club that was going to be dissolved might be valuable to a member's creditors ; but this would be a rare case, and I can find nothing written about it. Some clubs endeavour by their rules to extinguish the right of a bankrupt member.

subscription.   (5) It ceases if in accordance with the rules he is expelled.   (6) His share—if of a share we may speak—is diminished whenever a new member is elected.   (7) He cannot demand a partition.   And (8) in order to explain all this, we have to suppose numerous tacit contracts which no one knows that he is making, for after every election there must be a fresh contract between the new member and all the old members.   But every judge on the bench is a member of at least one club, and we know that, if a thousand tacit contracts have to be discovered, a tolerable result will be attained.   We may remember that the State did not fall to pieces when philosophers and jurists declared that it was the outcome of contract.

There are some signs that in course of time we may be driven out of this theory.   The State has begun to tax clubs as it taxes corporations[1].   When we have laid down as a very general principle that, when a man gains any property upon the death of another, he must pay something to the State, it becomes plain to us that the property of a club will escape this sort of taxation.   It would be ridiculous, and indeed impossible, to hold that, whenever a member of a club dies, some taxable increment of wealth accrues to every one of his fellows.   So the property of the "unincorporated body" is to be taxed as if it belonged to a corporation.   This is a step forward.

Strange operations with *Miteigenthum* and *Vertrag* must, I should suppose, have been very familiar to German jurists in days when corporateness was not to

---

[1] Customs and Inland Revenue Act, 1885, sec. 11.

be had upon easy terms.   But what I am concerned to remark is that, owing to the hard exterior ,shell provided by a trust, the inadequacy of our theories was seldom brought to the light of day.   Every now and again a court of law may have a word to say about a club ; but you will find nothing about club-property in our institutional treatises.   And yet the value of those houses in London, their sites and their contents, is very great, and almost every English lawyer is interested, personally interested, in one of them.

A comparison between our unincorporated *Verein* and the *nicht rechtsfähige Verein* of the new German code might be very instructive ; but perhaps the first difference that would strike anyone who undertook the task would be this, that, whereas in the German case almost every conceivable question has been forestalled by scientific and controversial discussion, there is in the English case very little to be read.   We have a few decisions, dotted about here and there ; but they have to be read with caution, for each decision deals only with some one type of *Verein*, and the types are endless.   I might perhaps say that no attempt has been made to provide answers for half the questions that have been raised, for example, by Dr Gierke. And yet let me repeat that our *Vereine ohne Rechts- fähigkeit* are very numerous, that some of them are already old, and that some of them are wealthy[1].

One of the points that is clear (and here we differ from the German code) is that our unincorporated

---

[1] I believe that all the decisions given by our Courts in any way affecting our clubs will be found in a small book : J. Wertheimer, *Law relating to Clubs*, ed. 3, by A. W. Chaster, 1903.

Verein is not to be likened to a *Gesellschaft* (partner-ship): at all events this is not to be done when the *Verein* is a "club" of the common type[1]. Parenthetically I may observe that for the present purpose the English for *Gesellschaft* is "Partnership" and the English for *Verein* is "Society." Now in the early days of clubs an attempt was made to treat the club as a *Gesellschaft*. The *Gesellschaft* was an old well-established institute, and an effort was made to bring the new creature under the old rubric. That effort has, however, been definitely abandoned and we are now taught, not only that the club is not a *Gesellschaft*, but that you cannot as a general rule argue from the one to the other. Since 1890 we have a statutory definition of a *Gesellschaft* :—"Partnership is the relation which subsists between persons carrying on a business in common with a view of profit[2]." A club would not fall within this definition.

The chief practical interest of this doctrine, that a club is not to be assimilated to a *Gesellschaft*, lies in the fact that the committee of an English club has no general power of contracting on behalf of the members within a sphere marked out by the affairs of the club. A true corporate liability could not be manufactured, and, as I shall remark below, our courts were setting their faces against any attempt to establish a limited

---

[1] It was otherwise with the unincorporated *Actiengesellschaft*; but that is almost a thing of the past. A few formed long ago may still be living in an unincorporated condition, e.g. the London Stock Exchange.

[2] Partnership Act, 1890, sec. 1. For the meaning of these words, see F. Pollock, *Digest of the Law of Partnership*, ed. 6.

liability. The supposition as regards the club is that the members pay their subscriptions in advance, and that the committee has ready money to meet all current expenses. On paper that is not satisfactory. I believe that cases must pretty frequently occur in which a tradesman who has supplied wine or books or other goods for the use of the club, would have great difficulty in discovering the other contractor. We have no such rule (and here again we differ from the German code) as that the person who professes to act on behalf of an unincorporated *Verein* is always personally liable[1]; and I think the tradesman could often be forced to admit that he had not given credit to any man, the truth being that he thought of the club as a person. I can only say that scandals, though not absolutely unknown[2], have been very rare; that the members of the club would in all probability treat the case as if it were one of corporate liability; and that London tradesmen are willing enough to supply goods to clubs on a large scale. If there is to be extraordinary expenditure, if, for example, a new wing is to be added to the building, money to a large amount can often be borrowed at a very moderate rate of interest. We know a "mortgage without personal liability"; and that has been useful. Strictly speaking there is no debtor; but the creditor has various ways by which he can obtain payment: in particular he can sell the land.

Deliktsfähigkeit is an interesting and at the present time it is perhaps a burning point. A little while ago English lawyers would probably have denied that

---

[1] B. G. B. § 54.   [2] See Wertheimer, op. cit. p. 73.

anything resembling corporate liability could be established in this quarter. Any liability beyond that of the man who does the unlawful act must be that of a principal for the acts of an agent, or of a master for the acts of a servant, and if there is any liability at all, it must be unlimited. But this is now very doubtful. Our highest court (the House of Lords) has lately held that a trade union is *deliktsfähig* : in other words, that the damage done by the organized action of this unincorporated *Verein* must be paid for out of the property held by its trustees. Now a trade union is an unincorporated *Verein* of a somewhat exceptional sort. It is the subject of special Statutes which have conferred upon it some, but not all, of those legal qualities which we associate with incorporation. Whether this decision, which made a great noise, is attributable to this exceptional element, or whether it is to be based upon a broader ground, is not absolutely plain. The trade unionists are dissatisfied about this and some other matters, and what the results of their agitation will be I cannot say. The one thing that it is safe to predict is that in England *socialpolitische* will take precedence of *rechtswissenschaftliche* considerations. As to the broader question, now that a beginning has once been made, I believe that the situation could be well described in some words that I will borrow from Dr Gierke:

"Vielleicht bildet sich ein Gewohnheitsrecht das die nicht rechtsfahigen Vereine in Ansehung der Haftung für widerrechtliche Schadenszufügung dem Körperschaftsrecht unterstellt[1]."

The natural inclination of the members of an English

---

[1] Gierke, *Vereine ohne Rechtsfähigkeit*, zweite Auflage, S. 20.

club would, so I think, be to treat the case exactly as if it were a case of corporate liability. It has often struck me that morally there is most personality where legally there is none. A man thinks of his club as a living being, honourable as well as honest, while the joint-stock company is only a sort of machine into which he puts money and out of, which he draws dividends.

As to the *Deliktsfähigkeit* of corporations it may not be out of place to observe that by this time English corporations have had to pay for almost every kind of wrong that one man can do to another. Thus recently an incorporated company had to pay for having instituted criminal proceedings against a man "maliciously and without reasonable or probable cause." In our theoretical moments we reconcile this with the *Fiktionstheorie* by saying that it is a case in which a master (*persona ficta*) pays for the act of his servant or a principal for the act of an agent, and, as our rule about the master's liability is very wide, the explanation is not obviously insufficient. I am not sure that this may not help us to attain the desirable result in the case of the unincorporated *Verein*.

Our practical doctrine about the *Vermögen* of our clubs seems to me to be very much that which is stated by Dr Gierke in the following sentence, though (for the reason already given) we should have to omit a few words in which he refers to a *Gesellschaft*[1].

"Das Vereinsvermögen...gehört...den jeweiligen Mitgliedern; aber als Gesellschaftsvermögen [Vereinsvermögen] ist es ein für den

---

[1] *Vereine ohne Rechtsfähigkeit*, S. 14.

Gesellschaftszweck [Vereinszweck] aus dem übrigen Vermögen der Theilhaber ausgeschiedenes, den Gesellschaftern [Vereinsmitgliedern] zu ungesonderten Antheilen gemeinsames Sondervermögen, das sich einem Körperschaftsvermögen nähert."

And then in England the *Sonderung* of this *Vermögen* from all the other *Vermögen* of the *Theilhaber* can be all the plainer, because in legal analysis the owners of this *Vermögen* are not the *Vereinsmitglieder*, but the trustees. It is true that for practical purposes this *Eigenthum* of the trustees of a club may be hardly better than a *Scheineigenthum*, and the trustees themselves may be hardly better than puppets whose wires are pulled by the committee and the general meeting. And it is to be observed that in the case of this class of trusts the destinatories are peculiarly well protected, for, even if deeds were forged, no man could say that he had bought one of our club-houses or a catholic cathedral without suspecting the existence of a trust: *res ipsa loquitur*. Still the *nudum dominium* of the trustees serves as a sort of external mark which keeps all this *Vermögen* together as a *Sondervermögen*. And when we remember that some great jurists have found it possible to speak of the juristic person as puppet, a not unimportant analogy is established.

"Der Verein kann nicht nur unter Lebenden, sondern auch von Todeswegen erwerben. Denn es besteht kein Hinderniss die jeweiligen Mitglieder in ihrer gesellschaftlichen [vereinschaftlichen] Verbundenheit zu Erben einzusetzen oder mit einem Vermächtniss zu bedenken[1]."

This is substantially true of our English law, though the words "zu Erben einzusetzen" do not fit into

---

[1] Gierke, op. cit., S. 21.

our system. A little care on the part of the testator is requisite in such cases in order that he may not be accused of having endeavoured to create a trust in favour of a long series of unascertained persons (future members) and of having come into collision with our "rule against perpetuities." The less he says the better. Substantially the *Verein* is *vermächtnissfähig*. Dr Gierke's next sentence also is true, though of course the first word is inappropriate.

"[Landesgesetzliche] Einschränkungen des Rechtserwerbes juristischer Personen können auf nicht rechtsfähige Vereine nicht erstreckt werden."

Since our lawyers explained away a certain statute of Henry VIII, which will be mentioned below, our *nicht rechtsfähiger Verein* has stood outside the scope of those *Gesetze* which forbad corporations to acquire land (Statutes of Mortmain). And this was at one time a great advantage that our *nicht rechtsfähiger Verein* had over the *rechtsfähige Verein*. The Jockey Club, for example, could acquire Newmarket Heath without asking the King's or the State's permission. Even at the present day certain of our *nicht rechtsfähige Vereine* would lose their power of holding an unlimited quantity of land, if they registered themselves under the Companies Acts and so became corporations[1].

As regards *Processfähigkeit*, our doctrine regarded the capacity "to sue and be sued" as one of the essential attributes of the corporation. Indeed at times this capacity seems to have appeared as the

---

[1] Companies Act, 1862, sec. 21.

specific *differentia* of the corporation, though the common seal also was an important mark. And with this doctrine we have not openly broken. It will be understood, however, that in a very large class of disputes the concerns of the *nicht rechtsfähiger Verein* would be completely represented by the trustees. Especially would this be the case in all litigation concerning *Liegenschaft*. Suppose a dispute with a neighbour about a servitude ("easement") or about a boundary, this can be brought into court and decided as if there were no trust in existence and no *Verein*. And so if the dispute is with some *Pächter* or *Miether* of land or houses that belong "in equity" to the *Verein*. There is a legal relationship between him and the trustees, but none between him and the *Verein* : and in general it will be impossible for him to give trouble by any talk about the constitution of the *Verein*. And then as regards internal controversies, the Court of Chancery developed a highly elastic doctrine about "representative suits." The beginning of this lies far away from the point that we are considering. It must suffice that in dealing with those complicated trusts that Englishmen are allowed to create, the court was driven to hold that a class of persons may be sufficiently represented in litigation by a member of that class. We became familiar with the plaintiff who was suing "on behalf of himself and all other legatees" or "all other cousins of the deceased" or "all other creditors." This practice came to the aid of the *Verein*. Our English tendency would be to argue that if in many cases a mere class (e.g. the testator's nephews) could be represented by a specimen, then *a fortiori* a *Verein* could be represented by its "officers." And we should do this without seeing that we were infringing the corporation's exclusive possession of *Processfähigkeit*[1].

But with all its imperfections the position of the unincorporate *Verein* must be fairly comfortable. There is a simple test that we can apply. For the last forty years and more almost every *Verein* could have obtained the corporate quality had it wished to do this, and upon easy terms. When we opened the door we opened it wide. Any seven or more persons associated together for any lawful purpose can make a corporation[2]. No approval by any organ of the State is necessary, and there is no exceptional rule touching *politische socialpolitische oder religiöse Vereine*. Many societies of the most various kinds have taken advantage of this offer; but many have not. I will not speak of humble societies which are going to have no property or very little: only some chess-men perhaps. Nor will I speak of those political societies which spring up in England whenever there is agitation: a "Tariff Reform Association" or a "Free Food League" or the like. It was hardly to be expected that bodies which have a temporary aim, and which perhaps are not quite certain what that aim is going to be, would care to appear as corporations. But many other bodies which are not poor, which hope to exist for a long time, and which have a definite purpose have not accepted the offer. It is so, for example,

---

[1] Our law about this matter is now represented by Rules of the Supreme Court of Judicature, XVI, 9.

[2] Companies Act. 1862, sec. 6.

with clubs of what I may call the London type: clubs which have houses in which their members can pass the day. And it is so with many learned societies. In a case which came under my own observation a society had been formed for printing and distributing among its members books illustrating the history of English law. The question was raised what to do with the copyright of these books, and it was proposed that the society should make itself into a corporation; but the council of the society—all of them lawyers, and some of them very distinguished lawyers—preferred the old plan: preferred trustees. As an instance of the big affairs which are carried on in the old way I may mention the London Library, with a large house in the middle of London and more than 200,000 books which its members can borrow.

Why all this should be so it would not be easy to say. It is not, I believe, a matter of expense, for expense is involved in the maintenance of the hedge of trustees, and the account of merely pecuniary profit and loss would often, so I fancy, show a balance in favour of incorporation. But apparently there is a widespread, though not very definite belief, that by placing itself under an incorporating *Gesetz*, however liberal and elastic that *Gesetz* may be, a *Verein* would forfeit some of its liberty, some of its autonomy, and would not be so completely the mistress of its own destiny as it is when it has asked nothing and obtained nothing from the State. This belief may wear out in course of time; but I feel sure that any attempt to drive our *Vereine* into corporateness, any *Register-zwang*, would excite opposition. And on the other hand a proposal to allow the courts of law openly to give the name of corporations to *Vereine* which have neither been chartered nor registered would not only arouse the complaint that an intolerable uncertainty was being introduced into the law (we know little of Austria) but also would awake the suspicion that the proposers had some secret aim in view : perhaps nothing worse than what we call "red-tape," but perhaps taxation and "spoliation."

Hitherto (except when the Stock Exchange was mentioned) I have been speaking of societies that do not divide gain among their members. I must not attempt to tell the story of the English *Aktiengesell-schaft*. It has often been told in Germany and else-where. But there is just one point to which I would ask attention.

In 1862 Parliament placed corporate form and juristic personality within easy reach of "any seven or more persons associated together for any lawful pur-pose." I think we have cause to rejoice over the width of these words, for we in England are too much accustomed to half-measures, and this was no half-measure. But still we may represent it as an act of capitulation. The enemy was within the citadel.

In England before the end of the seventeenth century men were trying to make joint-stock com-panies with transferable shares or "actions" (for that was the word then employed), and this process had gone so far that in 1694 a certain John Houghton could issue in his newspaper a price list which included the "actions" of these unincorporated companies side by side with the stock of such chartered corporations as the Bank of England. We know something of the structure of these companies, but little of the manner in which their affairs were regarded by lawyers and courts of law. Then in 1720, as all know, the South Sea Bubble swelled and burst. A panic-stricken Parliament issued a law, which, even when we now read it, seems to scream at us from the statute book. Unquestionably for a time this hindered the formation of joint-stock companies. But to this day there are living among us some insurance companies, in particular "the Sun," which were living before 1720 and went on living in an unincorporate condition[1]. And then, later on when the great catastrophe was forgotten, lawyers began coldly to dissect the words of this terrible Act and to discover that after all it was not so terrible. For one thing, it threatened with punishment men who without lawful authority "presumed to act as a corporation." But how could this crime be committed?

From saying that organization is corporateness English lawyers were precluded by a long history. They themselves were members of the Inns of Court. Really it did not seem clear that men could "presume to act as a corporation" unless they said in so many words that they were incorporated, or unless they usurped that sacred symbol, the common seal. English law had been compelled to find the essence of real or spurious corporateness among comparatively superficial phenomena.

Even the more definite prohibitions in the Statute of 1720, such as that against "raising or pretending

[1] F. R. Relton, *Fire Insurance Companies*, 1893.

to raise a transferable stock," were not, so the courts said, so stringent as they might seem to be at first sight. In its panic Parliament had spoken much of mischief to the public, and judges, whose conception of the mischievous was liable to change, were able to declare that where there was no mischievous tendency there was no offence. Before " the-Bubble Act" was repealed in 1825 most of its teeth had been drawn.

But the *unbeschränkte Haftbarkeit* of partners was still maintained. That was a thoroughly practical matter which Englishmen could thoroughly understand. Indeed from the first half of the nineteenth century we have Acts of Parliament which strongly suggest that this is the very kernel of the whole matter. All else Parliament was by this time very willing to grant: for instance, active and passive *Processfähigkeit*, the capacity of suing and being sued as unit in the name of some secretary or treasurer. And this, I may remark in passing, tended still further to enlarge our notion of what can be done by "unincorporated companies." It was the day of half-measures. In an interesting case an American court once decided that a certain English company was a corporation, though an Act of our Parliament had expressly said that it was not.

And if our legislature would not by any general measure grant full corporateness, our courts were equally earnest in maintaining the unlimited liability of the *Gesellschaftsmitglieder.*

But the wedge was introduced. If a man sells goods and says in so many words that he will hold no one personally liable for the price, but will look

only to a certain subscribed fund, must we not hold
him to his bargain? Our courts were very unwilling
to believe that men had done anything so foolish.; but
they had to admit that personal liability could be
excluded by sufficiently explicit words. The wedge
was in. If the State had not given way, we should
have had in England joint-stock companies, unin‑
corporated, but contracting with limited liability. We
know now-a-days that men are not deterred from
making contracts by the word "limited." We have
no reason to suppose that they would have been
deterred if that word were expanded into four or
five lines printed at the head of the company's letter-
paper. It is needless to say that the directors of a
company would have strong reasons for seeing that
due notice of limited liability was given to every one
who had contractual dealings with the company, for,
if such notice were not given, they themselves would
probably be the first sufferers[1].

---

[1] In England development along this line stopped at this point,
because *wirtschaftliche Vereine* became corporations under the *Gesetz*
of 1862. English law had gone as far as the first, but not, I believe,
as far as the second of the two following sentences. : "Es steht
namentlich nichts im Wege, eine rechtsgeschäftliche Verpflichtung
der Mitglieder so zu begründen, dass jedes Mitglied nur mit einem
Theil seines Vermögens, dass es insbesondere nur mit seinem Antheil
am Vereinsvermögen haftet. Ist aber eine solche Abrede wirksam,
so kann auch von vornherein durch die Satzung die Vertretungsmacht
des Vorstandes dahin eingeschränkt werden, dass er die Mitglieder
nur unter Beschränkung ihrer Haftung auf ihre Antheile verpflichten
kann" (Gierke, op.-cit. 39). Then as regards our clubs, there is, as
already said, no presumption that the committee or the trustees can
incur debts for which the members will be liable even to a limited
degree.

In England the State capitulated gracefully in 1862. And at the same time it prohibited the formation of large unincorporated *Gesellschaften*. No *Verein* or *Gesellschaft* consisting of more than twenty persons was to be formed for the acquisition of gain unless it was registered and so became incorporate. We may say, however, that this prohibitory rule has become well-nigh a *caput mortuum*, and I doubt whether its existence is generally known, for no one desires to infringe it. If the making of gain be the society's object, the corporate form has proved itself to be so much more convenient than the unincorporate that a great deal of ingenuity has been spent in the formation of very small corporations in which the will of a single man is predominant ("one-man companies"). Indeed the simple *Gesellschaft* of English law, though we cannot call it a dying institution, has been rapidly losing ground[1].

In America it has been otherwise. As I understand, the unincorporate *Aktiengesellschaft* with its property reposing in trustees lived on beside the new trading corporations. I am told that any laws prohibiting men from forming large unincorporated

---

[1] A distinction which, roughly speaking, is similar to that drawn by B. G. B. §§ 21, 22 was drawn by our Act of 1862, sec. 4:—"No company, association or partnership consisting of more than twenty persons [ten persons, if the business is banking] shall be formed for the purpose of carrying on any business that has for its object the acquisition of gain by the company, association or partnership, or by the individual members thereof unless it is registered." I believe that in the space of forty years very few cases have arisen in which it was doubtful whether or not a *Verein* fell within these words.

partnerships would have been regarded as an unjusti-
fiable interference with freedom of contract, and even
that the validity of such a law might not always be
beyond question. A large measure of limited liability
was secured by carefully-worded clauses. I take the
following as an example from an American "trust
deed."

> The trustees shall have no power to bind the shareholders
> personally. In every written contract they may make, reference
> shall be made to this declaration of trust. The person or corpora-
> tion contracting with the trustees shall look to the funds and
> property of the trust for the payment under such contract...and
> neither the trustees nor the shareholders, present or future, shall
> be personally liable therefor.

The larger the affairs in which the *Verein* or
Gesellschaft is engaged, the more securely will such
clauses work, for (to say nothing of legal require-
ments) big affairs will naturally take the shape of
written documents.

Then those events occurred which have inseparably
connected the two words "trust" and "corporation."
I am not qualified to state with any precision the
reasons which induced American capitalists to avoid
the corporate form when they were engaged in constructing the greatest aggregations of capital that the
world had yet seen; but I believe that the American
corporation has lived in greater fear of the State than
the English corporation has felt for a long time past.
A judgment dissolving a corporation at the suit of the
Staatsanwalt as a penalty for offences that it has committed has been well-known in America. We have
hardly heard of anything of the kind in England since

the Revolution of 1688. The dissolution of the civic corporation of London for its offences in the days of Charles II served as a *reductio ad absurdum*. At any rate "trust" not "corporation" was the form that the financial and industrial magnates of America chose when they were fashioning their immense designs.

Since then there has been a change. Certain of the States (especially New Jersey) began to relax their corporation laws in order to attract the great combinations. A very modest percentage is worth collecting when the capital of the company is reckoned in millions. So now-a-days the American "trust" (in the sense in which economists and journalists use that term) is almost always if not quite always a corporation.

And so this old word, the "trustis" of the Salica, has acquired a new sense. Any sort of capitalistic combination is popularly called a "trust" if only it is powerful enough, and Englishmen believe that Germany is full of "trusts."

VI.

And now let me once more repeat that the connection between Trust and Corporation is very ancient. It is at least four centuries old. Henry VIII saw it. An Act of Parliament in which we may hear his majestic voice has these words in its preamble[1].

Where by reason of feoffments…made of trust of…lands to the use of…guilds, fraternities, comminalties, companies or brotherheads

---

[1] Stat. 23 Hen. VIII, c. 10.

erected...by common assent of the people without any corporation...
there groweth to the King...and other lords and subjects of the
realm the same like losses and inconveniences...as in case where
lands be aliened into mortmain.

We see what the mischief is. The hedge of
trustees will be kept in such good repair that there
will be no *escaeta*, no *relevium*, no *custodia*, for behind
will live a *Genossenschaft* keenly interested in the
maintenance of the hedge, and a *Genossenschaft* which
has made itself without asking the King's permission.
Now no one, I think, can read this Act without
seeing that it intends utterly to suppress this mischief[1].
Happily, however, the Act also set certain limits to
trusts for obituary masses, and not long after Henry's
death Protestant lawyers were able to say that the
whole Act was directed against "superstition.". Perhaps
the members of the Inns of Court were not quite
impartial expositors of the King's intentions. But in
a classical case it was argued that the Act could not
mean what it apparently said, since almost every town
in England—and by "town" was meant not *Stadt*
but *Dorf*—had land held for it by trustees. Such a
statement, it need hardly be said, is not to be taken
literally. But the trust for a *Communalverband* or for
certain purposes of a *Communalverband* is very ancient
and has been very common : it is a "charity.". There
was a manor (*Rittergut*) near Cambridge which was
devoted to paying the wages of the knights who
represented the county of Cambridge in Parliament[2].

---

[1] The trust is to be void unless it be one that must come to an
end within twenty years.

[2] Porter's Case, 1 Coke's *Reports*, 60 : "For almost all the lands

It is true that in this quarter the creation of trusts, though it was occasionally useful, could not directly repair the harm that was being done by that very sharp attack of the *Concessionstheorie* from which we suffered. All our *Communalverbände*, except the privileged boroughs, remained at a low stage of legal development. They even lost ground, for they underwent, as it were, a *capitis diminutio* when a privileged order of *communitates*, namely the boroughs, was raised above them. The county of the thirteenth century (when in solemn records we find so bold a phrase as "die Grafschaft kommt und sagt") was nearer to clear and unquestionable personality than was the county of the eighteenth century. But if the English county never descended to the level of a governmental district, and if there was always a certain element of "self-government" in the strange system that Gneist described under that name, that was due in a large measure (so it seems to me) to the work of the Trust. That work taught us to think of the corporate quality which the King kept for sale as a technical advantage. A very useful advantage it might be, enabling men to do in a straightforward fashion what otherwise they could only do by clumsy

belonging to the towns or boroughs not incorporate are conveyed to several inhabitants of the parish and their heirs upon trust and confidence to employ the profits to such good uses as defraying the tax of the town, repairing the highways...and no such uses (although they are common almost in every town) were ever made void by the statute of 23 H. 8." Some of the earliest instances of "representative suits" that are known to me are cases of Elizabeth's day in which a few members of a village or parish "on behalf of themselves and the others" complain against trustees.

methods ; but still an advantage of a highly technical kind. Much had been done behind the hedge of trustees in the way of constructing *Körper* ("bodies") which to the eye of the plain man looked extremely like *Korporationen*, and no one was prepared to set definite limits to this process.

All this reacted upon our system of local government. Action and reaction between our *Vereine* and our *Communalverbände* was the easier, because we knew no formal severance of Public from Private Law. One of the marks of our *Korporation*, so soon as we have any doctrine about the matter, is its power of making "bye-laws" (or better "by-laws"); but, whatever meaning Englishmen may attach to that word now-a-days, its original meaning, so etymologists tell us, was not *Nebengesetz* but *Dorfgesetz*[1]. And then there comes the age when the very name "corporation" has fallen into deep discredit, and stinks in the nostrils of all reformers. Gierke's account of the decadence of the German towns is in the main true of the English boroughs, though in the English case there is something to be added about parliamentary elections and the strife between Whig and Tory. And there is this also to be added that the Revolution of 1688 had sanctified the "privileges" of the boroughs.

[1] Murray, *New English Dictionary*. It will be known to my readers that in English books "Statute" almost always means *Gesetz* (Statutum Regni) and rarely *Statut*. Only in the case of universities, colleges, cathedral chapters and the like can we render *Statut* by "Statute." In other cases we must say "by-laws," "memorandum and articles of association" and so forth, varying the phrase according to the nature of the body of which we are speaking.

Had not an attack upon their "privileges," which were regarded as *wohlerworbene Rechte*, "vested rights," cost a King his crown? The municipal corporations were both corrupt and sacrosanct. And so all sorts of devices were adopted in order that local government might be carried on without the creation of any new corporations. Bodies of "commissioners" or of "trustees" were instituted by *Gesetz*, now in this place, and now in that, now for this purpose, and now for that; but good care was taken not to incorporate them. Such by this time had been the development of private trusts and charitable trusts, that English law had many principles ready to meet these "trusts of a public nature." But no great step forward could be taken until the borough corporations had been radically reformed and the connection between corporateness and privilege had been decisively severed.

A natural result of all this long history is a certain carelessness in the use of terms and phrases which may puzzle a foreign observer. I can well understand that he might be struck by the fact that whereas our borough is (or, to speak with great strictness, the mayor, aldermen, and burgesses are) a corporation, our county, after all our reforms, is still not a corporation, though the County Council is. But though our modern statutes establish some important distinctions between counties and boroughs, I very much doubt whether any practical consequences could be deduced from the difference that has just been mentioned, and I am sure that it does not correspond to any vital principle.

I must bring to an end this long and disorderly

paper, and yet I have said very little of those *Communalverbände* which gave Dr Redlich occasion to refer to what I had written. I thought, however, that the one small service that I could do to those who for many purposes are better able to see us than we are to see ourselves was to point out that an unincorporated *Communalverband* is no isolated phenomenon which can be studied by itself, but is a member of a great genus, with which we have been familiar ever since the days when we began to borrow a theory of corporations from the canonists. The technical machinery which has made the existence of "unincorporated bodies" of many kinds possible and even comfortable deserves the attention of all who desire to study English life or any part of it. What the foreign observer should specially remember (if I may be bold enough to give advice) is that English law does not naturally fall into a number of independent pieces, one of which can be mastered while the others are ignored. It may be a clumsy whole; but it is a whole, and every part is closely connected with every other part. For example, it does not seem to me that a jurist is entitled to argue that the English county, being unincorporate, and having no juristic personality, can only be a "passive" *Verband*, until he has considered whether he would apply the same argument to, let us say, the Church of Rome (as seen by English law), the Wesleyan "Connexion," Lincoln's Inn, the London Stock Exchange, the London Library, the Jockey Club, and a Trade Union. Also it is to be remembered that the making of grand theories is not and never has been our strong

point. The theory that lies upon the surface is sometimes a borrowed theory which has never penetrated
far, while the really vital principles must be sought for
in out-of-the-way places.

It would be easy therefore to attach too much
importance to the fact that since 1889 we have had
upon our statute-book the following words :—" In this
Act and in every Act passed after the commencement
of this Act the expression 'person' shall, unless the
contrary intention appears, include any body of persons
corporate or unincorporate[1]." I can imagine a country
in which a proposal to enact such a clause would give
rise to vigorous controversy ; but I feel safe in saying
that there was nothing of the sort in England. For
some years past a similar statutory interpretation had
been set upon the word " person " in various Acts of
Parliament relating to local government[2]. Some of
our organs of local government, for example, the
" boards of health " had not been definitely incorporated, and it was, I suppose, to meet their case that
the word " person " was thus explained. It is not
inconceivable that the above cited section of the Act
of 1889 may do some work hereafter ; but I have
not heard of its having done any work as yet ; and
I fear that it cannot be treated as evidence that we
are dissatisfied with such theories of personality as
have descended to us in our classical books.

One more word may be allowed me. I think that
a foreign jurist might find a very curious and instructive story to tell in what he would perhaps call

[1] Interpretation Act, 1889, sec. 19.
[2] Public Health Act, 1872, sec. 60.

the publicistic extension of our Trust *Begriff*. No one, I suppose, would deny that, at all events in the past, ideas whose native home was the system of Private Law have done hard work outside that sphere, though some would perhaps say that the time for this sort of thing has gone by. Now we in England have lived for a long while in an atmosphere of "trust," and the effects that it has had upon us have become so much part of ourselves that we ourselves are not likely to detect them. The trustee, "der zwar Rechtsträger aber nur in fremdem Interesse ist" is well known to all of us, and he becomes a centre from which analogies radiate. He is not, it will be remembered, a mandatory. It is not *Vertrag* that binds him to the *Destinatär*. He is not, it will be remembered, a guardian. The *Destinatär* may well be a fully competent person. Again, there may be no *Destinatär* at all, his place being filled by some "charitable" *Zweck*. We have here a very elastic form of thought into which all manner of materials can be brought. So when new organs of local government are being developed, at first sporadically and afterwards by general laws, it is natural not only that any property they acquire, lands or money, should be thought of as "trust property," but that their governmental powers should be regarded as being held in trust. Those powers are, we say, "intrusted to them," or they are "intrusted with" those powers. The fiduciary character of the *Rechtsträger* can in such a case be made apparent in legal proceedings, more or less analogous to those which are directed against other trustees. And, since practical questions will find an answer in the elaborate statutes

which regulate the doings of these *Körper*, we have
no great need to say whether the trust is for the
State, or for the *Gemeinde*, or for a *Zweck*. Some
theorists who would like to put our institutions into
their categories, may regret that this is so; but so it is.

Not content, however, with permeating this region,
the Trust presses forward until it is imposing itself
upon all wielders of political power, upon all the
organs of the body politic. Open an English newspaper, and you will be unlucky if you do not see
the word "trustee" applied to "the Crown" or to
some high and mighty body. I have just made the
experiment, and my lesson for to-day is, that as the
Transvaal has not yet received a representative constitution, the Imperial parliament is "a trustee for the
colony." There is metaphor here. Those who speak
thus would admit that the trust was not one which
any court could enforce, and might say that it was
only a "moral" trust. But I fancy that to a student
of *Staatswissenschaft* legal metaphors should be of
great interest, especially when they have become the
commonplaces of political debate. Nor is it always
easy to say where metaphor begins. When a Statute
declared that the *Herrschaft* which the East India
Company had acquired in India was held "in trust"
for the Crown of Great Britain, that was no idle
proposition but the settlement of a great dispute. It
is only the other day that American judges were
saying that the United States acquired the sovereignty
of Cuba upon trust for the Cubans.

But I have said enough and too much[1].

[1] It did not seem expedient to burden this slight sketch with

many references to books; but the following are among the best treatises which deal with those matters of which I have spoken:— Lewin, *Law of Trusts*, ed. 10 (1898); Tudor, *Law of Charities and Mortmain*, ed. 3 (1889); Lindley, *Law of Partnership*, ed. 6 (1893); Lindley, *Law of Companies*, ed. 6 (1902); Pollock, *Digest of the Law of Partnership*, ed. 6 (1895); Buckley, *Law and Practice under the Companies Act*, ed. 8 (1902); Palmer, *Company Law*, ed. 2 (1898); Wertheimer, *Law relating to Clubs*, ed. 3 (1903); Underhill, *Encyclopædia of Forms*, vol. 3 (1903), pp. 728—814 (Clubs). As regards the early history of "uses" or trusts, an epoch was made by O. W. Holmes, "Early English Equity," *Law Quarterly Review*, vol. I. p. 162.

THE TEACHING OF HISTORY[1]

THE following essays were to have been ushered into the world by Lord Acton. That he is unable to perform for them this good office will be deeply regretted both by their writers and by their readers. Of what he would have written only this can be said with certainty, that it would have added greatly to the value of this book. Still it is not apparent that these essays, proceeding from men who have had much experience in the teaching of history, imperatively demand any introduction. A few words about a matter of which the essayists have not spoken nor been called upon to speak, namely, about the history of the teaching of history in the English universities, are all that seem necessary, and may be suffered to come from one who can look at schools of history from the outside.

The tale need not be long, and indeed could not be long unless it became minute. The attempt to teach history, if thereby be meant a serious endeavour to make historical study one of the main studies of the universities, is very new. We can admit that it has attained the manly estate of one-and-twenty years and a little more. But not much more. Some of those

[1] *Essays on the Teaching of History.* Cambridge, 1901.

who watched its cradle are still among us, are still active and still hopeful.

The university of Oxford, it is true, came by a professorship or readership of ancient history in times that we may well call ancient, especially if we remember that only in 1898 did the university of Cambridge permanently acquire a similar professorship. But those ancient times were in some respects nearer our own than are some times that have intervened. The professorship at Oxford was established by William Camden in 1622 at the end of a life devoted to history, and the founder numbered among his friends many eager and accomplished explorers of the past: Selden and Ussher, Spelman and Godwin, Savile and Cotton. Much had been done for history, and more especially for English history, in the age that was closing: an age that had opened when Matthew Parker set scholars to work on the history of the English church and was in correspondence with the Centuriators of Magdeburg. The political and ecclesiastical questions which had agitated mankind had been such as stimulated research in unworked fields. Learning had been in fashion, and much sound knowledge had been garnered.

For a moment it seemed probable that Cambridge would not long be outstripped by Oxford. One of her sons, Fulke Greville, Lord Brooke, who was murdered in 1628, founded or endeavoured to found a readership of history, which would have balanced Camden's foundation. He sought to obtain Vossius from Leyden, and obtained from Leyden Dorislaus as an occupant for the chair. After two or three lectures the lecturer was in trouble. His theme was Roman history and he said somewhat of the expulsion of kings : a matter of which it is not always safe to talk at large. That he would take part in trying an English king for treason he did not foresee, nor the vengeance that followed, nor the public funeral in Westminster Abbey, nor the exhumation of bones that polluted a royal sanctuary. What at the present moment concerns us more is the loss of an annuity that Lord Brooke meant, so it seems, to be permanent. Apparently our historians have as yet found no more concrete cause to which they may assign this disaster than "the iniquity of the times." So Oxford had a professor of ancient history and Cambridge had none. Cambridge, however, had for a while "a reader of the Saxon language and of the history of our ancient British churches": two branches of learning which since Parker's day had been united. The reader was Abraham Wheelock : he also professed Arabic but edited ancient English laws. As reader of Saxon he was paid by Henry Spelman, upon whose death in troublous days (1641) the endowment lapsed. Opportunities had been lost. The age of fresh and vigorous research went by. Cambridge should have had an historical professorship recalling the name of Parker. A line of professors that began with G. J. Vossius would have begun famously.

A decline of interest, or at least of academic interest, in history may be traced by anyone who with a list of the Camden professors before him seeks for their names in that *Dictionary of National Biography* which is among the best historical products of our own time. During the seventeenth century the Camden professors were men who in some way or another left a mark behind them.   Degory Wheare, for example, the first of them, wrote a book on The Method and Order of Reading Histories : a book that can still be read and such a book as a professor should sometimes write.   Lewis Dumoulin was a remarkable member of a remarkable family.   "Dodwell's learning was immense," said Gibbon.   Then, however, there was a fall.   Thomas Hearne, the under librarian at Oxford, who was a truly zealous student, might, so he said, have filled the chair if he would have bowed the knee to an usurping dynasty.   Apparently learning and loyalty were not to be found in combination.   Late in the eighteenth century occurs the name of William Scott, who as Lord Stowell was to expound law for the nations.   His lectures were well attended (so we are told) and were praised by those whose praise was worth having.   His name is followed by that of Thomas Warton, who had already been professor of poetry.   His title to the one chair and to the other is not to be disputed, at all events if history is to include the history of literature ; and the versatile man wrote a history of the parish of Kiddington as "a specimen of a history of Oxfordshire."   But we need trace no further the fortunes of ancient history.   It might be considered as a branch of "the classics" or of "humane letters," and the study of it, though flagging, was likely to revive.

We must turn to speak of a royal benefactor. George I, the king, whose title to the crown of Great Britain the learned Hearne would not acknowledge, had "observed that no encouragement or provision had been made in either of the universities for the study of modern history or modern languages." Also he had "seriously weighed the prejudice that had accrued to the said universities from this defect, persons of foreign nations being often employed in the education and tuition of youth both at home and in their travels." It may well have struck His Majesty that, if it was a defect on his part to speak no English, it was a defect on the part of his ministers to speak no German. Also it may have struck him that a knowledge "rerum Brunsvicensium," and, to speak more generally, a knowledge of the Germanic Body and its none too simple history was not so common in England as it might reasonably be expected to be in all parts of His Majesty's dominions. Also it is not impossible that a prince of that house which had Leibnitz for its historiographer may have thought that such historiographers as England could show hardly reached a creditable standard. So he founded professorships of modern history at Oxford and Cambridge (1724). Out of the stipends that were assigned to them the professors were to provide teachers of the modern languages.

The university of Cambridge, if it wanted learning, was not deficient in loyalty, and effusively thanked the occupier of the throne for his "noble design," his "princely intentions." The masters and scholars "ventured...to join in the complaint that foreign tutors had so large a share in the education of our youth of quality both at home and in their travels." They even dared to foresee a glad day when "there should be a sufficient number of academical persons well versed in

the knowledge of foreign courts and well instructed in
their respective languages; when a familiarity with the
living tongues should be superadded to that of the
dead ones; when the solid learning of antiquity should
be adorned and set off with a skilful habit of convers-
ing in the languages that now flourish and both be
-accompanied with English probity; when our nobility
and gentry would be under no temptation of sending
for persons from foreign countries to be entrusted with
the education of their children ; and when the appearance of an English gentleman in the courts of Europe
with a governor of his own nation would not be so
rare and uncommon as it theretofore had been."

Such were the phrases with which these representatives of English learning welcomed the royal gift.
This we know; for if the university of Cambridge was
slow to produce a school of history, the borough of
Cambridge once had for its town clerk a compiler of
admirable annals.   The foreigner, we observe, was
to be driven from the educational market, and the
English gentleman was to appear in foreign courts
with a "governor" of his own nation : in other words
the professor of modern history was to be the trainer
of bear-leaders : the English leaders of English bears.
This being the ideal, it is not perhaps surprising that
the man who at that time was doing the best work
that was being done in England as a systematic
narrator of very modern history was the Frenchman
Abel Boyer, or that he should have belonged to the
hateful race of foreign tutors.   The remoter history of
England might be read in the pages of M. de Rapin,
or, if "familiarity with the living tongues" would not

extend so far, then in the translation which Mr Tindal was about to publish. In academic eyes modern history was to be an ornamental fringe around "the solid learning of antiquity." As to the wretched middle ages, they, it was well understood, had been turned over to "men of a low, unpolite genius fit only for the rough and barbarick part of learning." One of these mere antiquaries had lately written a History of the Exchequer which has worn better than most books of its time. Also he had written this sentence: "In truth, writing this history is in some sort a religious act." But the spirit which animated Thomas Madox was not at home in academic circles.

It may be that some of the regius professors ably performed the useful task with which they were entrusted. Statistics which should exhibit the nationality of the tutors who made the grand tour with young persons of quality would be hard to obtain, and no unfavourable inference should be drawn from the bare fact that the professor's mastery of history was seldom attested by any book that bore his name. Of one we may read that he is the anonymous author of "The Country Parson's Advice to his Parishioners of the Younger Sort"; of another that "he was killed by a fall from his horse when returning...from a dinner with Lord Sandwich at Hinchinbroke." Macaulay has said that the author of the Elegy in a Country Churchyard was in many respects better qualified for the professorship than any man living. That may be so; but "the habits of the time made lecturing unnecessary" (so Mr Leslie Stephen has told us), and as a teacher of modern history Thomas Gray must be for us a mute, inglorious potentiality.   Historical work was being done even at Cambridge.   David Wilkins published the collection of English Concilia which still holds the field and edited the Anglo-Saxon laws ; but he, like -Wheelock, was professor of Arabic ; also he was a German and his name was not Wilkins.   To find a square hole for the round man was apparently the fashion of the time.   Conyers Middleton professed geology.

If Gibbon learnt much at Oxford he was ungrateful, and yet he was the only member of the historical "triumvirate" in whom an English university could claim anything.   Modern history was at length earning academic honour north of the Tweed when Robertson reigned at Edinburgh.   Hume found that history was more profitable than philosophy and consumed less time.   His rival in the historical field could in the interval between Peregrine Pickle and Humphrey Clinker turn out history at the rate of a century a month ; but he was another beggarly Scot.   The demand for history was increasing ; the notion of history was extending its bounds.   Burke began a history of the laws of England and should have written more than ten pages.   Anderson, another Scot, had compiled a solid history of British commerce.   Dr Coxe of the house of Austria showed that the travelling tutor might become an industrious and agreeable historian.

About the beginning of the nineteenth century it became usual to appoint to the chairs of modern history men who would take their duties seriously and who either had written or might be expected to write history of one sort or another.   Thus Prof. William Smyth, of Cambridge, published lectures that were admired, and Prof. Nares, of Oxford, wrote about Lord Burleigh a book, which as Macaulay's readers will remember, weighed sixty pounds avoirdupois. Thomas Arnold's name occurs in the Oxford list, and, besides all else that he did, he introduced the teaching of modern history into a public school. Nevertheless if we look back at the books that were being produced during the first half of the century, we must confess that a remarkably large amount of historical literature was coming from men who had not been educated at Oxford or Cambridge. One and the same college might indeed boast of Macaulay, Hallam, Thirlwall and Kemble. On the other side stand such names as those of James Mill, Grote, Palgrave, Lingard, Carlyle, Buckle, Napier; and we must not forget Sir Archibald Alison and Sharon Turner; still less such archivists as Petrie and the two Hardys. We cannot say that any organized academic opinion demanded the work that was done by the Record Commission, by the Rolls Series, or by the Historical Manuscripts Commission, or that the universities cried aloud for the publication of State Papers and the opening of the national archives. But some Niebuhr was translated and then some Ranke, and it became plain that the sphere of history was expanding in all directions.

Then the great change came, soon after the middle of the century. The professors at the two universities were among the first men that would have been mentioned by anyone who was asked to give the names of our living historians. An opportunity of teaching, and of teaching seriously was being provided

for them.   Gradually the study of history became the
avenue to an " honours degree."   It was not among
the first of "the new studies" that obtained recognition
at Cambridge.   The moral sciences and the natural
sciences took precedence of it.   For a while the moral
-sciences included a little history (1851).   Then (1858),
a small place was found for it in the Law Tripos.
Then for a few years there was a Law and History
Tripos (1870) in which, however, law was the predominant partner.   The dissolution of partnership
took effect in 1875.   History was emancipated.   A
similar change had been made at Oxford some few
-years earlier (1872).   At Oxford the class list of the
school of Modern History has now become nearly if
not quite the longest of the class lists.   In Cambridge
the competition of the natural sciences has been
severer, but the Historical Tripos attracts a number
of candidates that is no longer small, and increases.
Some new professorships have been founded.   Oxford
has two chairs of modern, one of ancient, one of
ecclesiastical history, besides readerships and lecture-
ships.   Cambridge has had a professor of ecclesiastical
history since 1884, a professor of ancient history since
1898. · Whewell, the historian of inductive science,
provided ample encouragement for the study of international law, which is closely related to modern
history.   Scholarships in " history, and more especially
ecclesiastical history," were endowed by Lightfoot,
the historian of early Christianity.   The establishment
of prizes for historical essays began at Oxford in the
middle of the century when the name of Thomas
Arnold was thus commemorated.   Other prizes came

from Lord Stanhope, who in various ways deserved well of history, and from Lord Lothian. At this point also Cambridge was somewhat behindhand; but the names of the Prince Consort, Thirlwall, and Seeley are now connected with prizes. A list of successful essays shows that in not a few cases the offer of an honourable reward has turned a young man's thoughts to a field in which he has afterwards done excellent work. It is a cause for rejoicing that among the teachers of history at the universities there have been men so justly famous, each in his own way, as Stubbs, Freeman, Froude, Creighton, Hatch, and Seeley—for we will name none but the departed—but when all men get their due a large share of credit will be given to those whose patient and self-denying labours as tutors and lecturers have left them little time for the acquisition of such fame as may be won by great books.

It is, then, of a modern movement and of young schools that these essays speak to us : of a movement which is yet in progress : of schools that have hardly outlived that tentative and experimental stage through which all institutions ought to pass. We may wish for these schools not only the vigour but also the adaptability of youth. And, if it be true, as will be said by others, that there are many reasons why history should be taught, let it not be forgotten that, -whether we like it or no, history will be written. The number of men in England who at the present time are writing history of some sort or another must indeed be very large. Very small may be the number of those who take the universe or universal mankind for their theme. Few will be those who aspire so high as the whole life of some one nation. But many a man is writing the history of his county, his parish, his college, his regiment, is endeavouring to tell the tale of some religious doctrine, some form of art or literature, some economic relationship, or some rule of law. Or, again, he is writing a life, or he is editing letters. Nor must we forget the journalists and the history, good, bad, and indifferent that finds a place in their articles ; nor the reviewers of historical books, who assume to judge and therefore ought to know.

All this is important work. It has to be done, and will be done, and it ought to be done well, conscientiously, circumspectly, methodically. Now it may be that no school of history can be sure of producing great historians ; and it may be that when the great historian appears he will perchance come out of a school of classics or mathematics, or will have given some years to metaphysics or to physiology. But even for his sake we should wish that all the departmental work, if such we may call it, should be thoroughly well performed. His time should not be wasted over bad texts, ill-arranged material, or assertions for which no warrantor is vouched. To help and at any rate not to hinder him should be the hope of many humble labourers.

That is not all. The huge mass of historical stuff that is now-a-days flowing from the press goes to make the minds of its writers and of its readers, and indeed to make the mind of the nation. It is of some moment that mankind should believe what is true,- and disbelieve what is false.

To make Gibbons or Macaulays may be impossible: but it cannot be beyond the power of able teachers to set in the right path many of those who, say what we will, are going to write history well or are going to write it ill. Unquestionably of late years an improvement has taken place in England; but still it is not altogether pleasant to compare English books of what we will again call departmental or sectional history with the parallel books that come to us from abroad. When the *English Historical Review* was started in 1886—at J. R. Green's suggestion, so Creighton has told us—England in one important respect stood behind some small and some backward countries. "English historians had not yet...associated themselves in the establishment of any academy or other organisation, nor founded any journal to promote their common object." Even of late Dr Gross has been sending us our bibliographies from the other side of the Atlantic. More co-operation, more organisation, more and better criticism, more advice for beginners are needed. And the need if not met will increase. History is lengthening and widening and deepening. It is lengthening at both ends, for while modern states in many parts of the globe are making new history at a bewilderingly rapid rate, what used to be called ancient history is no longer by any means the ancientest: Egypt, Assyria, Babylonia, and even primeval man are upon our hands. And history is widening. Could we neglect India, China and Japan, there would still be America, Australia, Africa, as well as Europe, demanding that their stories should be told and finding men to tell them well or to tell them badly. And history is deepening. We could not if we would be satisfied with the battles and the protocols, the alliances and the intrigues. Literature and art, religion and law, rents and prices, creeds and superstitions have burst the political barrier and are no longer to be expelled. The study of interactions and interdependences is but just beginning, and no one can foresee the end. There is much to be done by schools of history; there will be more to be done every year.

LAW AT THE UNIVERSITIES[1]

THE Cambridge Law Club was founded in 1888, and in the summer of 1889 I was appointed its Secretary: in other words it has existed for 14 years and during nearly the whole of that time I have been its only officer. This afternoon I am going to place my resignation in your hands, with thanks to you for your kindly toleration of the least business-like secretary that any club ever had. Even if there were no circumstances of the particular case I should be inclined to decide that thirteen years is by at least three years too long a time for anyone to manage such affairs as we have, and that the aged should make room for the young: but as you are aware there are some circumstances of the particular case which make my retirement necessary. A secretary *in partibus infidelium* is of little use to you, and if the spirit is willing the flesh is weak.

In those spacious days when conveyancers were paid by length and no self-respecting person was allowed to leave the world until he had set his hand to a handsome array of common law folios it was usual to make a testator say that though weak in

---

[1] A paper read to the Cambridge Law Club, 1901.

27—2

body he was of a whole and disposing mind.   It is,
so I hope, with a whole and disposing mind that I
make and publish my last will and testament in
manner following (that is to say) :—

I observe with penitence that a Club which began
by meeting twice a term in accordance with its rules
now meets but once a term, against the form of the
statute in that case made and provided.   I acknowledge my fault.   At the same time I should like to
observe that the competition for the honour of reading
a paper to the Club has not been keen : members
bearing essays in their hands have not had to shoulder
each other out of the way that leads to the Secretary's
rooms.   I hope that my successor's ardour and vigour
will after a little while bring back the Club into the
old path of constitutional duty.   For I believe (and
this is what I have to say this afternoon) that the
Club has a useful function to perform.

I think it a matter of importance that all those
who are engaged in teaching law at Cambridge should
meet each other in what I may call socially pleasant
circumstances.   I will not dwell on the mere pleasantness except by saying this :—Cambridge is a curious
place.   We all live so much under the influence of
time tables that it is very possible for a man to reside
here and to take a fairly active part in university
affairs and yet hardly ever to see some other men
whom he would be very glad to meet.   On most days
I go to the University Library at about the same
hour.   As I go and return I daily see the same men
at about the same places, while other men (whom
perhaps I like much better) I never see at all.   They

go out earlier or they go out later. You know what I mean and I will not enlarge upon it.

Nor upon the mere pleasantness of our meetings will I dwell. Only this I will say that having had a little experience of two Special Boards of Studies besides the Law Board I think we law men may congratulate ourselves upon the pleasantness of our intercourse and the despatchfulness of our official organ. Jealous critics may ascribe this to our laziness or to the *vis inertiae* of the law. I am disposed to attribute some little influence to our Club. I do not want to fall into platitude, still I think it true as a general rule that the more men see of each other, the better they understand each other, and the better they understand each other the better they like each other. I hope that this is not an unduly optimistic creed.

Majora canamus. I have used the phrase our official organ, meaning thereby the Special Board for Law, and you will not suppose for one moment that I am in revolt against that august body if I say that I like to think of our Law Club as our unofficial organ—the unofficial moot of the lagemanni de Grentebrigia. I do not undervalue the pleasure or the profit that has accrued to us by some very interesting papers that we have heard: papers on legal problems and legal history—but I am going to suggest that a little new blood might be introduced into a body that I can hardly call full-blooded and that in course of time the number of meetings might be raised to the constitutional standard if it was understood among us that the most acceptable subject for a paper is some question affecting the teaching of law in Cambridge. Each of us has his own study—it may be Roman law, it may be Indian law or what not, each of us is necessarily a bit of a specialist and I can well understand that each of us is a little unwilling to put some bit of specialism into a paper for the Club. ' He must be brief, he is by no means certain that he will really be interesting or intelligible to more than two or three of his hearers, and he does not think that the few remarks that his paper will evoke are likely to be of very high value to himself. On the other hand there is one subject in which we all are interested— the study of law at Cambridge : and I think that we ought to have a good deal to say to each other about it.

Before I go further let me make two or three remarks about the Law Board. I hope that it is a representative body. Still it cannot comprise all the men who are teaching law in Cambridge, and in particular it cannot comprise all the younger men. Now it is I am sure no conventional untruth that I utter when I say that the opinions of the young are highly valued by the old. If for the moment I make myself the spokesman of the aged I would say that we are well aware of the always widening gulf that separates us from the undergraduates, and we are well aware that any schemes for improvement, any adaptations of our machinery to the new wants of new times will fail unless the opinions of the young are attentively considered. Then again, the Law Board is a business body, and I think that I may call it a business-like body. We all feel—at least I feel—that the Board Room is not the place where abstract questions can be pleasantly and profitably discussed. Now I think that one of us may often have something to say that would be of great interest to his fellows though he is not prepared to end with a motion which, if carried, would aim at the alteration of some statute or ordinance of the University. What is more, having some half-formed project in his head he may well be desirous of ascertaining the opinions of other people and seeing how the land lies—and I think that, in such a case, this Club might provide the occasion for discussions and conversations of a most useful kind.

Let me read from the book the minutes of what I thought at the time a very profitable meeting...

You will understand that I have not read these minutes as a precedent for confining our discussions to proposals for changes in Examinations; far from it. I think that there are many other matters of a somewhat similar character that might be debated. In a hasty way I will name two or three.

Can we get more money? That sounds like a selfish and a vulgar question. But in my opinion it is vital in the interests of English jurisprudence. I think that we might with some confidence ask the question—What has been done for law in England by professors and other endowed teachers of law. I will not go back to Blackstone's commentaries and I will spare your blushes by saying nothing of Cambridge. But take the men who are or lately have been teaching law at Oxford and take the books that they have written—are not those books among the very best books about law that modern England has produced, and would they have been written if there had been no endowments? I think that a question that we may ask with great confidence. As matters now stand an endowed office is almost the only reward that can attract a man from the beaten and lucrative paths of practice and induce him to write about law something that will not be of direct use to legal practitioners. I have spoken of professorships and readerships and the like as rewards and I am now going to say something that will sound to you extremely selfish—but as it seems to me to be true I will say it all the same. I think that as matters now stand in England there would be a great need of professorships as prizes even if the professor when appointed generally fell at once into his dotage. To take by way of example a matter in which just at present I am much interested. How am I as literary director of the Selden Society (such is my title) to induce young men to learn enough about the law of the fourteenth century to enable them to edit the Year Books. I live in terror lest the Savigny Stift or the École des Chartes should undertake an edition. But there, I am only saying what you all must feel in the studies that you have made your own—and the question whether there is any hope of improvement is just one of those questions that the Club might advantageously discuss. Heaven forbid that the Club should become a trade union, still that dirty economic factor unfortunately is a factor that we cannot eliminate. To be concrete—I have long thought that we ought to have a readership in Roman Law and Jurisprudence. Could we get one?

Our position as regards this and similar matters is beset by difficulties. In the present state of the finances of the University a plea for more money is not likely to meet with much attention unless those who urge it can say that more teaching is requisite and that the teachers will have numerous hearers. And unfortunately that is not what we can say with any great confidence. If the number of candidates for the Law Tripos is increasing at all it is not increasing very rapidly. What is more (and here I am expressing a difficulty of my own) I am not sure that we ought to wish for any great increase. When I try to take an impartial view of the matter and ask myself whether if I had a son at Cambridge I should wish him to read for the Law Tripos—I find myself saying that the answer would depend upon my hypothetical income. Place that income at either end of the scale I might answer Yes. I might say— My son is to be a solicitor—it is highly important that he should get to work at once and for this reason I think that the amount of law that he can learn at Cambridge will be decidedly more valuable to him that an equivalent amount of history, natural science or the like. And then at the other end of the scale I might be saying—my son is not going to work for his living, he will be a country gentleman, sit on the county bench, go into parliament perhaps, and some knowledge of law is likely to be as useful as any other kind of knowledge that he will acquire at the University. But then I must confess to you that if the boy was a bright boy looking forward to a career at the bar and there was no great hurry for his first few guineas, I might be inclined to say, Well you are going to work at law all your life, you had better take a look round at something else before you make your plunge into the *oceanus iuris*— in particular (so I should say) a look at history or at ethics and political economy. So you see that I—and some of you may feel yourselves in the same position— can hardly bring myself to preach the virtues of the Law Tripos with that penetrating and unquavering voice which might gain an audience in a place where everyone is calling aloud for coin. And then on the other hand what I feel in my own mind to be the real want is not one which will be felt by the University or the world at large. I want to see a great deal done that is not being done in the way of unremunerative work—work done for the history of law and for the theory of law—and it is only I think with the aid and stimulus of endowments that such work will be done at all.

It is not an easy case to argue—and in particular it is not an easy case to argue before the rulers of the Inns of Court. What can be made intelligible in that august quarter is that there ought to be a bar examination and that teaching which leads to that examination should be provided. Now so far as I can learn this part of their duty is upon the whole satisfactorily performed. I do not think that we are in a position to demand a really severe examination, indeed I think that to demand that would be a mistake. There is, as we all know, a great difference at this point between the two professions of law and medicine—the layman chooses his own medical adviser and the State may well be right in insisting that the medical student shall have been examined many times over before he obtains a licence to practise. On the other hand, the barrister is selected by one who himself is an expert: and really I cannot say with any certainty that the work done by barristers would be better done if the bar examination were severer. Moreover—and this remark comprises both branches of the profession—the qualities desirable in a lawyer are to a very large extent qualities that cannot be tested by written questions and answers. So I think that in honesty we have to make the admission that the people who control legal education in London do fairly well what they are likely to regard as the whole of their duty. And I should be ungrateful if I did not add that (owing largely to the efforts of certain judges of whom Cambridge is proud) three of the Inns of Court have subsidized the Selden Society. More than this it is difficult to expect. If anything is said about the provision of higher teaching—the teaching that will not fill rooms—a natural answer is that this is work for the Universities.

I have heard it said to me by well-disposed persons—Now you at the Universities teach the theory—then we in London will see to a working knowledge of English law. That sounds plausibly, and I think it very possible that there are among us here some who think that a sort of theory of law—the *generalia* of jurisprudence—can be profitably taught to those who as yet know nothing of any concrete system. Now that is just one of the questions which might promote a fruitful discussion in our Club. My own opinion is that we get our men too young for us to be able to deal with them in the manner that is thus suggested. I won't say but that a man who has seen a little of the world and taken in law through the pores might not intelligently read what we call general jurisprudence before he studied the law of Rome or England or Germany. Our freshmen are too ignorant of life. When I lecture to them I adjure them to read the newspapers, more especially the *Times*. If I could have quite my own way with them I would plunge them at once into Dr Kenny's *Case Book of Criminal Law*. All this I know to be a disputable point, but you will see how my opinion about it affects my opinion about some other matters. To a very large extent our Tripos must be an elementary examination in very concrete English law and therefore we are obliged to keep a good deal of our teaching on a pretty low level. Still I am not sure that we are doing all that might be done towards meeting that opinion which would assign to the Universities the office of teaching theory and to the Inns of Court the office of teaching practice. I have never concealed my opinion that the distribution of papers between the two parts of the Law Tripos is not quite that which I should myself have proposed. I should like to see English Criminal Law and Jurisprudence changing places. My main reason is this— that on the one hand we try to teach some legal theory to those whose heads are as yet so empty of concrete rules that, though they may be able to repeat what they have been taught, they are in no position to understand it, and that on the other hand when a youth is beginning to know some concrete rules and to perceive their play in practical life then we in effect say to him—Don't bother yourself about theories any more; they are for children; you have put aside childish things; leave your rules and work your problems.

All this has been said before. But it seems to me that two events have lately happened which go far towards the removal of certain difficulties, which have hitherto stood in the way of the sort of change which I should like to see. In the first place, we have come by two books on English Criminal Law which (as I think) have made it as good a subject for beginners as any subject could possibly be. I will say this in Dr Kenny's presence for I would say it in his absence:—I cannot imagine two books better fitted to give a freshman his first ideas about law. And then, in the second place, we have Mr Salmond's new volume. I don't want to jump at it at once— before I recommended it I should like to hear the opinions of all members of the Law Club—but it is the sort of book for which I have long been looking, a book which would give our Second Part men a liberal and liberating interest in their study of English law. However I must not wander down this bye-path.

Then there is the question whether the colleges or any of them could be induced to do more than they are doing. Now as mere prizes for our young men I would very rarely ask for fellowships—and indeed I don't know that I would ever ask for them. But of course the fact that our Tripos is not a high road to fellowships hurts us in a good many ways, and (so I fear) is destined to hurt us more and more.

The competition of the history school is becoming severe, and I think will become severer, especially if a certain important college continues the course that it has of late pursued. Not the least among the good deeds of the late Lord Acton was this, that he raised history by many degrees in the estimation of those whose opinions are influential in the college afore-said—and we are seeing the result. It would be hard, however, for any man to do as much for law, for I do not think that law is a subject about which young men are likely to write dissertations which will, if I may so say, bear their excellence on their outside. However I think that here again we have one of those matters to which our attention ought to be directed in friendly converse, and if we could agree upon any plan of missionary endeavour something might come of it. We are few and don't count for many on a division in the Senate House, but Cambridge is a place in which men are willing to listen, and if we can't get all that we want we may get part of it. I betray no secret in saying that the Squire Law Library came of asking. If we had not been urging the demand for a Library for some time past, the liberality of the testatrix would have found another channel. If these History men had not been so perversely modest, if they had not deserted us and turned their backs in the day of battle they might now have room enough for Lord Acton's books.

Also (to bring this paper to an end) I want to see some more prizes like the Yorke Prize and some more Scholarships like the Whewell Scholarships now that the tenure of the Whewell Scholarships has been amended. What I want above all things is to provide some stimulus and reward for men who are no longer undergraduates which will set them to work at law but a little outside the beaten path that leads to briefs and fees. I have often wished and wish still that the George Long Prize and the Chancellor's Medal were prizes for dissertations, open to men for two or three years after the first degree. That is the time when a young man may be saved from success on the one hand and disappointment on the other and be made a happy man for life by an interest in what can be the most enthralling of all studies.

But I have said enough and too much. I hope that under the guidance of a more vigorous secretary the Club will have these and similar matters debated—especially by the younger of its members—and will become a centre of organized opinion.

A SURVEY OF THE CENTURY[1]

LAW.

THE century which has just come to an end, the century which lies between the Code civil des Français and the Bürgerliches Gesetzbuch of the German Empire, is likely to be memorable in the history of law. When its exploits in the field of jurisprudence are surveyed from a great distance, the most valuable and permanent part of its work will, perhaps, be found partly in a vast extension of the territorial dominion of civilized law, and partly in a grand simplification of the legal map of the world. The provincial customs have disappeared from France; the laws of the several German states are falling into a secondary and subordinate place. Unified and codified French law rules a compact domain, and has been a model for all people who speak versions of the Latin language, to say nothing of Turks and Japanese and Dutchmen. If it has of late been expelled from Elsass and Baden, and other parts of Western Germany, it may plausibly claim to have materially modified the new code of the victors, though a Prussian can proudly remember that

[1] *The Twentieth Century*, Jan. 1901.

not Napoleon, but Frederick the Great was the first of the modern codifiers. The unifying of law has gone hand in hand with the making or re-making of great nations, and, at least for the moment, the future fate of jurisprudence seems to be involved in the future fate of a few, a very few, national systems.

Among these is the English. The system which in 1601 prevailed in the southern half of a small island has thence spread outwards until it has become the greatest system that the world has known. This we may say if we think of square miles or if we count heads; but, after a little seemly hesitation, we may say it also when we have distinguished greatness from mere bigness, and have refused to call a legal system great merely because it governs the actions of many men in many lands, or merely because it is our own. For a moment, however, we dwell on size. If the eighteenth century as it neared its end had in a somewhat bellicose fashion prepared in divers quarters of the globe a way for the destined expansion of English law, still for the nineteenth century (which, when all has been seen of its quarrelsomeness, will appear to students of its predecessors as reasonably pacific) remained the task of filling with law the void that arms had made. And now courts which are administering what is in origin and inmost texture the Common law of England are, to use the old phrase, "speaking right and deeming doom," not only throughout by far the greater part of those countries of which Queen Victoria is the sovereign lady, but also throughout the whole or nearly the whole of one immense country into which her writ will not run.

The important exceptions that must be made before we can identify the territorial sphere of the English legal system with the lands that are subject to our Queen are full of past and future history. Scotland has every right to be tenacious of its law. At a critical time Scotchmen showed themselves to be in legal as in other matters more willing than Englishmen were to listen to foreign teaching, and the age was one in which foreigners had much that was good to teach. Since then Scotland, besides sending many an able son to administer English Law in England and elsewhere, has on more than one occasion served as the instructor of the southern kingdom. Lately also we heard a voice from Louisiana protesting that some clear French ideas of legal relationships ought not to be overwhelmed by the advancing flood of indefinite Englishry. To such protests, whether they come from New Orleans or from Edinburgh, we shall always do well to listen. Perhaps the most beneficial trait of an arrangement which brings to the parts of Westminster appeals from all the ends of the earth is that it compels a certain number of English lawyers and judges to make the acquaintance of law that is not of English origin, and, it may be, to doubt whether our insular jurisprudence is just that perfection of wisdom which it sometimes seems to those to whom it has brought both fame and riches. At all events for the present, it is for the good of the whole British Commonwealth that a code modelled after the French code should prevail in the province of Quebec, that the French code should prevail in Mauritius, and that what is called Roman-Dutch law, extinct in Holland, should be extant in British South Africa. The time has not yet come when we should desire to thrust some parts of our law, and notably of our cumbrous and antiquated land law, upon countries which have hitherto escaped its sway. But still better is it that numerous legislatures—in all, about a hundred, if to our own commonwealth we add the United States— should be freely building upon one and the same traditional foundation. The science of legislation will for a long time be an experimental science, and it is plain already that plenteous and daring experiments will be made by English-speaking men before the twentieth century is very old. By success, or by failure, New Zealand, for example, will soon be teaching us much about the good and ill of social-democracy. In its capacity to assimilate new material and thus to meet new needs, we may find the justification for our statement that the English system is not merely big but great. It is seriously doubtful whether any other body of law has ever shown a greater power of rapid but peacefully continuous development. At the beginning of the century Jeremy Bentham was advising the Americans "to shut their ports against the common law as they would against the plague." At the end of the century we see that a loyal and well-nigh romantic devotion to this same common law has been no hindrance to marvellous progress, and if we look to American legislatures for novelties, we now look to American law-schools for antiquities.

But, despite the sterling good that lies in experimentation and local variation, the demand for uniformity will come. It may come very quickly, as the size of the world, when measured in time, grows rapidly less. Merchants are likely to feel always more keenly the evils of a multitude of differing laws, and the number of those inhabitants of this island who have material interests elsewhere will be yearly augmented. Already we may see that a well-devised statement of the law of England about bills of exchange or the sale of goods or partnership will be speedily adopted by British legislatures all the world over. Uniformity in the law about bills of exchange, a uniformity to be secured by the voluntary adoption of a single set of rules by many independent legislatures, this was the utmost legal unity that Germans could secure in 1847. From that point outwards the movement spread, until first a Commercial, and ultimately, after more than twenty years of assiduous labour and minute discussion, a Civil Code had been fashioned and enacted. Already the penal code which Macaulay drew for India has been showing its adaptability to other countries, and we may feel fairly sure that a penal code which was drawn for England by Sir J. F. Stephen, and revised by Lord Blackburn, will not always lie useless in the pigeon-holes of an office. The century that is opening may end in something very great, greater than the French codes and the German ; even in an accurate and artistic statement of the English system, though in what quarter of the globe the work will be done we cannot guess. A toilsome task it will be, but hardly more arduous than that which Germany has lately achieved. The ideal may be distant, but unless it be kept in view, there is a serious danger that one of the strongest bonds that hitherto have kept together all parts of the English-speaking race will be weakened.

Meanwhile, there is much to be done, but no cause for despair. The century that we are leaving behind us was in the field of law a busy time. Distant, indeed, from us seem the days when the reforming and conservative forces were embodied in the persons of Jeremy Bentham and Lord Eldon, the days when trial by battle was legally possible, when procedure was encumbered by countless fictions, when fines were being levied and recoveries were being suffered, when John Doe and Richard Roe were, or seemed to be, alive. Distant even seem the days when law and equity were separately administered, and the suitor was bandied from court to court in search of a remedy. That short reign of William IV, when the reforming tide was in flood, will stand out in our legal annals with all the distinctness that marks an age that is truly great. It swept away much useless and pernicious lumber, the scarcely intelligible relics of bygone times. Since then good work of many sorts and kinds has been done, destructive and constructive. Not that there has yet been enough destruction. Far from it. Englishmen who are quick to remove patent grievances are slow to perceive the latent but real and deep-seated mischief that is being done by the retention of out-worn theories and obsolescent ideas. On more than one occasion in recent years our Parliament has turned out work that was inexcusably bad, and this because it had not the courage of its opinions, and tried to tinker the untinkerable. There is a great deal in our so-called law of real property which is thoroughly unworthy of a new century, and which no rational lecturer can teach without a blush or a sigh. We have never fairly cleared up that great medieval muddle which passes under the name of feudalism, and until that be done, English law cannot be stated in terms that would befit the modern code of a self-respecting nation. That clearness must be effected, and the sooner that the various legislatures fairly face the problem, the greater is the likelihood of its being solved deliberately, and not under the stress of some revolutionary impulse. If the mother-country will not take the lead, she will some day have to sit at the feet of one of her own daughters.

How in some yet distant age men will see or fancy that they see the time in which we live, is a question that even the most ignorant of us should not readily answer. But we may believe that in the universal history of law a century which struck out from all moderately civilized law books, all chapters on slavery and on serfage will not seem idle. We can imagine also that something in its praise will be said on the score of an endeavour to protect the weak against the strong. It may be noted, too, that strenuous endeavours to improve the law were not impeded, but forwarded by a zealous study of legal history. If at one time it seemed likely that the historical spirit (the spirit which strove to understand the classical jurisprudence of Rome and the Twelve Tables, and the Lex Salica, and law of all ages and climes) was fatalistic and inimical to reform, that time already lies in the past. Men, who were profoundly versed in history bore a willing and helpful hand in the unification of German law.   Now-a-days we may see the office of historical research as that of explaining, and therefore lightening, the pressure that the past must exercise upon the present, and the present upon the future.   To-day we study the day before yesterday, in order that yesterday may not paralyse to-day, and to-day may not paralyse to-morrow.

LINCOLNSHIRE COURT ROLLS AND YORKSHIRE INQUISITIONS[1]

"HAVING, through the kindness of the lord of the manor, been afforded the opportunity of transcribing and studying at my leisure the court rolls of a Lincolnshire manor, which form an unusually complete series, and seem to me of special interest, I have thought it worth while to print the results in the interests of county history, and I am even ambitious enough to hope that my abstracts may be found to have a still wider historical value."

WITH these words the rector of Ormsby prefaces a book which deserves perusal by all who are studying the rural economy of medieval England. In the first place we must always be grateful to those who will give us the substance of legal records that are in private hands, so great is the danger of their remaining unknown and even of their perishing. In the second place Mr Massingberd is right in thinking that the rolls of Ingoldmells have some special claims upon our attention. The manor lay in the extreme east of England, its lord was not a religious corporation, and it has been remarked before now that we have in print comparatively little information concerning eastern manors and concerning manors which

---

[1] *English Historical Review*, Oct. 1903.

were in the hands of laymen. What Mr Massingberd gives us is enough to show that from such manors we yet have much to learn. If he is right, then in one most important respect this manor of Ingoldmells differed widely from what we might call the classical type. The rolls begin in 1291, and yet, "during the time the rolls cover there was no demesne farm at Ingoldmells." In other words, as we understand the matter, there was no land there which was the lord's demesne in the narrowest sense of that term : no land the produce of which went into his barns. Nor is this all. There is no agricultural land which has been demesne and has been let in one mass to a farmer together with the right to exact labour from the villeins. From his villeins—of whom there were plenty—the lord got money; but he got no work. Their whole time was their own. And yet it must be understood that this manor was not some little trifle which might be set down as an anomaly. "In 1295 the rents of the free and bond tenants were £51. 17s. 1d. inclusive of £10 of tallage, but exclusive of fines, perquisites of courts etc., amounting to £18. 11s. 8d." These are handsome amounts.

We have spoken hypothetically. We have said that this is so if Mr Massingberd is right. The extracts that he prints give us no reason to doubt his word : quite the contrary. But his assertion concerning the non-existence of any seignorial demesne is of so much importance that we should wish to see it amply proved. And apparently there are account rolls where the proof lies. These are at the Record Office and therefore accessible to all ; but we very

much hope that Mr Massingberd, with a full sense
of the gravity of the task, will complete the investigation that he has begun, for he has learned so much
of Ingoldmells that those account rolls would give
up their story more easily to him than to strangers.
It is a serious thing to find a large, handsome, profitable manor without demesne land, without labour-
service, in the year 1291. We are far from saying
that there were not many similar estates, but the
establishment of one good instance beyond the possibility of doubt would be a meritorious deed.

Mr Massingberd gives us English instead of
Latin, pleading that he cannot give us both ; and
as such books cannot be remunerative the plea must
be allowed. On the whole, his English is such as
to inspire confidence. But we would point out to him
the desirability of putting in a Latin word whenever
there can be any doubt of its meaning. As an
example we will take a case in which he has seen
the desirability of doing what we could wish that he
had done more frequently. According to him, pre-
sentments are frequently made that women have been
"chastised"; whereupon those women are amerced.
Thus in 1313 Beatrice, Joan, and Matilda "have been
chastised." The sort of offence of which they had
been guilty will be guessed by those who have seen
manorial rolls, and Mr Massingberd, as we may learn
from his introduction, knows what it was. But why
"chastised"? We should have been left to speculate
about some queer use of *castigata* which made it the
opposite to *casta*, if the editor had not on one occasion
revealed the secret. The Latin word appears to be

allopantur, and this, so it seems, he has connected
with *alapa* and not that somewhat mysterious Anglo-
French *aloper* which is the origin of our *elope*.
Apparently, "seduced" would be better than "chastised." Similarly, when he tells us that the usual
habendum on the admission of a tenant to bond-land
was "to him and his boys," we should like to know
what is the Latin word that is rendered by "boys,"
for if it is *pueris* we might have been inclined to
go as far as "children" or even as "issue." But we
cannot say that we are often in serious doubt as to
what it is that he has seen upon the rolls, and the
few instances in which a lawyer might have suggested
a better, or at all events a more orthodox, translation
than that which he has adopted are not of great
importance.

The lately issued volume of *Yorkshire Inquisitions*
covers the period between 1281 and 1302. Of the
earlier volumes notice has been taken in these pages.
It is among the best features of Mr Brown's work
that he gives us a good deal of Latin. He is a
translator whom we trust not the less but the more
because he allows us an opportunity of questioning
the accuracy of the words "twelve quarters of wheat
(*siliginis*)" which stand on the first page of his book,
for we thought that in our medieval Latin *siligo* always
stood for rye. An example of a more serious kind
is a translated petition to the king and council,
presented, so we read, by "the ten burgesses" of
Scarborough, who assert that the two hospitals in the
town were "founded by the ancestors of the said
ten burgesses." But the original French is printed

in a footnote.   In it the petitioners call themselves *les diz Burgeys*, and say that the hospitals were *foundous de les auncestres les diz Burgeys*.   We submit that *les diz* is not "the ten" but "the said," though it is true that in the French of English clerks a final *z* was often written where a final *s* would have been better, just as it is true that the use of *foundu* for *foundé* was a very common error.   It is true also that no burgesses are mentioned before *les diz Burgeys* appear.   But the document begins thus : *Uncore au Rey e a sun Counseyl prient les diz Burgeys*, and the *Uncore* seems to show that in this, as in many other instances, a string of petitionary clauses written on a single piece of parchment was converted by a knife into a number of separate documents after it had been presented.   We do not wish to speak dogmatically, but we are glad that Mr Brown gave us the French as well as the English, for the patronage over these municipal hospitals is a matter of no little interest to those who study the development of municipal corporations.

We hope that the society which is fortunate enough to have Mr Brown for its secretary is well supported. Perhaps there is no class of documents better suited for publication by similar societies than that which consists of inquisitions *post mortem* and *ad quod damnum*.   Apart from matters of purely local interest, there are some large open questions of national history of which they will supply the solution.   For example, there is the question whether the kings used the Statute of Mortmain in furtherance of a deliberate and continuous policy, or readily sold licences to the detriment of their successors. Mr Brown's industry and accuracy are supplying us with excellent materials for an answer to this inquiry.

It is almost needless to say that such documents as he and Mr Massingberd have been translating let in light into out-of-the-way corners. In spite of what has been done in the publication of ecclesiastical service books, we are glad to get from the verdict of a jury the words used by a bridegroom and his father where there was to be an endowment *ex assensu patris.* The son said the English for " De anulo isto te disponso, et de corpore meo te honoro, et de tercia parte omnium terrarum Willelmi patris mei te doto." The father said the English for " Et ego predicte donacioni assensum prebeo." Then, to turn back to Mr Massingberd's book, we see a curious illustration of the manner in which the jurisprudence of the royal courts played upon local usage. In 1341 we find a husband concerned to assert that his wife is a bondwoman, for if she is not a bondwoman she can have no right in bond-land. To this it is replied that she is a free woman because she is a bastard. A jury finds that until ten years past the custom of Ingoldmells did not exclude bastards from claiming rights in bond-land. Apparently the custom had just yielded to what had lately become the doctrine of Westminster, namely that illegitimate children are always born free. This and other entries have induced Mr Massingberd to paint the condition of the Ingoldmells villein in colours that are by no means lugubrious, and he seems to show pretty clearly that in the sixteenth century the "unearned increment" due to changes in the value of money came not to the lord, but to the villeins or their successors in title. But, as already said, we hope that he will return to his theme. "The condition of England question" is to be answered by account rolls.

THE LAWS OF THE ANGLO-SAXONS[1]

THOUGH Dr Liebermann has still something in store for us in the way of notes, index, glossary, and the like, the time has already come when we may rejoice in the possession of a really good edition of the oldest English laws, an edition which will bear comparison with the very best work that has hitherto been done upon any historical materials of a similar kind. That this task should have been performed by a German scholar at the instance of a German academy, and with the support of a German trust fund, may not be what we in England should have liked best, but must not detract from the warmth of our welcome and our praise. If Englishmen cannot or will not do these things, they can at least rejoice that others can and will.

The German occupation of a considerable tract of English history has been a gradual process. The sphere of influence becomes a protectorate, and the protectorate becomes sovereignty. The shore is surveyed and settled; and now with colour of right far-reaching claims can be made over an auriferous hinterland. How and why all this happened it would

[1] *Quarterly Review*, July 1904.

be long to tell, but a small part of the story should be remembered.

Few words will be sufficient to recall to our minds the nature and extent of the territory which, so we fear, is slipping from our grasp.   Any one who, at the present day, desired to study, even in outline, the first six centuries of English history—those centuries which intervene between the withdrawal of the legions and the coming of the Normans—would find himself compelled, whether he liked it or not, diligently to peruse a certain small body of laws.   We cannot, indeed, say that, were it not for these monuments of ancient jurisprudence, the only tale that he would have to tell would be of battles between "kites and crows."   Certain great men—an Alfred, for instance, or a Dunstan—might be seen and portrayed, though without a background. There would still be something to be learnt about heathenry and Christianity, about religious doctrines and ecclesiastical organisation, about poetry and prose, about arts and crafts.   One of those old-fashioned chapters or appendixes touching "the manners and customs of the people" might be rewritten with truer insight and apter illustrations.   But if from the sum total of what we know about our forefathers we subtracted what has been directly or indirectly taught us by legal documents, the residue, it must be confessed, would be both incoherent and precarious.   Not only could we make no attempt to see the nation as an organised and growing whole, but our great men, our Alfred and our Dunstan, would be far more shadowy than they are.   Nay, even our battles would have little good fighting in them, and our very "kites and crows" would be phantasmal. Moreover, if we owe to these laws a certain sum of assured knowledge, we owe to them also—and this is hardly less valuable—a certain sum of assured ignorance. When they do not satisfy they at all events stimulate a rational curiosity; and where they do not give us intelligible answers they prompt us to ask intelligent questions—questions which go deep down into the pith and marrow of our national history, but questions that would never have occurred to us if we had nothing to read but chronicles and the lives of saints.

We have spoken of a small body of laws, and small it certainly is. Without translation and apparatus it might be handsomely printed in a hundred and fifty octavo pages. We fancy that in the days of flamboyant draftsmanship a single Act of Parliament sometimes contained more words than have come to us from all the law-givers that lived in England before the Norman Conquest. We have, it will be remembered, a little priceless matter from our first Christian king, from Æthelberht of Kent. To use round figures, we may say that it comes from the year 600. We have a little from his successors upon the Kentish throne; we have more from the West Saxon Ine (circ. 700), which, however, has passed through the hands of Alfred (circ. 900); and we have a considerable amount from Alfred himself. Then legislation becomes commoner. The tenth century and the first years of the eleventh are illustrated by laws of Edward, Æthelstan, Edmund, Edgar, and Æthelred; and the series ends with the respectably lengthy and luminous code of Cnut the Dane. Besides this, we have a few short statements of legal or customary rules coming to us, not from law-givers, but from presumably learned men—little formularies and so forth, which were transcribed along with the laws and have been slowly disengaged from them by the skill of recent editors.

Such was the territory which was to be explored and cultivated by modern science ; and such was the territory which, as some of our neighbours saw, was lying derelict and inviting annexation. Exploration, it is true, was no easy task, especially because—unlike the parallel laws of the continental nations, Goths and Lombards, Franks and Saxons—these old "dooms," as they call themselves, were written, not in Latin, but in the vernacular, or, in other words, in a language which, for a long time past, has been far less intelligible than Latin to the great mass of fairly educated mankind. Just for this reason, however, these English dooms might claim a prerogative right. Up to a certain point Latin, and even the worst Latin of a dark age, may be generally intelligible ; but, as many investigators have of late had occasion to remark, the thoughts of barbarous Teutons were sadly contorted in the process of latinisation. Many a passage, for example, in the code of the Salian Franks, the famous *Lex Salica*, would by this time be far less obscure than it will ever be had it been transmitted to us, not in Latin, but in Frankish words. In this respect, therefore, our English dooms have a singular, a unique, value. It was a value which could but slowly be turned to account, but it became an effective asset as the old English language was gradually reconstructed; and nowadays, in the eyes of every serious student of early medieval history, the Anglo-Saxon laws appear, not merely as good but as supremely good material.

But to speak at greater length of the extent and fertility of the ground that we have lost or are losing would be needless. The control of the Anglo-Saxon laws, which henceforward we shall have to know as "Die Gesetze der Angelsachsen," implies a protectorate, to say the least, over some six centuries of English history. Nor is that all, for, as will be remarked below, the people who taught us the word "hinterland" have taught us also how a hinterland should be treated. But in order to understand what they have done we must go back a little way.

In the middle of the sixteenth century the Anglo-Saxon laws began, if we may so say, to awake from a long sleep. That there had been such things had never been quite forgotten, for a well-known chronicle contained large extracts from one of those Latin translations that were made soon after the Norman Conquest. But, diligent as our lawyers had been in their hunt for ancient documents—and the amount of old manuscript that Anthony FitzHerbert had perused and digested may well astonish us—a limit was set to their investigations. As far back as the boundary of legal memory, as far back as Glanvill, they could pursue their researches not only with interest, but with professional profit. What lay on the other side of that line seemed to belong to another world, and had no points of contact with their practical work. As to an original Anglo-Saxon text, they could hardly have understood one word of it. The fact that their own technical language was not even English but debased

French tended to widen a gulf which in any case
would have been wide enough.

As Dr Liebermann rightly remarks, the Anglo-
Saxon renaissance began in another quarter. We
might call it a by-product of the Reformation. So
soon as the quarrel with Rome became acute, "divers
sundry old authentick histories and chronicles" were
being explored by important people; and a charter in
which an English king appeared as a "Basileus" was
passing from hand to hand and exciting comment. A
little later, and it seemed possible that, expressed in an
unknown tongue and a barely legible script, there lay
title-deeds of a national church—title-deeds which told
not only of independence, but of purity. And, as a
set-off to the dismal tale of pillaged libraries, we may
remember that the tools had at length come to those
who would use them—the rescued manuscripts to the
hands of those who would be at pains to read them.
Pains were required. The casting of a fount of type
that would imitate the Old English characters shows
us how outlandish to Elizabethan Englishmen was the
speech of their forefathers. For the service performed
in the cause of history by Matthew Parker, John
Joscelyn, and Laurence Nowell we must always be
grateful; nor should Bale and Foxe be forgotten,
though it was no purely scientific spirit that guided
them in their enterprises. It was reserved, however,
for Nowell's pupil, that sound lawyer William Lambard,
to publish an edition of the Anglo-Saxon laws; and
we now have Dr Liebermann's authority for saying
that he did his work wonderfully well. That in every
five lines or thereabouts of his Latin version he should

be guilty of a mistake which his successors can call gross, is only what was to be expected. He was a pioneer in an unknown land.

The first half of the seventeenth century may be regarded as the heroic age of English legal scholarship. Great questions were opening, and on all sides an appeal was being made to ancient law and ancient history. It is true that, as regards very old times, little that was of real value came from the imperious dogmatist who dominated the jurisprudence of his time. When he was on unfamiliar ground Sir Edward Coke was, of all mankind, the most credulous. There was no fable, no forgery, that he would not endorse; and a good many medieval legends and medieval lies passed into currency with his name upon their backs. But in Selden and Spelman England produced two explorers of whom she might well be proud. We are glad to say that in Dr Liebermann's sketch of the work that was done by his predecessors Sir Henry Spelman comes by his rights; and we think it worthy of observation that it was what we nowadays call the comparative method which enabled these illustrious Englishmen to put new life into English history. It has been said with some truth that the man who "introduced the feudal system into England" was not William the Conqueror, but Henry Spelman; and if, as is usual in such cases, similarities were seen before dissimilarities, still to have begun the comparison was a great achievement; for very true it is that England will never be known to those who will know nothing else. There are many other names that deserve remembrance—the names of diligent antiquaries.

Marvellously diligent they were.   Contending with
difficulties and discomforts which their luxurious successors can but faintly imagine, they copied and
collated and edited.   Prynne, for example, munching
his crust of bread as with burning zeal he deciphered
decaying documents in the filth and stench of the
White Tower, is an heroic figure.   If we have done
little else to help Dr Liebermann, we may at least
hope that " Englands edle Gastfreundschaft " (we are
glad to see the phrase) has enabled him to do his
work in pleasant surroundings.

In his judgment the editions of the Anglo-Saxon
laws which were published by Abraham Wheelock in
1644 and by David Wilkins in 1721 owe their merits
more to others than to their editors, who marched
rather behind than in front of the linguistic science
of their times.   That the man whose edition held
the field for a century and upwards was of Prussian
descent, and that his real name was not Wilkins but
Wilke, might be represented as a forecast shadow of
future events ; but there is little or nothing to show
that this industrious professor and archdeacon brought
to his task any equipment of foreign learning.   Meanwhile linguistic science had been advancing ; and, if in
this quarter the help of a De Laet and a Dujon had
been useful, George Hickes, the nonjuring bishop, had
surely shown that at this point England could as yet
hold her own.

But general interest in the old laws was failing.
They had disappointed reasonable expectations.   It
is plain enough, for example, that Blackstone does not
know what to make of them.   And what is one to

make of laws which leave it somewhat doubtful whether our Saxon forefathers were possessed of our glorious constitution, with trial by jury and "habeas corpus," and all other bulwarks, palladia, checks, balances, commodities, easements, and appurtenances? Unfortunately the forgeries and the fables, the legends and the lies, were much more to the point than those meagre, enigmatical, and altogether "Gothic" sentences which defied the resources of gentlemanly scholarship.

The study of the old texts never died out altogether. We might tell of good deeds, but they were done, for the more part, in the antiquary's fashion, and seldom by men of great power. Then in the nineteenth century came the critical moment. Would Englishmen see and understand what was happening in Germany? Would they appreciate and emulate the work of Savigny and Grimm? In particular, would they set themselves to investigate the growth of law and institutions with scientific accuracy and scientific zeal, and, inspirited by big thoughts, hold no labour too laborious, no text too obscure, no detail insignificant until all should be known? It can hardly be said that they rose to the occasion. We had our swallows, and beautiful birds they were; but there was spring in Germany. We had our *guerrilleros*; they were valiant and resourceful; but in Germany an army was being organised. Grimm's pupil, Kemble, was in the field, fighting a brave battle for the study of the Old English language and the Old English laws. The great Palgrave was in the field; surely a great commander if an army had been forthcoming. But our English forces, if forces they might be called, were irregulars. Discipline was not their strong point, as the chequered tale of the Record Commissions amply shows. Chequered indeed were the books in which public money was invested; the scandalously bad elbowed the admirably good.

The official edition of the *Ancient Laws and Institutes of England*, which was published in 1840, fell midway between the two extremes. Dr Liebermann, who is scrupulously fair to his forerunners, goes no farther than truth compels when he says that the book did not meet just expectations. The proof came soon. In 1858 Reinhold Schmid, a professor of law at Bern, without being able to visit England, and consequently without seeing the manuscripts, published a much better edition. A very good book it was, and those who now are laying it aside must feel that they are parting from an old and trusty friend. From that moment the English official edition was superseded. There the matter rested, so far as England was concerned. That the failure should be officially recognised and a new edition put in hand was not to be expected—such confessions of failure are made in Germany; but no Englishman came forward to meet the German challenge, though it must have been sufficiently plain that an edition made by one who had not seen the manuscripts could not be final. The next edition was to be made by Felix Liebermann, at the instance of the Bavarian Academy, at the cost of the Savigny Trust; it was to be beautifully printed at Halle; it was to be dedicated to Konrad von Maurer, or to his memory.

Konrad Maurer—the "von" came afterwards—
was one of our conquerors. He was the son of that
George Ludwig von Maurer who explored village
communities, gave Greece a criminal code, was a
prominent statesman in the Bavaria of Lola Montez,
died in 1872, and lives for Englishmen in the pages
of Sir Henry Maine. Early in the fifties of the last
century Konrad reviewed Kemble's book in a series
of papers which, though not always to be found even
in the best of English libraries, marks a dividing
line between two periods. In his hand the study of
Anglo-Saxon law passed into a more scientific stage,
because it became part of a much larger whole, "die
Germanische Rechtsgeschichte." Already in 1845 he
had won his doctor's degree by a piece of sober comparative jurisprudence, a study of the growth of the
noble class among the Teutons; and the Teutonic
inhabitants of England had received a full share of his
attention. Then, while still a young man, he wrote
those memorable papers about Anglo-Saxon law, and
he gave the rest of a long life to the subjugation of the
Scandinavian north. In 1902, after encouraging and
helping Dr Liebermann to the last, he died full of
years and honours. None of the honours were English;
but he must have known that he had left his mark
very deep in the current version of the oldest English
history. And so to "Konrad von Maurer, dem Altmeister der Germanischen Rechtsgeschichte," this
edition of our old laws is dedicated.

There is another of Dr Liebermann's dedications
to which it is pleasant to turn. One of the tracts in
which he has been giving to the world the result of his

researches bears on its forefront these words, "Dem Andenken an William Stubbs, den Meister der Erforschung und Darstellung Englischer Geschichte im Mittelalter." Every one of these words is well weighed and well deserved. The grand figure of William Stubbs seems to be destined to become grander and more solitary as the years roll by. Now the extent to which, in his reconstruction of the age before the Conquest, Dr Stubbs adopted the theories of German pioneers might easily be exaggerated; and exaggeration we have seen. He was a sturdily independent and conservative Englishman, not easy to lead, not easy to persuade, and wholly free from the vanity that parades what is new and what is foreign. Still it is unquestionable that he had learned much from Waitz and Schmid and Maurer; and his willingness to look for good books beyond the four seas was an essential trait in his greatness. Also it was natural that the German influence should be most perceptible in the most purely legal part of his work. Englishmen were beginning to think of talking about "comparative jurisprudence" while Germans had been steadily making it. That prematurely ambitious theories, "evolved from the depths of the inner consciousness," had seen the light in Germany no one would deny. But their short reign was over, and sanity, modesty, and caution were in the order of the day. If we must name one example of the sort of work to which we refer, let it be Wilda's *Strafrecht der Germanen*; and let the date upon its title-page, 1842, be noted. Was it, then, unnatural that Dr Stubbs should look abroad? How much remained to be done before the Anglo-Saxon laws and the law-books of the Norman age would be a well-mapped country he was fully aware. How he welcomed Dr Liebermann to England, Dr Liebermann has told ; and we wish that we could repeat the terms in which the Bishop of Oxford explained to the University of Cambridge how well this German visitor deserved his honorary degree; we have warrant for saying that they were warm and forcible.

Whether the study of the Old English language, and the family of languages to which it belongs, flourished in England of the nineteenth century with all desirable prosperity is a question about which we offer no decided opinion, though we fancy that here also the tale that has to be told is rather of rare swallows than of genial spring. The main deficiency, so it seems to us, did not lie in this quarter. The laws, on the interpretation of which the whole historical scheme depends, were left severely alone, while Bede and the Chronicle and the homilies attracted editors, and Asser was supremely fortunate in the hands of Mr Stevenson. But where schools of law do not flourish the history of law will not be adequately studied, and the consequence will be that the march of the whole historical army, and especially of those new regiments, economic and social history, will be seriously retarded. Whether we like it or not, the fact remains that, before we can get at the social or economic kernel of ancient times, we must often peel off a legal husk that requires careful manipulation. It will not be supposed that we are bringing any general accusation against such law schools as we have had. Of late years there has been a very marked improve-

ment in our text-books of current law—in the
"dogmatic" of law, as a German would say—and
it is directly traceable to a few men who have believed
that law can be taught.   We freely admit that this is
far more important work than that of training editors
for barbarous codes.   Nor do we in any way regret
the gallant efforts that have been made to keep a few
Englishmen interested in the classical law of Rome.
All things considered, this may have been the best
available preventive against that fatal disease of
contented insularity which so easily besets us.   Still
the Victorian age came and went without Englishmen
having written a tithe of the legal and institutional
history that might reasonably have been expected of
them.   We have not forgotten Sir Henry Maine.
Who could forget the world-wide horizon, the penetrating glance, the easy grace, the pointed phrase?
But, to blurt out an unfashionable truth, there were
qualities in his work, or in his presentment of his
work, which would have served to better purpose in
a land of laborious pedantry than where men are
readily persuaded that hard labour is disagreeable
and that the signs of hard labour are disgusting.
That old fable needs revision.   Perhaps the Frenchman is a little reluctant to do more than "cultivate his
garden"—a well-arranged garden it is nowadays; it
is the German who seeks the wilderness, while the
Englishman remains at the fireside or elegantly strolls
down "the high priori road."

When once it was apparent that our own old laws
would only become eloquent when they were placed
among their kinsfolk, the question was whether English-

men would master foreign law, or whether foreigners would master English law. That question was soon closed ; or rather we pay ourselves too high a, compliment if we suppose that it ever was open. Extravagance could go no farther than to expect that an Englishman would devote his life to an edition of—we will not say of the *Sachsenspiegel* or the *Grágás* or the *Siete Partidas*—but of those Norman custumals which are almost English. It is all very well to be modest, to believe that foreigners know their own business, to believe that M. Tardif or M. Viollet knows more of Normandy than you will ever learn ; but in these days of international science we must be invaders or invaded, and if we will not dump we must not complain of dumping ; no tariff can protect us. There came a Russian scholar to teach us, among many other interesting things, that all that we had been saying about the folk-land was untrue. We bowed our heads in meek submission, and not one English lance was broken in defence of orthodoxy. Happily Oxford's " edle Gastfreundschaft "—to her great honour be it said—saved the situation, and made a professor of Dr Vinogradoff.

The sureness of Dr Liebermann's tread in a province that Englishmen have almost abandoned gives occasion for one other remark. The province to which we refer is the history of ecclesiastical law. Now it is unquestionable that in Victorian England a vast part of the best work that was done for medieval history was done by clerks in holy orders. It would be far too little to say that in this, as in many other quarters, the Church of England fully maintained her reputation as a learned Church. What is more, it was the clergyman that taught the lawyer about the Middle Ages, not the lawyer that taught the clergyman. Nevertheless it must be confessed that a field which lies (if we may so say) within view from the vicarage window is not being tilled very zealously or in conformity with the methods of modern science. To be concrete, we might ask whether Stubbs's edition of the English Councils is always to remain a fragment. We might ask how it came about that an extraordinarily interesting tract written by a canon of York concerning the relation between Church and State was carried off as lawful prize for the *Monumenta Germaniae* from under the guns of the Cambridge divines. We might ask whether Boehmer's indictment of Lanfranc as one of the most unscrupulous of forgers is to be answered, or whether the fair fame of an archbishop of Canterbury is to have no defender. We might ask why a young German student of divinity should have a chance of writing so good and so new a book as Boehmer's *Church and State in England and Normandy.* We should have thought that the whole story of papal encroachments—a story that might be told not in vague outline but realistically out of countless edited and unedited documents—would have been singularly attractive to some of our learned clerks, for there is much in it on which Anglicans might dwell with pride. The fault is not theirs. They have had none to guide them among legal snares and to tell them of the revolutionary work that has been accomplished in Germany and Italy and France. Where law schools do not flourish ecclesiastical history may be good as far as it goes, but it will never go to the end.

When we turn from our own modest output to the

tons of books concerning legal history which Germany produced in the nineteenth century, it is right to remember that during a great part of that period our neighbours were being spurred forward by an incitement to study such as we have never felt and they are not likely to feel again. When the famous "historical school" began its career, the legal condition of Germany was deplored by all those for whom Germany was more than a name. How could this miserable state of affairs be remedied? To what causes was it due? Whence would deliverance come? From a closer study of those Roman texts which constituted such "common law" as Germany possessed? from the disinterment of old Germanic principles? from the observation of neighbouring and less unfortunate nations? We do not detract from the scientific value of the best work that was done if we remember that the motive force was not mere curiosity. When once the impulse had been given, men would labour in regions far remote from the practical life of their own time with no hope of any reward except a few new grains of truth. Still the impulse, a patriotic, a national, and we might even call it a utilitarian impulse, was requisite. And now we see the result of it all. This people of pedants and dreamers, of antiquaries and metaphysicians, after discussing the history of every legal term and every legal idea, has made for itself what is out and away the best code that the world has yet seen.

It is currently said that this interdependence of historical research and practical endeavour is now being illustrated in another way. It is said that legal history is losing its interest ; that young Germans will study nothing but the *Bürgerliches Gesetzbuch* ; that famous teachers have now no time for anything else ; that even Roman law is being deserted. A warning issued by Bekker, Brunner, Mitteis, and Mommsen is, we should suppose, likely to receive attention in the proper quarter. If not, the world will be the poorer and Germany will not be the richer, except perhaps in the wealth that perishes. One title to honour will have been forfeited, and neither success in arms nor success in commerce will wholly fill the vacant place. Dr Liebermann's book, however, speaks of no decadence, but of the great age when men reconstructed the praetor's edict and discovered the origin of trial by jury and tracked the false Isidore to his lair. And, since we have mentioned German wealth and German honour, we will allow ourselves two remarks, one of which may deserve consideration in some English, and the other in some German circles. We believe that the man who put fourteen years of the hardest drudgery into an edition of the Anglo-Saxon laws had, as some Englishmen would reckon, no valid reason for living "laborious days," but "scorned delights," which he might have tasted to the full. We believe also that this man, whom we in England can regard as a good representative of what is best in Germany, is one whom what is worst in Germany, the blatant sham science of her Philistines, would ban as "ungermanisch." Well, there are fools everywhere ; but we in England are not going to dispute the Englishry of our great Sir Francis Palgrave.

On the present occasion we will say but little of

what has been done for the Anglo-Saxon laws, properly so called, for, as already said, some notes are yet to come. But already we have a translation of a very excellent kind—a translation from which even those who have but a slight acquaintance with the Old English tongue may gather both what a laconic legislator has said, and also what he has meant to an editor skilled in the early history of Teutonic law. We shall run no risk in saying that by this new version all older versions are superseded. As to the text, we do not like to speak of finality, but have great difficulty in imagining what more could have been done. In particular, students of language will, so we think, be hard to please if Dr Liebermann has not given them material enough. Rejecting less exhaustive methods, he has printed in parallel columns the texts that are given by all the leading manuscripts. We open the book; we see alongside each other three different English texts of the laws of Cnut and three different Latin versions of the same, while the new German translation fills the bottom of the page. It looks like the full score of an opera, and some time must be spent before we can master the manifold typographical devices which have been invented to save time and space. At first sight the editor seems to have a rooted objection to printing six consecutive words without a change of type; and the natural man sighs for the simplicity of a pianoforte arrangement. But unquestionably all this elaborate technique, which must have taxed to their uttermost the resources of a great printing house, will be highly valued by philologists. Want of imagination has been a common fault in editors. A little difference in spelling, for example, seems to you too trivial for notice. A few years go by ; science strides forward ; you can be accused of jumbling two dialects together ; and then your work must be done over again. Never, it is rightly said, is a long day ; but we fancy that a long day will pass before Dr Liebermann is charged with insufficiently minding his p's and q's. It would be admitted on all hands nowadays that the oldest monuments of the English language deserve as much care as an English, or any other, editor would un-grudgingly spend upon the most worthless scrap of classical Greek ; but we fear that we have been slow to take this truth to heart. A characteristic example occurs on Dr Liebermann's first page. There is a word, now partly illegible, in the only medieval manu-script that gives the very earliest of all the laws. The English editor can only tell us of a guess. It struck Dr Liebermann that what cannot be read now could perhaps be read in the sixteenth century by one of those antiquarian worthies who sometimes copied the more accurately because they hardly aspired to under-stand what they were copying. And so a very "secondary source," Francis Tate's transcript of a manuscript that is still in our hands, solves the diffi-culty. Why did not we think of it?

But we shall be on yet surer ground if we turn to the law-books of the Norman time, for during the last twelve years or thereabouts Dr Liebermann has been slowly telling his tale about them in various pamphlets, and we hardly know where to lay our hands upon better specimens of modern research. It is true that his pamphlets are not always easy reading. In his desire for compression he becomes algebraic. We very much wish that he would now be persuaded to step, as it were, between his severer self and an ignorant, but not unteachable, British public. After all this fatiguing research a little "high vulgarisation," as the French call it, would be a pleasant kind of relaxation. Many scattered remarks show that he has a good eye for men and movements as well as for laws and language. He might teach us much of parties and policies, of efforts and ideals, much even that Freeman did not teach and could not; for, with reverence be it said, Freeman's healthy contempt for lawyers did not always improve the quality of his work when "past politics" were to be discovered in legal documents.

We have spoken of a hinterland. It is curious that these law-books of the Norman age should naturally present themselves as a hinterland, as a region into which we can penetrate only by passing through the laws of a yet older time, or as a mass of matter whose destined place is the appendix. Yet that is the traditional, and it still seems the right place. What is under examination refuses to look like a prologue; it is an epilogue. These books—"book" is rather too grand a name for some of them—are the product of a very strange, and perhaps we might say a unique, state of affairs. The conquering Frenchmen have no written laws, or none to speak of, and they have no law-books of their own. The conquered Englishmen have a considerable mass of written laws ending with the code of Cnut. The official theory tells of unbroken continuity. William has inherited the crown from his cousin, and, upon the whole, is well satisfied with the rights that

the old English laws will give him.   And yet, despite
official theory, the whole law is being rapidly changed,
until at length the theoretic crust falls in and a new
formation is displayed in Glanvill's orderly treatise.
The honest books of this confused and confusing time
try their best—a very bad best it often is—to reconcile
theory and fact; and then people who are not
scrupulously honest begin to tinker and to tamper,
to forge and to fudge in the interest of classes and
professions and programmes.   A wild hinterland it
has been, full of gins and snares, peopled by uncouth
monsters, "anthropophagi and men whose heads do
grow beneath their shoulders."   Roads were slowly
made into it.   No admiration for "the last German
book" must induce us to forget how much good road-
making was done by Selden and Spelman, by Twysden
and Somner, by Allen and Palgrave, by Schmid and
Stubbs.   Still it is the simple truth that the credit of
having surveyed the whole territory, of having classified
its grotesque fauna, of having reduced the savage inhabitants to order, falls to Dr Liebermann.   There
are warnings in legible German now over most of the
pitfalls, and even where the hill is dangerous to cyclists.
The chimera can no longer prey upon the reasonably
cautious traveller, and will soon be harnessed to the
historian's plough.   And let it be remembered that
this hinterland is auriferous.   A stage in the history
of law and thought and manners which is represented
in England by these obscure texts is represented elsewhere by an obscurer silence.   The English twilight
between moon and sun, between the laws of Cnut and
Glanvill's treatise, is not very brilliant; but there is
dark night in other lands.

One of the most interesting of the strange people, the anthropophagi, whom Dr Liebermann has interviewed is the latest of them, a Londoner of John's day, so it seems, who forges in the interest of a political and municipal programme. In some respects it was a by no means irrational programme, though the manner in which he sought to forward it was singularly unscrupulous. An imperialist he was with a witness. In his view the King of England was by rights lord or emperor not only of Wales and Scotland, but also of " all the adjacent islands with their appurtenances," a very extensive region floating in a haze of mysterious geography. Round his cave were human bones in plenty. Some of his products had, indeed, long been known as the lies that they were—not fables, but lies told with intent to deceive. But here for the first time his offences are brought home to him. The indictment is long, and it comprises, among its many counts, a crime of the first order, the concoction of that famous letter which Pope Eleutherus did not write to Lucius, King of Britain. For some time past this letter, which used to play a part in Anglo-Roman controversy, has been stigmatised as forger's work, though Dr Liebermann is able to say, to our surprise, that so late as 1892 it was seriously cited. But who was the forger? A singularly convincing argument enables us now to hold with some certainty that he was the man who interpolated his civic and imperialistic conceits into the laws of Alfred and Ine, and that the scene of his nefarious operations was not remote from the Guildhall of London. It is pleasant to remember that an article in the *Quarterly Review* delivered mankind

from the tyranny of the false Ingulf[1].   To see the
pseudo-Eleutherus writhing under Dr Liebermann's
cross-examination would have delighted Sir Francis
Palgrave.

But by far the most important of these men of the
twilight is the most puzzling of them all.   He is the
man who schemes a comprehensive law-book which
Dr Liebermann, with fairly good warrant, calls the
Quadripartitus.   He is also the man who, having but
little English, painfully translates into some sort of
Latin the Anglo-Saxon laws, returning again and
again to his task as his knowledge increases.   He
is also the man who composes the treatise that we
know as the *Leges Henrici.*   A most puzzling person
he is, even when Dr Liebermann has written a life of
him.   That life is of necessity a series of inferences.
Some of them we may dispute ; but the biographer
always allows us to see precisely what he is doing.
If from time to time he seems to be acuter than a man
should be, recalling those dear Red Indians of our
youth and the Sherlock Holmes of to-day, he always
tells us what is the basis of ascertained fact upon
which he proposes to build.   If, for example, we are
told that this man is not of English race, that he is
not a monk, that he is a cleric, that he has served the
Archbishop of York, that he has the run of a considerable library, that he is a justice of the King's Court,
we know the premises from which these conclusions
are deduced.   Dr Liebermann is not one of those who,
in the name of a false art, pull down the scaffolding
when the house is built—one of the worst crimes

[1] *Quarterly Review*, No. 67 (June 1826).

against history that the historian can commit. We can climb if we please, and form our own opinions as to the strength of the structure, for all is visible. For our own part we have struggled long against one of Dr Liebermann's conclusions, namely, that this queer being, striving to make himself understood, is not only professionally engaged in the work of the law but sits among King Henry's justices. But the evidence that is brought to bear upon this point is not easily resistible; and Dr Liebermann helps us in many ways to understand the legal, political, social environment in which a royal justice, who was also a churchman with some unusual erudition, could aim so high and fall so low: could be so ambitious, so learned, so industrious, and yet so incapable of arranging his materials or explaining his thoughts. *

Keen criticism of literary style is one of the tools in Dr Liebermann's workshop. It is a highly useful weapon when anonymous products are to be dated or a forger is to be confronted with his handiwork, and yet we fancy that it will be almost news to many Englishmen that this weapon can be used not only— no one would doubt that—where literary style is reasonably good, but also, and with even greater effect, where style is abominably bad. As a relic of the old belief "that all the Middle Ages lived at the same time," there remains, we will not say a belief, but a disposition to think that all "low" Latin is equally low. Really, however, the style of these *Leges Henrici* is as distinctive as style could be: marvellously different from the glib Latinity of Lanfranc and his scholars. It is a highly distinctive compound of the worst sort of windy rhetoric and the mere dog-Latin of a man who is thinking in French about Anglo-Saxon technicalities. There is a repellent preface to one of his works. We fear that an English editor would have thought that he had done enough for the sorry stuff when he had complained of its turgidity. Not so Dr Liebermann. The miserable man is not allowed to finish his first sentence before the detective has found a clue. " Did you say *nullis aduersitatum liuoribus obatrescit*? Pardon me, but that is a Firmicianism. You have come under the influence of the astrologer, Julius Firmicus Maternus ; and that is another link between you and Archbishop Gerard, who, to the scandal of all right-thinking Christians, died—at least, so the High Church people said—with this necromancer's book under his pillow." But it will be easier for Englishmen to recover any ground that they may have lost in this literary quarter than to appear once more as the best interpreters of ancient English law. Those who, like Dr Brunner, have seen it, not in taciturn isolation, but in the converse of the family circle, have been Dr Liebermann's guides and must for a long while be ours.

One pressing task remains. We have lost the Anglo-Saxon laws. Can we retain the Anglo-Saxon charters, those numerous " land-books " which must be re-edited if the first period of English history is ever to be well understood? Kemble was a great man, but, even according to the standard of his own time, he was not a very good editor of legal documents ; and now, owing to the progress that has been made by various studies, linguistic, legal, and diplomatic, the standard has been raised by many degrees. That it is not unattainable by Englishmen, Professor Napier and Mr Stevenson have fully proved by their masterly treatment of a few lucky charters which had escaped less expert hands. Dr Liebermann salutes their work as the beginning of a new era. At this point we have a great advantage. All else may go; but those very acres that the old kings "booked" lie where they always lay, and the identification of places and the perambulation of boundaries is a highly necessary part of the work that awaits the coming editor. Moreover, at the hither end of the charters stands Domesday Book; and that book is not the riddle that it was when Mr Round began his brilliant researches. We have a long start, a favourable handicap, but, to continue the metaphor, the odds are against us. It may be that Berlin will emulate the enterprise of Munich, that the "Savigny-Stiftung" will make yet another grant in aid of British indigence, and that the England that the Normans conquered will be not less thoroughly conquered a second time.

THE MAKING OF THE GERMAN CIVIL CODE[1]

THE system of law under which we live, its merits and defects, its relation to other living systems, these are themes which—so I imagine—might and ought to have a place in a scheme of social and political education. Do we Englishmen think enough about them? I am not persuaded that we do; though, as a teacher of English law, I feel at this point the danger of professional or professorial prejudice. No doubt we are often deeply interested in some law or another. For some weeks our newspapers are full of talk about the law concerning Trade Unions; and then, for some months, we are all discussing an Elementary Education Bill. We become excited about these matters; we make them the issues at General Elections; we use hard words of those who disagree with us; we are ready to argue by the hour; and some of us can argue closely and cogently. Let that be allowed. But turn from laws to Law. Turn from bits of our legal system to the system as a whole. Do we often think of it?

[1] A Presidential Address delivered to the Social and Political Education League. *Independent Review*, August 1906.

Do we often ask ourselves whether it compares well with its neighbours and rivals, whether it is in all respects rational, coherent, modern, worthy' of our country and our century? I fear that we do not.

That answer, you may say, betrays the academic mind; and I may be told that we English are a practical race. But bold propositions concerning national character often seem to mé the riskiest of all assertions; and I am not fully convinced that we English are pre-eminently practical. Sometimes it seems to me that a little more practicality would improve us.

Can you remember the time—unfortunately I can —when it was usual and plausible to paint the German as an unpractical, dreamy, sentimental being, looking out with mild blue eyes into a cloud of music and metaphysic and tobacco smoke? Was it not the German who evolved the camel out of the depths of his own inner consciousness, while the Englishman went forth to study the beast in the desert? It is in quite other fashion that we paint our German now. Some of the portraits that we draw of him, like some portraits of John Bull that are drawn in Germany, seem to me scandalously bad : the work of envy, malice, and uncharitableness. There is room for an amendment of manners on both sides of the sea ; and not only of manners but of morals. Still I think that we are right in no longer painting our German as unpractical. The practical man is the man who does things. The eminently practical man is the man who does great things. The German has done some great things. Among the great things that he has done is this : he has codified the greater part and the most important part of his law ; he has set his legal house in order ; he has swept away the rubbish into the dustbin ; he has striven to make his legal system rational, coherent, modern, worthy of his country and our century.

The greatest among his exploits is a Civil Code ; and about the making of it I propose to say a few words, for I think the story instructive.

First, however, we may observe that there were special reasons why some codification should be desired in Germany. By "special reasons" I mean such as cannot move us in England, though, as a matter of fact, they have at various times come into play in most European countries. From a very remote time England stood out among the European kingdoms as the land which had uniform law, law common to the whole of it. Into the geographical and historical causes of this big fact we need not go. It was being established in the twelfth century, and was secure in the thirteenth. A big fact it was ; and it gave us many and great advantages over our neighbours. The thought, however, may occur to us, that what is an advantage at one time may become a disadvantage later on. If there had been half-a-dozen different systems of provincial law in England, should we not have been compelled to abolish them, and put in their stead some uniform system worthy in all respects of modern times ? I cannot answer that question. It is too indeterminate; and, very possibly, in the supposed case we might hastily and foolishly have done something of which at our leisure we should have repented. We might, for example, have tried to find our law in the Roman or Byzantine books ; and that would, I think, have been a disastrous error. Be that as it may, we may observe that, ever since the sixteenth century, the main force which has made for codification has been a desire for uniform national law. The inconvenience of a state of affairs in which, to use Voltaire's phrase, you change your law when you change your post-horses, is an inconvenience of a palpable kind, obvious to every plain man. Add to this, that the enlightened despotism of the eighteenth century found its action hampered by discordant provincial laws. Frederic the Great must have a code for Prussia, Maximilian for Bavaria, Maria Theresa for the Austrian dominions. And then, in the nineteenth century, when a nation which had long been torn into fragments once more became united, a single uniform system of law appeared not only as a matter of convenience, but as a symbol and guarantee of the political union that had been achieved. Frenchmen, Italians, Spaniards, Germans—in short, I think, most peoples—have had reasons for code-making such as have not appealed to Englishmen since time immemorial. True it is that, within our island, within Great Britain, we have had, and we still have, two systems of law, the one north, the other south of the Tweed. Still, this has not been enough to bring home to us in an acute form those evils which have plagued our neighbours. I read that in 1845 there were in Silesia —and Silesia is not a very large part of Germany—no less than sixty different schemes of marital property law.

When Germany pulled itself together after 1870,

there certainly were reasons enough why Germans should wish to see some large changes made in the field of jurisprudence. Legally, Germany was still a patch-work quilt. Leaving out of account multitudinous minor causes of variation, there were three or four great and flourishing systems, each with its territory. We may notice, by the way, that a large, wealthy, and populous part of Germany—I am not speaking of the two provinces which had recently been taken from France—was still ruled by French law. About fourteen per cent. of the German nation lived under the untranslated French code; and the Badeners lived under a translated and slightly modified version thereof. A Frenchman might say: "Napoleon's legions may be expelled; but where his code has once been introduced, there it stays." The German was not able to contradict him, and sometimes would frankly admit that, of all the systems obtaining in the Fatherland, the French was in some respects the most enlightened. No doubt too it was felt that a great code of laws would be, in the eyes of the world, a sign and token that the disruptive forces were for ever vanquished, and that the union of Germany was an accomplished and irreversible fact. We shall think none the worse of a law-book because some national pride, even perhaps some national vanity, went to its making. If we needs must swagger, there are worse things to boast of than a code which we say is the best that has yet been made.

However, you must not suppose that the task was easy. If German civil law was to be unified, there would of necessity be much interference with established rules. Men of business and others become attached to the rules under which they live. They may allow that those rules are not the best; and yet they will deprecate interference. You call on them to make some sacrifice, to change their usages, to go to school once more. Then, so soon as there is talk of a code, all the people who have projects of social regeneration will be let loose. Everyone of them will think that the hour for his pet scheme has struck. As to the lawyers, the fact that several different systems were actually in force was not likely to diminish the opposition that was to be expected in this quarter so soon as any project of a code was published. Moreover, the past history of Germany had, for reasons into which we cannot go, made German jurisprudence a highly controversial science. In England, the would-be codifier, if he existed, would not have to take a side in the quarrels of rival schools. But in Germany there were rival schools, with dogmas and watch-words—schools somewhat given to belabouring each other in books and pamphlets. Lastly, German lawyers were, I think, fully persuaded that a hasty and slip-shod code would be far worse than no code at all. If there was a country in which the danger of premature codification had been persuasively preached, and the short-comings of the Prussian Code and the French Code had been eloquently denounced, that country was Germany. That however was, in reality, a hopeful factor in the situation.

Now let us see what was done. In 1874 a Commission of eleven distinguished lawyers was appointed to prepare a project. They took thirteen years and

more over the work. It was published in 1888, together with five vast volumes of "motives," giving the
why and wherefore for all that was proposed. What
then happened is, I think, well worthy of notice ; for
it shows that a nation can become profoundly interested
in its legal system. A tornado broke loose. It rained,
it poured books and pamphlets. At that time, I made
a habit of looking through a weekly list of books published in Germany ; and it struck me that no German
could find anything to write about except this embryonic code. The project was criticised from every point
of view ; and, though the lawyers may have been
keenest in the fray, they were by no means the only
combatants. The whole nation seemed to convert
itself into a large debating society, in which, however,
everybody spoke at once. The general result of the
debate was unfavourable to the draft. It was condemned as too abstract, pedantic, "doctrinaire," too
Roman and too un-German ; and, besides all this,
countless objections were taken to particular provisions.
One might have thought that the whole scheme would
perish. But the Germans are a persevering people.
So a second Commission was appointed : this time a
commission of twenty-two ; and upon it, not merely
legal science and legal practice, but commerce and
industry and agriculture and other great interests were
well represented. The Commissioners took up the
draft, revised it, and made large and important changes;
indeed they turned much of it inside out. They published their project—the Second Project—in parts ;
so that the public criticism of their performances went
on while they laboured. They were at work for four

years ; and, profiting by criticism, they issued a second edition of this Second Project. This Second Project gave much greater satisfaction than the First. Then the Federal Council, which, as you know, represents the various federated governments, took up the draft, and in January 1896 laid the Third Project before the Reichstag.

What then happened gives us, so I think, good cause to admire—perhaps to envy—our neighbours, and also good cause to think hopefully of parliamentary institutions. Between January and July, 1896, a parliamentary assembly, roughly comparable to our House of Commons, passed a code of 2385 sections. Now of course we shall not think of Germany as a country without political parties. Party spirit runs high there ; and I should suppose that the lines which divide the various groups are, to say the least, as deep as any that we see in England. Moreover, the organised political groups are more numerous than our English parties. A very little obstruction, a very little obstructive coalition between the various groups, would have killed the projected code. And do not suppose that a civil code merely settles legal details : those small rules which will interest none but lawyers. This draft, this Bill, dealt with the most vitally important of all human affairs. Think, for example, of marriage and divorce, and all that we indicate when we speak of the law of husband and wife. Take one out of a thousand questions : one that gave rise to a close division ·in the Reichstag. The hopeless insanity of one of the parties to a marriage, ought it to be a cause for a divorce ? Every one can, most people will, give you an answer to that question ; and some will give it passionately. The settlement of that question will not be made any easier by the fact that the different systems current in the country have contradicted each other at this point. Compulsory civil marriage had already been enacted in the days of the *Kulturkampf.* But it was to be re-enacted in the code ; and, to speak mildly, it was profoundly distasteful to a powerful party, the Catholic Centre. To take another instance, a vast question, concerning the terms upon which the advantage of corporateness could be acquired by societies of divers sorts and kinds, was opened; and, as you might suppose, the different political parties held very different opinions about this matter, "the liberty of association." Then there were the Socialists —such Socialists as we hardly know in England—and the code was, in their eyes, a statement of those indi-vidualistic, "capitalistic," and "bourgeois" principles, which are for them the hateful thing. But there was no obstruction; there was wonderful forbearance. The draft was laid before a committee of twenty-one, on which all political parties were represented, and a con-siderable number of changes were made in it ; but the utmost care was taken not to damage the artistic character of the work. The amendments moved in the full House were by no means numerous. Just a few questions of the utmost importance were raised and debated—very well debated, I should say. Every now and again some group would declare that if one of its demands was not satisfied, it would think about wrecking the code ; but there was no wrecking, and there was much self-restraint. If you read the proceedings, you may be amused at finding that the briskest of all the debates took place over the two little words "and hares" in a section relating to damage done by wild animals. Powerful language is used; and, for a moment, the whole of this mighty project seems to be endangered by the conflicting interests of sport and agriculture. That is the touch of humour required as a relief for so much civic virtue.

Civic virtue, that is what we may see in these debates; and especially do I admire what is said by some of the Socialists :—" Put your 'bourgeois' law in shape, in the best possible shape; we will not try to prevent you; incidentally we shall strive for and we shall obtain some not unimportant concessions; and at any rate, when your code is made, all will see what your 'bourgeois' system really is." The jealousy which will not let "the other fellows" get the credit of doing things, or which seeks to spoil the detail of their measures—this civic or uncivic vice I cannot detect, though I fear that it is not unknown in parliamentary assemblies. Also I think it well worthy of remark, that there was no departure of any great moment from the ordinary procedure of parliamentary assemblies. Every member of the Reichstag was free to propose any number of amendments; and, if I remember rightly, no debate was closured.

So the Reichstag did its work in six months. The code was sanctioned by the Federal Council; and then it was published as law on August 24, 1896. It came into force on January 1, 1900, at what some people thought to be the beginning of a new century. Altogether, men were hard at work upon it from 1874 to

1896 : that is, for more than twenty years ; and, during the last eight years, a project had been lying before the nation and exciting the keenest debates—debates not less thorough or less effectual because they were not carried on within the four walls of a chamber. Never, I should think, has so much first-rate brain power been put into an act of legislation ; and never, I should think, has a nation so thoroughly said its say about its system of law. Yet there was less talk in the Reichstag over a Civil Code of 2385 sections, than there will be talk in Parliament over this Education Bill.

Well, I do not know how this strikes you ; but it strikes me as a great achievement, and as a just cause for national pride. Germans feel it to be that ; and I do not think that they are wrong. Their new code is being admired in many parts of the world ; and, assuredly, it will exercise a powerful influence far outside the boundaries of the Empire. It is being carefully studied in France, and wins high praise from French lawyers who have no predilection for Germany. Frenchmen cannot but feel that their own Civil Code, which, for all its hastiness and other defects, has had a splendid history, is becoming antiquated, and is no longer that light to lighten the nations that it was for nearly a century. Also I notice that one nation, an enterprising nation in the far East, has already been fetching its civil law from Germany. The Japanese have, I think, shown us that they know what and where to borrow. They also have been making a Civil Code. It is a highly interesting piece of work. It preserves a great deal of genuinely Japanese matter,

especially in that part of it which concerns the family.
But much has been taken from Europe ; and most of
what has so been taken bears on its face the legend
"made in Germany." That is an act of homage of
which German lawyers may well be proud. I sadly
fear that our Japanese friends are not likely to regard
our English system as a model of lucidity and technical
excellence.

But it is not of technical excellence that I would
speak ; nor will we plunge into the old question touching the relative merits of codified and uncodified law.
What strikes me forcibly is this : that our German
neighbours have brought their law up to date, and
are facing modern times with modern ideas, modern
machinery, modern weapons. I ought to interject the
remark that the Civil Code, of which I have been
speaking, is by no means their only exploit ; they have
a Commercial Code also, and a Criminal Code. Now,
of course, a great deal of the law that is to be found in
these books is, in one sense, by no means new. Take
any rule that stands there. Perhaps you will find that
it has a long history, reaching back to the golden age
of Roman jurisprudence or to the customs of medieval
Germany. But all this stuff, wheresoever obtained,
has recently been passed through modern minds, has
been debated, criticised, refined ; and an endeavour
has been made to present it as a single, coherent,
homogeneous whole. Could anything of the same
sort be said of us ? Are we facing modern times with
modern ideas, modern machinery, modern weapons ?
I wish that I could think so. Some of our ideas seem
to be antiquated ; some of our machinery seems to me

cumbrous and rusty; some of our weapons I would liken to blunderbusses, apt to go off at the wrong end.

No Englishman is likely to admire all things German. Certainly I do not. In some important respects I think that we—that "we" must include our American cousins—are still leading the world; and at many other points there is much to be said for the course that we take, though no one else may be ready to take it. But there are some departments—large departments—of English law which seem to me thoroughly discreditable to us. I would mention in particular a great deal of what we call the Law of Real Property. It seems to me to be full of rules which no one would enact nowadays unless he were in a lunatic asylum. And surely that should be the test. Would you enact that rule nowadays? Can you conceive that any sane man would enact that rule nowadays?

To say that a rule is historically interesting is not to the point. For myself, I happen to think that legal history is a fascinating matter for study. It is pleasant, and I even believe that it is profitable, to trace the origin of legal rules in the social and economic condition of a by-gone age. But any one who really possesses what has been called the historic sense must, so it seems to me, dislike to see a rule or an idea unfitly surviving in a changed environment. An anachronism should offend not only his reason, but his taste. Roman Law was all very well at Rome; medieval law in the Middle Age. But the modern man in a toga, or a coat of mail, or a chasuble, is not only uncomfortable but unlovely. The Germans have been deeply interested in legal history; they were the

pioneers; they were the masters. That has not prevented them from bringing their own law up to date.
Rather I should say that it encouraged them to
believe that every age should be the mistress of its
own law.

We in England are not within a measurable distance
of a Civil Code. There is much to be done first; and
I cannot honestly say that our legislators seem inclined
to do it, or even to be aware that it wants doing.
I wish that Parliament could be persuaded to place
itself for a while in the humble position of a teacher
of English law—not for the sake of teachers (they
don't matter) but for the sake of the nation at large.
I see our Land Law growing always a heavier burden.
Almost yearly Parliament adds something to the
weight. Exceptions are piled upon exceptions; but
the old rules are never cleanly abolished. It was not
always so. In the 'thirties of the last century, the days
of the Radical Reform, some good destructive work
was done; and destructive work is as necessary and as
honourable as constructive. One of the primary functions of a legislature is, I conceive, to sweep into the
dust-bin the rubbish that inevitably accumulates in the
course of legal history. We cannot, I fear, affirm that
Parliament adequately performs this scavenger's task;
and, from the very nature of the case, it cannot be
performed by the judges. Much they can do in the
way of accommodating old law to new wants; but they
never can say that the old rule is rubbish and must go
to the dust-bin. Yet that is what some one ought to
be saying, sternly and effectually. Next year there
will be more new Acts to read; but still we shall be
expounding medieval doctrine, and a thrice accursed

statute of Henry VIII. We drag an ever lengthening chain. Parliament, it is true, goes about with its spud, digging up a plantain here and a plantain there. But it never drops sulphuric acid into the hole; and a little sulphuric acid is what we want. It is not of lack of zeal that we have to complain, nor of lack of knowledge: but there is apparently some lack of imagination. People do not see what I fear is the truth, namely, that our Land Law as a whole is becoming a more intricate labyrinth every year, owing to the improvements that Parliament makes in it. To this we must add, that a great deal of the work that should be done is unattractive to our Parliament men, because it would bring them little applause or none. It is the old tale. If the prophet bade them do some great thing, they would do it; but " Just you clean up this here mess " is the hardest of all commandments. The consequence is, that German Land Law seems to me to be about a century ahead of English Land Law.

Well, I must not weary you longer with this jeremiad. I suppose that we shall, as the phrase goes, "muddle along" somehow, and show our practicality by passing some more of those timid and half-hearted Acts about the transfer of land which are monuments of futility. If ever a catastrophe happens, and our system collapses under its own weight, we may find that by that time our Japanese friends have a code that we can borrow—rational, coherent, modern. However, I hope for better things. The German mess—that also was a bad mess, worse in some respects than our own; and yet, by dint of skill and courage and perseverance, the great work has been accomplished.

STATE TRIALS OF THE REIGN
OF EDWARD I.[1]

ONE of the virtues which is placing Mr Tout in the very front rank of our historians is his determination to leave no stone unturned, no thicket unbeaten. Out of the thicket may fly a bird worth powder and shot. Under the stone may lurk a toad with a jewel in its head. Every historian of Edward I's reign must say a little of the judicial scandal of 1289, the appointment of auditors to hear complaints against the judges, and the purgation of the bench. If he writes on a large scale he will probably say something of Ralph Hengham and Adam of Stratton, of Thomas Weyland and Solomon of Rochester. The chroniclers are not dumb about this matter. Far from it. They are vociferous. But what they tell us, when we have blown away some effervescent froth, lacks precision. We infer that behind the smoke there must be fire, but the extent of the conflagration is very uncertain. Clearly there had been some scoundrels in high places; but were all the king's judges a pack of knaves? Was there none that did good, no, not one, save only John of Mettingham, whose rectitude is positively tiresome?

[1] *English Historical Review*, Oct. 1896.

Professor Tout, having heard that there were at the Record Office two large rolls, on which were set forth the proceedings of the auditors, decided to grapple with this promising yet repulsive material. Here was a stone to be turned, a thicket to be beaten. Regarded as thickets, legal records, with their technical phrases, their *etceteras*, their unfinished words, are dense and thorny. Regarded as stones they are apt to break up, as we lift them, into little fragments, and the dust thereof gets into our eyes and obscures the view. But Mr Tout is not easily repelled or discouraged. He sets to work upon these rolls, and when he could no longer find time for the task of transcription Miss Johnstone relieved him. By means partly of long extracts, partly of an ingeniously constructed calendar, they give us the sum and substance of the information that can be obtained from a great mass of parchment. Then in an excellent introduction, which is the work of Miss Johnstone, we find judicious generalisation. I do not think that the book could have been better planned, and the execution, so far as I can judge, seems wonderfully good. Any one who hereafter wishes thoroughly to know the England of Edward I will be bound to study these pages, or at all events the introduction. One reader can honestly thank the editors for a good many hours of unalloyed pleasure.

Instead of endeavouring to sum up the conclusions at which they have arrived—conclusions so succinctly stated that no summary is needed—we may notice that incidentally light is thrown into some dark corners of legal history. For example, one of these records offers much the earliest proof that I can remember to have seen of the fact that the indicting jury received "bills" handed to it by a judge. Every one, we are told, is free to deliver a bill of indictment to any of the justices in eyre. Then the justice delivers the bill to the jurors, and they, if they think its contents true, make a presentment to that effect. In all essentials we have here the procedure which ᵣobtains at the present day. Not only are these already bills of indictment, but they pass through the hands of a judge, who thus has an opportunity of talking about them to the jurors. This is by no means the only bird that has flown out of the well-beaten covert, but it may serve as a specimen. A loyal member of the Selden Society feels a little jealous.

In matters of law the editors acquit themselves so well that a professional lawyer might envy their sureness of foot. At the same time it ought to be known—for it is a fact—that the work of copying plea rolls is by no means easy. One can, for example, expand the little syllable *iur'* in many different ways. Any one who has been engaged in this work is likely to feel that he has in his time been guilty of many crimes, and a superannuated copyist may endeavour to quiet his conscience by discovering mistakes in what is done by other people. I will venture to suggest a few small amendments by way of proving that I have read with attention and enjoyment. I ought to add that some parts of these rolls are very ill to read, and that the courage and skill with which Miss Johnstone has encountered some really great difficulties seem to me worthy of high admiration.

It is much to be hoped that she will continue her labours in a field in which she has already done excellent service. Meanwhile I submit my *corrigenda*. Even if all of them are acceptable they do not indicate many flaws.

P. 6, l. 29.　For *se tamen* read *se tantum*, meaning *he alone.*

P. 8, l. 33.　There seems no reason for changing *suus* into *suis.* Have we not here the *Suo A. suus B.* of the polite letter-writer?

P. 9, l. 1.　For *mandatum* read *inauditum*, meaning *unheard of.*

P. 21, l. 10.　In *sex de predicto panello iuratores fuerunt* read *iurati* instead of *iuratores.* Six of the jurors were already sworn. Then, going back to p. 19, l. 30, we can improve on *sex de illis iur*[*atores et*]. I seem to see a barely legible *iurassent.*

P. 36, l. 15.　For *nichil sciuit de hoc* read *nichil sciuit. De hoc.* A full-stop is badly needed here, just because one does not at once see the need of it.

P. 37, l. 5.　Is not *quod precepit* [not *preceptum*] *cap*[*ere*] *non capiendum* what is wanted? Hengham ordered the arrest of one who ought not to have been arrested.

P. 38, l. 19.　The *prouiti*, which I cannot construe, should, I think, be *promti* [ready], but I have to suppose that the scribe omitted a few words.

P. 39, l. 18.　For *valitate* read *vtilitate.*

P. 47, l. 3.　Read *et super hoc exiuit breue eiusdem Radulfi de iudicio capitali iusticiario* [not *capitalis iusticiarii*] *de Hibernia.* This is a really difficult passage, but I think the key to it is the fact that the term *breue de iudicio* had become a sort of compound substantive. It means a "judicial writ," that is, a writ proceeding from a court of law as contrasted with a *breue originale* issuing from the chancery. (Compare our modern "judgment summons.") Perhaps the scribe would have done better had he written *breue de iudicio eiusdem Radulfi exiuit*; but that also would have been ambiguous. I construe thus: "A judicial writ of (i.e. tested by) Ralph Hengham issued to the chief justice of Ireland."

P. 48, l. 10.　For *placito noto* read *placito moto.*

P. 48, l. 16.　For *ut tenemus* read *ut tenemur*, meaning *as our duty is.*

P. 49, l. 7. For *contra iusticiarios* read *contra iusticiam*. According to the complainant justice was on one side and the justices were on the other.

P. 51, l. 8. For *saluo...iuratore suo* read *saluo...iure suo*.

P. 69, l. 7. For *plures iuratores* read *plus iuris*. The prior had more right in his demand than Henry in his defence. Compare the *maius ius* which soon follows. That the roll gives *plus* is duly noted by the editors.

P. 69, l. 26. In the phrase *et si non sit verum quod deniant illam billam* might we not read *demant*? A Lat. *deniare* made from Fr. *denier* is not impossible. But a subjunctive seems to be wanted, and see the *iudicium demptum* on p. 36. The jurors are, I think, to "dash the bill."

P. 78, l. 9. The *acupamento* of roll and footnote is, I fancy, better than the *acusamento* of the text. In year-book French the words *acoupement, encoupement* (hardly distinguished from each other) are common, while I cannot remember *acusement*.

P. 91, l. 20. For *conuincatur* read *commitatur*.

The very interesting record concerning the prior of Butley and John Lovetot (p. 62) might have been more completely published if the editors had known that a copy of the record of a later stage of this case was partially printed by Sollom Emlyn in his notes to Hale's *Pleas of the Crown* (ii. 298). It is an important case in the history of trial by jury, and also in the history of villeinage, and we may regret that, owing to the bad condition of the roll, the editors were unable to tell the whole story, or perhaps to see how exceptionally interesting it is. One of the errors laid to the charge of the justices was that they had maintained the doctrine that free blood could not be made servile by long continued performance of villein services. The auditors, on the other hand, declared that this liberal maxim was *omnino falsum*. Then they were bidden to send the case to the King's Bench, where there was more pleading. I do not know that the judgment of that court has yet been found. This is one of those cases which make us think that there were two sides to the stories told against King Edward's justices. A man who was trembling on the verge of villeinage obtained a judgment against a prior who had ejected him. The prior complained to the auditors, who reversed the judgment; but the ejected tenant was not yet beaten, and is last seen pleading for land and liberty before a regular court.

Besides the records the editors have printed a *Passio Iudicum* which throws a queer light upon medieval religion. It is a short satire or squib made up of a large number of Biblical texts which are jocosely perverted. One knows not whether to call it ribald or to say that in an age of faith ribaldry was impossible. The editors have done for it all that could be asked of them, and they must have been very happy when they saw that *fons Babylonis* is Babwell.

WILLIAM STUBBS, BISHOP OF OXFORD[1]

No readers of the *English Historical Review*, no English students of history, no students of English history can have heard with indifference the news that Dr Stubbs was dead. A bright star had fallen from their sky. This is not an attempt to speak on behalf of those who had been his close friends, or even of those who, without being his close friends, yet knew him well. Evidently there is much to be told which only they are privileged to tell of a man who was good as well as great, of a kindly and generous, large-minded, warm-hearted man. Then there is the bishop to be remembered, and the professor, the colleague in the university, and the counsellor of other historians, whose ready help is acknowledged in many prefaces. Evidently also there is something to be added of good talk, shrewd sayings, and a pleasant wit. Of all this some record has been borne elsewhere, and fuller record should be borne hereafter. But to this journal rather than to any other there seems to fall the office of endeavouring to speak the grief of a large but unprivileged class—namely, of those to whom Dr Stubbs was merely

[1] *English Historical Review*, July 1901.

the author of certain books, but who none the less cordially admired his work and who feel that within our English realm of historical study there has been a demise of the crown, or rather that they have had a king and now are kingless.

Representatives of this unprivileged multitude would, I take it, be hard to find among Oxford men unless they were too young to remember the days when the great books were coming from the press. It is with many misgivings that I shall endeavour to say a little part of what should be said. But when I was asked to do so, some battered and backless volumes told me of happy hours and heavy debts. Also I was not sorry that an opportunity for some expression of gratitude to the historian of the English constitution should be given to one whose lot is that of teaching English law.

The bishops of London and Oxford have but just left us, and our thoughts may naturally go back to the year 1859, when Hallam's death was followed by Macaulay's. It is to be remembered, however, that some years have already fled since Stubbs and Creighton retired from the active service of history. Already we may think of them as belonging to a past and a remarkable time. Was there ever, we might ask, any other time when an educated, but not studious Englishman, if asked by a foreigner to name the principal English historians, would have been so ready with five or six, or even more names ? Freeman and Froude, Stubbs, Creighton, Green, and Seeley he would have rapidly named, and hardly would have stopped there, for some who yet live among us had already won their spurs. It is fair to say that the English historian who wishes to have numerous readers in his own country had better give to that country a large share of his attention. I fancy that Creighton gained the public ear somewhat slowly, and that the well-known Seeley was not the Seeley who wrote of Stein. Still it was a remarkable time, prolific of work that not only was good but was generally praised. Also we may notice the close connexion that existed between these masters of history and the English universities, but more especially the university of Oxford. The time when the active labourers had been Grote and Carlyle, Buckle and Palgrave, men in whom neither Oxford nor Cambridge could claim anything, and Edinburgh could not claim much, had been followed by a time when Oxford had become a centre of light whence historians proceeded and whither they returned. History seemed to be in the ascendant, and an Historical Review was needed. Now it might be too much to say that if a laurel crown had been at the disposal of the public that reads history this prize would certainly have fallen to Dr Stubbs, but there can, I think, be little doubt about its destination if the only awarders had been the generally recognised historians and votes for self (which in some cases may properly be given) had been excluded. Of some weighty voices we can be very sure, for they have spoken in prefaces and dedications.

At least there should, so it seems to me, be no doubt about the award that should be made in this journal. The greatness of historians can be measured along many different standards, and far be it from any one to speak slightingly of the man who, without adding to what was known by the learned, has charmed and delighted and instructed large masses of men. His place may be high, and even the highest, provided that he be honest and reasonably industrious in the search for truth. But such a man will find his reward in many places. Here we have to think first of the augmentation of knowledge—the direct augmentation which takes place when the historian discovers and publishes what has not been known, and the indirect augmentation which takes place when his doings and his method have become a model and an example for other scholars. And here Dr Stubbs surely stood supreme.

No other Englishman has so completely displayed to the world the whole business of the historian from the winning of the raw material to the narrating and generalising. We are taken behind the scenes anc shown the ropes and pulleys ; we are taken into the laboratory and shown the unanalysed stuff, the rerts and test tubes; or rather we are allowed to seehe organic growth of history in an historian's mind nd are encouraged to use the microscope. This " actical demonstration," if we may so call it, of the htorian's art and science from the preliminary hunfor manuscripts, through the work of collation and filïion and minute criticism, onward to the perfected talthe eloquence and the reflexions, has been of incalcıble benefit to the cause of history in England and far ore effective than any abstract discourse on methodoy could be. In this respect we must look to the ry greatest among the Germans to find the peers ofr

Stubbs, and we must remember that a Mommsen's productive days are not cut short by a bishopric. The matter that lay in the hands of our demonstrator was, it is true, medieval, and the method was suited to the matter, but in those famous introductions are lessons of patient industry, accurate statement, and acute but wary reasoning which can be applied to all times and to every kind of evidence. The very mingling of small questions with questions that are very large is impressive. The great currents in human affairs, and even "the moral government of the universe," were never far from the editor's mind when he was determining the relation between two manuscripts or noting a change of hand, and then if he turned for a while to tell big history it was with a mind that still was filled to the full with tested facts and sifted evidence.

In 1857 a project in which the honour of England was deeply concerned took shape: the Rolls Series was planned. Looking back now we may see that a considerable risk was run. A supply of competent editors was wanted, and the number of men who had already proved their fitness for the task was by no means large. We may fairly congratulate ourselves over the total result, though some indifferent and some bad work saw the light. In such matters Englishmen are individualists and libertarians. The picture of an editor defending his proof sheets sentence by sentence before an official board of critics is not to our liking. We must take the ill along with the unquestionable good that comes of our free manners. It would be in the highest degree unjust were we in the present case so to distribute light and shade that one bright figure should stand out against a gloomy background. There were accomplished men and expert and industrious men among the editors. There was the deputy keeper himself, and Dr Stubbs, who measured his words of praise, called Sir Thomas Hardy illustrious. Luard there was, and Madden and Brewer; but we have no wish to make what might look like a class list. However, it must be past all question that Dr Stubbs raised the whole series by many degrees in the estimation of those who are entitled to judge its merits. Not a few of his fellow editors would gladly have admitted that they learned their business from him, and that they were honoured when their books were placed on one shelf with his. We cannot say that without him there would have been failure, but the good work would have had some difficulty in floating the bad. His output was rapid, and yet there was no sign of haste. In the course of twenty-five years seventeen volumes were published, besides such a trifle as the *Constitutional History*; and every one of those volumes might fearlessly be put into the hands of learned foreigners as an example —a carefully chosen example, it is true—of English workmanship. Praise was not grudged by learned foreigners. When extracts from the English chronicles were being published in the *Monumenta Germaniae*, men who well knew good from bad work, and the best work from the second best, carefully examined what Dr Stubbs had done, and pronounced it perfect. His knowledge of the manuscript contents of English libraries, episcopal registries, muniment rooms, and similar places must have been unrivalled, and he seemed to have at his fingers' ends all the information that had been collected by the Hearnes and Bales and Tanners. But also from the first he was distinguished by the sureness with which he trod on foreign ground, and though no Englishman will blame him for devoting his best powers to English history we may often wish that he had interpreted medieval Germany, or even modern Germany, to Englishmen. Though very English he was never insular.

Meanwhile it was becoming evident that under the pretext of introducing chroniclers Dr Stubbs was writing excellent history on a large scale. Whether in an adequately governed country he would have been allowed to do this we need not inquire. A " brief account of the life and times of the author" was permitted by official instructions, and " any remarks necessary to explain the chronology" might be added. These elastic terms were liberally construed. Sir Thomas Hardy must have seen that he had found the right man, and the vicar of Navestock proceeded to explain chronology in his own manner and to the delight of many readers. To begin with, he explained the chronology of the crusades so freshly and so vigorously that after many years we turn back with joy to his explanation. There is room for differences of opinion touching the relative merit of the various introductions: each of us may choose his favourite. The Hoveden was the first that I read, and, perhaps because it is an old friend, there is none that I like better. Into these earliest introductions Dr Stubbs poured the contents of a mind that was brimming over not merely with facts but with thoughts. What, we may ask, could be better conceived or better executed than the sketch of Henry II's foreign policy and its consequences? Where but in the "Walter of Coventry" shall we look for the quarrel between John and Innocent? Whither do we go for the age of Dunstan or for the age of Edward II? Then there is the gallery of portraits in which the statesmen and the prelates and the men of letters of the twelfth century stand before us real, solid, and living. We feel that every scrap of available knowledge about them and their families and their surroundings has been fused and utilised by a constructive and sympathetic mind which has found details and has given us men—"erring and straying men." Dr Stubbs's men err and stray in a most life-like manner.

The worst of this plan of writing history in the guise of introductions was that Dr Stubbs never received at the hands of the large public just that palm which the large public was competent to bestow. He was, so it seems to me, a narrator of first-rate power: a man who could tell stories, and who did tell many stories, in sober, dignified, and unadorned but stirring and eloquent words. If an anthology were to be made of tales well told by historians, and the principle of selection paid no heed to the truthfulness of the passages, but weighed only their verisimilitude and what may be called their æsthetic or artistic merits, Dr Stubbs would have a strong right, and hardly any among the great historians of his day would have a stronger, to be well represented. But the large public knows or guesses that constitutional history is arid; the little book on the early Plantagenets is highly compressed; some of the seventeen lectures are—as many lectures may

properly be—a little too garrulous to be good reading; and the well-told stories and the life-like portraits
are where the large public will not look to find them.

It is not a little surprising that a man who could
paint men so well, and so well tell stories, a man (we
may add) who loved a pedigree and was fond of tracing
the hereditary transmission of landed estates and psychical traits, should have decided to make the great
effort of his life in the history of institutions. That
he had a strong taste for law—and the history of institutions is the history of public law—cannot be denied.
It has often seemed to me that if he had changed his
profession he might have been a very great judge.
But if there was taste there was also—this often appears—a strong conviction that constitutional history
is the absolutely necessary background for all other
history, and that until this has been arranged little
else can be profitably done. I do not suppose that
the great task was irksome, but still it was a task to
which duty called.

What are we to say of the *Constitutional History* ?
Perhaps I have just one advantage over most of its
readers. I did not read it because I was set to read
it, or because I was to be examined in it, or because
I had to teach history or law. I found it in a London
club, and read it because it was interesting. On the
other hand it was so interesting, and I was so little
prepared to criticise or discriminate, that perhaps I fell
more completely under its domination than those who
have passed through schools of history are likely to
fall. Still, making an effort towards objectivity, must
we not admire in the first instance the immense scope

of the book—a history of institutions which begins
with the Germans of Caesar and Tacitus and does not
end until a Tudor is on the throne?   Then the enormous mass of material that is being used, and the ease
with which this immense weight is moved and controlled.   Then the risks that are run, especially in the
earlier chapters.   This last is a point that may not be
quite obvious to all ; but is it not true that the historian
runs greater and more numerous dangers if he tells of
the growth and decay of institutions than if he writes
a straightforward narrative of events?   Would Gibbon's
editor find so few mistakes to rectify if Gibbon had
seriously tried to make his readers live for a while
under the laws of Franks and Lombards ?   Then,
again, we recall the excellent and (to the best of my
belief) highly original plan which by alternating
"analytical" and "annalistic" chapters weaves a web
so stout that it would do credit to the roaring loom
of time.   While the institutions grow and decay under
our eyes we are never allowed to forget that this process of evolution and dissolution consists of the acts of
human beings, and that acts done by nameable men,
by kings and statesmen and reformers, memorable acts
done at assignable points in time and space, are the
concrete forms in which the invisible forces and ten-
dencies are displayed.   When compared with other
books bearing a like title Stubbs's *Constitutional History* is marvellously concrete.

It is possible that by trying to blend or interlace
two styles of history Dr Stubbs sometimes repelled
two classes of readers.   The man who wants events
and actions, characters and motives, may find more

than he likes of institutional development and even of technical law, while there may be too many facts and details, names and dates and moral judgments for those who desire a natural history of the body politic and its organs. But to both these classes of students it may be suggested that in the present state of our knowledge concerning men and their environment both methods must be used, and that our highest praise should be reserved for one who can use them concurrently. Also Dr Stubbs's book is extremely "well documented," as the French say, and those who have had occasion to criticise any part of it would willingly confess that its footnotes were the starting points of their own investigations. A word too should surely be said of the art—unconscious art, perhaps, but still art—whereby our interest is maintained not only throughout the long crescendo but also throughout the long diminuendo. Dr Stubbs saw English history and taught others to see it in a manner which, if I am not mistaken, was somewhat new. Somewhere about the year 1307 the strain of the triumphal march must be abandoned; we pass in those well-known words "from the age of heroism to the age of chivalry, from a century ennobled by devotion and self-sacrifice to one in which the gloss of superficial refinement fails to hide the reality of heartless selfishness and moral degradation." It was no small feat for an historian who held this opinion to keep us reading while the decades went from bad to worse, reading of "dynastic faction, bloody conquest, grievous misgovernance, local tyrannies, plagues and famines unhelped and unaverted, hollowness of pomp, disease and dissolution." And yet he kept us reading, and even those whose unfortunate experience compels them to think of the book chiefly as one whence pupils must be taught can, if they get a spare hour, still read and still admire. It is so solid and so real, so sober and so wise ; but also it is carefully and effectively contrived.

As regards permanence, probably we ought to distinguish. It is difficult to believe that the account of the twelfth and three next following centuries will become antiquated until many a long day has gone by, though mistakes will be found and additions will be made. On the other hand it would be foolish to say that Dr Stubbs knew the earlier centuries as he knew the twelfth. That is impossible; the evidence is too small in quantity and too poor in quality. Many an investigator will leave his bones to bleach in that desert before it is accurately mapped. It may be doubted whether Dr Stubbs himself was fully aware of the treachery of the ground that he traversed. He had studied the evidence for himself with his usual thoroughness. Nevertheless he was under the guidance of German explorers. This an Englishman who means to do good work in those ages is likely to be. The Germans have some advantages over us. For one thing, legal education has been good in Germany, and consequently the German historian, be he lawyer or no, can use a much more accurate set of terms and concepts than such as are at our disposal. This may lead him to make about old times theories that are too sharp to be true, but he sees possibilities that are concealed from us in our fluffier language, and the sharp one-sided theory will at least state the problem that is to be solved.

Dr Stubbs chose his guides well. In particular any one who is praising his first chapters should turn aside for a moment to do reverence to the great Konrad Maurer. It is pleasant to think that Dr Liebermann has been able to dedicate his edition of the Anglo-Saxon laws to this veteran scholar—*dem Altmeister der germanischen Rechtsgeschichte.* When Dr Stubbs published his book those first chapters well represented the best learning of the time ; but *die germanische Rechtsgeschichte* did not stop in 1873, and Dr Stubbs stopped there or thereabouts. No doubt the author of a work which is obviously becoming classical has a difficult question before him when new editions are demanded. How much to alter in order that the book may keep abreast of advancing knowledge? How much to leave unaltered in order that the book may still be itself? Dr Stubbs made some changes, but not many that were of importance. It is allowable to regret that he made so many and yet so few. He sometimes leaves us doubting whether he is deliberately maintaining in the nineties a position that he held in the seventies. It is apparent that he was slow to change opinions when he had once formed them; but we do not always know precisely how much he is reaffirming and how much he is simply leaving alone. To have altered the footnotes would have been laborious, for the books, especially the German books, to which students were rightly sent in 1873 can hardly have been the first to which the bishop would have wished to send them in 1897. Conservat[1]sm, however, is the note of the methodological preface prefixed to the last edition of the *Select Charters,* which one of its readers must

confess that he does not altogether understand. Some
one is being reprimanded. But who? Fustel de
Coulanges? We can only guess. A laudable desire
to avoid controversy, coupled with a desire to warn
the young against seductive guides, seems to have
made the bishop's words for once obscure, and this
at an interesting moment, for he was publishing what
might be called his last will and testament. But
whether those early chapters are destined to wear ill
or to wear well, they represented an almost immeasurably great advance beyond anything that had previously
been written in England; nor can we say that, as a
general picture of the first age of English history,
they are likely to be superseded in the near future.
This being so, the conservatism that their writer displayed was, to say the least, pardonable. He wished
to hold fast that which had been good.

Conservative Dr Stubbs was in another sense, but
it may be a testimony to his fairness and to his rigorous
and praiseworthy exclusion of modern politics from the
middle ages if I say that it was possible to know the
Constitutional History fairly well and yet not know
how its author would vote at a parliamentary election;
my own guess would have been wrong. It even seems
possible that at some time hence those who, ignoring
the contents of English ballot-boxes, assign to historiographers their respective places in the thought of the
nineteenth century, will reckon Dr Stubbs's version of
English history among the progressive rather than
among the conservative forces. If the study of history
had in some sort made him "sad," he was hopeful;
and he was hopeful at a time when great changes were

following each other in swift succession. Was there ever so profound a medievalist who was so glad when he had done with the middle ages? "The charm," he said, "which the relics of medieval art have woven round the later middle ages must be resolutely, ruthlessly broken." Even his high-churchmanship, if it is more apparent than anything that could accurately be called political conservatism, is by no means prominent in the *Constitutional History.* A large collection might be made of passages in which archbishops, bishops, monks, and clergy are castigated in terms which a layman would have scrupled to use. I open the second volume by chance at a page where the clergy of the fourteenth century "are neither intelligent enough to guide education nor strong enough to repress heresy"; the best prelates are apparently being blamed for being "conservative rather than progressive in their religious policy," while the lower type represented by Arundel is charged with "religious intolerance." Certainly Stubbs was just, and to read his great book is a training in justice.

To those for whom he was no more than a writer of books the seventeen lectures revealed him in some new lights. We will pass by the pleasant chat and the too frequent groans over statutory lectures. The attempt to formulate "the characteristic differences between medieval and modern history" might, so I venture to think, be taken as an instance of the sort of work which Dr Stubbs could not do very well. He loved the concrete, and was not happy among abstractions of a high order, such as a contrast between "rights, forces, and ideas." We think how Seeley's

agile mind would have played round, and perhaps
played with, such a theme.   On many pages, however,
Dr Stubbs indicated the shape that some comparatively
modern history would take if he wrote it.   For example,
a dislike for the puritans, or at any rate for the puritan
cause, came out strongly.   These indications were new
to some of us who stood outside.   That his history was
not carried beyond 1485 is deeply to be regretted.   The
two admirable lectures on Henry VIII are tantalising,
though worthy of the man who drew Henry II.   We
see that he sees the great problem, and a solution is
suggested; but we are left to doubt whether an unwillingness to admit that many people wanted Henry
to do what he did in ecclesiastical affairs is not compelling the historian to imagine not only a king who is
almost super-human in his self-will, but also a clergy
and a nation which are sub-human in their self-abase-
ment.   Still, though he seems inclined to steer a course
that looks difficult, Dr Stubbs was so wise and equitable and sympathetic that it is possible, and more than
possible, that he would have kept his head where many
heads have been lost, and would have done good justice
both to papist and to puritan.   Certain it is that those
statesmen and churchmen whose cause he thought the
good cause would at times have felt the weight of his
chastening hand.   He never spared a friend who erred
and strayed.

Nothing has yet been said of the *Councils and
Ecclesiastical Documents*.   What is published is enough
to make us wish that Dr Stubbs had given one of many
lives to the Anglo-Saxon charters.   Other lives should
have been devoted to the constitutional history of Scot-

land and France and Germany; yet another to a history
of medieval scholarship. Nothing, again, has been said
of the *Select Charters*—that fertile book, which, is becoming the mother of a large family in England and
elsewhere. Few books have done more to make a
school than that book has done, and the school at
Oxford may well be proud of it. Nothing, again, has
been said of the laborious and lucid historical appendix
which redeems the report of certain commissioners
from the limbo to which such things tend. It may be
doubted whether history can be written upon commission, for the historical inference, when it is set to do
practical work, is apt to degenerate into the legal
dogma. Still, even when it was produced under unfavourable conditions, Dr Stubbs's work could never
fail to be good.

But I must end. The last words of the great
history are familiar, so familiar that I will not repeat
them. Few historians have a right to speak in that
solemn strain about the attainable maximum of truth
and the highest justice that is found in the deepest
sympathy with erring and straying men. Few indeed
have had a better right to speak in that strain than
had Dr William Stubbs. His place among historians
we do not attempt to determine. Assuredly it will be
high. I fancy that those who fix it high among the
highest will be those who by their own labours have
best earned the right to judge.

LORD ACTON[1]

It was from the first but a hopeless sort of hope that we had of Lord Acton's return to Cambridge. And now it has passed away. Early in the vacation there came to us the news of his death. Since then we have had time to think of our irreparable loss. The more we think of it, the heavier it seems.

Of it I should not dare to say a word, were it not that when the *Cambridge Modern History* was hardly yet an embryo, I (being then one of the Syndics of the Press) was allowed the privilege of seeing the great project take shape in the hands of one, who, as I thought then, and think now, had at last found a long-sought opportunity of teaching the world some part of what he had learned in the course of a laborious life. Comparing what I then saw and heard with what has since been published in the newspapers, it seems to me that there is some little danger that an imperfect estimate of our misfortune may pass current even in Cambridge.

The learning we may take for granted. All who as yet have ventured to write of it have agreed that it was immense. Whether any other Englishman,

---

[1] *The Cambridge Review*, Oct. 16th, 1902.

whether any other human being, ever knew more of Universal History than Lord Acton knew—in truth it is some such question as this that we are prompted to ask, and the name of the man of whom we ought to ask it does not occur to us. If with a laudable wish to avoid extravagance we recall the giants of a past time, their wondrous memories, their encyclopædic knowledge, we must remember also how much that Lord Acton knew was for them practically unknowable. This is a truth that he was fond of teaching by examples. "Where Hallam and Lingard were dependent on Barillon, their successors consult the diplomacy of ten governments."

The immensity of the learning being unquestionable, some disposition to question the use that was—or was not—made of it was to be expected, and has in fact been observed. That "daily consumption of a German octavo," did it benefit him and the world, or was it only a stupendous feat of intellectual voracity? Reference to the catalogue of the University Library might give point to the question. One lecture, an inaugural lecture, delivered in 1895, one letter written in 1870, a German letter written to a German bishop—these, so the inquirer might say, appear to be all the published works of John Emerich Edward Dalberg, first Lord Acton. He might also notice that this letter seems to have taken a quarter of a century or thereabouts in reaching our shelves, and might not be there now, had not Dr Hort acquired a copy. Some want of interest among the generality of Englishmen in a great historic event of their own time, some unwillingness to believe that a German letter to a

German bishop could contain matters of importance, might thus be established incidentally ; but the main question would not lose its edge. Was ever such disproportion between intake and output?

Now no one who heard him talk or read what he wrote or borrowed a book from the most generous of book-lenders would for one moment think of him as reading idly, for amusement, for distraction, to pass the time. It was serious work the reading of history, calling not only for a chair, but for a table, pencil, pen and abundant slips of paper. The day's book was mastered. If it was of any value, certain facts had been ascertained from it, and they had been correlated with countless other facts. And the author had been judged : not vaguely consigned to a class, but judged in a reasoned judgment : often condemned. You had but to ask and you might hear the sentence, plain, decided, not what you had expected, for, though there was reticence, though there was irony, a plain question about book or man brought a plain answer and an unconventional. Once it happened that a solemn filler of many volumes, a German too and an historian, whom I supposed to be highly respected, was dismissed with "mountainous jackass." Some years ago an adversary in high place, who feared Lord Acton and his then associates, charged them with "the ruthless talk of undergraduates." In the accusation or the compliment there was, so it seems to me, some truth that we here can understand. He could speak straight out, from heart and head. Age, experience and erudition had not taught him to minish and mince. On the other hand, readers of anecdotes will do well to remember that he was by no means incapable of casting a pearl of irony in the way of those who would mistake it for pebbly fact.

No, if the reading had been idler, less purposeful, more might have been written and published. " Everybody has felt...that he knew too much to write." These are words that he applied to Döllinger, his friend and master, and in some sort they were true of himself. But the obstacle did not consist merely in the enormous weight of the mass that was to be moved. Huge it was, but in his hands not unwieldly. There was also an acute, an almost overwhelming sense of the gravity, the sanctity of history. He was not the man wearily to preach upon this or any other text. A little irony, a little raillery would do more good than the set sermon. Yet read the reviews that he signed, and beneath the playful, witty, enigmatic phrases, you see the solemnity of the historian's task. Lord Acton's favourite metaphors came, not from the laboratory, but from the court of justice. It is judicial work to be done without fear or favour in the midst of the subtlest temptations. Not merely is it the historian's duty to see that individual rogues shall not escape, more especially the rogues of his own nation, his own party, his own creed, but there is the universe—nothing less—at the bar of the court, called upon to give an account of its behaviour before an inexorable judge. Even to the verge of paradox—and some would say a little further—he bore the standard of high morality. Once he spoke a light word of "that rigid liberalism which, by repressing the time test and applying the main rules of morality all round, converts history into a frightful monument of sin." But with some theoretical concessions to a "sliding scale" to be established hereafter by a science " that is yet in its teens," and with some (not very much) leniency in the Middle Age, his own precept and practice hardly fell short of this "rigid liberalism." " It is," he said, " the office of historical science to maintain morality as the sole impartial criterion of men and things." We have had other definitions of the historian's duty. This was Lord Acton's.

It may seem to some a plain untruth that he was more deeply interested in certain great problems of a philosophical kind than in any concrete presentment of particular facts. They may well have thought of him as the man who with wonderful exactitude knew and enjoyed all the bye-play in the great drama :—at home, no doubt, upon the front-stairs, but supreme upon the back-stairs, and (as he once said) getting his meals in the kitchen : acquainted with the use of cupboards and with the skeletons that lie therein ; especially familiar with the laundry where the dirty linen is washed ; an analyst of all the various soaps that have been employed for that purpose in all ages and all climes. Disclaiming all esoteric knowledge and reading only what all may read I cannot think of him thus. When he was observing, recording, appreciating the incidents, the bye-play, he was intent on a main plot difficult to apprehend : " fatalism and retribution, race and nationality, the test of success and of duration, heredity and the reign of the invincible dead, the widening circle, the emancipation of the individual, the gradual triumph of the soul over the body, of mind over matter, reason over will, knowledge over ignorance, truth over error, right over

might, liberty over authority, the law of progress and
perfectibility, the constant intervention of providence,
the sovereignty of the developed conscience." Plenty
of men are troubled about these matters; plenty of
men make theories, "alluring theories," about them;
but then they are not the men who know the back-
stairs or get their meals in the kitchen; not the men
who have toiled in the archives, hunting the little fact
that makes the difference. For Lord Acton, so it
seems to me, nothing was too small because nothing
was too large. The whole lay in every part and
particle: there and there only to be discovered, there
and there only to be judged. A conception of history
so abstract and so concrete, so unitary and so manifold,
so bold and so minute, would have paralysed a weaker
man. It did not paralyse him. He worked while the
light lasted. But to "seek a little thing to do, find it
and do it," to give all his thought to a century, a
nation, a fragment—"no, that's the world's way."

Of this, however, I am very sure, that when all has
been collected that can be collected, and all has been
told that ought to be told, it will be clear to the world
that the acquisition of knowledge was for Lord Acton
not end but mean. The late, the very late, arrival
upon our shelves of that open letter to a German
bishop—an "open letter" in more senses than one—
should remind us that few indeed are the men in
Cambridge or in England who have even a rudi-
mentary acquaintance with what was no episode but
perhaps the chief theme of his earnest life. Some
day the story may be told. His friends have no cause
to fear the truth. If there was failure, surely it was

heroic failure; and the end is not yet. Really one must live in Little Pedlington and never transgress the parish boundary if one is to inform the British public that Lord Acton and his "hoarded knowledge" counted for nothing in the Europe and Christendom of the nineteenth century[1]. That was not the judgment of those who had crossed swords with him in a world-wide arena and had felt the strength of his wrist. Deeply convinced that the history of religion lies near the heart of all history, he was isolated from the bulk of his fellow-countrymen by religious and from the residue, or the bulk of the residue, by historical convictions, and, this being so, he was not likely to find or to seek an audience in the market-place. Nor was it given to him to beat the big drum outside the patriotic show and call that historiography. Moreover he had home-truths to tell, and they could best be sent home by a few words written for the few. But it is safe to say that there are, for example, some forty pages in the *English Historical Review* for 1890 which will still be shining when most of our justly applauded histories have sunk beneath the horizon.

Opportunities were taken when they were offered. Friends were lavishly helped. This man who has been called "a miser" was in truth a very spendthrift of his hard-earned treasure and ready to give away in half an hour the substance of an unwritten book. A journal was edited; it was dreaded and denounced. A great deal of reviewing was done, and reviewing of so admirable a kind that the review has become, for all wise

[1] See a letter in the *Daily News* of July 8th, 1902.

readers of the book, an indispensable appendix. And
at last came the great opportunity : at last and too
late. We saw with wonder how eagerly it was seized,
and how a project that might have been pedestrian
took horse, took wings and soared. All modern
history—the scheme was large enough. Twelve stout
volumes—there would be room enough for minutely
truthful work. Stored knowledge, big thoughts, an
acknowledged primacy, polyglot correspondence, rami-
fying friendships, the tact of a diplomatist, the ardour
of a scholar, all were to be subservient in a noble cause;
to the greater glory of truth and right : to the greater
glory, be it added, of a Cambridge that he had learned
to love. It was Napoleonic. I know no other word,
and yet it is not adequate. I felt as if I had been
permitted to look over the shoulder of a general who
was planning a campaign that was to last for five
centuries and extend throughout the civilised world.
No doubt there was some overestimate of health and
endurance and mere physical force, some forgetfulness
of the weight of accumulating years. We feared it
then ; we know it now. But of such mistakes, if mis-
-takes they be, the brave will be guilty. And about
mental power there was no mistake. With whatever
doubts I had gone to his rooms, I came away saying
to myself that if contributors failed, if the worst
came to the worst, or perhaps the best to the best,
Lord Acton could write the twelve volumes from
beginning to end, and (as the phrase goes) never turn
a hair. But it was too late : too late by ten or fifteen
years.

The execution of his project in his large spirit is the memorial that he would have desired. Our best have undertaken the task. At this moment it would not be right to say more than that we are deeply grateful to them.

Another memorial might be thought of. Those who sat or stood in the crowded Divinity School can never forget the majestic act of pardon and oblivion which was the preface of the inaugural lecture. "At three colleges I applied for admission, and, as things then were, I was refused by all. Here, from the first, I vainly fixed my hopes, and here in a happier hour, after five and forty years, they are at last fulfilled." As it is written, *Lapidem quem reprobaverunt ædificantes, hic factus est caput in angulo.* Those who most revere these words will be the last to say that they teach no practical lesson. Well, intolerance is a foolish thing, and an apology based upon unintended consequences is an apology of just the sort that aroused Lord Acton's indignation. Still to some of his hearers must have occurred the thought :—" Were you not the gainer by our churlishness? Had Cambridge then received you, no doubt you would have been a very learned man and by this time Regius Professor. But would you have been quite such a master of contemporary history, quite such an impartial judge of modern England, so European, so supernational, so catholic, so liberal, so wise, so Olympian, so serene?" And even now, so I cannot but think, the pride and sorrow with which Cambridge writes Acton's name on the roll of her illustrious dead is not unalloyed by an uncomfortable suspicion that just those qualities that were most distinctive of his work and most admirable, are but exotic flowers in our Cambridge garland. An effective resolve that never hereafter shall there be cause for such an abatement of our pride is the debt that we owe to his memory. Meanwhile a little —remorse will do us no harm. The pardon was freely granted. We have yet to earn it.

SIR LESLIE STEPHEN[1]

How great a man went from among us when Leslie
Stephen died becomes apparent if we think for a
moment how much might appropriately be said in this
place of him and his work, and then think how large
a part of him and his work would still remain unnoticed.
If, as perhaps we ought, we try to leave out of sight
the critic, the essayist, the biographer, if we shut our
eyes to the "Sunset from Mont Blanc," refuse to listen
to the "Praise of Walking," and endeavour to forget
the "Forgotten Benefactors," we still see the historian
of philosophic thought, the scientific moralist, the
rational assailant of theology, the organizer of the
grandest historical enterprise that the England of our
age has seen.   But if ever man was one and indivisible,
that man was Leslie Stephen: a great contemner of
boundaries, whom no scheme of the sciences, no delimitation of departments, would keep in the highway
if he had a mind to go across country.   And across
country he would go, thinking freely and speaking
plainly.

Leslie Stephen was born on Nov. 28, 1832.   He
was younger by three and a half years than his brother

[1] *Proceedings of the British Academy.*

the future Sir James Fitzjames. One contrast between them soon disclosed itself. Leslie was a very delicate child. It long was doubtful whether he would ever be capable of any strenuous exertion of mind or body. To stimulate his intellect or his imagination was unnecessary; on the contrary, doctors prescribed life in the open air and a strict abstention from poetry, for poetry went to his head like wine. Even stories of adventure were too exciting. When he was eight years old he for about a year attended a school at Brighton, but only as a day boy. In the spring of 1842 he went to Eton, but again only as a day boy. He left Eton when he had just turned fourteen. Though he had not much bullying to complain of, he could afterwards recall the sufferings of "a pale, delicate boy with thin limbs and spider fingers, and a sensitive organization, set down amidst some hundreds of lads as mischievous and thoughtless as monkeys—a poor little fragment of humanity, kicked contemptuously aside, and heartily ashamed of himself for his undeniable atrocity." He had shown ability and diligence in his school work, especially in such mathematics as were taught at Eton; but his tutor "spoke strongly of his want of success in composition," and his father removed him, thinking that time enough had been wasted in an unsuccessful attempt to produce Etonian elegiacs. For a short time he went to a school at Wimbledon, but only as a day boy, and afterwards for about two years he was by way of going to King's College, London, but his attendance there was intermittent, and two winters had to be passed in the warmth of Torquay. In the October of 1850, when he was not yet eighteen, he began his career at Cambridge as an undergraduate at Trinity Hall. By this time his robust brother was finishing his course at Trinity. A small college—it was then a very small college—was chosen for Leslie, because it was thought that the examinations at Trinity would be too severe a tax for his strength, and Trinity Hall was chosen as being the college of which his father, who by this time had quitted the Colonial Office, and become Professor of Modern History, was a distinguished member. Leslie became enamoured of Cambridge. His health was rapidly improving. He read mathematics diligently, and in the tripos of 1854 was twentieth wrangler: he was a very young competitor, and to the last was being warned against over-work.

Before the end of the year a certain "bye fellowship," which was in effect a sort of chaplaincy, was bestowed upon him, and in the spring of 1856 he became one of the two "presbyter fellows" and tutors of Trinity Hall, having been ordained a deacon in December, 1855. By this time he had become a vigorous, though not in all respects a strong man, keenly enjoying all manner of sports and capable of some wonderful feats of endurance. His first visit to the Alps he paid in 1857, and very soon he was in the front rank of English mountaineers. The prospect of a career at Cambridge was extremely attractive to him, and though, as he afterwards said, "he took a good deal upon trust," there is no reason whatever to doubt that his religious opinions lay well within the limits of Anglican orthodoxy, even in 1859 when he became a priest. As a college tutor he was brilliantly successful. Pupils of his say that it must be doubtful whether any tutor has been more "worshipped," and attribute to him a decisive influence upon the rapid growth of Trinity Hall. While admitting that his enthusiastic encouragement of rowing and other sports was one main cause of their worship, they speak with no less warmth of more serious matters. Those who were very intimate with him knew, for example, that on his long walks he could recite poetry by the mile. When therefore in 1862 he said that he could no longer read the service in chapel and resigned the tutorship, he was abandoning a career that he dearly loved, and his courageous resolution was the outcome of an acutely painful struggle. He was very uncertain whether he was likely to succeed in any other walk of life. Beyond translating Berlepsch's *Alps* (1861) for the purpose of improving his German, he had done nothing in the literary way, and he was then and ever afterwards exceedingly diffident. He could not at once tear himself from Cambridge. He lingered there for two years and a half, reading philosophy and political economy, examining in the moral sciences, straying further and further from the paths of orthodoxy, writing an article for *Macmillan's* which was rejected, and another on "An American Economist" which was accepted, walking matches against runners, championing his friend Henry Fawcett in divers electoral enterprises, serving as editor, sub-editor, and staff of a "campaign newspaper" (the *Brighton Election Reporter*), pamphleteering about "The Poll Degree," and ardently advocating the cause of the North against all comers with "outbursts of burning eloquence," which have not been forgotten by those who heard them. His enthusiasm

for the northern cause induced him to visit America in
1863.   He went as far west as St Paul and St Louis,
slept under canvas with Meade's army in Virginia, had
some words with Seward and a word with Lincoln, his
object being the collection of powder and shot for the
warfare in which he was engaged at Cambridge; but
incidentally he saw Lowell, Longfellow, Emerson,
Hawthorne, Holmes, and other men of letters.   Lowell
and he became from that moment fast friends, and this
friendship, as also that with Professor C. E. Norton,
were of the greatest service to Stephen when a few
years later he was diffidently making his first serious
efforts as an author.   Few incipient authors have stood
in greater need of encouragement.   A more proximate
result of the journey to America was a spirited onslaught
upon the *Times*, which took the form of a pamphlet
published by "L. S." in 1865.   In 1864 he was still
hesitating.   He had to earn his living; his Fellowship,
which he yet retained, would expire if he married.   At
the end of the year he resolved to settle in London, and
try his hand at journalism.

His diffidence is the more remarkable because by
this time his brother had been ten years in London,
and, while labouring successfully at the bar, had already
done an immense amount of writing for newspapers
and magazines.   Leslie at once found favour with the
editor of the *Saturday Review* who was willing to take
all that he would write, if it were not about politics or
religion.   Then the *Pall Mall Gazette* was founded
(1865) and among his first contributions to it were the
"Sketches from Cambridge by a Don" which in the
same year appeared as his first book.   It is less

generally known that in 1866 he became the English correspondent of the New York *Nation,* and that to it for some seven years he sent a fortnightly letter dealing with current politics as well as other events. He attended important debates in Parliament and had strong opinions about what went on there. Indeed, it was not because he was no politician, but rather because he was an uncompromising politician that he did not seek employment as a writer of "leaders." Among magazines *Fraser* and the *Cornhill* were open to him, and *Fraser* was willing to receive outspoken articles about religious matters such as he was desirous of writing. He left Cambridge with the idea of a great book in his mind. It was to have been a work on political theory; but, as he read, the history of religious speculation became more and more interesting to him, and politics fell into the background. Though he read deeply as well as widely, he could hardly find time for the composition of a lengthy book. He was desirous of freeing himself from journalistic drudgery; but by this time he was married (1867) and had lost his fellowship. He was even compelled to think of being called to the bar, and began "eating dinners" at one of the Inns of the Court. However, in 1871 he acquired a little more liberty by becoming editor of the *Cornhill.* Then came book after book: from 1871 the *Playground of Europe*; from 1873 *Free thinking and Plain speaking*; from 1874, 1876, and 1879 the *Hours in a Library.* Meanwhile in 1876 the *History of English Thought in the Eighteenth Century* had conclusively proved that, besides being an admirable essayist and a vigorous thinker, he had become a man of unusual learning. When this heavy piece of work was off his hands, he began to meditate the *Science of Ethics*, which was not published until 1882. In rapid succession he wrote *Johnson*, *Pope*, and *Swift* for the series of "English Men of Letters," to which he afterwards added the *George Eliot* and posthumously the *Hobbes*. His mastery in books of this order was admitted on all hands. A request that he would write the life of his friend Henry Fawcett was answered affirmatively by return of post, and the book that was then written was surely a model for all biographers. Meanwhile, however, towards the end of 1882, he took charge of the projected *Dictionary of National Biography*. He was hard at work upon it for two years before the first volume was published. Gradually he discovered that the task was far more laborious than he had expected, and when it became apparent that the Dictionary, however highly it might be praised, was not going to be a financial success, this only made Stephen the more anxious to do with his own hand all that he possibly could. The incessant work began to tell upon a frame which had its weak as well as its strong points. In 1888 there was an alarming illness, directly attributable to mental strain; there was another in 1889. In 1891 the editorship was transferred to Mr Sidney Lee, who from the beginning had been Stephen's right-hand man and in 1890 had become joint editor. From that time onward Stephen could only work at what he regarded as half pressure, and sorrows came upon him thick and fast; but the tale of what he did is amazing. He had projected a sequel to his *History of English Thought in the Eighteenth*

Century.   Often it had to be laid aside and as often it was resumed.   It at length appeared in 1900 as three volumes on the *English Utilitarians*.   To this we must add the *Agnostic's Apology* (1893), which some think the best of all his books, the life of his brother Fitzjames, which is worthy to stand by the side of the life of Fawcett, two volumes called *Social Rights and Duties* (1896), four volumes called *Studies by a Bio-grapher* (1900 and 1902), the *Letters of J. R. Green* (1901), the Ford Lectures for 1903, which he was not strong enough to deliver and which were published a few days before his death, and the *Hobbes* (1904), which he never saw in print.   He wrote until he could no longer hold a pen and read until his eyes closed.   It is a splendid record.

In his last days he would sometimes say that he had "scattered himself" too widely, that he was jack of all trades and master of none, not a scholar, not a philosopher, not an historian, only an amateur.   Possibly in these pages it ought to be admitted that there is a particle of truth in this judgment, and fairly certain it is that if Leslie Stephen had done less, he would seem to have done more, for we are apt to think that anything that he does is bye-work lying outside his proper province.   But such an amateur, if that be the right term, such a contemner of the conventional boundaries, so untrammelled a thinker, so sincere a speaker is worth more to the world than many professionals, especially if he is as incapable of affectation as he is incapable of pedantry.   So much might be allowed by those who knew Leslie Stephen only upon paper.   Those who knew the man have another tale to tell of a noble life, of tender love and warm-hearted friendship, of heavy sorrows gallantly borne, and of last days that were like some glorious sunset—even the Sunset from Mont Blanc.

HENRY SIDGWICK [1]

" I THINK your book is one of a rare class—the class of biographies which are good in the sense in which good novels are good; I mean biographies which do not merely give the reader the feeling that the writer has performed a task incumbent on him in a competent manner, but which give him the peculiar pleasure and instruction that can only be given by the full unfolding of the intellectual and moral quality of a rare mind that has lived, developed, and produced important social effects in interesting circumstances."

It was thus that Henry Sidgwick wrote to Mr Wilfrid Ward concerning *W. G. Ward and the Catholic Revival*; and it seems to me that judicious readers will find themselves silently addressing some very similar words to the authors of the recently-published memoir of Henry Sidgwick. He dated the "consulship of Plancus" in A.D. 1860–65; and in 1895 he retrospectively spoke of "the *forward* movement of the thought" of those hopeful years when "Hebrew old clothes" were being discarded. Then it was that he "took service with Reason." That Forward Movement, with Reason as recruiting sergeant, may not yet

---

[1] *Henry Sidgwick: A Memoir.* By A. S. and E. M. S. London: Macmillan & Co., 1906. *Independent Review*, June, 1906.

have found its historian; but, if less picturesque upon
the surface, surely it was not less worthy of remembrance than the Catholic Revival, which without offence
—none is intended—might, I suppose, be called a Backward Movement.   Altogether "the circumstances" of
Sidgwick's life, though not exciting, may well be deemed
adequately "interesting," by those who look beneath
the surface of current history; and there can be no
doubt that we are here enabled to see "the full unfolding of the intellectual and moral quality of a rare
mind"—a very rare mind—and, be it added, of a
singularly lofty and beautiful character.

Still loftier than his friends, or some of his friends,
suspected? I think so; and, just about this one matter,
I will venture, at the editor's instance, to write a few
lines without making the pretence that I am reviewing
a book.

It is not mine to speak from the vantage ground of
intimacy. Sidgwick, throughout his life, had deeply-
attached and intimate friends, to whom, as sufficiently
appears in these pages, he unbosomed himself unre-
servedly. Nor indeed have I any right to speak, except
in the first person singular, though I have good reason
to suppose that what I saw was what was seen by many
other of his acquaintance who stood outside that innermost circle. And the first trait upon which I will lay a
little stress is one that may not be—I do not feel sure
about it—sufficiently evident to all readers of this
memoir. May not some of them gather from it the
notion that Sidgwick was so much engaged in self-
scrutiny, self-criticism, perhaps even self-torment, that
he can have had little time or energy for other pursuits,

or, at any rate, that the native hue of resolution must
have been sicklied o'er with the pale cast of thought?
I do not think that any reasonably careful reader ought
to draw this inference, or that the writers of the memoir
are in any degree to blame if so grave a mistake be
committed. Apart from what they tell us, there is, on
the face of Sidgwick's own letters, ample evidence of
the extremely keen interest that he took in all manner
of human affairs. But what I may call the introspec-
tive passages, excerpted from letters and journals, are
so deeply, and sometimes, it may be, so painfully interesting, that possibly they may throw the residue of
story into the background. I can even imagine the
habitual skipper skipping in search of more "revela-
tions," though assuredly he will be a loser if he skips.
Therefore it may not be out of place to say, that a man
who seemed less self-conscious or less self-centred than
Sidgwick was not to be met; nor one who, to all
appearance, so steadily and easily kept himself at an
objective point of view. There are, for example, in
this memoir, paragraphs written by distinguished col-
leagues of his, which, if they attract their proper share
of attention, will give the right idea of Sidgwick's
ceaseless activity in the affairs of the University of
Cambridge; but it should, I think, be added with
some emphasis that whatever he did was done with
ungrudging cheerfulness, and most of it with apparent
enjoyment. One wondered whether there was any
practical question that he would not study with zest;
one wondered whether he could be bored, whether he
could be irritated. If ever he was weary of well-doing,
he kept his weariness very much to himself. Nobody

—I need hardly say this—could have been less like the philosopher of traditional caricature, who carries his head in the clouds and does not see where he is going. The next step was, for the time being, the all-important step, and well worthy of the best thought that could be given to it. But further, I should have said that from any of those failings which betoken the habitual "introspector" (is there such a word?) Sidgwick's behaviour was markedly free. His range of sympathy was astonishingly wide. He seemed to delight in divining what other people were thinking, or were about to think, in order that he might bring his mind near to theirs, learn from them what could be learnt, and then, if argument was desirable, argue at close quarters.

What was thus visible in the course of business was still more visible in the course of free conversation. Sidgwick was a wonderful talker ; a better I have never heard. But Mr Bryce and Mr Benson and Leslie Stephen have said some part of what might be said of this matter ; and I have nothing to add, save one small remark suggested by what I have just been writing. Sidgwick's talk never became, and never tended to become, a monologue. He seemed at least as desirous to hear as to be heard, and gave you the impression that he would rather be led than lead. Even more than the wit and the wisdom, the grace and the humour, it was the wide range of sympathy that excited admiration when the talk was over. To see with your eyes, to find interest in your interests, seemed to be one of his main objects, while he was amusing and instructing and delighting you. As a

compliment that was pleasant; but I cannot think
that it was a display of mere urbanity. Sidgwick
genuinely wished to know what all sorts of people
thought and felt about all sorts of things. His irony
never hurt, it was so kindly; and, of all known forms
of wickedness, "Sidgwickedness" was the least wicked.
Good as are the letters in this book, I cannot honestly
say that they are as good, or nearly as good, as their
writer's talk. A letter, being a monologue, cannot represent just what seemed most to distinguish him from
some other brilliant talkers. I imagine that superlatively good letters—I mean letters which will be called
superlatively good when they are printed and published
and read by strangers—are hardly to be written unless
among their ingredients is a pinch—not more, but still
a pinch—of egotism; and this is a spice which we
cannot detect in Sidgwick's epistles, at any rate in
those that were written after the consulship of Plancus.
He was a most unegotistical talker, and a most unegotistical man. But as to egoism in a philosophic sense,
it has sometimes struck an old pupil of his that "the
selfish system of morality" might be plausibly rehabili-
tated by any one who paid more regard to the practice
than to the preaching of a certain professor of moral
philosophy. That conflict between duty and enlightened self-interest, between "altruistic hedonism" and
"egoistic hedonism"—did Sidgwick really know, could
Sidgwick really know, anything about it from personal
experience? It seemed hardly credible—so cheerfully,
naturally, spontaneously, was every duty done. Much
pains would be taken to ascertain the path of duty.
An observer might readily guess that this philosopher's

"method of ethics" involved a calculation of consequences near and remote. Sidgwick's mind was large;
but it was also full, and, consequently, it required much
"making up." Any one, it may be parenthetically observed, can quickly pack a portmanteau if he has only
a sleeping suit to put in it. But, when once the path
of duty was ascertained, the step was at once taken;
and it seemed to be taken not only gallantly but gaily.
Sidgwick appeared to be so happily constituted that he
found his greatest pleasure in active, though thought-
ful, beneficence. That was how it struck an outsider.
We could not say the same of all very good and dutiful
persons.

And now we may know more, we "friends at a
distance" who honoured and admired him. I do not
think that we are or ought to be surprised or saddened;
but I think that we are and ought to be profoundly
grateful. Notwithstanding all his powers, attainments,
virtues, Sidgwick never seemed to us in the least in-
human, even when some of us sat on benches and he
stood on the further side of the chasm that lies somewhere between twenty and thirty-two. But he seems
yet more human now, when we can see something of
effort and conflict and suffering beneath the serene
surface. I will pass by what he called his years of
"storm and stress." As we read the letters of those
years the thought may come to us, and if it comes it
will be painful, that possibly he may miss his vocation.
Of his going wrong, in any serious sense of that phrase,
there cannot be even a momentary fear. But there
does seem to be a chance that this man, to whom so
many brilliant careers are open, may not choose the

noblest but most arduous of them all; and there does at times seem to be a chance that, while he is choosing, he may fall a prey to the insidious disease that is, called " scholar's paralysis." To say this, however, is only to say that if Sidgwick had not been Sidgwick he would have been somebody else. And when, because of religious scruples, he thinks of resigning his fellowship, and reveals his inmost thoughts to his friends, though his distress must pain us, we do not feel inclined to avert our eyes, for there is nothing sickly or morbid or unlovely to be seen : only scrupulous veracity and unflinching courage. It is an inspiriting sight, though perhaps we are in some sort glad when it is over, and the " sun is shining and all shapes of life evolving overhead " (p. 200).

Passing to a later time, we see much that is attractive ; but I will only mention what will move some of us most of all. We may have known something of it, and guessed a little more ; it is here to be seen by all who can read this book with sympathetic eyes : namely, Sidgwick's singular truthfulness. Of course this does not mean merely that he did not tell lies, or profess doctrines that he did not believe ; it means that, beyond most other men, and, I fancy, beyond most other philosophers, he was honest with himself. A little self-deceit or self-mystification over the great ultimate problems of philosophy and religion, is it not very common, very easy, and even very excusable ? Down here, among mundane matters, beliefs which are the offspring of desire fare badly. They come into collision with hard facts, and they perish soon. But up in those aerial regions where most of us soon feel dizzy, I fear that it is otherwise. A small change in a delicate scheme of values, a little shifting of scarcely ponderable weights, or of measures that can never be absolutely rigid, may satisfy the cravings of the heart without offending the head, unless that head be trained to severe sincerity. Now a very slight degree of moral obliquity, hardly enough to be seriously condemned, might, so it seems to me, have made Sidgwick the most plausible and popular of modern sophists, or (it is the same thing) of modern prophets. All other requisites were there : ingenuity, subtlety, resource, circumspection, erudition, besides a reserve of rhetorical and literary power upon which he seldom drew. Even by way of exercise for our imagination, we could not suppose him capable of maintaining what he did not believe; but, had it not been for his perfect probity, and that vigilant self-criticism which, so I gather from the public papers, has come as a surprise to some of those who knew and revered him, he might, as others often do, have forgotten the exact point where proof ended, and only hope remained. And then what a sophist or what a prophet he might have been, and what a "school" he might have founded!

The temptation was not wanting. In choosing to be a philosopher, he had chosen a thorny path. I do not know that a philosopher's career must needs be exceptionally arduous. Whether it requires better brains and harder labour to write a good book on philosophy than to write a good book on physics, I cannot say. But if you take philosophy very seriously, it may distress you in a manner in which you will never be distressed by chemistry or philology or jurisprudence.

The riddle of the universe may oppress and persecute you as no minor puzzles will, especially if you are truly solicitous about the welfare of your fellows, and the time is one when old theories and creeds are called in question on every hand. Sidgwick took philosophy very seriously: as seriously, I should suppose, as it was ever taken; and it is not precisely of the "consolations of philosophy" that this book will make us think, but rather of the burden of thought. There is a good deal of *Weltschmerz* (p. 277) in it. Sidgwick felt

> "The heavy and the weary weight
> Of all this unintelligible world."

Or rather, we ought to say, of this morally irrational world. Unless certain theses could be established, the universe was for him morally chaotic, and therefore distressful. Perhaps we others, we of the grosser clay, who know more of toothache than of *Weltschmerz*, cannot fully make his feelings ours. Moreover, I can see no room for pity here. We read of a very happy life. Fate aimed at Sidgwick—to her credit be it said —no one of her crushing blows. But what, so I think, we may all admire, is the watchful honesty which will not suffer any hope, however ardent, or any desire, however noble, to give itself the airs of proof. "Well," wrote Sidgwick in 1891, "I myself have taken service with Reason, and I have no intention of deserting. At the same time I do not think that loyalty to my standard requires me to feign a satisfaction in the service which I do not really feel." These words give us the core of the matter, which is stated more fully and with more emotion elsewhere. Is it painful reading ? Not wholly painful, I think, especially if we remember, as at this point we must, that the *Welt-schmerz* and the long continued conflict between head and heart did not cripple Sidgwick, or make of him a moral valetudinarian, but rather seem to have braced him for the service, the active, cheerful, spontaneous service, of his fellow men. In an able, appreciative, and affectionate review of this book, I saw it suggested that some "paradox" has been set before us in this quarter. It may be so. I have no skill in psychology, theoretic or applied; and certainly I could not sum up the character of Henry Sidgwick in any form of words. Still it seems to me that, somehow or another, all that we now learn blends with all that we remember. Rare the total result may be; but it is harmonious. Complex the character may be; and yet, in another sense, it is beautifully simple.

The prediction of the fate of *Memoirs* is, I should imagine, a peculiarly hazardous kind of prophecy; and perhaps it should never be undertaken by those who knew, even at a distance, the men whose lives are in question. Yet may we hope with some confidence that, even when many years have gone by, this book will still have for a few discerning readers some part of the charm that it has for many of us now. The whole of that charm they can never know; but they may at least see that one of the acutest, profoundest and most influential thinkers of our time was a true and good and noble man; and in some degree they may feel that he is even for them an encouraging master, a wise counsellor, and a delightful companion.

MARY BATESON[1]

To many residents at Cambridge it still seems hardly credible that Miss Mary Bateson is no longer at work among them. We thought it so certain that twenty years hence her generous enthusiasm for learning, her dogged tenacity of purpose, her cool and sober common sense, would still be serving mankind, that we might well be dazed by the disaster that has befallen us. Yet some things are clear. If we have to think of promise, we can also think with some comfort of performance. For much more we confidently hoped; but we have much that cannot be taken away. I shall not endeavour to tell the whole tale, but will speak only of the last book. The admirably edited *Records of the Borough of Leicester* and the brilliant papers on the "Laws of Breteuil" had shown that Miss Bateson's knowledge of the history of our medieval towns was almost, if not quite, unrivalled. Thereupon she was asked to undertake for the Selden Society a sort of digest of the borough custumals, published and unpublished. The first volume appeared in 1904; the second and last appeared this summer, with a long and learned introduction, which is in truth a full and elaborate com-

---

[1] *The Athenæum*, 1906.

mentary. When the first volume only had been issued, the Lord Chief Justice told the Selden Society that Miss Bateson knew more about English legal history than nine lawyers out of ten. After seeing the second volume, his lordship may doubt whether his words were quite strong enough. Such a book cannot make its mark in a couple of months, nor yet in a couple of years. It cannot attract "the general reader"; it can be only a book for a few students of history. Moreover, Miss Bateson, a true daughter of Cambridge, felt such scorn for what she would call "gas" that it was difficult to persuade her that a few sentences thrown in for the benefit of the uninitiated are not to be condemned by the severest taste. Of such a work I should not like to speak confidently at short notice. But it was my good fortune to see this book in every stage of its growth: in manuscript, in slip, and in page. Good fortune it was. The hunger and thirst for knowledge, the keen delight in the chase, the good-humoured willingness to admit that the scent was false, the eager desire to get on with the work, the cheerful resolution to go back and begin again, the broad good sense, the unaffected modesty, the imperturbable temper, the gratitude for any little help that was given— all these will remain in my memory, though I cannot paint them for others. As to the book—friendship apart—I do think it good. Given the limits of space and time, which were somewhat narrow, I do not see how it could have been much better. Given those limits, the name of the Englishman who both could and would have done the work does not occur to me.

Unless I am much mistaken, that book will "sup late," but in very good company. I see it many years hence on the same shelf with the *History of the Exchequer* and the *History of Tithes.* Neither Thomas Madox nor yet John Selden will resent the presence of Mary Bateson.

INDEX

M. III.

CAMBRIDGE: PRINTED BY JOHN CLAY, M.A. AT THE UNIVERSITY PRESS.

WS - #0023 - 110823 - C0 - 229/152/31 - PB - 9781331288459 - Gloss Lamination